Imagining the Modern

Chris Grimley
Michael Kubo
Rami el Samahy

Imagining the Modern

Architecture and Urbanism of the Pittsburgh Renaissance

THE MONACELLI PRESS

ROSEN BAUMS
Blatz

SHERATON HOTEL
SHERATON HOTEL
SHIELDS RUBBER Co.
RUBBER FOR INDUSTRY

FULTON

^ **Pittsburgh skyline,** Brady Stewart Studio, 1952.

^^ **Demolition of the Better Homes Exposition buildings,** Paul Slantis, c. 1949.

^^^ **Men at the base of the Civic Arena's dome,** William V. Winans Jr., 1960.

With generous support from

Graham Foundation

Bill and Janet Hunt

Carnegie Mellon University Architecture Archives

Furthermore: a program of the J.M. Kaplan Fund

PRESERVATION PITTSBURGH

Contents

LESSONS FROM PITTSBURGH

Raymund Ryan
Curator of Architecture,
Heinz Architectural Center.
Carnegie Museum of Art

Imagining the Modern began as an experiment, the first in a series here at the Heinz Architectural Center, the architecture department of the Carnegie Museum of Art. The claim to experimentality is justified on several, complementary counts. First, the installation contained comparatively few original drawings or models; the visitor instead was presented with copious quantities of photographs, drawings, and newspaper articles in reproduction. Second, architecture students, from neighboring Carnegie Mellon University, were physically present – actively embedded – in the galleries, envisioning future urban scenarios. Third, original research underpinned the presentation, enriched iteratively by the students' work and by a series of public encounters – "salons" – here in the galleries.

This multi-part experiment, its aims and its structure, determined by Chis Grimley, Rami el Samahy, and Michael Kubo. Grimley and el Samahy are partners in the Boston-based practice, OverUnder. Frequently in collaboration with Michael Kubo, an architectural historian, and with a third partner at OverUnder, Mark Pasnik, they have mounted smart exhibitions revisiting the recent urban history of Boston, an endeavor captured in their initial book with the Monacelli Press, *HEROIC: Concrete Architecture and the New Boston*. In addition, el Samahy knows Pittsburgh well, having taught urban design studios for a decade at Carnegie Mellon.

They thus seemed like perfect candidates to tackle Pittsburgh, both its unique characteristics and those it shares with other urban centers.

The Carnegie Museum of Art dates back to Pittsburgh's extraordinary economic and urban growth in the late nineteenth century. *Imagining the Modern* addresses the city's second great burst of activity a full half-century later, in the aftermath of World War II and on the cusp of suburban flight. As the authors deftly demonstrated at the museum and now in these pages, the Steel City was in the forefront of commissioning such singular works of architecture as the Alcoa and U.S. Steel Headquarters (both by the Manhattan firm of Harrison & Abramovitz) and the urban renewal of entire neighborhoods (The Lower Hill, Allegheny Center, East Liberty).

It may well be this focus on neighborhood that is the key lesson from *Imagining the Modern*. In part due to its topography of rivers, hills, and valleys, the Pittsburgh conurbation is an archipelago or jigsaw of many small towns and settlements typically keenly aware of their own personalities and history. This attention to neighborhood opens the conversation up from the trap of abstract planning or aesthetic interest in signature buildings to prioritize the civic realm, to embrace housing, landscape, and infrastructure.

Curiously, as far as we can tell, there had been no comparable exhibition of postwar Pittsburgh prior to OverUnder agreeing to this challenge, this mission they decided to accept. And there has not, until now, been a publication dedicated to the presentation of these complex postwar phenomena in logical and interconnected ways. This book results therefore from an experiment that began in preliminary conversations between OverUnder and the Carnegie Museum of Art now some years past and that continued in situ in the Museum's galleries.

With the foresight of the Monacelli Press, those conversations, research, and analysis have led to this document, these lessons for all those interested in the past, present, and future of great American cities.

Reimagining the Modern

WORLD'S FINEST CANDY
CLARK
CLARK CANDY BAR
Enjoy a
CLARK CANDY BAR

PITTSBURGH AS PROJECT: REIMAGINING THE MODERN

Chris Grimley
Michael Kubo
Rami el Samahy

We shall not be able to say that we have created a modern style until Architects cease to condemn all that is modern, or all that belongs to the past.

James A. Mitchell & Dahlen K. Ritchey, 1937 1

In 1946, in celebration of the year-long Diamond Jubilee of his department store in downtown Pittsburgh, owner Edgar Kaufmann commissioned the young architecture and planning office of Mitchell & Ritchey to produce *Pittsburgh in Progress*, an exhibition that offered a visionary projection of the city's future. Led by Kaufmann as client and James Mitchell and Dahlen Ritchey as designers—all three among the principal advocates for modern architecture in Pittsburgh after the 1930s—the exhibition imagined a radically new era for a city then shrouded in pollution, threatened with the loss of its industrial base, and in need of significant reinvention following economic and physical stagnation during the Depression and the Second World War. In their accompanying publication, Mitchell and Ritchey described their ambition to provide "an exploration of Pittsburgh's possible future" that might envision "what the city and its region can become" at the outset of the postwar boom.2 This transformation, they wrote,

> calls for a partnership between us and our descendants for the continuous improvement of living.... [It] has been prepared on the premise that there will be an expansion in the civilized use of intellect, heart, science, and technology and that the atomic age will be one of construction.3

The following year, the newly formed Allegheny Conference on Community Development (ACCD) issued a publication of similar format, titled *Pittsburgh: Challenge and Response*. In explaining its mission, the ACCD compared its ambitions for postwar Pittsburgh to the democratic origins of the U.S., arguing that large-scale redevelopment was both urgently needed and crucial to the city's future. Pittsburgh's environmental and urban problems, according to the Conference, required visionary thinking at a scale commensurate with

> the genius of our country which has been its love of progress, its restless explorations, its unwillingness to relax in the smug worship of things as they are. Each generation of Americans has

< **Overview: View of Alcoa Building and Hill District**
Clyde Hare, 1952.

> gone farther, and produced more, that than which came before it. The broad sweep of the Conference program can be found in its profound acceptance of the inevitability of change.[4]

Together, these parallel documents marked out the breathtaking ends of urban redevelopment in Pittsburgh as well as the means by which this change would be effected. Both initiatives were driven by private interests in alliance with government: companies with leadership invested in the economic welfare of the city and determined to improve it. These corporate leaders sought out the talents of architects, planners, landscape architects, and engineers to help them envision a city renewed, one that was advertised to members of the public and elected officials alike as a necessary path toward a desired future. Viewed from the present, both documents reflect the great divide between that era and ours in terms of the power of architecture and planning—real and perceived—to reshape the built environment. What is today regarded as hubristic was, at the outset of Pittsburgh's redevelopment, seen as both idealistic and urgent.

Imagining the Modern revisits the complex history of urban change that followed pronouncements like these, during the period that came to be known locally as the Renaissance and elsewhere as the urban renewal era. An ambitious program of revitalization in the 1950s and '60s transformed Pittsburgh and quickly became a model for other U.S. cities. Politicians, civic leaders, and architects worked together through sweeping local and federal initiatives that aimed to address the social, economic, and environmental problems that confronted the postwar city. This era of superlatives has often been identified with visionary mayors and business leaders, powerful urban planning authorities, and architects and designers of international as well as local renown.[5] Yet Pittsburgh's progress also included less-well known designers, writers, photographers, and community groups who played important roles in envisioning, projecting, and contesting the modern project from their particular vantage points. The result was a contentious legacy of intervention whose social impacts continue to be debated, but whose buildings and landscapes remain among the most powerful examples of modern architecture and urbanism anywhere in the U.S.

This book extends from a research initiative and exhibition of the same title held at the Heinz Architectural Center of the Carnegie Museum of Art in 2014-15. As curators and "architects in residence" for the nine months of the exhibition, we were invited to unravel the city's complicated relationship with modern architecture and planning through an archival history of the sites, actors, and voices of intervention that shaped the Pittsburgh Renaissance. The material presented in this book builds on these efforts, offering a nuanced view of this crucial moment through original documents, photographs,

Aerial view of the U.S. Steel Building during construction, 1969–70.

and drawings supplemented by scholarly essays, analytical maps and diagrams, and interviews with key protagonists of the city's transformation. Addressing both positive and negative impacts of the era, *Imagining the Modern* examines what the Renaissance meant then and now, what was gained or lost, and what reengaging these histories might suggest for the future of the contemporary city. In looking to Pittsburgh as a specific case, we seek to reassess the broader narrative of urban renewal in U.S. cities, arguing for a deeper understanding of the complexities and concerns which underlay the evolution of architecture and urbanism.

RENAISSANCE AND RENEWAL

It is important to revisit the factors that sponsored the optimistic mindset behind urban renewal in Pittsburgh and elsewhere. Uniquely among the protagonists of the World War II, the U.S. emerged with its physical and industrial fabric relatively unscathed, the only industrialized nation whose economic engines were not devastated, but rather vastly empowered, by the conflict. In 1950, the country, containing roughly half a percent of the world's population, was responsible for more than a third of the world's economic output.[6] By 1960, the U.S. share of the world's production increased to 40%.[7] By this time the gross national product had more than doubled in the fifteen years since the end of the war, growing from $200 billion to more than $500 billion.[8]

In this climate of postwar prosperity, both civic institutions and private corporations shared a willingness to fund ambitious construction projects following the stagnation of the Depression and the war years, particularly in Pittsburgh, a national industrial center that was actively seeking to reshape its urban fabric and its image. At the same time, the end of the war drove a need to retool the economy, and the nation, for the imperatives of the Cold War as well as for the needs of an expanding population and a booming consumer culture.[9] The steel and aluminum industries, both with significant ties to Pittsburgh, redirected their production from the war effort to more domestic concerns, in the process developing new needs for their materials. These included a wide range of new building and consumer products, from the development of new structural possibilities in steel to the use of aluminum for everything from vases to facades.

At the same time, major metropolitan areas faced real and pressing challenges. The need to house returning veterans and their families dominated political discussions and led to sweeping new programs of federal legislation. The American Housing Act of 1949 widened federal subsidies for low income housing, while the Federal-Aid Highway Act of 1956 inaugurated the construction of a 41,000-mile network of interstate highways at a cost of $26 billion, the most ambitious infrastructural project in the nation's history. Together, these new mechanisms transformed the American landscape, nowhere more so than in its cities. In Pittsburgh, such federal initiatives were preceded by local environmental efforts to clean the city's heavily polluted air and water and reduce traffic congestion, thereby shedding its national reputation (as well as its persistent image) as "the Smoky City."[10] After the war, the city began to enforce a law passed in 1941 that required factories to use treated coal. Combined with the introduction of natural gas piped into most residential buildings and the transition of regional railroads from coal to gas, these efforts had a profound—and seemingly instantaneous—effect on the city's air. Not least among the benefits of this transformation was a vastly altered visual landscape, from a dark atmosphere of haze and pollution to a bright setting for luminous new buildings that reflected the economic and material abundance of the renewed city.

In postwar Pittsburgh, national efforts toward urban renewal were bolstered by the unusual combination of civic authorities with a profound desire to meet basic needs and a wealthy corporate class willing and empowered to do so. Indeed, the story of the Pittsburgh Renaissance is deeply interwoven with the city's attempt to evolve from a wartime industrial powerhouse to a peacetime corporate and civic center. These particularities of Pittsburgh's situation led it to become one of the first cities out of the urban renewal gate, for better or worse. The city's transformation in this period includes some of the earliest instances of successful public-private partnerships as well as grassroots efforts, both in support of and in opposition to urban renewal efforts. These complex relationships and competing aspirations were made manifest in the types of projects that were built—including corporate headquarters and suburban office parks, public landscapes, cultural and recreational facilities, university buildings, and housing districts—and in their aesthetic expression, often as a direct reflection of local means of production in steel, glass, aluminum, and brick. Meanwhile the press releases, brochures, newspapers, and magazines that narrated and promoted this construction boom were frequently filled with superlative boasts: Pittsburgh celebrated the world's first aluminum-clad building (Alcoa), the largest retractable dome (the Civic Arena), and the tallest exposed steel structure (U.S. Steel). In this sense, the Renaissance is what we might refer to as Pittsburgh's "Dubai moment:" an era when the world's eyes were turned to the city's spectacular firsts as emblems of the future metropolis.

ARCHITECTURE AND URBANISM

As architects and historians, our interest in Pittsburgh's modern heritage stems not only from our appreciation of its buildings and landscapes, but from the experimental spirit that these projects continue to embody. The best products of the era share an expressive confidence that can be found in works built in other cities at the time, but there is a distinctiveness to their formal and material manifestation in Pittsburgh that makes them worthy of renewed attention. Renewal efforts in Boston, for example—also among the cities that received the largest proportion of urban renewal funds relative to their size—were dominated by governmental initiatives to remake the public sphere, often without the support of the city's wealthy Brahmin class and expressed primarily through robust civic and institutional buildings in concrete.[11] By contrast, the Pittsburgh Renaissance was largely wrought in shimmering glass and metal, propelled largely through private interests in consortium with a cooperative local government.

Many of Pittsburgh's finest buildings of this era were built

Workmen installing the first aluminum panel on downtown's Alcoa Building, Newman-Schmidt Studios, 1951.

as national or regional headquarters for industrial corporations. The period is bracketed by Harrison & Abramovitz's towers for Alcoa (1953) and U.S. Steel (1971), both of which played key roles in reshaping the downtown area known as the Golden Triangle into a symbol of the city's progress and power. Moreover, both buildings stood as essays in developing a corporate expression by pushing the boundaries of what was technologically possible for the industrial materials associated with each entity. At Alcoa, the architects deployed the company's products to numerous ends, including the first aluminum stamped panel facade system, the first aluminum wiring and plumbing, and the first combination of acoustic ceiling panels with a radiant heating and cooling system.[12] Harrison & Abramovitz made similar use of U.S. Steel's material expertise to create its corporate headquarters two decades later. Here exposed plates of weathering steel, known as Cor-Ten, snap into an exposed steel frame to create a rugged exterior that recalls the dark atmosphere formerly associated with the city's steel industries, now chemically absorbed into the building's surface. Situated on a difficult triangular site, the innovations of U.S. Steel extended to structure, with six massive supporting columns positioned outside the building envelope, and to systems, including the fireproofing of these external columns via a pioneering water-based solution.

Such technical achievements were not reserved for industrial headquarters alone. The external structural diagrid of the IBM Building (Curtis & Davis, 1963), clad in stainless steel, was also the first of its kind. Nor were the city's architectural and material innovations exclusively the domain of corporations. The Civic Arena (Mitchell & Ritchey, 1961), originally conceived as a home for the Pittsburgh Civic Light Orchestra, boasted the world's first large-scale retractable dome, comprising nearly 3,000 ton of stainless steel supported by a single cantilevered arm. Innovations also occurred on a more modest scale, as when architect Tasso Katselas designed a non-standard brick for the construction of low-income housing in East Liberty, incorporating a notch in the brick to accommodate the mason's maximum reach and thereby save time and labor.[13]

Perhaps the project that best exemplifies Pittsburgh's eagerness to innovate in this period is Mellon Park Square, designed by architects Mitchell & Ritchey and landscape architects Simonds and Simonds and completed in 1955. The project was the brainchild of Richard King Mellon, then president and chairman of Mellon Bank, who sought to keep Alcoa from moving to New York City by aggregating properties in the Golden Triangle to create a site for Alcoa's headquarters next to a new public plaza at the center of the city. The design of Mellon Square addressed the change in grade between Smithfield Street and William Penn Place through the first integrated design of a modern park above a garage, accommodating seven floors of parking below grade and lining the exposed edge along Smithfield Street with retail to create a modernist, multi-level open space in the heart of downtown.[14] Significantly built through private initiative with the full backing of city government, Mellon Square remains one of the city's most popular landscapes.[15]

Beyond the built legacy of the Pittsburgh Renaissance, a number of ambitious unbuilt proposals for the city continue to loom large in the architectural imagination. The most significant of these are Frank Lloyd Wright's two proposals for the Point Park Civic Center.[16] Wright was approached at the behest of Edgar J. Kaufmann in the late 1940s to reenvision the Point following his magisterial design of Fallingwater, Kaufmann's summer house southeast of Pittsburgh (1934–37), at roughly the same time that Kaufmann commissioned Mitchell & Ritchey to design the *Pittsburgh in Progress* exhibition.[17] Wright proposed an enormous corkscrew ramp, nearly a quarter-mile in diameter, that would provide access to a variety of large-scale cultural and entertainment venues, including an opera house, a planetarium, an aquarium, exhibition halls, and a sports arena. The complex was to be connected via two multi-level bridges to the North Side and the South Side, with a third connection leading to a 500-foot tower at the confluence of Pittsburgh's three rivers. Following a muted reaction from the Point Park Committee, Wright proposed a second, slightly more subdued version, featuring two cable bridges hanging from a shorter 100-foot tower and retaining the mammoth ramp as a parking podium. This second scheme met with no more success than Wright's initial design, and the project was abandoned.

Other corporate patrons commissioned visionary schemes to remake vast areas of the city for cultural and commercial uses. In the early 1960s, Harrison & Abramovitz were hired by the Oakland Corporation, a consortium of private interests, to look at the potential of Panther Hollow, a ravine in the heart of Oakland that divided the University of Pittsburgh and the Carnegie Museums from Carnegie Tech (now Carnegie Mellon University). The firm designed a megastructure that would have filled the entire 150-foot deep gorge to the brim, a mile-long research city linking Oakland's academic and cultural institutions and expanding Schenley Park with rooftop terraces culminating in a hanging garden at Panther Hollow Lake. In the same years Skidmore, Owings & Merrill (SOM) was hired to design a center for the arts on the Lower Hill, envisioned by civic leaders as "a cultural Acropolis."[18] Lead designer Gordon Bunshaft and his team proposed a vast plinth containing an art museum and symphony hall at opposite ends of a landscaped plaza that would have afforded dramatic views of downtown Pittsburgh. A large glass box encasing the symphony hall was flanked by monumental travertine columns supporting a waffle-slab portico and roof, while the three-story art museum was to be enlivened with an undulating roof structure of low vaults.

At the same time, other designers were developing counter-projects for Pittsburgh's neighborhoods that were extremely different in their methods but no less visionary in their intended impact. In the late 1960s, Community Design Associates, led by Troy West, worked with residents of the Lower Hill to produce "Our Way," an ambitious response to the city's official plans for the area. The project strategically located programs in two long buildings on both sides of the existing Our Way Alley, with the larger of these two bars organized in a stepped mass containing multiple types of housing units. A superstructure covering the upper floors was to be planted to provide residents with shading and food. West's ambitious proposal, developed through innovative methods of community-led design, synthesized concerns for housing, environmental conditions, and food production in a radically modern project that was in many ways the antithesis of the top-down planning that typified other schemes for the neighborhood.

While these neighborhood-scale projects never made it past the planning stages, they had a significant impact on the development of the city as well as on discussions of urban renewal era beyond Pittsburgh. These proposals often helped galvanize support for subsequent plans that did come to fruition, in some cases leading to the critical rethinking of designs that were ultimately built. Moreover, the national attention garnered by these proposals affirmed the

Our Way, model, Community Design Associates, 1971.

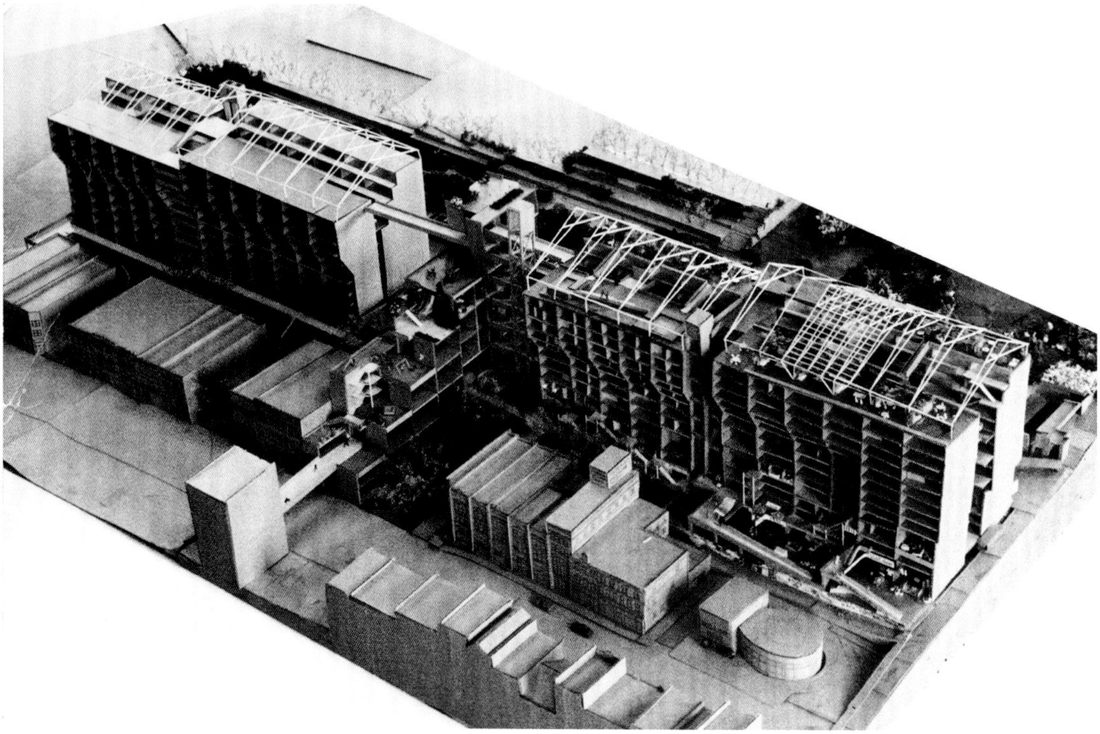

importance of Pittsburgh's transformation as a touchstone for postwar debates on architecture and urban planning, one that provided architects with new models for thinking about large-scale solutions to contemporary urban problems.

REIMAGINING THE MODERN

This book explores the manifold ways in which the modern was imagined in Pittsburgh. The extraordinary range of media through which the Renaissance was staged offers a case study in how modernity was envisioned, discussed, drawn, promoted, contested, constructed, and documented in a city undergoing immense transformation. Excavating this archive from the overlapping viewpoints of curators, designers, historians, and critics, the material gathered in *Imagining the Modern* reflects the dramatic scope of efforts to construct new realities for the postwar city and records how those visions were projected through mediatic and physical manifestations.

The first section of the book, **Positions**, presents essays that reassess Pittsburgh's urban renewal era from an array of contemporary disciplinary perspectives. Architect and urbanist Kelly Hutzell examines the Renaissance through the lens of urban planning, placing the city's transformation within a national context and situating its intellectual framework. Historian Caroline Constant surveys the city's modern landscapes, specifically those of the landscape architect John O. Simonds, who forged his career in the city. Archivist and writer Martin Aurand describes the broader project of modernity in Pittsburgh—one that extended across the domains of infrastructure, planning, architecture, and landscape design—through its creation of profoundly new experiences, and his **Mapping Networks** diagrams trace the various civic, corporate, and institutional connections that made the Renaissance possible.

The book's second section, **Media**, collects a plethora of artifacts through which images of the modern were conceptualized, advertised, and realized in this period. The spectrum of representations through which the Renaissance took shape included visionary documents that set the stage for new visions of the city; planning reports and polemics that laid the practical and theoretical foundations for modernism in Pittsburgh; visualizations using the tools of design, from sketches and models through which ideas were conceived and tested to renderings meant to persuade, to orthographic drawings and technical documents for construction; publications including periodicals, promotional materials, and magazines that chronicled Pittsburgh's progress, as well as a wide range of photographic practices through which the actualities of urban renewal, both positive and negative, were recorded and made visible. While all of these media were essential to the processes of envisioning, marketing, and realizing the modern project in Pittsburgh, in their diversity they also weave a multivalent story, reflecting the competing voices and interests that surrounded the city's transformation.

The third section, **Sites**, examines the six areas of the city that were primary subjects of the intense planning and design efforts that marked this era, from built works to unbuilt speculations. The chapter begins with early downtown projects for Point and the Golden Triangle, continues through attempts to remake the Lower Hill as a contemporary cultural acropolis and Oakland as a vast educational, scientific, and research center, and ends with the replanning of East Liberty and Allegheny Center, both attempts to wrest back retail primacy from the growing allure of suburban malls. In each of these areas, differing circumstances and constraints resulted in urban interventions that varied widely in their methods of planning and execution, as well as in their perceived successes or failures in relation to the city's communities.

The final section of the book, **Perspectives**, presents different voices from the era's participants as well as reflections on the Renaissance from a range of contemporary scholars, practitioners, and critics. Interviews with three key protagonists provide insight into their involvement in the city's transformation: Robert Pease, the director of the Urban Redevelopment Authority (URA) in these years; architect Tasso Katselas, perhaps the most prolific of Pittsburgh's postwar modernists; and Troy West, a designer, activist, artist, and professor whose work offered a powerful model of counter-planning in the midst of urban renewal. It also includes four salon discussions that took place at the Carnegie Museum of Art in the spring of 2016, convened by the authors as part of a series of programs over the nine months of *Imagining the Modern*. These conversations brought together local and national experts to debate the legacy and meaning of the Renaissance today and speculate on Pittsburgh's futures. The four salons featured historians including Lizabeth Cohen, Kai Gutschow, Albert Tannler, Joel Tarr, and Gwendolyn Wright; architects, planners, and preservationists including Matt Falcone, Ray Gastil, Justin Greenawalt, Christine Mondor, Susan Rademacher, and Corey Zehngebot, and critics and authors including Martin Aurand, Charles Rosenblum, and Mimi Zeiger.

Pittsburgh's postwar architecture and urbanism represented a transformative moment in its history. At a point when the city is currently experiencing a new resurgence in energy, *Imagining the Modern* is especially relevant to those who seek to understand an era when Pittsburgh was at the center of the world stage. Using the city as a case study, this book frames questions that extend beyond the region, reassessing this important period in twentieth-century architecture at a time when many of its products are under threat across the nation.

1 James A. Mitchell and Dahlen K. Ritchey, "Impressions and Reflections, Part 2," *Charette*, August 1937, 2.
2 James A. Mitchell and Dahlen K. Ritchey, *Pittsburgh in Progress Presented by Kaufmann's* (Pittsburgh: Kaufmann's, 1946), 1.
3 Ibid.
4 *Pittsburgh: Challenge and Response* (Pittsburgh: Allegheny Conference on Community Development, 1947), 3.
5 See Albert M. Tannler, *Pittsburgh Architecture in the Twentieth Century: Notable Modern Buildings and Their Architects* (Pittsburgh: Pittsburgh History & Landmarks Foundation, 2013).
6 Michael French, *U.S. Economic History Since 1945* (Manchester, UK: Manchester University Press, 1997), 199.
7 Peter Dicken, *Global Shift: Transforming the World Economy*, 3rd edition (New York: Guilford Publications, 1998), 28.
8 French, *U.S. Economic History Since 1945*, 199.
9 See Lizabeth Cohen, *A Consumers' Republic: The Politics of Mass Consumption in Postwar America* (New York: Vintage Books, 2003). On the reorientation of architects and planners during the Second World War to the anticipated tasks of postwar renewal in U.S. cities, see Andrew M. Shanken, *194X: Architecture, Planning, and Consumer Culture on the American Home Front* (Minneapolis: University of Minnesota Press, 2009).
10 See Joel A. Tarr, *Devastation and Renewal: An Environmental History of Pittsburgh and Its Region* (Pittsburgh: University of Pittsburgh Press, 2005).
11 We have elsewhere described this period of concrete construction in Boston and other U.S. cities as the Heroic era. See Mark Pasnik, Michael Kubo, Chris Grimley, ed., *Heroic: Concrete Architecture and the New Boston* (New York: Monacelli Press, 2015).
12 On the material innovations of Alcoa's aluminum facades in contrast to the glass skins typical of other postwar office buildings, see Thomas Leslie, Saranya Panchaseelan, Shawn Barron, Paolo Orlando, "Deep Space, Thin Walls: Environmental and Material Precursors to the Postwar Skyscraper," *Journal of the Society of Architectural Historians* 77, no. 1 (March 2018): 77–96. Following their invention at Alcoa, Harrison & Abramovitz designed similar aluminum cladding systems for corporate clients in other U.S. cities including Republic Bank in Dallas (1954) and Socony-Mobil in New York City (1954–56), though no longer symbolically associated with the products of their respective companies.
13 Rami el Samahy and Chris Grimley, Interview with Tasso Katselas in *Imagining the Modern: HACLab Pittsburgh* Broadsheet #3 (April 2016), 7.
14 In its combination of a surface-level urban park with a subterranean garage, Mellon Square was preceded by Union Square in San Francisco, a nineteenth-century park to which underground parking was added in 1938–42 after three years of research on the feasibility of its construction. See Gregory J. Nuno, "A History of Union Square," *The Argonaut* 4, no. 1 (Summer 1993). Union Square was among Mellon's inspirations for creating a modern landscape in Pittsburgh that was integrally designed for the first time to combine park space with shops and a multi-level garage.
15 See Susan Rademacher, *Mellon Square: Discovering a Modern Masterpiece* (New York: Princeton Architectural Press, 2014).
16 On the evolution of Wright's designs for the Point, see Neil Levine, "The Point Park Civic Center and Traffic Interchange for the Heart of Downtown Pittsburgh, 1947," in *The Urbanism of Frank Lloyd Wright* (Princeton: Princeton University Press, 2016), 261–333.
17 Wright also designed Kaufmann's office for his downtown department store (1935–37) in the same years as Fallingwater. See Richard Louis Cleary, *Merchant Prince and Master Builder: Edgar J. Kaufmann and Frank Lloyd Wright* (Pittsburgh: Heinz Architectural Center, 1999).
18 William Mallet, "Redevelopment and Response: The Lower Hill Renewal and Pittsburgh's Original Cultural District," *Pittsburgh History* (Winter 1992), 182.

POSITIONS
WORDS AND ESSAYS

PITTSBURGH'S PLANS: TRIUMPHS AND TRIBULATIONS OF URBAN RENEWAL

Kelly Hutzell

Urban renewal in America is often regarded as a failure: a top-down effort characterized by an over-reliance on highways, inadequate and insufficient housing, and an aesthetic alien to the city and its residents. The projects associated with the Pittsburgh Renaissance are no exception. Yet each of these projects was the result of different sets of goals, actors, funding, processes, and outcomes. As a result, each reveals a more nuanced story of urban renewal in Pittsburgh. In this sense, the city's successes and shortcomings can be seen within the larger framework of the development of American comprehensive planning, a process that began in the decades preceding urban renewal and in which Pittsburgh was a key participant.

GEOLOGY IS DESTINY

One cannot begin to talk about Pittsburgh's built environment without first addressing its geology, as it created the natural resources that made the city possible, and the terrain that made its growth challenging. Western Pennsylvania is essentially an upper flatland plateau, eroded by rivers and ravines. The entire area was once covered by an inland sea, periodically advancing and retreating, leaving rich deposits of organic matter that would eventually become natural gas, oil, and most abundantly, coal. After a collision of tectonic plates pushed up ridges, glacial forces flooded the region, eroding the plateau and creating two swift-flowing rivers (the Monongahela and the Allegheny) that form at a third (the Ohio), which flows to the Mississippi River and beyond to the Gulf of Mexico. The carving of each river through the terrain resulted in broad flatlands at their banks. This compressed geography provided the ideal adjacencies of resource extraction, industrial production, and river transportation.[1]

Due to its strategic location, the area had long been in contention between Native Americans and French and English armies when, in 1784, the surveyor George Woods and his teenage assistant Thomas Vickroy were hired on behalf of the newly independent United States to hastily extend John Campbell's original military plan of four blocks along the Monongahela River. This was no easy task: the triangular point at the junction of the two rivers included the 80-foot high "Grant's Hill," and an existing informal settlement. They chose to plat two grids, one parallel to the Monongahela and one to the

Allegheny. As a result, a disruption occurs through the heart of downtown, creating a series of triangular blocks where the two grids meet, purposely misaligned.[2] This seam, now Liberty Avenue, extended out from the tip of the Triangle to its eastern edge, and served as a main rail conduit into the city during the industrial age.

High-volatile bituminous coal and the steel that it forged fueled Pittsburgh's industrial economy. In 1865 the region's multiple massive iron and steel complexes "accounted for forty percent of national iron production and by 1900, thirty percent of national steel-making capacity."[3] Carnegie Steel – the region's largest metals manufacturer at the turn of the century – was a colossal industrial force. From 1888 to 1900 the company increased production almost tenfold to 4 million tons. To put this in perspective, this was 80% of the total output for all of England at the time.[4] Upon visiting Pittsburgh in 1866 to see the magnitude of production, a writer from *The Atlantic Monthly* climbed a bluff to view the smoke and fire below and remarked that it was like "looking over into – hell with the lid taken off."[5] Fig.1

With the growth of the steel industry, Pittsburgh experienced an enormous population boom. In 1860, the population was just over 46,000; by 1910, it had grown to more than 533,000, the overwhelming majority of whom were either immigrants or the children of immigrants.[6] As the population grew, so did the city. During this period, Pittsburgh annexed numerous adjacent municipalities, growing from less than two to more than twenty-eight square miles. Downtown began to take shape. In the 1890s the first "skyscrapers" appeared. This was followed by an intensive escalation in urban construction and a corresponding growth of the surrounding suburbs.[7]

Fig.1 Pittsburgh, Allegheny & Birmingham, Otto Krebs, 1871.

PLANNING PITTSBURGH'S RISE | 1900–1930

If the origins of the city require a discussion of geology, then its rise to prominence cannot be considered without an understanding of the professionalization of planning in the late-nineteenth and early-twentieth centuries. As industrial cities increased in density, city officials began to hire engineers and landscape architects, the former to manage urban growth, the latter to design open space in the form of parks and boulevards.

Civil engineer Edward Bigelow, Director of Pittsburgh's Department of Public Works, has become known as the "first truly great planner in Pittsburgh."[8] He brokered a land donation to create Schenley Park, and he assembled individual parcels of farm land to create Highland Park. Inspired by the precedent of New York's Central Park (1867), he appointed British landscape architect William Falconer to serve as park superintendent to design these parks, which were adopted by ordinance in 1889. As Head of City Planning, Bigelow set about to create a system of grand boulevards to connect the parks. This park system was designed primarily for the benefit of the prominent members of society who lived on the upper plateaus. However, it could not mask the squalor and smoke rising from below.

Owing to the poor quality of life emanating from its industrial base, Pittsburgh was chosen as the focus of a pioneering sociological survey financed by the Russell Sage Foundation. The six-volume report, *The Pittsburgh Survey*, concluded that "never before has a great community applied what it had so meagerly to the rational purposes of human life."[9] Conceived of and led by a business and professional elite from across the nation, its primary project was urban reform. The survey sought to record working conditions, working class life, and the effects of industrialization on the environment. The results paved the way for the establishment of the Pittsburgh Civic Commission in 1909.

In 1909 the Commission retained Frederick Law Olmsted Jr. to prepare a comprehensive plan that would address the rapid growth within this unique geography. The commission must have given Olmsted pause. As he outlined a few years later: "A glance also indicates the almost unparalleled problems of this city because of the large amount of territory 25 per cent or over in grade.... Consequently, Pittsburgh must exercise greater ingenuity and foresight than other cities..." Given that Woods and Vickroy's early plan was created by a surveyor's chain "an inch too long for every ten feet,"[10] Olmsted emphasized the necessity of accurate surveys and topographical maps, as well as the need to align streets and level hills.

Olmsted's proposal prioritized mobility within the downtown commercial core, to accommodate the railroad and streetcar system, the rise of the private automobile, and pedestrian routes. He concluded: "Of the 530 miles of main thoroughfares within a radius of seven miles of City Hall, less than one and one-half percent have room for passage between cars and vehicles, slow-moving or standing at curb."[11] As a result, Olmsted highlighted the state legislation that facilitated the widening of streets, and he drew diagrams incorporating turning radii, not unlike Frank Lloyd Wright and Le Corbusier's later drawings for their own urban visions. He recommended a new enlarged system of downtown roads negotiating its steep slopes, citing precedents of Bern, Budapest, and Lyon. In addition to the proposed parkways (Boulevard of the Allies along the Monongahela hillside), his comprehensive vision was bracketed by a system of plazas (Schenley Plaza), parks (Nine Mile Run), and promenades (the downtown promenade with vehicular and pedestrian traffic above the Monongahela wharf).

Olmsted's plan, *Pittsburgh: Main Thoroughfares and the Down Town District: Improvements Necessary to Meet the City's Present and Future Needs*, was completed in 1911. The report consisted of five parts outlining recommendations for the downtown district, main thoroughfares, surveys, and a city plan, notes on parks and recreational facilities, and special reports on The Market, The Hump Cut, and The City and Allegheny River Bridges. His father's revolutionary design of 1879 for Boston's Back Bay Fens, combining picturesque landscape design with the larger amelioration of ecological systems, surely influenced the son's holistic approach. He remarked of the Point: "Poetically, this spot, at the meeting of the rivers, stands for Pittsburgh.... Never can a single feature of The Point safely be designed independent of the rest, if worthy results are to be obtained. And what is true of this great monumental feature is true in large measure of all public improvements in relation to a comprehensive city plan."[12]

Shortly after Olmsted completed his proposal for Pittsburgh, he led the formation of the American City Planning Institute (ACPI). It differed radically from the British Town Planning Institute and the French Société Française des Urbanistes that were composed of architects. By contrast, the ACPI was dominated by landscape architects and engineers.[13]

As one of the largest American cities at the time, Pittsburgh was at the forefront of seeking best practices in American planning.[14] At the behest of Mayor William Magee the Pittsburgh Civic Commission's initiative led in 1911 to the establishment of the City Planning Commission, with a focus on practical affairs. In the same year, the Municipal Art Commission was formed to address the "City Beautiful," a nation-wide civic beautification movement that sought to improve cities through grandeur and monumentality. Pittsburgh native Frederick Bigger, who had earned his architectural degree from the University of Pennsylvania, was appointed assistant of the Art Commission in 1914.[15] In 1918, he helped found the voluntary Citizen's Committee on City Plan (CCCP) and served as its chief technical advisor. This organization led Pittsburgh's comprehensive planning efforts, starting with six well-regarded reports from 1920 to 1923 on playgrounds, streets, public transportation, parks, railroads, and waterways. A key advisor for the CCCP reports was Harland Bartholomew, the first full-time planner employed by an American city (Newark, NJ) in 1914 and planner of St. Louis (1915–1950), heralded at his death as "the Dean of City Planners."[16]

The CCCP planning impetus was inspired in part by New York City's adoption of zoning in 1916. In late 1918, the CCCP founders and officers Charles Armstrong, president of Armstrong Cork Company, and Richard B. Mellon, CEO of Mellon Bank, outlined the "need to secure for the city the benefits of scientific planning such as is now being applied elsewhere in order to control its proper development, both industrially and socially."[17] Work began on a Pittsburgh zoning ordinance in 1920, which was narrowly passed in 1923.[18] Bigger, then Pittsburgh's leading professional planner, became chairman of the City Planning Commission (1924–1954).

In the 1920's the city's industrial supremacy peaked, marking the end of six decades of job growth in manufacturing.[19] This came with a price: severe environmental degradation. Environmental historian and Carnegie Mellon University Professor Joel Tarr states, "There is no city that surpasses Pittsburgh in terms of the scope of its air, land, and water pollution history and the extent to which its landscape has been altered and shaped."[20]

PITTSBURGH'S MOVES TO MODERNIZE | 1930-1950

By the onset of the Great Depression, it was clear that the industrial successes of the previous sixty years begat both environmental and economic woes. Unlike Detroit, St. Louis, or Cleveland, Pittsburgh failed to diversify its economy, so that when the demand for steel fell rapidly, the city suffered disproportionately. In 1934, one third of the labor force was unemployed, and those with jobs earned a fraction of their previous salaries.[21] Downtown property values plummeted, and vacancies rose. Combined with the ongoing environmental disasters (smoke pollution and recurring floods, including the devastating Saint Patrick's Day Flood of 1936), Pittsburghers endured a low quality of life.

Despite this weakened state, or perhaps because of it, Pittsburgh's corporations strove to find new relevance in a changing world. The New York World's Fair of 1939 brought new technologies and modernism to the masses and Pittsburgh's industrial products were featured prominently among the exhibitions. The Electrical Products

Building featured Westinghouse products. Pittsburgh Plate Glass constructed a glass house as part of the exhibition "The Town of Tomorrow."22 The Heinz building had a race car as its centerpiece; it was here that Howard Heinz met the famed New York City Parks Commissioner Robert Moses.23

Known as "master builder" of the New York metropolitan region, Moses had a reputation for accommodating the private automobile by creating roadways, parkways, and bridges that facilitated development of the suburbs.24 Later that year Heinz hired Moses to create an arterial plan for Pittsburgh, having met his fee by securing personal donations from leaders in the Pittsburgh Regional Planning Association.25 Fig.2 From the scale of the appliance to the building to the city, Pittsburgh was preparing to modernize.

Moses's vision for the "Golden Triangle" of downtown Pittsburgh included leaving the Point and Manchester bridges in place (they were removed in 1959 and 1969 respectively), easing traffic congestion by eliminating the trolley system, adding parking facilities, and clearing the railroad tracks and dilapidated buildings at the Point to create a park in which a large column of black granite, glass, steel, and aluminum, was to be installed as "a tribute of the modern City of Steel."26

Moses differed greatly from St. Louis' Harland Bartholomew, who also embraced the age of the automobile, yet pressed for the inclusion of social and land use criteria to inform freeway design. Moses proposed three new routes through the city: first, uninterrupted travel along and parallel to the Allegheny River (a version of today's Tenth Street Bypass), second, a parkway along the Monongahela River from downtown to Wilkinsburg (today's Penn-Lincoln Parkway East), and third, a boulevard connection between the Allegheny and the Monongahela (today's Crosstown Boulevard). Of the third, he said: "Incidentally, this will wipe out a slum district [the Lower Hill] that is no credit to Pittsburgh, and which has a depressing effect on available surrounding property," an ominous harbinger of things to come.27

Moses' sweeping approach to urban renewal in New York City

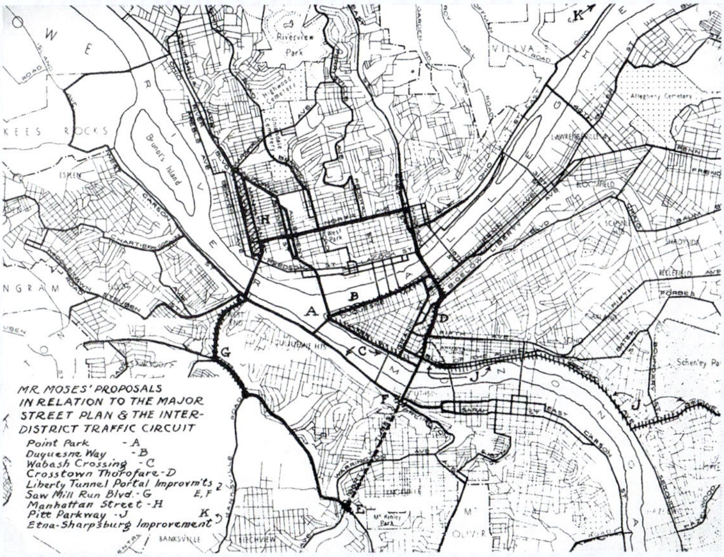

Fig.2 Arterial plan for Pittsburgh, Robert Moses, 1939.

proved no different when it came to Pittsburgh. While the document he completed was entitled Arterial Plan for Pittsburgh, the Pittsburgh Press reported on his recommendations with the headline "Highways to Suburban Areas." Historian and University of Pittsburgh Professor Emeritus Edward K. Muller remarked that "Moses didn't come up with anything particularly, but he grabbed the attention of the civic leaders. His visit galvanized interest and became a critical moment in the fore steps of the Renaissance."28 Though World War II interrupted Pittsburgh's infrastructural ambitions, the Moses report had enormous influence on the plans that would be realized in the postwar era.

The economics of the war effort may have saved Pittsburgh financially, but continued to exacerbate inherent issues within the city. With industrial plants running at full production, workers who were not drafted easily found employment. An over-reliance on the steel sector increased, while the improvements championed by business leaders, including smoke elimination, flood control, and blight removal, were put on hold.

One such leader was Richard K. Mellon, heir to the Mellon fortune and one of the region's most influential financiers. He provided unifying leadership and was considered a consensus builder amongst the city's corporate titans. As founder of the Golden Triangle Division of the Chamber of Commerce in 1939, he led the organization at a time when it was regarded as duty-bound to address civic problems. He also headed the Pittsburgh Regional Planning Association and served as Vice President of the national ACTION organization, which advocated on behalf of for-profit private urban renewal projects. After serving in the Army during the war, Mellon played a key role in the creation of the Allegheny Conference on Community Development (ACCD), whose mission was to develop "an overall community improvement program" for Pittsburgh. Twenty-four chief executives of Pittsburgh's top corporations were asked to participate, as citizens, in face-to-face dialogue.29

At the same time, Democratic boss David Lawrence continued his rise in local and state politics. Having served as chairman of both the Allegheny County Democratic Committee (beginning in 1920) and the Pennsylvania Democratic Party (from 1934), Lawrence ran for mayor of Pittsburgh in 1945, embracing the state's Republican initiative for construction of a new Point Park and a limited-access highway in a nine-mile stretch connecting downtown to eastern suburbs. Stating that "the future of Pittsburgh demands teamwork," he won handily.30 He presided as mayor of Pittsburgh from 1946 to 1959, when he left that office for the governor's mansion.

These two men—Democratic Mayor David Lawrence, and Republican financier R.K. Mellon—consolidated power in their respective spheres, recognized the mutual benefits of collaboration, and jump-started what would become the Pittsburgh Renaissance with a series of joint initiatives. Lawrence and Mellon launched Pittsburgh's Renaissance in 1946 with a view towards environmental improvements and modernization of the city's infrastructure. The Commonwealth of Pennsylvania's Urban Redevelopment Law of 1945 led to the establishment of the Urban Redevelopment Authority of Pittsburgh (URA) in November 1946, with Lawrence as its first chairman. The URA quickly established a parking authority, a public auditorium authority, a sanitation authority, and a tunnel authority. Programs initiated earlier were now restarted: the discharge of integrated waste into the rivers was ordered to cease in 1945, the Allegheny County Sanitary Authority (ALCOSAN) was established in March 1946, and a Smoke Control Ordinance was enacted in April 1946.

Despite the national euphoria at the end of the war, the situation in Pittsburgh had become desperate, and by 1945 the need for action was acutely felt. Not only were the land, air, and water toxic, but the economic vitality of the central business district was on a precipice. Alcoa, U.S. Steel, and Westinghouse were looking beyond Pittsburgh to New York City to base their future operations. Lawrence began a series of meetings with Mellon's corporate network in an effort to form public-private partnerships towards creating investment partnerships, as suggested by the national resources organization, the Committee for Economic Development. Top business leaders became main partners with the government, with the city's many universities as secondary participants. Throughout the initial decades of the Pittsburgh Renaissance, there was little, if any input solicited from the general public.

Nonetheless, the public was engaged in a number of ways, chief among them, as viewers of informative exhibitions. Many were held in department stores, which had become centers for the consumption of modern products and ideas in the postwar era. This occurred throughout the nation, with Pennsylvania as an early adopter.[31]

On the occasion of the 75th anniversary of Kaufmann's Department Store, owner Edgar Kaufmann engaged architects James A. Mitchell and Dahlen K. Ritchey to develop a report looking 75 years into the future, leading to the exhibition *Pittsburgh in Progress* displayed at the downtown Pittsburgh store in 1946. Fig.3 In the architects' imagination, "the Point is a spacious triangle of green. Towering office buildings are set in the midst of the expanding green of nature. The North Side with its metropolitan and commercial center is relieved of its congestion."[32] Ultimately,

Fig.3 *Pittsburgh in Progress* exhibit, 1946.

their fantastical vision became the new template for the city.

A MODEL THROUGHOUT THE NATION | 1950S

The businessmen and politicians who had coalesced around Mellon and Lawrence had the resources to actualize Mitchell and Ritchey's visions. In three early projects, Pittsburgh led the way, introducing new large-scale urban transformations as well as new economic models for their realization. These included a state-funded park, a privately-funded commercial district, and a cultural center and housing district that utilized a combination of philanthropic, developer, and federal housing funds.

Based on reports by Olmsted, Moses and others, the ACCD had begun to consider alternative futures for the Point before the war. In 1947, the year following *Pittsburgh in Progress*, Kaufmann, as chair of the ACCD committee on the Point, invited Frank Lloyd Wright, who had designed his summer house at Falling Water, to consider a large-scale civic intervention at the site. Wright made two radical proposals: the first an enormous circular building housing an opera house, movie theaters, and a convention hall; and the second, a tower holding bridges across the Allegheny and the Monongahela. Neither scheme moved forward, as Kaufmann's peers hesitated at the scale and cost of Wright's schemes.

The site was ultimately approved for state funding as a park. The 36-acre historic and recreational Point State Park was designed by landscape architect Ralph Griswold and architect Charles M. Stotz, with additional assistance from Gordon Bunshaft of Skidmore, Owings & Merrill, beginning in 1949. Although construction took decades to complete, with the park finally opening in 1974, the site was fairly easy to assemble. With state funding, a limited number of residents, and the power of eminent domain, the city had the means to compensate property owners without much political price to pay. A handful of property owners, objecting to the designation of their properties as "blighted," a necessary step for invoking eminent domain, took the city to both state and supreme court, but the city's actions were upheld.

The initiative included another ambitious project, the Gateway Center. Understanding the transformative potential of a new park at the Point, city officials and the business community seized the opportunity to revitalize the adjoining 23-acre area. By appointing the mayor to head the URA, the city had signaled its seriousness in redeveloping the area. When business leaders approached the Equitable Life Assurance Society of New York in a bid to convince it to relocate to Pittsburgh, the company agreed and saw fit to finance the Gateway Center development.

The project was both typical of CBD redevelopment of the era and unusual in a number of ways. As in subsequent downtown revitalizations (e.g. Baltimore, Philadelphia, Detroit), this was largely a private initiative, with government providing the tools for development, chiefly eminent domain. The design was not created by architects or planners, however. When Olmsted first proposed a new vision for the Point, he had called for comprehensive planning, but that was not to be the case for Gateway Center. Instead the redevelopment plan included no maps or zoning ordinances. Written by a lawyer in 1950, it was essentially a contract between the URA and Equitable Life.[33]

Initially envisioned as a super block of eight cruciform towers in a park (reminiscent of Le Corbusier's Plan Voisin for Paris of 1925), the plan was modified over the years, and only three aluminum-clad cruciform towers were constructed. Originally planned as the world's first stainless steel buildings, their cladding material was changed at the outbreak of the Korean War. Subsequent buildings were more varied in form and materials, but all were designed in a modernist corporate language. These included Four Gateway Center (Harrison & Abramovitz), the Bell Telephone Building (Dowler & Dowler), the State Office Building (Altenhof & Bown), the IBM building (Curtis & Davis), and the Westinghouse Building (Harrison & Abramovitz). The project was grounded by the landscape, notably Equitable Plaza (Collins, Simonds and Simonds), which provided pedestrian connectivity across a number of parcels. Among the first urban renewal projects in the nation, Gateway Center's success made Pittsburgh a model for other cities across the country. The project also spurred other private development in the Business District, most notably, Mellon Square and the Alcoa Building and the U.S. Steel-Mellon Bank Building.

With the early successes of the downtown projects, Pittsburgh's civic leaders set their sights on the adjacent neighborhood of the Lower Hill. At this time a predominately African-American quarter in poor condition, the neighborhood had been eyed for redevelopment in Moses's plan of 1939. The 100 acres of the Lower Hill was regarded as the cultural and commercial heart of black Pittsburgh, but its proximity to downtown drew civic leaders to consider it as a site for a new—and different—cultural center.

This proposed cultural district, composed of museums, convention auditoria, and symphony halls, would, according to the Allegheny Conference, "remove the lingering conception of Pittsburgh as a 'milltown' that is bereft of any beauty and grace."[34] According to Robert Pease, former executive director of both the URA and the ACCD, Mayor Lawrence believed that the city needed to become "big league" to compete with other cities: "we have to have major league stadiums and major league symphony halls."[35] The Lower Hill was the preferred location for this "cultural acropolis," but reservations remained due to the high cost of relocating the thousands of residents who called the densely populated neighborhood home.

It was the 1949 Housing Act, the first urban renewal legislation, that opened up a path to remove and relocate residents. In the following year, the URA obtained $15 million in federal funds to build "a glittering new Hill District to match the Point Park Development."[36] The land was declared blighted and cleared in a record two years. A series of projects began, including a master plan for the entire site by Mitchell & Ritchey. The architects were also selected to design the Civic Auditorium, an 18,000-seat facility that boasted the largest dome in the world at the time of its construction, with many of the components and systems manufactured in Pittsburgh.[37] Other components of the master plan included a Center for the Arts complex, funded by the Howard Heinz Foundation and designed by Gordon Bunshaft, as well as three new residential towers designed by I. M. Pei for developer William Zeckendorf.

Although the Civic Auditorium was completed to great fan-fare, other components would subsequently stall or collapse. Zeckendorf's three tower scheme was reduced to one, and Heinz, whose funding had been contingent upon the city clearing the adjacent residential blocks, withdrew his offer and invested in a symphony hall downtown. Both projects succumbed in part due to neighborhood resistance. The Lower Hill renewal project began with the support of the local African-American community, who believed that the plan would include improved housing for residents. While some housing projects were built or expanded, city officials were unwilling or unable to keep pace with the relocation process. As it became increasingly clear that its needs were not being met, the local community saw less advantage in supporting the program, and by the 1960s it stood firmly in opposition to the project.

In the 1950s, however, it still seemed as if Pittsburgh could do no wrong. In the space of a decade it had decreased smoke pollution, controlled the flood waters, completed Mellon Square and two new skyscrapers around it, and begun construction on Point Park, Gateway Center, and the Lower Hill. New buildings and public spaces were materializing in which local corporations showcased advanced materials and technologies and new plazas designed in bold geometries offered novel open spaces for downtown use – and for viewing from the new office towers. National media celebrated the city's successes; politicians and planners from other cities came to view the "Pittsburgh Renaissance" in person. Pittsburgh's progress graced the pages of numerous national magazines, including *Fortune* (May 1952), *Life* (May 14, 1956), and *Holiday* (March 1959). Views of the Golden Triangle figured prominently in the 1956 film *American Engineer* (sponsored by Chevrolet) that celebrated the use of technology to improve the built environment. **Fig. 4** Once again Pittsburgh was seen – and presented – as a dynamic city, replete with new pollution controls, a revitalized central business district, and national acclaim.

It was in this context that David Lawrence was invited to Harvard in 1956 by Josep Lluís Sert, Dean of the Graduate School of Design and President of the International Congress of Modern Architecture (CIAM). That year Sert convened his first conference, with the aim of establishing urban design as a distinct discipline at the intersection of architecture, landscape architecture, and planning. Lawrence participated at the two day event with architects, landscape architects, planners and professors, "with an eye toward the development and reshaping of American cities."[38] Edmund Bacon, executive director of the Philadelphia City Planning Commission, expressed the urgency of the moment in his opening remarks, saying: "The action of the Congress of the United States in appropriating one billion dollars to create a new urban environment places on all of us a responsibility we cannot duck."[39]

Lawrence, the only politician invited to participate, presented Pittsburgh as a case study response to the postwar challenge: "We think that civilization cannot be a string of country villas, or a sprawl across the landscape of incomplete satellites revolving around nothing. We think there must be a center where the highest skills may congregate and exchange ideas and services, where the rare and the beautiful may be exalted, where the art of administration may be practiced to meet the increasing complexities of both industry and government; where the human need for mingling with one's fellows can be met. That has been the philosophy of our design for Pittsburgh."[40]

Extolling the necessity of private funding,

Fig. 4 Cover of *Fortune*, June 1952.

Lawrence elaborated: "A community...cannot live on public works alone. The test of our design, the test of our planning, comes when we make the best possible reconciliation of public powers and controls with the drive and initiative of private enterprise." He described the interaction between government and citizen representation as "a two-way flow. Perhaps some of it has come from government; at least as much has come *to* government from the citizen representation of the Allegheny Conference on Community Development."[41]

Referring to the Point and the Gateway Center as "a greenbelt border at the heart of our central business district," he made reference to the massive infrastructural changes afoot but acknowledged the power of architecture and public spaces in garnering the spotlight. "We have worked hard in the fields of air and water purification, in public health, in flood control. We feel that we have largely conquered the nuisance of smoke and air pollution, and just last week, we began the physical construction of a $100,000,000 sewage system. But the most obvious things – the symbols, the attention drawers – are buildings and new land uses."[42]

THE SECOND WAVE / THE RESISTANCE | 1960s

Despite the many strides made in the 1950s, various critiques were offered of the planning processes and its outcomes in the subsequent decade. Some critics took exception to a decision-making process that appeared to include only elites, other felt that the projects were not moving fast enough. A third criticism came from within the power structure, by powerful groups who were not a part of the initial success. These opinions paralleled the general disenchantment with urban renewal that was beginning to be felt nationwide.

That dissatisfaction was articulated most clearly by Jane Jacobs, who also participated in the Harvard conference, where she urged planners to "respect strips of chaos" such as "the plaza, the marketplace and the forum."[43] Her 1954 series for Fortune magazine praised Bacon's plans for Philadelphia, which impressed the "eminence grise of American urbanism," Lewis Mumford, and the *Fortune* editor, William H. Whyte, Jr.

Upon later visiting Philadelphia at Bacon's invitation, however, Jacobs rescinded her praise, shocked at what had been built, and credited him in particular for inspiring her to develop what became known as the most vigorous attack on the urban renewal order. Speaking of Bacon she said, "not only did he and the people he directed not know how to make an interesting or humane street, but they didn't seem to care."[44] Her critique continued in an essay she wrote for Whyte's 1958 book *The Exploding Metropolis*, titled "Downtown is for People." At an urban design conference at the University of Pennsylvania that same year, where she was invited to speak with

Kevin Lynch, I. M. Pei, Lewis Mumford, and Louis Kahn, Jacobs caught the attention of the Rockefeller Foundation, which sponsored the work that culminated in *The Death and Life of Great American Cities* (1961). Shortly thereafter, Jacobs spoke at a panel discussion at the Museum of Modern Art, where she endorsed more urban renewal and planning, but only if it was based on a new attitude, incorporating "urbanity." In the span of five years, Jacobs became a leading figure in American urbanism.[45]

Jacobs arrived in Pittsburgh at the invitation of a University of Pittsburgh lecture committee in September 1962, the same year she was named Woman of the Year by the British *Architect's Journal*.[46] Her comments proved as provocative as they were in her book. The best account of her trip comes from James Cunningham, who as associate director of ACTION-Housing was engaged in the effort to bring better housing to the city. "In one appearance after another," he wrote, "she hit hard on her theme of the city's need for variety, better design, high densities and preservation of the old."[47] She lambasted city planners, community development groups, and citizen groups. A consummate controversial critic of urban renewal and modernist planning, she famously concluded that "Pittsburgh is being rebuilt by city haters."[48] She certainly did not endear herself to her hosts. In a meeting with Chancellor Edward Litchfield and other University of Pittsburgh administrators, Jacobs "declared the university's plan to redevelop its surrounding neighborhood to be a blunder and a bungle, likely to destroy the diversity and life of the area."[49] Cunningham may have been the only one to cast a positive light on Jacobs's critique, remarking, "if the function of the critic is to stir public interest and discussion of an important human problem and to cause professionals to re-examine their principles and practices— she fulfilled the function well."[50]

In a sense, the three major Pittsburgh projects of the 1960s can be read as distinctive responses to these early critiques of urban renewal. Each exemplifies a different trend in American city planning with regard to its impetus and implementation. Unlike the renewal of the Point, the Golden Triangle, and the Lower Hill, which were essentially top-down partnerships between the corporate world and local politicians, these three projects involve different sets of actors, ranging from universities and institutions as the drivers of development in Oakland, a corporation as developer/builder at Allegheny Center, and retail merchants who instituted a participatory planning process in East Liberty.

The earliest of these transformations began in Oakland and was led by the many educational and cultural institutions that called the neighborhood home. Oakland's development was driven in large part by the University of Pittsburgh, the largest of these institutions. It was led by its ambitious chancellor Edward Litchfield (1956–1965), who was keen to grow the university academically and physically. By the end of the 1950s, with support of the university Board of Trustees and working closely on a campus plan with Harrison & Abramovitz (who were so crucial to the transformation of Pittsburgh's downtown), Litchfield announced a dozen major capital projects. These included three new residential towers on Forbes Avenue (later renamed in his honor), new sports facilities, and a new complex comprised of a library and six professional schools (business, law, social work, education, public and international affairs) on the site of Forbes Field, the stadium previously used by the Pittsburgh Pirates.

In his essay "Some Blessings of Urban Renewal" noted housing expert Charles Abrams outlined how the renewal "inducements," with its power of eminent domain and write-down costs, could spur institutional expansion as well as cultural centers, etc.[51] While Abrams's insights encompass the Lower Hill project (which Litchfield had vociferously opposed for fear of losing the Carnegie Museum of Art from its home in Oakland), the University of Pittsburgh projects were university-funded and, as a result, did not benefit from the tools of urban renewal such as eminent domain or federal funding. At the same time, they were not subject to the same degree of public scrutiny to which other projects of the era might have been. Provided that the university could bear the costs, it had substantial freedom to develop these ambitious projects.

To achieve his most ambitious project, the development of Panther Hollow, Litchfield adopted a different mechanism: The Oakland Corporation created in 1961 following the Pittsburgh Regional Planning Association's long-range master plan for the redevelopment of Oakland. Comprised of seven non-profits with interests in the neighborhood (with Litchfield as chairman and the University of Pittsburgh with 50% ownership) OakCorp was tasked with acquisition and development of the property. Unlike the institutions that owned the company, it was to sell stock, make a profit, and pay taxes. OakCorp immediately set about to develop an enormous research park (designed by Harrison & Abramovitz) in the ravine that divided the Carnegie Museum from Carnegie Tech. Announced to great fanfare in 1963, the Panther Hollow project filled in the ravine with what was touted as the "world's greatest research park," containing a total of 18 million square feet of offices, support spaces, residences, and cultural spaces. Although ground broke in 1964, the project could not attract sufficient tenants, and OakCorp disbanded the following year—the same year Litchfield resigned as chancellor amidst questions regarding overspending.[52]

If Oakland's development was driven by its educational and cultural institutions, Allegheny Center can be considered through

Fig.5 Aerial view of Allegheny Center and downtown Pittsburgh, A. Church Photographers, 1935.

the lens of the industrial corporation. A vast reconfiguration at the heart of Pittsburgh's Northside, Allegheny Center comprised thirty-six blocks of the original Allegheny City urban fabric, rebuilt as a single car-free super block. **Fig.5** It consisted of a mall, two office buildings, several residential apartment buildings, and a parking garage holding nearly 2,800 cars. The project was thoroughly modern: Deeter Ritchey Sippel master planned and designed much of it, with contributions from Tasso Katselas and the Office of Mies van der Rohe (following Mies's death). A national competition was held for the main public plaza, which was won by William Berger, a former employee of Walter Gropius.

Financed in large part by Alcoa, Allegheny Center showcased aluminum in a number of ways. The walls of the shopping mall, which occupies a third of the super block, featured "the unique use of a variegated bronze-colored Duranodic aluminum insulated panels." An office building marked the first use of a thin wall aluminum casting curtain wall, allowing for wide views and a flush facade. Even the central plant, which provides heating and cooling to the entire complex, sports "unusual extruded Alcoa aluminum columns that support 80 foot span steel trusses."[53]

Alcoa's involvement came as no surprise, as they were deeply interested in using their products for construction. In a 1964 *Fortune* magazine article entitled "The Third Force in Urban

Renewal" Hubert Kay identified the role of Big Aluminum in urban renewal, stating "to date, ... the most interesting and significant leaders of the new movement are the big aluminum companies, Alcoa and Reynolds. Both companies are neck-deep in the lagging and bitterly criticized urban renewal program."54 In 1959 Reynolds created a subsidiary specializing in housing and hired Albert M. Cole, who as a congressman had helped write the 1949 Housing Act, and who under Eisenhower had administered the associated federal housing program. In 1960 Alcoa entered the real estate market, and by the mid-1960s, building products accounted for a quarter of the entire aluminum market. In the early 1950s aluminum companies experimenting on the level of the building; by the following decade they engaged in reshaping entire swaths of the city.55

East Liberty's transformation was not driven by academic institutions or industrial titans, but by local merchants. In the late 1950's, concern about the middle-class exodus to the suburbs, poor traffic circulation, and an increasingly deteriorated building stock led East Liberty retailers to petition the URA to conduct what would eventually become the city's largest redevelopment project to save Pittsburgh's "Second Downtown." URA Executive Director Robert Pease assigned the project to Allan Jacobs, who later became well known as San Francisco's Director of Planning and a professor at University of California, Berkley. Pease and Jacobs made a point of leading a planning process that engaged the public; in the course of developing the plan, the URA staged more than 280 public meetings, an average of three nights a week.56

As a result, the plan left more than half of the 254-acre project untouched, while reconceiving the remaining road and built up area in an effort to restore East Liberty to its former status as the commercial heart of the East End. A few short years after Victor Gruen's master plan pedestrianized downtown Fort Worth—a project much lauded by Jane Jacobs—Pittsburgh followed suit. The main commercial corridors were to become a car-free pedestrian mall supported by new housing. A loop road diverted through-traffic, while those who wanted to shop would utilize new parking lots and entries at the backs of the stores. More than 1,800 new dwelling units and 2,000 new parking spaces were planned. East Liberty Mall was designed by landscape architect Simonds and Simonds, the signage and wayfinding by modernist Peter Muller-Monk Associates, and the housing by architect Tasso Katselas.57

The East Liberty plan was approved in 1960 and land acquisition began the following year. Nevertheless, it took the better part of the decade to complete the project. Work on the pedestrian mall did not begin until 1965, and it was completed in 1969. The city took advantage of federal dollars to provide much of the project's funding; a $7.56 million grant was allocated to kick start the project in 1960, and the housing was funded by urban renewal grants.[58] As a result, what was initially planned as middle-class housing was converted into low-income housing during the course of the project. Delays in construction, the changed demographic of residents, middle-class flight to the suburbs, and the rise of the enclosed suburban shopping mall doomed the project once lauded as "a new village within a city."[59]

One wonders if it ever had a chance. With workplaces migrating to the suburbs, the white population followed. Pittsburgh's population high of 676,806 occurred in 1950; it lost half of its population in the second half of the century, while the suburbs grew and flourished. The agricultural land of Monroeville gave way in 1954 to the Miracle Mile Shopping Center near the Pittsburgh Interchange of the Pennsylvania Turnpike. In 1969, the Monroeville Mall was completed. At its opening, it was the largest shopping mall in the U.S., with nearly 1.5 million square feet of leasable space and 6,500 parking spaces. Easily accessible by the highway system and considered safe, it proved overwhelming in its appeal.

CONCLUSION

The Pittsburgh Renaissance was not an aberration in the city's history; it represented the continuum of a long history of urban planning and built upon these foundations. The Renaissance began as the exemplar of what could be achieved with a solid public-private partnership; through deft positioning, this partnership was able to marshal funding and organizational capacity to initiate creative large-scale projects. By the mid-1950's the first urban renewal prototypes of this new approach to urban planning were appearing. As circumstances evolved and new models were needed, planning for Pittsburgh developed into a series of alternative experiments in an attempt to respond to the times: by involving educational institutions as cultural players, by creating developer driven projects, and by responding to merchant requests to begin a participatory planning process.

Nor was the Renaissance an aberration in the national context, as Pittsburgh played an important role in the national move towards a modern approach to planning. Successful public-private cooperation began in Pittsburgh, and other American cities soon followed suit, spawning ad hoc organizations of downtown business interests, working in increasingly close partnership with City Hall. Moreover, the involvement in Pittsburgh of Frederick Law Olmsted Jr., Robert Moses, and Jane Jacobs – three key voices in modern American planning – emphasizes the city's relevance in a national dialogue about American comprehensive planning that began in the early-twentieth century and with which we continue to engage.

1 Joel Tarr, *Devastation and Renewal: An Environmental History of Pittsburgh and Its Region* (Pittsburgh: University of Pittsburgh Press, 2005), 13.
2 Sarah Hutchins Killikelly, *The History of Pittsburgh: Its Rise and Progress* (Pittsburgh: B.C. & Gordon Montgomery Co., 1906), 59.
3 Gregory J. Crowley, *The Politics of Place: Contentious Urban Redevelopment in Pittsburgh* (Pittsburgh: University of Pittsburgh Press, 2005), 31.
4 Ibid., 31.
5 James Parton, "Pittsburgh," *Atlantic Monthly*, no. 1 (January 1868), theatlantic.com/magazine/archive/1868/01/pittsburg/536130/
6 "Pittsburgh, Pennsylvania Population 2018," World Population Review, worldpopulationreview.com/us-cities/pittsburgh-population/ Accessed August 3, 2018.
7 Crowley, *The Politics of Place*, 33.
8 William Loeffler, "City Parks: A Legacy to Cherish – The Fledgling Pittsburgh Parks Conservancy Works to Preserve, Restore Urban Breathing Spaces," *Pittsburgh Tribune Review*, January 16, 2000, web.archive.org/web/20070928063010/phlf.org/news/mediaclips/2000/000116tr.html.
9 Walter Kidney, *Pittsburgh's Landmark Architecture* (Pittsburgh: Pittsburgh History & Landmarks Foundation, 1997), 128.
10 Frederick Law Olmsted Jr., *Pittsburgh Main Thoroughfares and the Down Town District Improvements Necessary to Meet the City's Present and Future Needs*. gutenberg.org/files/49972/49972-h/49972-h.htm. Accessed August 23, 2018.
11 Ibid.
12 Ibid.
13 Stephen V. Ward, *Planning the Twentieth-Century City: The Advanced Capitalist World* (Chichester, Wiley Press, 2002), 113.
14 In his book, Edward Muller states, "The city was engaged in urban planning from the 1890s to World War II and was among the leading cities in urban planning during the first decade of the 1900s... By 1920, we were the fifth or sixth largest metropolitan area in the country. At that time, to be engaged in urban planning was forward thinking. We were in the forefront with New York, Boston, and the other large cities." Patricia Lomando White also puts this argument forth in her essay "Pittsburgh Has Long History of Urban Planning." chronicle.pitt.edu/story/pittsburgh-has-long-history-urban-planning. Accessed August 18, 2018.
15 Roy Lubove, *Twentieth Century Pittsburgh: Government, Business, and Environmental Change* vol. 1 (Pittsburgh and London: University of Pittsburgh Press, 1995), 57.
18 Joan Cook, "Harland Bartholomew, 100, Dean of City Planners" *New York Times*, December 7, 1989. nytimes.com/1989/12/07/obituaries/harland-bartholomew-100-dean-of-city-planners.html. Accessed July 28, 2018.
19 Crowley, *The Politics of Place*, 34.
20 Tarr, *Devastation and Renewal*, 3.
21 Crowley, *The Politics of Place*, 34.
22 "1939 New York World's Fair Town of Tomorrow folder #4 Pittsburgh House of Glass." 1939nyworldsfair.com/worlds_fair/wf_tour/town_to-morrow/House-04.htm. Accessed October 3, 2018.
23 John Bauman and Edward Muller, *Before Renaissance: Planning in Pittsburgh, 1889-1943* (Pittsburgh: University of Pittsburgh Press, 2006), 252.
24 Paul Goldberger "Robert Moses, Master Builder, is Dead at 92" *New York Times*, July 30, 1981. nytimes.com/learning/general/onthisday/bday/1218.html. Accessed September 12, 2018.
25 Bauman and Muller, *Before Renaissance*, 252.
26 Robert Moses, *Arterial Plan for Pittsburgh*, prepared for the Pittsburgh Regional Planning Association, 1939, 7.
27 Ibid., 17.
28 As quoted in Patricia Lomando White, "Pittsburgh Has Long History of Urban Planning" *PittChronicle*, January 2008. chronicle.pitt.edu/story/pittsburgh-has-long-history-urban-planning, Accessed August 18, 2018
29 Lubove, *Twentieth Century Pittsburgh*, 108.
30 As quoted in Crowley, *The Politics of Place*, 44.
31 Pittsburgh was not the only city in the Commonwealth with public exhibitions that promoted city planning. In September 1947, the year following the *Pittsburgh in Progress* exhibit, Edmund Bacon assisted Oscar Stronorov, Louis Kahn, Robert B. Mitchell, and others to stage the *Better Philadelphia Exhibition* at the Gimbel's Department Store in Center City. The widely viewed exhibition built tremendous public consensus in the city and became Bacon's playbook as he assumed the role of executive director of Philadelphia's City Planning Commission from 1949 to 1970. Eric Mumford, *Defining Urban Design: CIAM Architects and the Formation of a Discipline, 1937-69*, (New Haven and London: Yale University Press, 2009), 64-69.
32 James Mitchell and Dahlen Ritchey, *Pittsburgh in Progress Presented by Kaufmann's* (Pittsburgh: Kaufmann's, 1946), andrew.cmu.edu/user/ma1f/PittsburghinProgress.pdf. Accessed August 8, 2018.
33 Roger Montgomery, "Improving the Design Process in Urban Renewal," in *Urban Renewal: The Record and The Controversy*, ed. James Q. Wilson

(Cambridge: MIT Press, 1967), 455.
34 William Mallet, "Redevelopment and Response: The Lower Hill Renewal and Pittsburgh's Original Cultural District," *Pittsburgh History* (Winter 1992): 182.
35 Ibid., 182.
36 "'Full Dress' Glitter Planned for the Hill," *The Pittsburgh Gazette,* August 25, 1950, 2.
37 "Civic Arena Construction Scenes," Historic Pittsburgh, historicpittsburgh.org/islandora/object/pitt:MSP285.B001.F17.I04. Accessed August 4, 2018.
38 "Conferencec Here on Urban Design Will Open Today," The Harvard Crimson, thecrimson.com/article/1956/4/9/conference-here-on-urban-design-will/. Accessed August 18, 2018. Other participants also included Reginald R. Isaacs, the Charles Dyer Professor of Regional Planning, who acted as chairman of the group; Charles Abrams, chairman of the New York Anti-Discrimination Commission; Douglas Haskell, editor of *Architectural Forum*; Gyorgy Kepes, professor of Design at MIT; Lloyd Rodwin, professor of Economics at MIT; Hideo Saski, assistant professor of Landscape Architecture; planner Ladislas Segoe; Ed Bacon; Luis Mumford; and Jane Jacobs, assistant editor of *Architectural Forum*.
39 "Urban Design," *Progressive Architecture* (August 1956): 108.
40 "Pittsburgh's Mayor Discusses Urban Design at Harvard Conference." *Charette*, May 1956, 25.
41 Ibid.
42 Ibid.
43 Christopher Klemek, *The Transatlantic Collapse of Urban Renewal: Postwar Urbanism from New York to Berlin* (Chicago & London: University of Chicago Press, 2011), 110.
44 As quoted by Nathaniel Rich in "The Prophesies of Jane Jacobs," *Atlantic Monthly*, November 2016. theatlantic.com/magazine/archive/2016/11/the-prophecies-of-jane-jacobs/501104/. Accessed July 30, 2018
45 Klemek, *The Transatlantic Collapse of Urban Renewal*, 109
46 Ibid., 121.
47 James V. Cunningham, "Jane Jacobs Visits Pittsburgh," *New City*, September 15, 1962, 4–7.
48 Ibid.
49 Ibid.
50 Ibid.
51 Charles Abrams, "Some Blessings of Urban Renewal" in Wilson, *Urban Renewal*, 558-82.
52 Robert C. Alberts, *Pitt: The Story of the University of Pittsburgh, 1787-1987* (Pittsburgh: University of Pittsburgh Press, 1987), 308-312.
53 Deeter Ritchey Sippel, *Allegheny Center* (1967), 18.
54 Hubert Kay, originally printed as "The Third Force in Urban Renewal," *Fortune* 70, no. 4 (October 1964): 130–33, 213–14, and reprinted as "The Industrial Corporation in Urban Renewal" in Wilson, *Urban Renewal*, 279.
55 Ibid., 280.
56 Dan Fitzpatrick, "East Liberty Then: Initial Makeover Had Dismal Results," *Pittsburgh Post-Gazette*, May 23, 2000. old.post-gazette.com/businessnews/20000523intro3.asp. Accessed August 23, 2018.
57 Justin P. Greenawalt, "Pittsburgh's East Liberty Project" (Master's thesis: Columbia University, 2010), 54.
58 Sorley Sheinberg, "Case Study, the East Liberty Urban Renewal Project: With a Brief History of the Events of the Pittsburgh Renaissance Leading to the Project" (internship report (MPA): University of Pittsburgh, Graduate School of Public and International Affairs, 1974), 28.
59 Dan Fitzpatrick, "The Story of Urban Renewal," *Pittsburgh Post-Gazette* May 21, 2000. old.post-gazette.com/businessnews/20000521eastliberty1.asp. Accessed August 23, 2018.

URBAN REVITALIZATION THROUGH LANDSCAPE: SIMONDS AND SIMONDS IN PITTSBURGH

Caroline Constant

Owing to the extensive contributions of landscape architect John O. Simonds and his brother, civil engineer Philip D. Simonds, landscape design was a significant component of the "Pittsburgh Renaissance" (1946–70). Graduate studies in landscape architecture at Harvard's Graduate School of Design (GSD) during the school's formative period of transformation led John Simonds (BLA 1939) to look to architecture chairman Walter Gropius and Dean Joseph Hudnut as mentors: Gropius for the value he placed on the social potential of modern design and Hudnut for his humanist ideals. Reflecting upon the diminished status of his chosen field of study at the GSD, Simonds later recalled: "When I asked my mentor, Dr. Gropius, what role he saw for landscape architecture in contemporary society, he looked at me long and thoughtfully without speaking. It was quite possibly one of the eloquent statement[s] ever never stated."[1] It was Hudnut who recommended that Simonds base himself in Pittsburgh, where he joined his brother in practice in 1939.[2] Although their early commissions centered on gardens for private residences and estates, this was a propitious decision, leading to the firm's active participation in the city's urban revitalization efforts that began in earnest in 1946 with the establishment of the Pittsburgh Urban Redevelopment Authority: the first such organization in the country. Under the provisions of Title 1 of the Housing Act of 1949, the city drew upon the power of eminent domain over areas designated as "blighted" to effect vast changes in the urban environment.[3]

Of the numerous projects that Simonds and Simonds carried out in collaboration with architects James A. Mitchell (Columbia MSc 1933) and Dahlen K. Ritchey (Harvard M.Arch 1934), the best known is Mellon Square (1949–55), the first modern garden plaza built atop an underground parking garage in the U.S. as well as the first such structure to incorporate commercial space. Mitchell and Ritchey had developed a reputation as pioneering modern architects in Pittsburgh, and John Simonds, who was principal spokesman for his firm, undoubtedly found resonance with their architectural values as he embraced related landscape means in pursuit of his civic ideals.

A number of factors contributed to the viability of these collaborative undertakings, especially the "remarkable alignment of civic groups, public agencies, and a new generation of business leaders," as a *Fortune* article devoted to the city's redevelopment efforts explained.[4] Not least was the patronage of Edgar Kaufmann, a local businessman and patron of the arts whose department store, Kaufmann's, was a prominent venue for advancing the cause of modern architecture and design. Kaufmann was active in the city's Urban Redevelopment Authority and a founding member of the Allegheny Conference on Civic Development, an organization of civic and business leaders established in 1943 "to stimulate and coordinate research and community development," which provided crucial support for the city's construction initiatives and efforts to address the unhealthy environmental conditions resulting from its industrial base, all intended to reinvigorate Pittsburgh's Golden Triangle as a dynamic urban core.[5]

To celebrate the seventy-fifth anniversary of his enterprise, Kaufmann enlisted Mitchell and Ritchey to develop a study envisioning the city in another seventy-five years, and the resulting exhibition, *Pittsburgh in Progress*, in which John Simonds participated, was exhibited at Kaufmann's in 1946.[6] Mitchell and Simond's vision for the future of downtown Pittsburgh has affinities with the proposal New York City Parks Commissioner Robert Moses made for the Regional Planning Association several years earlier, when he recommended clearing the obsolete structures at the tip of the triangle where the Allegheny and Monongahela Rivers meet to form the Ohio to create a new Point Park and reconfiguring the highways at its perimeter.[7] Images of this sector displayed in *Pittsburgh in Progress* include an urban core of office towers and apartment buildings set amid broad avenues and open parkland, a vision far removed from the grimy, sooty environment to which its residents had grown accustomed. Fig.1 Indebted to the radical urban propositions that Swiss/French architect Le Corbusier had been proposing since 1922, this "idea of clearing a whole slum at the confluence of two rivers, and turning it into a shining new city-in-a-park," as *Architectural Forum* subsequently

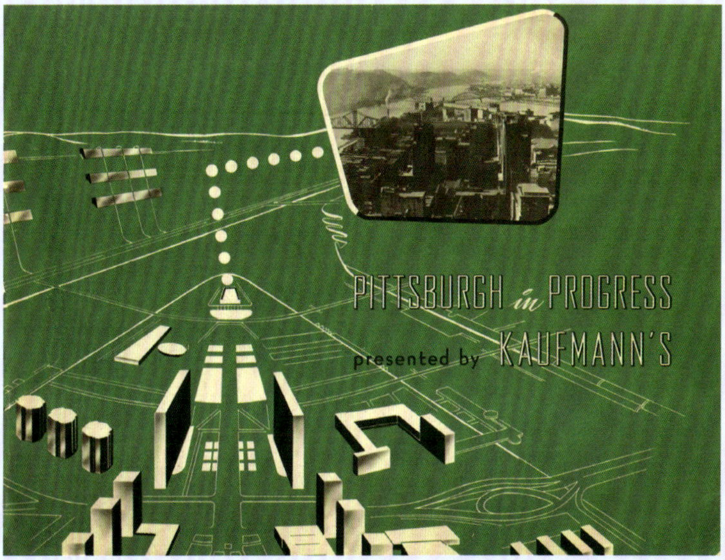

Fig.1 Cover of *Pittsburgh in Progress presented by Kaufmann's*, 1946.

termed the phenomenon, would become a governing principle of the Pittsburgh Renaissance.8

As Simonds noted, the "cause of landscape architecture" was advanced in Pittsburgh when the local Home Builders Association, in planning its Better Homes Exposition for 1949, turned to the local chapters of the American Institute of Architects and the American Society of Landscape Architects, whose advocacy of inter-disciplinary collaboration led to their joint effort to create the "House of Beautility." For an associated exhibition highlighting the work of local landscape architects in the adjacent Civic Exhibition Hall, brochures "designated to familiarize the public with the term landscape architect, and to outline the scope of his service" were distributed in an attempt to foster public understanding of the discipline—an aspiration that would underlie much of Simonds's career.9

The idea for Mellon Square originated that same year with philanthropist Richard K. Mellon, chairman of the Mellon Bank, former chairman of the Pittsburgh Regional Planning Association, and financial backer of the Allegheny Conference.10 In a successful effort to dissuade Alcoa and U.S. Steel from relocating their corporate headquarters to New York City—initiatives that were well underway at the time—he asked the Regional Planning Association to study the feasibility of creating a combination park-and-parking structure, inspired by the model of Union Square in San Francisco, where a parking garage had been erected beneath an historic urban park in 1942.11 The Planning Association enlisted Mitchell & Ritchey to create a scheme for a "Parking Park" to address the shortage of parking in the urban core by combining an underground garage

Fig.2 Parking Park study, Mitchell and Ritchey with Simonds and Simonds, 1949.

with a public amenity—a counterpart to the city's Point Park then in development—for a hilly site flanked by the existing Mellon Bank and two unspecified office buildings. Working with Simonds and Simonds, the architects revised their proposal of April 1949 with input from various civic groups, while funding from three Mellon foundations enabled Mellon Square park to be realized atop the architects' partially sunken six-story parking garage.12

The design team initially envisioned the park as a pedestrian enclave; based on the precedent of New York City's Rockefeller Center (Raymond Hood et al., 1930–39), it was contiguous on three sides with the new office towers and existing buildings and included a skating rink.13 To accommodate the Planning Authority's requirement of two additional parking levels, the collaborators were compelled to elevate the park, isolating it within traffic lanes and providing a tier of shops surmounted by a restaurant and dining terrace along the street at the lowest part of the site. Although Simonds and Simonds are not credited in Mitchell & Ritchey's proposal of 1949, their park design is fully represented in its plan and axonometric views. Fig.2 Consistent with John Simonds's design philosophy—as well as with the version realized in 1955—it is described as avoiding "the heavy monumentality and stereotypical symmetry usually associated with such projects.... It provides for constantly changing perspective views, rendered colorful and alive with fountains, planting, flags, etc."14

John Simonds rationalized the resulting "oasis in an asphalt desert" in terms of the beneficial effects of the park's internal experience: losing "by elevation and sight lines the street and traffic confusion" and enhancing its spatial effects, as "the apparent limits of this volume were extended beyond the screened-off streets to the facades of the flanking buildings."15 The park thus foregrounds the surrounding buildings from within, he added, while also serving as a focal point for the new office towers: the thirty-story Alcoa Building (1950–53) and the forty-two story U.S. Steel-Mellon Building (1948–51), both designed by the New York firm of Harrison & Abramovitz with Mitchell & Ritchey as local architects of record. While most design and business journals focused their coverage on the buildings, only *Architectural Record* published an extensive photo essay on the park.16

Simonds intended Mellon Square to be an urban set piece evoking "the uplifting spirit of civic monumentality."17 To that end, its tiered levels feature dense plantings, a vibrant triangular paving pattern in roughly-textured black and gray terrazzo, and the soothing aural and visual effects of water. Jets of water shoot upward from a rectilinear basin at the uppermost terrace as well as from nine circular cast bronze fountains, from which it spills back into the basin. Water also cascades down a series of pools that descend toward the lower

Fig.3 Mellon Square, Simonds and Simonds, 1955.

street, beckoning visitors to mount a broad stairway to gain access to the park, while its shimmering, reflective qualities are amplified by glazed paving tiles—in eleven colors in the main pool and three in the cascades.[18] Fig.3 Urban activist and *Architectural Forum* associate editor Jane Jacobs lauded this particular component of the park for capitalizing on the city's distinct topography, thus contributing to its individuality: "Pittsburgh is on the right track at Mellon Square (an ideally located focal point), where the sidewalk gives way to tall stairways, animated by a cascade. This is a fine dramatization of Pittsburgh's hilliness, and it is used naturally where the street slopes steeply."[19] A pair of shallow ramps providing access at the top of the hill corresponds to flights of stairs at the bottom, so that no sidewalks interrupt the garage entry and exit points to either side. Buffering the park from the streets are a set of shops at its lowest level and tiers of limestone-covered planters on its other three sides, fulfilling, in Simonds's words, the "need of strong plan forms at the perimeter to withstand the traffic's force of erosion."[20] Planters lining the slope of the hill are cantilevered over the garage entrances, amplifying their massive effects.

Thanks to the publicity campaign undertaken by the Allegheny Conference on Civic Development, Mellon Square was hailed as a significant component of the Pittsburgh Renaissance, as Mayor David Lawrence proclaimed at the groundbreaking ceremony in

September 1953: "This will be the very center, the heart, of the new Pittsburgh."[21] Following the opening Greater Pittsburgh asserted about the project: "nationally it has been one of the most publicized undertakings in Pittsburgh's renaissance."[22] Although considerably smaller than the city's typical redevelopment projects, Mellon Square was ultimately more successful than the other renewal efforts in which Simonds and Simonds participated with Mitchell & Ritchey, owing largely to the density and diversity of its urban context.

Equitable Plaza (1958–62), the firm's second commission to design a park in combination with a parking facility, constitutes an effort to mitigate the negative consequences of urban renewal in the Gateway Center, a group of office buildings set in an open landscape next to Point Park at the tip of the Golden Triangle. Sponsored by the Equitable Life Assurance Society, this urban redevelopment project originated with three cruciform office towers built atop a vast three-story parking garage. Although Mitchell & Ritchey were not involved in this initial phase of development, its layout, formulated in 1949 by the Real Estate Department of the City Investment Company, adhered to the spirit of their *Pittsburgh in Progress* exhibition.[23] The dominance of the automobile in this corporate landscape is reflected not only in its extensive subterranean parking garage but also in its bordering highways. In contrast to the success of Mellon Square in revitalizing its urban context, the Gateway Center elicited widespread criticism. In a 1949 issue of *Architectural Forum* devoted to "Pittsburgh Renascent," Douglas Haskell maintained about the original Gateway complex:

> The arrangement of the towers in the park is purely mechanical; the landscaping between them makes no fresh statement about our grand new world, but is simply a weak Versailles; and the steel-clad structures are an equally weak modernique, lacking in proportion, texture, and dignity, let alone mystery or power as that would differentiate them from "up-ended diners."[24]

Three office slabs added to the complex in the late 1950s—the Bell Telephone Company (Dowler and Dowler, 1956–58), the State Office Building (Altenhof and Bown, 1955–57, demolished 1980s), and Four Gateway Center (Harrison & Abramovitz, 1958–60)—constituted the immediate context for Simond and Simonds's plaza, which mediates between the cruciform towers of the initial development and Point Park at the tip of the peninsula. Deeming this "procession of odd metallic toys" to be "pretty much of an architectural flop," a critic for *Architectural Forum* did not mention Simond and Simonds's contribution.[25] Owing to the need to limit the structural load on the three-story parking garage, their design features shallow planting beds raised above its roof deck that incur restrictions on the vegetation. The plaza is enlivened by a combination of irregular planted areas and rectilinear pools with water jets, which are set within a tartan-grid paving pattern in gray and white terrazzo. In contrast to Clarke and Rapuano's more conventional, geometrically ordered gardens at the base of the cruciform towers, the irregular layout of Simond and Simonds's plaza is directed to intensifying pedestrian experience, signaling the innovative spirit of the newer complex. As John Simonds explained: "Here the street bends, the giant building forms shift from cruciform to slab, the plaza level rises above the street, the eye rests comfortably upon irregularity and color. Still under the shadow of giants, the pedestrian is partially set free from the heavy 'project' environment of much of the Gateway Center."26

Fig.4 Equitable Plaza, Simonds and Simonds, 1958–62.

Prior to completion of Equitable Plaza and its adjoining buildings, Jane Jacobs succinctly summarized the differences between Gateway Center and Mellon Square: "Look at Pittsburghers by the thousands climbing forty-two steps to enter the very urban Mellon Square, but balking at crossing the street to enter into the ersatz suburb of Gateway Center."27 Expanding upon this critique in *The Death and Life of Great American Cities* (1961), she contrasted the popularity of Mellon Square during a pleasant afternoon to the emptiness of the open spaces in the new urban core. Drawing an analogy with Le Corbusier's radical urban proposition of 1933, Jacobs maintained:

> Gateway Center is a Radiant City office and hotel project with the buildings set here and there in empty land. It lacks the degree of diversity of Mellon Square's surroundings.... City park users simply do not seek settings for buildings; they seek settings for themselves. To them parks are foreground, buildings background, rather than the reverse.28

In seeming recognition of the truth of this maxim, Equitable's brochure celebrating Gateway Center as "the nation's first comprehensive downtown business redevelopment accomplished without federal aid" features color images of Simond and Simonds's plaza foregrounding its gleaming cruciform towers of steel, aluminum, and glass.[29] Fig.4

Other aspects of the Pittsburgh Renaissance in which Simonds collaborated with Mitchell & Ritchey—and with Ritchey alone after Mitchell left the partnership in 1957—have been subjected to greater critical scrutiny, particularly the Lower Hill Redevelopment (1954–61). Speaking at the GSD's first urban design conference in 1956, Mayor David Lawrence anticipated that "redevelopment of the Lower Hill ... will be the greatest of our Pittsburgh projects." Simonds and Simonds contributed to Ritchey's plan for the area, which drew upon the collaborators' previously established aesthetic principles. As envisioned in *Pittsburgh in Progress*, it incorporated cultural, commercial, and recreational facilities, including a civic auditorium with a retractable roof for athletic events and musical performances, along with different types of housing. As Mayor Lawrence elaborated, the plan involved "a new street pattern, the consolidation of parcels into large areas susceptible of commercial and apartment developments with relatively low land coverage, parking, and the auditorium and other recreational and cultural uses."[30] Although Jane Jacobs viewed "the Lower Hill Auditorium and apartment project" as typical of such renewal efforts in which "each project will look very much like the next one," the development's social ramifications were of greater consequence than its aesthetics.[31] As was often the case with such examples, there were disproportionate effects on the urban poor who either suffered or benefitted only marginally from insufficient efforts to rehouse the residents of these "blighted" urban sectors. Ninety-five acres of land at the base of the Golden Triangle were razed, displacing 8,000 of the neighborhood's predominantly African-American residents to build Mitchell & Ritchey's Civic Arena (1954–61, demolished 2012) and the Crosstown Expressway but with little of the associated housing, increasing racial and economic segregation in the city's other residential sectors.[32]

Just as Pittsburgh led the country in urban redevelopment with what *Architectural Forum* in 1949 termed "[t]he biggest real estate and building story in the U.S. today," so the city's efforts to address the poor environmental conditions that emanated from its industrial base were equally groundbreaking.[33] Simond and Simonds's increasing involvement in planning during the 1960s led to their efforts to improve the environmental health of the city, particularly the quality of its river water. The firm's 1963 study of Twelve Mile Island in the Allegheny River provided an opportunity to enhance the recreational value of the riverfront and participate in the city's efforts to mitigate water pollution, thereby gaining cognizance of the regional implications of the river's watershed.[34] As Mitchell & Ritchey had imagined in *Pittsburgh in Progress*: "[t]he rivers are now devoted to the many pleasures offered only by lake and seaside cities. The Allegheny becomes a major riverway for swimming, yachting, boating, and water sports ... a broad flowing stream free of pollution."35 Moreover, planning for such sites led John Simonds to advocate orienting projects toward Pittsburgh's prominent waterways as positive aspects of its urban development, accentuating the city's unique geography.

Simonds and Simonds were also active in public park development. An Allegheny Conference study of 1958 recommending potential sites for a regional park system prompted grants from the same Mellon family foundations that had funded Mellon Square Park to purchase 3,600 acres of undeveloped land in the urban periphery. A new Department of Regional Parks was created, and three local landscape architecture firms, including Simonds and Simonds, were asked to consult on the creation of six parks.36 Although each office was initially assigned two sites to prepare land-use studies, master plans, and detailed development plans, the requirement to maintain a degree of standardization while taking full advantage of the distinct natural features of each site led to the decision to joint venture on the work. By 1963 details concerning water supply, roadways, drainage, footpaths, signage, and park furniture had been approved and a reforestation program begun.

In 1966 Simonds and Simonds formulated a long-range development plan for Allegheny Commons, Pittsburgh's oldest urban park and original grazing area. It involved erecting boundary walls to limit park access, while mounding up to their interior surfaces to conceal their presence from within. Zones for active or passive play were to be set within discrete clearings distributed about the wooded site, making discovery of these components a fundamental principle of the park experience. A series of mounds providing grassy sitting areas would inhibit lengthy vistas, providing a further impetus for imaginative exploration. Although these aspects of the proposal were not carried out, Simonds and Simonds reconfigured the formerly picturesque Lake Elizabeth into an irregularly configured trapezoidal, concrete-lined pool in an explicit expression of the constructed essence of an urban park. A related intensification of the park experience had resulted in 1952 from the firm's design for the landscape sequence inside its innovative aviary: a large area in which birds are unconfined, together with separate exhibit rooms replicating the natural habitats of hummingbirds, toucans, and a rain forest.37 A variation on the aviary expansion scheme that Simonds and Simonds envisioned in their park development plan was realized thirty years later, after the complex was awarded the status of National Aviary.

By the early 1960s John Simonds had begun to lament the priority given to vehicular traffic in Pittsburgh's urban redevelopment, which Robert Moses had advised in his *Arterial Plan for Pittsburgh*

(1939).38 Over the course of his career Simonds had witnessed the growing proliferation of automobiles from "[t]wentieth-century beetles burrowing under a twentieth-century garden" in Mellon Square and Equitable Plaza to the "roaring, fuming, four-wheeled monster[s]" that provided a rationale for the expressways plying the surfaces of Pittsburgh's hilly terrain.39 Echoing Jane Jacobs's criticism of the widespread propensity for urban renewal to involve highway construction that severed urban centers from their surrounding communities, Simonds developed projects to mitigate the effects of these "lethal lines of force," as he termed them.40 With an interdisciplinary team of professionals, including fellow GSD graduate Lawrence Halprin, he contributed to a federal study, *The Freeway in the City: Principles of Planning and Design* (1968), intended t o redress such segmentation of the urban environment.

The Allegheny Conference was instrumental in promoting the region's efforts on smoke abatement, flood control, treatment of river pollution, creation of parks and recreational facilities, highway and bridge development, and airport expansion, as well as the city's revitalization. By the mid-1960s, however, community response to the devastating social consequences of urban renewal, together with a decline in federal funding for such projects, led to the collapse of the public-private partnership reflected in the alliance of Democratic Mayor David Lawrence (1946–59) and Republican philanthropist Richard K. Mellon, with the result that the group was no longer able to wield such power over public policy formation. Simonds and Simonds were increasingly becoming involved in planning work, with offices in Washington, D.C., and Miami Lakes, Florida, as well as Pittsburgh. The firm's growing national reputation led to numerous commissions in landscape design and community and regional planning in the eastern United States and the Midwest.

John Simonds's interest in furthering the cause of his discipline also led to his work in landscape education. As a member of the American Society of Landscape Architects (ASLA) Committee on Education (1952–53), he viewed that organization as "the best hope and vehicle of co-operative effort for the good of our profession." Citing "too much emphasis on the 'garden art' concept of landscape architecture," he maintained: "In our opinion, landscape architectural education and training have been in the past, and are today, the matrix from which we have developed and are developing the majority of great city planners, housing planners, park planners, and planners of other related fields."41 From 1955 to 1967 Simonds taught courses in landscape architecture and community, urban, and regional planning to architecture students at Carnegie Institute of Technology (now Carnegie Mellon University), and his book *Landscape Architecture: The Shaping of Man's Natural Environment* (1961) grew out of that experience. Although intended to introduce architects, landscape architects, and planners to the landscape planning process, rather than as a textbook, *Landscape Architecture* was widely used in academic programs in the various design fields, supplanting Henry Vincent Hubbard and Theodora Kimball's long-outdated *Introduction to the Study of Landscape Design* (1917). At every scale, from site selection to regional planning, Simonds's emphasis in *Landscape Architecture* was on the potential for planning and design decisions to enhance the qualities of lived experience, "to realize to the fullest our human potential." As he elaborated: "One plans not places, or spaces or things—one plans experiences."[42]

Reflecting a growing environmental awareness nurtured by his experiences living and working in Pittsburgh during the city's so-called first Renaissance, Simonds maintained: "Somewhere in the complex process of evolving his living spaces, cities, and traffic ways, modern man has become so absorbed in the power of his machines, so absorbed in the pursuit of his new techniques of building, so absorbed with the new materials of construction that he has neglected man himself." In response to humankind's growing alienation from the natural world, he echoed aspects of Jane Jacobs's salient critique in endorsing the "intensification of the natural landscape character through sympathetic handling of man-made spaces and forms."[43] Such a symbiotic relationship among natural and constructed elements was fundamental to Simonds's disciplinary ethos, as he later summarized: "Landscape architecture ... is the art and science of preserving or creating compatible relationships between people and their activities and the natural world around them."[44]

1 John O. Simonds to Stuart Dawson, September 11, 1991, cited in *Mellon Square, Discovering a Modern Masterpiece*, ed. Susan M. Rademacher (New York: Princeton Architectural Press, 2015), 26.
2 John O. and Philip D. Simonds practiced as partners in Simonds and Simonds (1939–52), followed by Collins, Simonds and Simonds (1952–70), with offices in Pittsburgh and Washington, D.C., and as Environmental Planning and Development Partnership (EPD, 1970–82), with offices in Pittsburgh and Miami Lakes, Florida. Lester Collins (MLA 1942) taught landscape architecture at Harvard from 1945 to 1950 and chaired the department from 1950 to 1952 before joining Simonds and Simonds as a partner based in Washington, D.C.; after 1970 he served as consultant to EPD. After John Simonds retired in 1982, he continued to consult for the firm. The GSD Alumni Directory of 1975 lists John C. [sic] Simonds and Philip D. Simonds among the landscape architecture students in the class of 1939, although Philip Simonds did not complete his degree.
3 Title 1 of the Housing Act of 1949 established the legal and financial basis for urban revitalization by granting cities the power of eminent domain over neighborhoods deemed "blighted," while providing funding for demolition and relocation of the affected urban residents. It extended the provisions of earlier housing acts, such as that of 1937, which privileged techniques of spot clearance and rehabilitation, particularly in deteriorating but still livable neighborhoods, as well as establishing a program of slum prevention. The term "urban renewal" was introduced with the amended Housing Act of 1954.
4 "Pittsburgh Rebuilds," *Fortune* 45, no. 6 (June 1952): 88–89.
5 Marshall Stalley, "Pittsburgh and the Allegheny Conference," *Landscape Architecture* 38, no. 4 (July 1948): 153. Stalley was assistant director of the Allegheny Conference; he presented this paper at the annual meeting of the ASLA in Pittsburgh, 1948.
6 James Mitchell and Dahlen Ritchey, *Pittsburgh in Progress Presented by Kaufmann's* (Pittsburgh: Kaufmann's, 1946), andrew.cmu.edu/user/ma1f/PittsburghinProgress.pdf. Although John Simonds is not credited in the exhibition catalogue, Marjorie Simonds attested to his involvement. See Rademacher, *Mellon Square*, 48 and 148, fn. 29. Also see "Pittsburgh in Progress: Toward a Master Plan," *Progressive Architecture* 28, no. 6 (June 1947): 67–72.
7 See Robert Moses, *Arterial Plan for Pittsburgh Prepared for the Pittsburgh Regional Planning Association* (November 1939).
8 Ogden Tanner, "Some Progress in Pittsburgh," *Architectural Forum* 112, no. 6 (June 1960): 119. See "Pittsburgh Renascent," *Architectural Forum* 91, no. 5 (November 1949): cover, 59–73, 110, 112.
9 John O. Simonds, "Pittsburgh Meets the Landscape Architect," *Landscape*

Architecture 40, no 3 (April 1950): 129.
10 See "Magnificent Square in the Triangle," *Greater Pittsburgh* 37 (October 1955): 19-22, 62-63.
11 Harrison and Abramovitz were well along in their design for a new Alcoa headquarters in Manhattan, where U.S. Steel had also purchased property for its intended move, necessitating the speed with which Mitchell and Ritchey assembled their proposal for the Pittsburgh site.
12 "Underground garage, park contract let," *The Pittsburgh Press,* March 13, 1952, 9. Mellon Square was listed on the National Register of Historic Places in 1985.
13 Rademacher, *Mellon Square*, 50.
14 James A. Mitchell, Dahlen K. Ritchey, and George S. Sanderson, *Parking Park Study: A City Park and Underground Parking Garage for Pittsburgh's Golden Triangle* (Pittsburgh: Regional Planning Association, 1949), 17. Sanderson was consulting engineer for the proposal.
15 John O. Simonds, "Mellon Square: An Oasis in an Asphalt Desert," *Landscape Architecture* 48, no. 4 (July 1958): 211.
16 "An Open Place at the Heart of a City," *Architectural Record* 121, no. 2 (February 1957): 195-98. For a model of Simonds's park proposal and plans of the parking garage, see "Off-Street Parking that Pays for Itself," *Architectural Forum* 91, no. 5 (November 1949): 71.
17 Simonds, "Mellon Square," 208.
18 Owing to damage sustained by the original glazed tiles in the Mellon Square fountains, they were replaced by unglazed equivalents in the late 1950s.
19 Jane Jacobs, "Downtown is for People," *Fortune* 57, no. 4 (April 1958): 240-41.
20 Simonds, "Mellon Square," 211. Sited a block from Kaufmann's department store, Mellon Square was the third park in the U.S. to be constructed over an underground parking structure; it was placed on the National Register of Historic Places in 1985.
21 "Mellon Square Park is due to open at 12:30 pm," *Pittsburgh Post-Gazette*, October 18, 1955, 15; also see "Mellon Square Transforms Area," Ibid.
22 "Magnificent Square in the Triangle," *Greater Pittsburgh,* October 1955, 19.
23 Although *Architectural Forum* noted that the cruciform towers were initially laid out according to a process in which "no architect has been retained or even consulted," the New York firm of Eggers and Higgins were designated architects for the complex. Owing to its superblock organization the magazine initially compared the Point Park development to Rockefeller Center and subsequently to Le Corbusier's Ville Contemporaine of 1922. See "Pittsburgh's 'Rockefeller Center,'" *Architectural Forum* 91, no. 5 (November 1949): 2; and "Point Park Development," Ibid., 62; "now at last ... Office Towers in a Park," *Architectural Forum* 99, no. 6 (December 1953): 113.
24 D. H., "An Editorial: Architecture: stepchild or fashioner of cities?" *Architectural Forum* 91, no. 5 (November 1949): 117.
25 Tanner, "Some Progress in Pittsburgh," 119.
26 John O. Simonds, "Equitable Plaza, Pittsburgh," *Landscape Architecture* 53, no. 1 (October 1962): 19; also see "Tower and Plaza Business Area Thrives: Equitable's Gateway Center in Pittsburgh includes Hotel and Apartments," *New York Times,* May 9, 1965. Harrison and Abramovitz were architects for the Gateway Center garage/park, while Schell and Deeter were associate architects for both the garage and Four Gateway Center. In 1959 Deeter and Ritchey formed a partnership with offices in Four Gateway Center. The Gateway Center is part of the Pittsburgh Renaissance Historic District, listed on the National Register of Historic Places in 2013.
27 Jacobs, "Downtown is for People," 134.
28 Jane Jacobs, *The Death and Life of Great American Cities* (New York: Random House, 1961), 106.
29 "Equitable Builds a Gateway" [undated brochure], in "Postwar Pittsburgh Architecture Bibliography," compiled by Martin Aurand, Carnegie Mellon University archives: andrew.cmu.edu/user/ma1f/EquitableBuildsAGateway.pdf.
30 "Pittsburgh's Mayor Discusses Urban Design at Harvard Conference," *Charette,* May 1956, 25.
31 Jacobs, "Downtown is for People," 134.
32 For analysis of the residents' successful protest of this effort to replace the Lower Hill neighborhood with "a cultural Acropolis" that would restore the district's falling property values, see William J. Mallett, "The Lower Hill Renewal and Pittsburgh's Original Cultural District," *Pittsburgh History* 75, no. 4 (October 1992): 176-90.
33 "Pittsburgh Renascent," 59.
34 Edward K. Muller, "Urban Blueways: John Ormsbee Simonds and Riverfront Planning," *Journal of Planning History* 11, no. 4 (November 2012): 308-29.
35 Part 4, "Land Use Plan," in *Pittsburgh in Progress* (1946), n.p.
36 Philip D. Simonds, "The Birth of A Regional Park System," *Landscape Architecture* 53, no. 4 (April 1963): 207-8. The other landscape architecture firms were Griswold, Winters and Swain and Ezra C. Stiles.
37 The idea for the aviary originated with architect Lamont Button who worked closely with the Director of Parks and Recreation and with specialists in horticulture and ornithology. See C. Richard Hays, "Floorscape: The Ever-Changing Pasturage," *Landscape Architecture* 57, no. 4 (August 1967): 279-82. For earlier versions of Simonds's design, see this source and Charles Birnbaum, "Dual Vision: Can we be Preservationists and Designers," *Land Forum* 13, no. 1 (January 2002): 27-28. Allegheny Commons was listed on the National Register of Historic Places in 2013.
38 John O. Simonds, "Toward a More Livable City" [presentation at regional ASLA meeting, Hershey, PA, October 1966], cited by Muller, "Urban Blueways," 314.
39 "An Open Place at the Heart of a City," *Architectural Record* 121, no. 2 (February 1957): 195; John O. Simonds, *Landscape Architecture: The Shaping of Man's Natural Environment* (New York, Toronto, London: McGraw Hill, 1961), 167.
40 Ibid., 166.
41 John O. Simonds, "Thoughts on Education," *Landscape Architecture* 42, no. 4 (July 1952): 157. Simonds was president of the ASLA, 1963–65.
42 Simonds, *Landscape Architecture*, 218, 225. Revised editions were published as *Landscape Architecture: A Manual of Site Planning and Design* in 1983 and 1998.
43 Ibid., 5, 17.
44 John O. Simonds, "Beyond Modernism," letter to the editor, *Landscape Architecture* 80, no. 5 (May 1990): 8.

A SENSATION OF FREE AND OPEN SPACE: EXPERIENCING PITTSBURGH'S MODERNISM

Martin Aurand

The modern introduced a new-made spaciousness into American cities. Influential modernist designers and planners prescribed broad spatial interventions to cure the ills of density and congestion, to accommodate machine-age urban infrastructure, and to foster contemporary ways of living. The modern promised the city room to breathe and grow. It delivered new patterns of occupation and dispersal. It gave rise to a sensation of free and open space that transformed the experience of the city.

In Pittsburgh, the modern reinforced the space of topography and nature embodied in rivers, hillsides, and newly cleaned air; unleashed the space of urban renewal measured in acres of cleared urban land; created the space of modern engineering, landscape design, and architecture realized in highways, parks, and buildings; and exploited the space of visual fields with viewfinders, eyecatchers, and new urban prospects. A sensation of free and open space was experienced in the city's trajectories, locus, channels, and poles of modernism.

TRAJECTORIES OF MODERNISM

Pittsburgh is sited at the confluence of three rivers on the Appalachian Plateau. Many landmasses rise to a common elevation that appears as a plain when viewed from the top of the plateau; but the rivers and streams (known as runs) dissect the land to form valleys and hollows in the plateau. Native Americans and eventually European interlopers moved across and within the plateau on trails, waterways, and military roads. Subsequently, roads, canals, railroads, and inclined planes mastered the terrain and fostered settlement and urban development. The modern coming of age of the automobile and aviation brought highways, airports, and a suburban milieu to the plateau.

The Pennsylvania Turnpike, the so-called "Dream Highway," mounted the plateau and largely eclipsed other land routes when the Pittsburgh interchange opened about fifteen miles east of Pittsburgh in 1951. It spurred the development of the local William Penn Highway in Monroeville as a suburban commercial strip.[1] After 1952, passengers could also alight onto the plateau from the sky at the Greater Pittsburgh Airport about twelve miles west of Pittsburgh. The airport, one of the largest in the country at 1,600 acres, spurred construction of the Airport Parkway access highway. In turn, the Penn-Lincoln Parkway, which had been imagined in part

Fig.1 Aerial view of the Penn-Lincoln Parkway West and the trajectory of the Fort Pitt Tunnel through Mount Washington, 1960.

since the 1930s, was substantially built by 1953 and was completed by 1960; it joined the routes of US22 and US30 over the course of about twenty miles between the William Penn Highway and the Airport Parkway, connecting the turnpike and the airport with downtown Pittsburgh.2 Fig.1

The Parkway's modern engineering confronted the terrain with cuts, fills, and ribbons of concrete laid with modulated grades of up to five percent. Viaducts and bridges spanned run valleys and the Monongahela River. Tunnels penetrated Squirrel Hill and Mount Washington. Topographically-driven interchanges featured mutant cloverleafs and one-of-a-kind ramps that didn't conform to highway standards then or now.3 The Parkway spawned modern development—notably corporate research campuses—in its path. After World War II, many companies recruited scientists to do corporate research in pastoral suburbs. Consequently, "Sites along parkways and highways broadcast pleasing panoramas of verdant corporate facilities to thousands of passing motorists."4 Mobay, Crucible Steel, Harbison-Walker, and Jacobs Engineering (the bronze cube suncatcher at Greentree) built facilities along the Parkway West. The U.S. Steel Research Center, PPG Glass Research Center, Koppers Research Center, and Alcoa Technical Center were all built east of Pittsburgh between 1955 and 1965. Even so, the eastern suburbs were Westinghouse territory.

Legacy Westinghouse facilities along the Pennsylvania Railroad, from factories in the Turtle Creek Valley to the Westinghouse Building in downtown Pittsburgh, were joined by new facilities aligned with the Parkway East. These ranged from the Westinghouse Nuclear Center (1971) at the turnpike, to a new Westinghouse Building (1969) downtown, to the Westinghouse Research and Development Center (1955–72) and the Westinghouse Telecomputer Center (1963, 1969) in between. Eliot Noyes, appointed to modernize the company's image in 1960, commissioned a new logo from Paul Rand, hired modern architects like SOM, and designed the Telecomputer Center himself (with Deeter & Ritchey).5 This building was an early icon of the information age, the first corporate building that was "'on line' in 'real time.'" Computers linking hundreds of Westinghouse offices, factories, and warehouses occupied a glass enclosure at the building's center.6 A later Noyes addition featured a stark window wall that minimized external views and distractions. Yet the inward-looking building was designed with a "vigorous exterior that would be seen and identified by passing cars."7 The blocky sign with the 'circle bar W' logo, the vast suburban lawn, and the edgy modern buildings were eyecatchers and markers of corporate visibility along the Parkway East. Fig.2

A drive along the Parkway *was* a modern corporate experience and a modern existential and perceptual experience. Sigfried Giedion, writing in the milestone modernist text *Space, Time and Architecture*, described the new experience of the parkway. “Freedom was given to both the car and the driver. Riding up and down the long sweeping grades produced an exhilarating dual feeling, one of being connected with the soil and yet of hovering just above it...The space-time feeling of our period can seldom be felt so keenly as when driving...up and down hills, beneath overpasses, up ramps, and over giant bridges.”[8] Pittsburgh’s Parkway offered a similar experience according to a 1953 promotional report. “As motorists travel the Penn-Lincoln Parkway, East they are impressed by a sensation of free and open space, both on the roadway and off to either side... The sensation is one akin to flying at low altitude as they skim along above buildings and the Monongahela River.”[9] The Parkway offered

Fig.2 Along the Penn-Lincoln Parkway East, c. 1970, Westinghouse Telecomputer Center, Eliot Noyes with Deeter & Ritchey, 1963 and 1969.

the experience of free and open space within its own trajectory and the new suburban countryside.

LOCUS OF MODERNISM

The Parkway West motoring experience climaxed in a long descent of Greentree Hill, a breach of Mount Washington through the Fort Pitt Tunnel, and an emergence onto the Fort Pitt Bridge elevated above the Monongahela River. The *New York Times* reported in 1977, “In all urban America there may be no more dramatic spectacle than the wonderland that bursts suddenly into view as one emerges from the Fort Pitt Tunnel and sees downtown Pittsburgh, the Golden Triangle, glittering across the Monongahela River.”[10] Key to this experience were the compression and framing of the tunnel, the subsequent dramatic expansion into free and open space at the exit, and the exposed bridge deck with a single directional flow of traffic, which ushered the motorist into the city's locus: the basin of the three rivers and the space of the Golden Triangle, a triangular promontory that was the city's downtown core. The Golden Triangle was deeply recessed within the plateau; its tip, the Point, witnessed the confluence of the rivers; and its buildings composed a striking skyline. **Fig.3** The tunnel was a portal and a viewfinder that opened a powerful new way to enter and see a city remade by the modern.

Modern architects and planners sought to merge the countryside and the city into a new urban landscape. Mitchell and Ritchey's 1947 *Pittsburgh in Progress* study diagnosed urban problems and aspired "to plan the rebuilding of the city in bold terms...The old city wilderness will be cleared away. New pioneers will have cleansed and opened the land for living areas of noble proportions." The new Pittsburgh would have ample expanses of free and open space targeted for transportation infrastructure, parks and greenery, and widely spaced tall buildings.[11] When urban renewal ultimately cleared fifty-nine acres at the Point, it was transformed into the Point Interchange, Point Park, and Gateway Center.

The Fort Pitt Bridge (1959) and Fort Duquesne Bridge (1969) are rare double-decked tied-arch bridges that cross the Monongahela and Allegheny Rivers upriver from the confluence. Their bowstring arches propel motorists through the Point Interchange, a twelve-acre mixing box of highways, ramps, and bridge approaches, bundled into a single thoroughfare that crosses the Point. The Portal Bridge (1963), an elegant pedestrian underpass beneath the interchange, was designed in part by Gordon Bunshaft of SOM. Bunshaft proposed a long, low arch, constructed as a concrete shell with three vaults.[12] Oblique approaches and a bridge over a water feature controlled pedestrian movement to and within the arch. The Portal Bridge was a portal and a viewfinder where the experience of compression and expansion dramatically transitioned the pedestrian from and into two distinct visual fields.

To the west, the Portal Bridge offered a pointward view of Point Park, which was slowly realized on twenty-four acres of cleared land between 1948 and 1972. The topographical setting inspired park designers to evoke the eighteenth-century landscape known to military vanguards and pioneers at the city's point of origin. In a modern simulacra of Penn's Woods, which equally evokes a well-planted suburban yard, Ralph E. Griswold et al. grouped specimen native trees into token forests and created a grassy meadow like a pioneer clearing.[13] They plotted and laid out the early French and British forts: Fort Duquesne (1754–58) and Fort Pitt (1759–61). All deferred,

Fig.3 Rendering of the Golden Triangle with the Point Interchange, Point Park, and Gateway Center, 1963.

however, to a visual axis where the "hills and rivers...would provide a majestic memorial far more impressive than any man-made monument." Where the "dramatic view to the west, down the Ohio River, the nation's first highway to the heartland of America, [would] be open and unimpeded."14

To the east, the Portal Bridge offered a cityward view of Gateway Center, a commercial precinct built on twenty-three acres of cleared land. Gateway Center was developed in part "to supply a setting for Point Park," a complementary tableau of new buildings on an adjacent site.15 This face of the city required a facelift. The twelve major buildings—including the cruciform One, Two, and Three Gateway Center (1952) to the north, and Four Gateway Center (1960), the IBM Building (1963), and the aforementioned Westinghouse Building to the south—comprised a clustered critical mass of modern architecture. Altogether, Gateway Center spanned the Point and displayed bold faces of modern architecture to Point Park and the Monongahela and Allegheny riverfronts.

CHANNELS OF MODERNISM

The convergence of urban renewal and the emerging environmental movement spurred the redevelopment of waterfronts to clean up industrial zones, create landscaped parks, and stimulate investment.16 Such objectives inspired the nascent redevelopment of Pittsburgh's riverfronts. What's more, Pittsburgh's river valleys offered natural channels of free and open space and visual fields replete with striking and potentially reciprocal scenic views over water from riverfronts or elevated viewpoints. The basin of the three rivers formed a great natural amphitheater around the Golden Triangle. When modern Pittsburgh rediscovered its rivers, it enhanced their appearance, and took in the views.

Point Park's riverfronts were lined with promenades and wharfs, and stone bleachers were built along the Allegheny River so parkgoers could watch boating events. Or they could listen to a performance of the American Wind Symphony on Point Counterpoint II (1976), a floating concert venue designed by Louis I. Kahn. With its metallic sheathing and large circular windows, this peripatetic venue took the modern onto the rivers when it wasn't tied to a park wharf. Or they could watch the mesmerizing Westinghouse sign (1967) across the river. Reportedly the first computer-controlled sign in the United States, it featured nine iterations of the 'circle bar W logo' that lit up in a seemingly infinite number of sequences of circles, bars, strokes, and dots.[17] The sign was an eyecatcher and a marker of corporate visibility on the riverfront.

A multipurpose sports stadium and a riverfront park were imagined as early as the late 1950s across the Allegheny River from the Point. The stadium was sited on eighty-four acres of cleared land that was proximate to new highways and visible "to those entering the city from the west" through the Fort Pitt Tunnel and to "those who will view it from office buildings in downtown Pittsburgh," explicitly including Gateway Center.[18] In 1959, Griswold, Winters, and Swain proposed a walking and driving park to front the stadium,

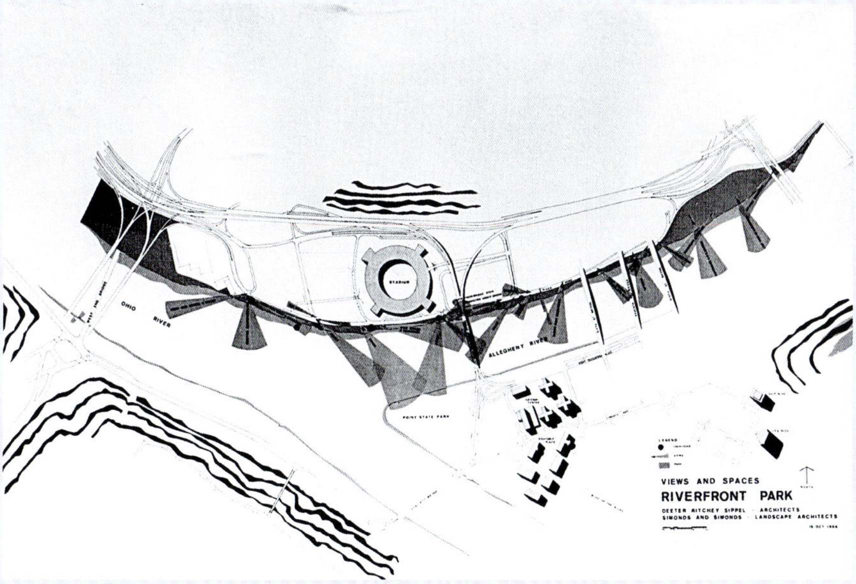

Fig. 4 Plan of spaces and views in Riverfront Park, Deeter Ritchey Sippel with Simonds and Simonds, 1968.

connect it to the river, and enhance views. The site, they noted, "is in the view from Point Park and Gateway Center across to the North Shore of the Allegheny River and is dismal in the extreme; but the North Shore Park would completely transform this landscape liability into a beautiful asset, in keeping with tremendous investment already completed in the Gateway scheme."19

Deeter & Ritchey's 1962 stadium proposal was a capacious venue and a viewfinder that opened toward Gateway Center and downtown. But when it was built as Three Rivers Stadium in 1970, the partly steel-framed horseshoe had morphed into a concrete donut, which minimized views. Riverfront Park (1971), reconceived by Deeter & Ritchey with Simonds and Simonds, emphasized views, as shown in a "Views and Spaces" site map that featured numerous outlooks and view cones. Fig. 4 Simonds argued that "riverfront redevelopment could unite communities, which rivers had separated. Activities on both sides must be planned to relate to each other." When partially executed as Roberto Clemente Memorial Park, and later expanded, the park enhanced views of the stadium from the Golden Triangle while it returned "views of the confluence of the three rivers, downtown's new skyline, [and Point Park]."20

On the south side of the Monongahela River, uphill and upstream from the Fort Pitt Tunnel, Mount Washington offered panoramas ranging from orthogonal views of the Golden Triangle to views that faced the Point more or less head-on. Views from almost any angle featured serendipitous attributes of unity, balance, distance, elevation, and sunlight. Griswold et al. proposed overlooks to structure the views from Mount Washington, which were later realized in part as the Grandview Avenue Overlook (1968). The hilltop Overlook comprised a linear progression of walkways studded with observation decks—concrete mushroom-shaped modern objects that projected into free and open space and showcased modern urban views for the spectator.

Crosstown Boulevard (1962–64), a spur of the Parkway East, was a manmade spatial channel that scribed the eastern edge of the Golden Triangle, separated downtown from the Lower Hill neighborhood, and made the Triangle into an island of sorts. Here Mitchell & Ritchey planned the ambitious Lower Hill Cultural Center (1953) on ninety-five acres of cleared land; but only their Civic Arena (1961) was built. A one-of-a-kind venue and engineering triumph, it featured a retractable dome composed of eight stainless-steel leaves hung from a mighty cantilevered steel arm. The shiny alien dome was an eyecatcher that opened as a viewfinder—a great eye with retractable lids—that looked across the boulevard toward downtown.21 It provided front-row seats to experience the modern skyline.

Fig.5 Rendering of the U.S. Steel Building, Harrison, Abramovitz & Abbe, 1971.

POLES OF MODERNISM

Modern Pittsburgh was well-stocked with corporate headquarters. The corporations built and occupied modern skyscrapers, many designed by Harrison & Abramovitz. The Pittsburgh version of corporate modern architecture favored metal frames and panels, products of the city's metallurgic heritage. The Golden Triangle's modern skyline boasted, among lesser companions, the various towers of Gateway Center, the Alcoa Building (1953) and the Mellon Bank/U.S. Steel Building (1953) that flanked Mellon Square, and before the era was over, a newer, bigger, and better U.S. Steel Building (1971) adjacent to Crosstown Boulevard. This skyscraper colossus was an 841-foot steel column that lifted high above the city. Triangular in plan, it was publicized as the "Steel Triangle in the Golden Triangle," an extrusion of the terrain on which it stood.[22] It doubled down on the Golden Triangle and raised a triangular acre in the sky, reportedly the largest, highest space atop a building anywhere. Fig.5

In parallel, Pittsburgh inserted another extraordinary skyline feature at the utmost tip of the Point. While Point Park sought to assimilate its natural heritage in the basin of the three rivers, it also aspired to enhance the drama of the meeting and mixing of the rivers. The Point Park Fountain (1974), was a marvel of modern hydraulic engineering. Its 150-foot column of water was scaled to the

Fig.6 Rendering of Point Park Fountain.

topographical and urban setting. A minimalist fountain without traditional sculptural iconography in a round one-acre pool, it was an extrusion of a geometric point at the Point. It doubled down on the three rivers and raised their confluence to a watery zenith in the sky.[23] Fig.6

The skyscraper colossus and the giant fountain were grand symbolic gestures that embodied Pittsburgh in modern forms. They were poles at opposite ends of the Golden Triangle that accentuated and framed the modern skyline. As the dominant eyecatchers in the modern city's visual fields, they acted as pilgrimage sites. The U.S. Steel Building, which rose above the plateau and was visible from far-flung vantage points, drew motorists onto the Penn-Lincoln Parkway and into the Golden Triangle to itself. The Point Park Fountain, which was visible from Mount Washington and other vantage points in the basin of the three rivers, drew pedestrians into Point Park and through the Portal Bridge to itself. The skyscraper and the fountain heightened and focused the experience of the modern city. They anchored modern Pittsburgh in free and open space.

CODA

As it turned out, the modern sensation of free and open space ranged from the sensory: hovering, bursting, mixing, compressing, expanding, viewing, anchoring; to the sensational: Dream highways! Dramatic portals! Green parks! Clustered towers! Scenic overlooks! A skyscraper colossus! A giant fountain! Or so modern Pittsburgh seemed to its champions at the time (though the free and open space came at a considerable physical and social price). And so—with some awareness and imagination—we experience Pittsburgh today. Some elements are faded and some are gone; but Pittsburgh's trajectories, locus, channels, and poles still offer the experience of the modern.

1 The Penn-Lincoln Parkway East extension (1962) took through traffic around Monroeville.
2 Robert Moses imagined the so-called Pitt Parkway as well as the Crosstown Boulevard. See Robert Moses, *Arterial Plan for Pittsburgh* (Pittsburgh Regional Planning Association, 1939), 17-22.
3 Charles R. Way, "Many Unusual Structures Feature [sic] Penn-Lincoln Parkway," *Civil Engineering* 26 (October 1956): 39-42.
4 Louise A. Mozingo, *Pastoral Capitalism: A History of Suburban Corporate Landscapes* (Cambridge, MA: MIT Press, 2011), 43, 51.
5 Noyes played a similar role at IBM.
6 John Harwood, "The White Room: Eliot Noyes and the Logic of the Information Age Interior," *Grey Room* 12 (Summer 2003): 7, 24.
7 "Westinghouse Computer Centre, Pennsylvania," *Architect & Building News* [London], November 24, 1965, 985.
8 Sigfried Giedion, *Space, Time and Architecture*, 5th ed. (Cambridge, MA: Harvard University Press, 1967), 825-31.
9 *Penn-Lincoln Parkway* (Harrisburg: Commonwealth of Pennsylvania, Department of Highways, 1953), 5.
10 William K. Stevens, "Pittsburgh, Revamped and Revitalized, Sheds Its Steel-Town Image," *New York Times,* April 16, 1977. See also: Paul Goldberger, "A Tempered Skyline Strengthens a City of Steel," *New York Times,* January 3, 1988. The portal experience was fetishized in the 2012 film *The Perks of Being a Wildflower*.
11 James Mitchell and Dahlen Ritchey, *Pittsburgh in Progress Presented by Kaufmann's* (Pittsburgh: Kaufmann's, 1946).
12 Robert C. Alberts, *The Shaping of the Point: Pittsburgh's Renaissance Park* (Pittsburgh: University of Pittsburgh Press, 1980), 154-57. Bunshaft consulted on the project while he was working on modern facilities for the H.J. Heinz Company in Pittsburgh.
13 Ralph E. Griswold, "From Fort Pitt to Point Park: A Turning Point for the Physical Planning of Pittsburgh," *Landscape Architecture* 46, no. 4 (July 1945): 200.
14 Alberts, *The Shaping of the Point*, 8.
15 Ibid., 86.
16 Edward K. Muller, "Urban Blueways: John Ormsbee Simonds and Riverfront Planning," *Journal of Planning History* 11, no. 4 (2012): 308-09, 321.
17 Ed Reis, "Westinghouse W's North Side Pittsburgh," *Western Pennsylvania History* (Fall 2010): 27-29.
18 Stadium Authority of the City of Pittsburgh, *Annual Report* (1965).
19 Griswold, Winters, and Swain, *A Master Plan for the Development of Riverfronts and Hillsides in the City of Pittsburgh* ([Pittsburgh]: [Department of Parks and Recreation], 1959), 8.
20 Muller, *Urban Blueways*, 320-21.
21 James D. Van Trump, "Pittsburgh's Pleasure Dome: The New Civic Arena," *Charette,* October 1961, 10.
22 *The Steel Triangle in the Golden Triangle* (Pittsburgh: c. 1971). Carnegie Mellon University Architecture Archives.
24 The fountain water is actually drawn from an aquifer, Pittsburgh's so-called fourth river.

Modern Networks

These network diagrams, conceived and researched by Martin Aurand, connect the major patrons and architects behind Pittsburgh's modern architecture with their projects and with each other. The extensive array of civic bodies, corporations, and institutions underscores the breadth of Pittsburgh's patronage of modern architecture. The roster of architects includes many names, but reveals that a few key firms—both local (Mitchell & Ritchey/Deeter Ritchey Sippel, Tasso Katselas) and national (Harrison & Abramovitz, Skidmore, Owings & Merrill)—played an outsized role in reshaping the city during the Renaissance era.

City of Pittsburgh, County of Allegheny, and State of Pennsylvania governments, in conjunction with organizations like the Allegheny Conference on Community Development, developed the hospitals and airports, sports and cultural facilities, and parks and plazas that were required by a city in the process of remaking itself. Pittsburgh's corporations (H.J. Heinz, Alcoa, U.S. Steel, Westinghouse) produced downtown skyscrapers, production and warehouse facilities, and suburban research and technology campuses stamped with Pittsburgh's own brands of corporate Modernism. Institutions (Carnegie Institute of Technology [now Carnegie Mellon University], University of Pittsburgh, Pittsburgh Board of Public Education, Carnegie Library of Pittsburgh) introduced modern architecture into the academy and the neighborhood in the form of university buildings, schools, and libraries.

The diagrams also record a number of aspirational projects—like Frank Lloyd Wright's Point Park Civic Center—that never quite got off the ground; and reveal the limited life spans of some built projects—particularly civic structures like Mitchell & Ritchey's Kane Hospital and Civic Arena—that proved susceptible to obsolescence, evolving social and economic forces, and changing taste.

CIVIC NETWORK MAP

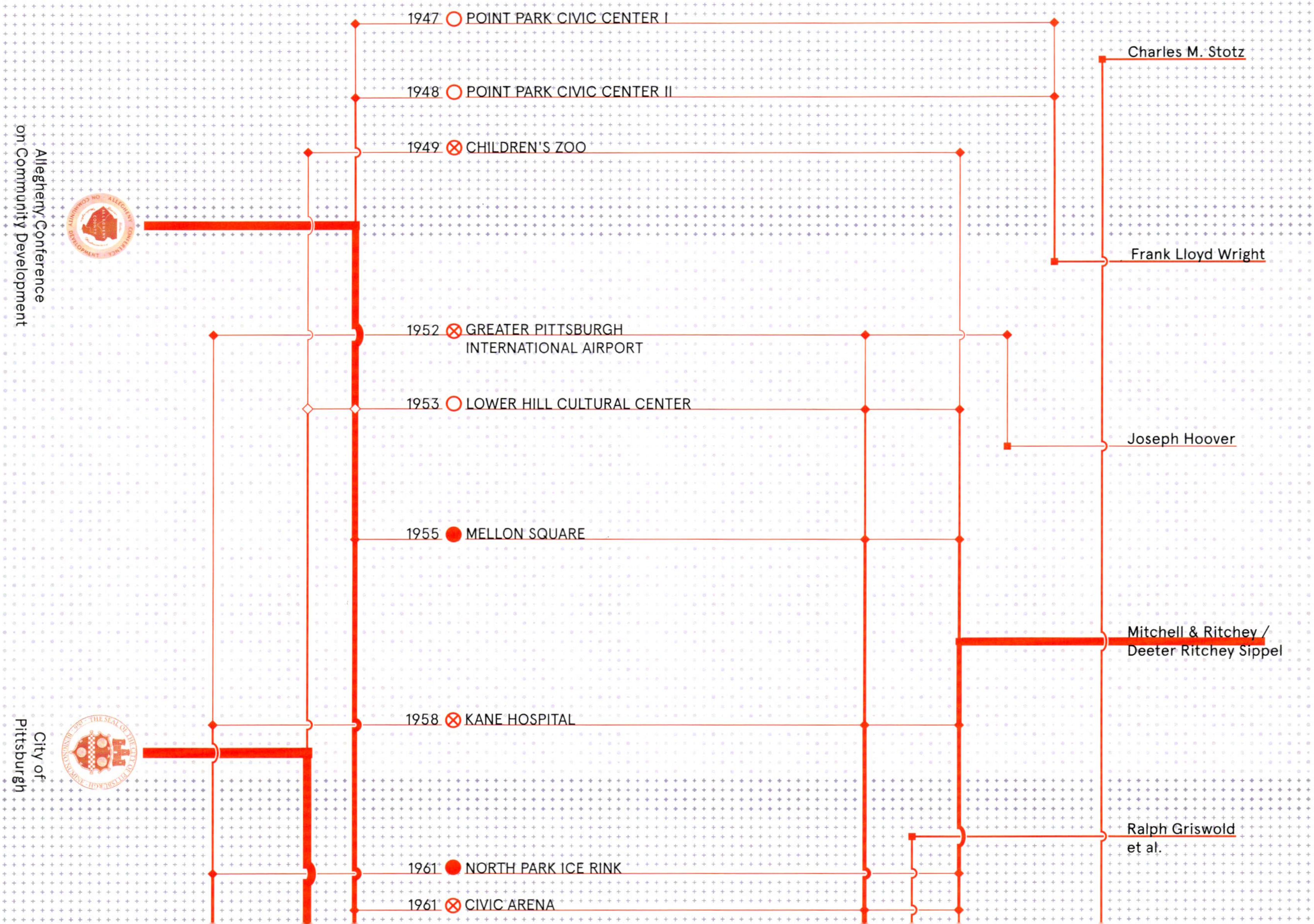

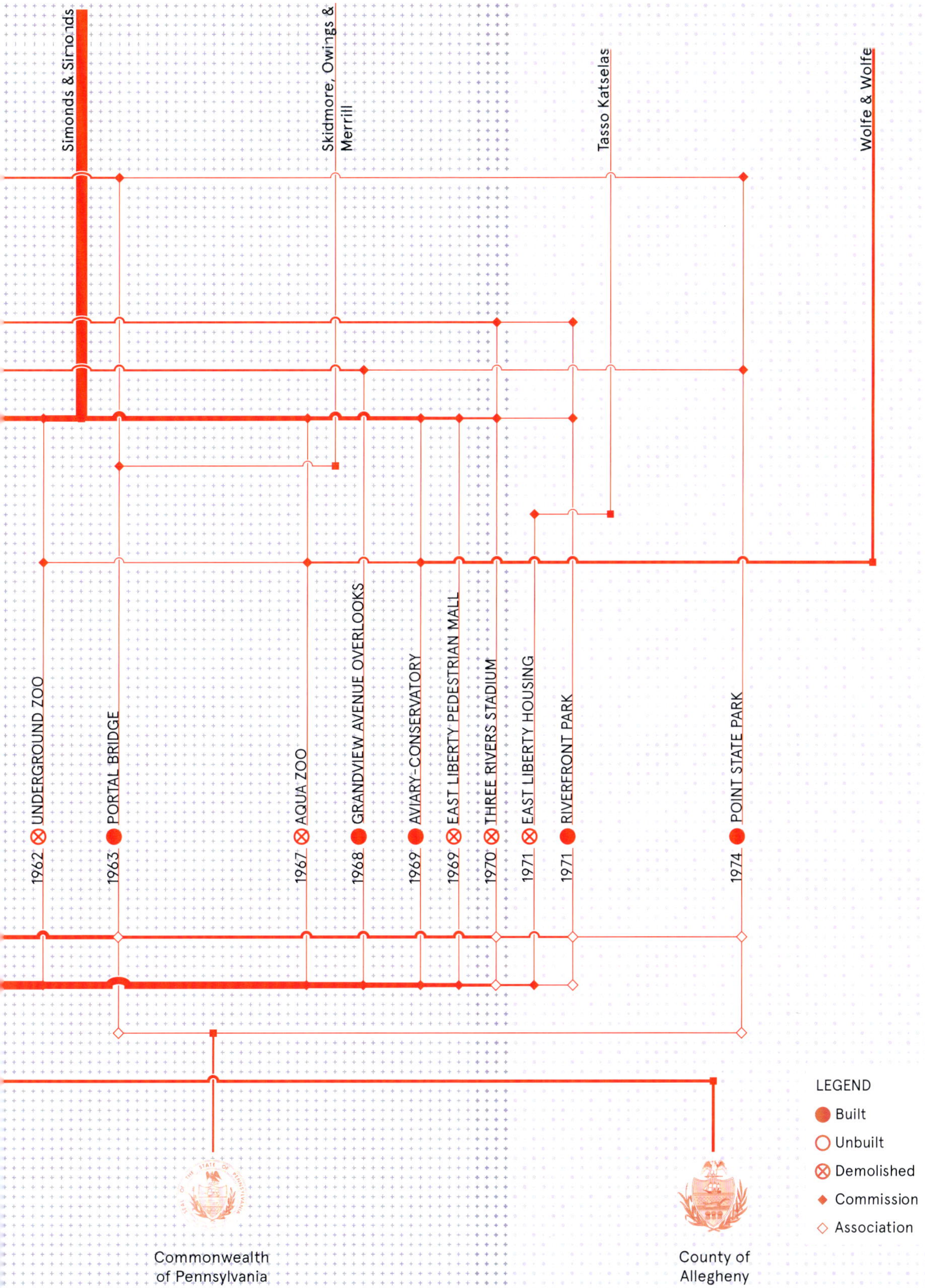
Simonds & Simonds
Skidmore, Owings & Merrill
Tasso Katselas
Wolfe & Wolfe
1962 UNDERGROUND ZOO
1963 PORTAL BRIDGE
1967 AQUA ZOO
1968 GRANDVIEW AVENUE OVERLOOKS
1969 AVIARY-CONSERVATORY
1969 EAST LIBERTY PEDESTRIAN MALL
1970 THREE RIVERS STADIUM
1971 EAST LIBERTY HOUSING
1971 RIVERFRONT PARK
1974 POINT STATE PARK
Commonwealth of Pennsylvania
County of Allegheny
LEGEND
Built
Unbuilt
Demolished
Commission
Association

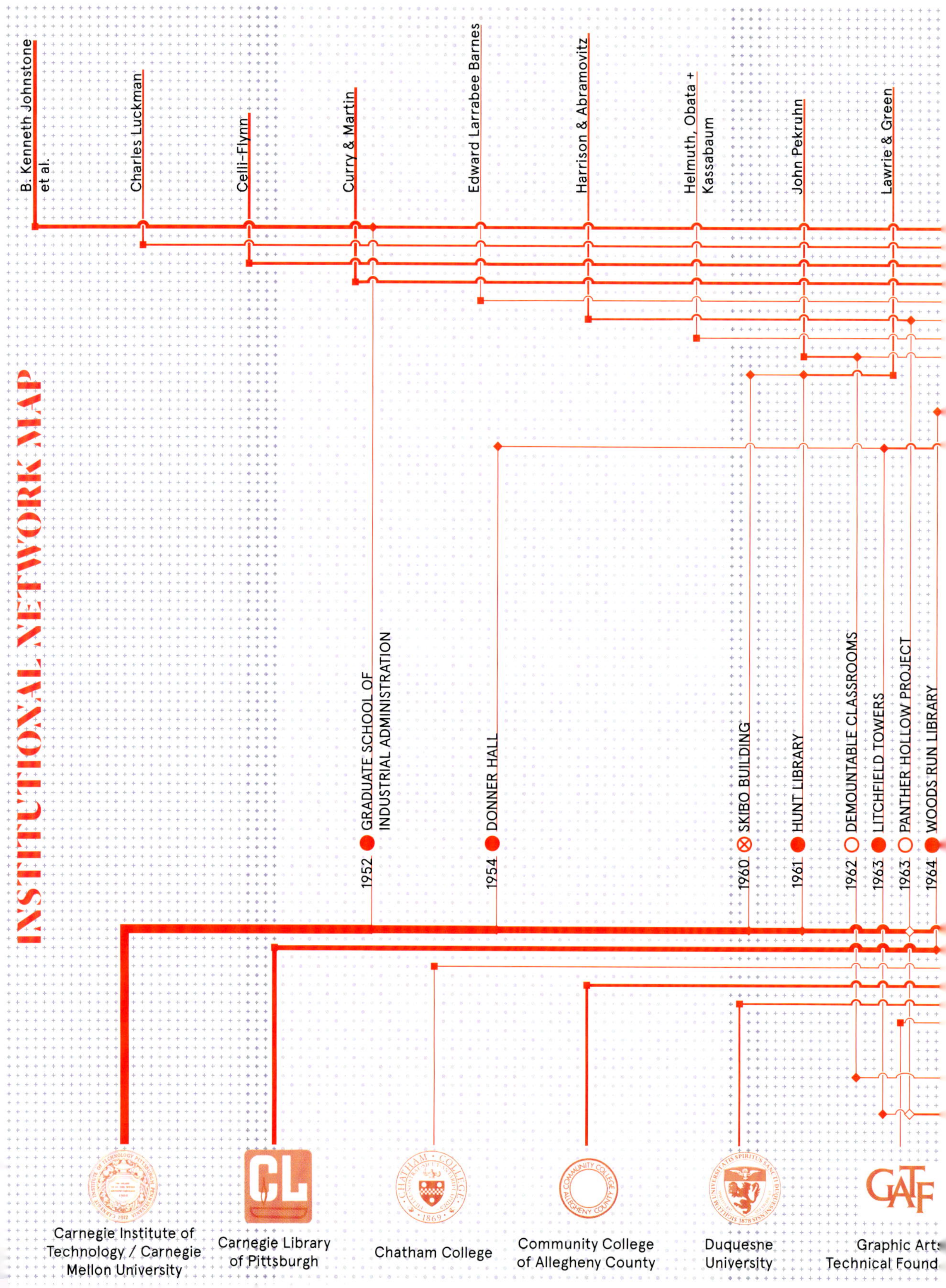
NSTITUTIONAL NETWORK MAP
B. Kenneth Johnstone et al.
Charles Luckman
Celli-Flynn
Curry & Martin
Edward Larrabee Barnes
Harrison & Abramovitz
Helmuth, Obata + Kassabaum
John Pekruhn
Lawrie & Green
1952 GRADUATE SCHOOL OF INDUSTRIAL ADMINISTRATION
1954 DONNER HALL
1960 SKIBO BUILDING
1961 HUNT LIBRARY
1962 DEMOUNTABLE CLASSROOMS
1963 LITCHFIELD TOWERS
1963 PANTHER HOLLOW PROJECT
1964 WOODS RUN LIBRARY
Carnegie Institute of Technology / Carnegie Mellon University
Carnegie Library of Pittsburgh
Chatham College
Community College of Allegheny County
Duquesne University
Graphic Arts Technical Found

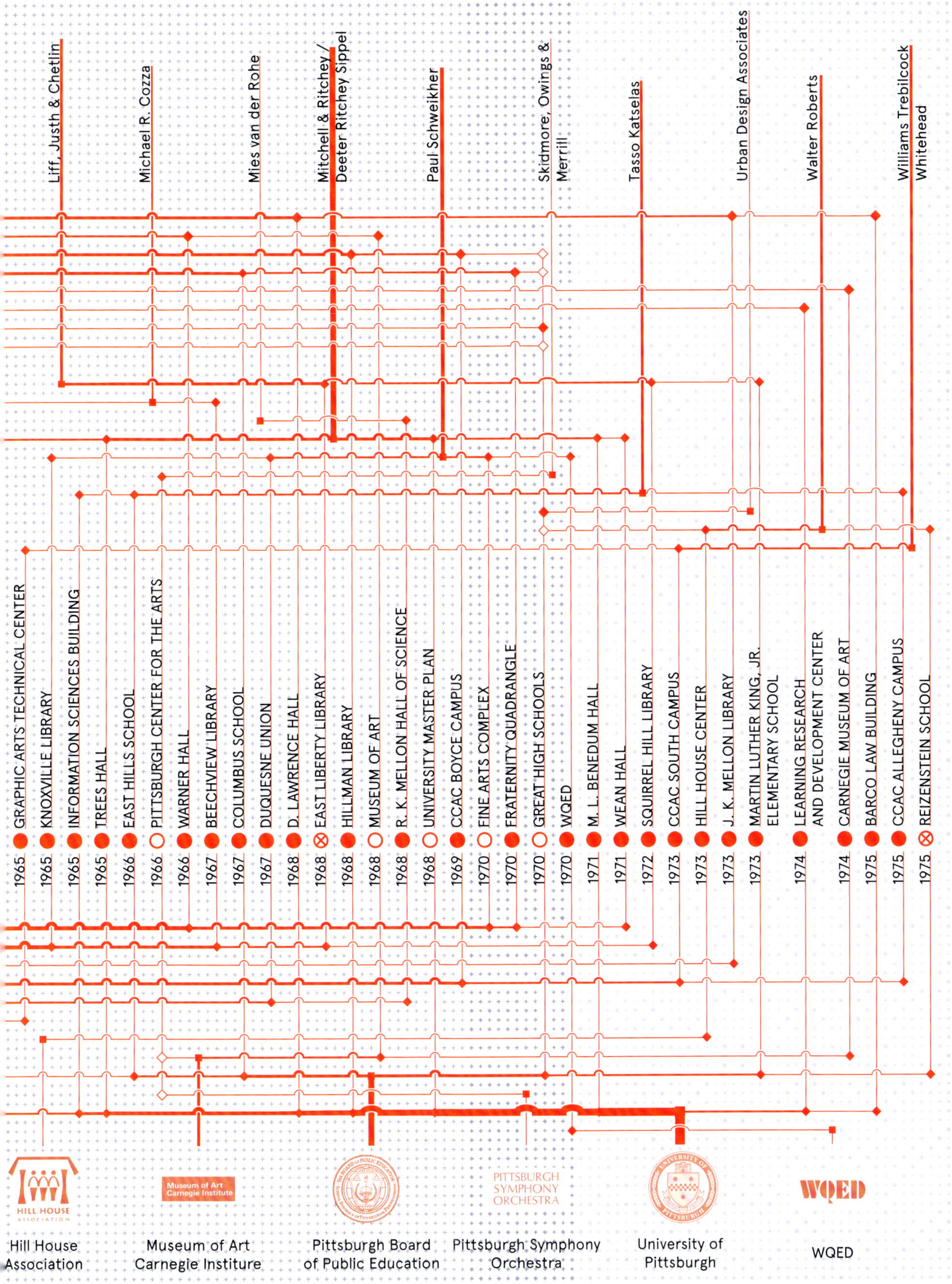

Liff, Justh & Chetlin
Michael R. Cozza
Mies van der Rohe
Mitchell & Ritchey / Deeter Ritchey Sippel
Paul Schweikher
Skidmore, Owings & Merrill
Tasso Katselas
Urban Design Associates
Walter Roberts
Williams Trebilcock Whitehead
1965 GRAPHIC ARTS TECHNICAL CENTER
1965 KNOXVILLE LIBRARY
1965 INFORMATION SCIENCES BUILDING
1965 TREES HALL
1966 EAST HILLS SCHOOL
1966 PITTSBURGH CENTER FOR THE ARTS
1966 WARNER HALL
1967 BEECHVIEW LIBRARY
1967 COLUMBUS SCHOOL
1967 DUQUESNE UNION
1968 D. LAWRENCE HALL
1968 EAST LIBERTY LIBRARY
1968 HILLMAN LIBRARY
1968 MUSEUM OF ART
1968 R. K. MELLON HALL OF SCIENCE
1968 UNIVERSITY MASTER PLAN
1969 CCAC BOYCE CAMPUS
1970 FINE ARTS COMPLEX
1970 FRATERNITY QUADRANGLE
1970 GREAT HIGH SCHOOLS
1970 WQED
1971 M. L. BENEDUM HALL
1971 WEAN HALL
1972 SQUIRREL HILL LIBRARY
1973 CCAC SOUTH CAMPUS
1973 HILL HOUSE CENTER
1973 J. K. MELLON LIBRARY
1973 MARTIN LUTHER KING, JR. ELEMENTARY SCHOOL
1974 LEARNING RESEARCH AND DEVELOPMENT CENTER
1974 CARNEGIE MUSEUM OF ART
1975 BARCO LAW BUILDING
1975 CCAC ALLEGHENY CAMPUS
1975 REIZENSTEIN SCHOOL
HILL HOUSE ASSOCIATION
Hill House Association
Museum of Art Carnegie Institute
Museum of Art Carnegie Institute
Pittsburgh Board of Public Education
PITTSBURGH SYMPHONY ORCHESTRA
Pittsburgh Symphony Orchestra
UNIVERSITY OF PITTSBURGH
University of Pittsburgh
WQED
WQED

CORPORATE NETWORK MAP

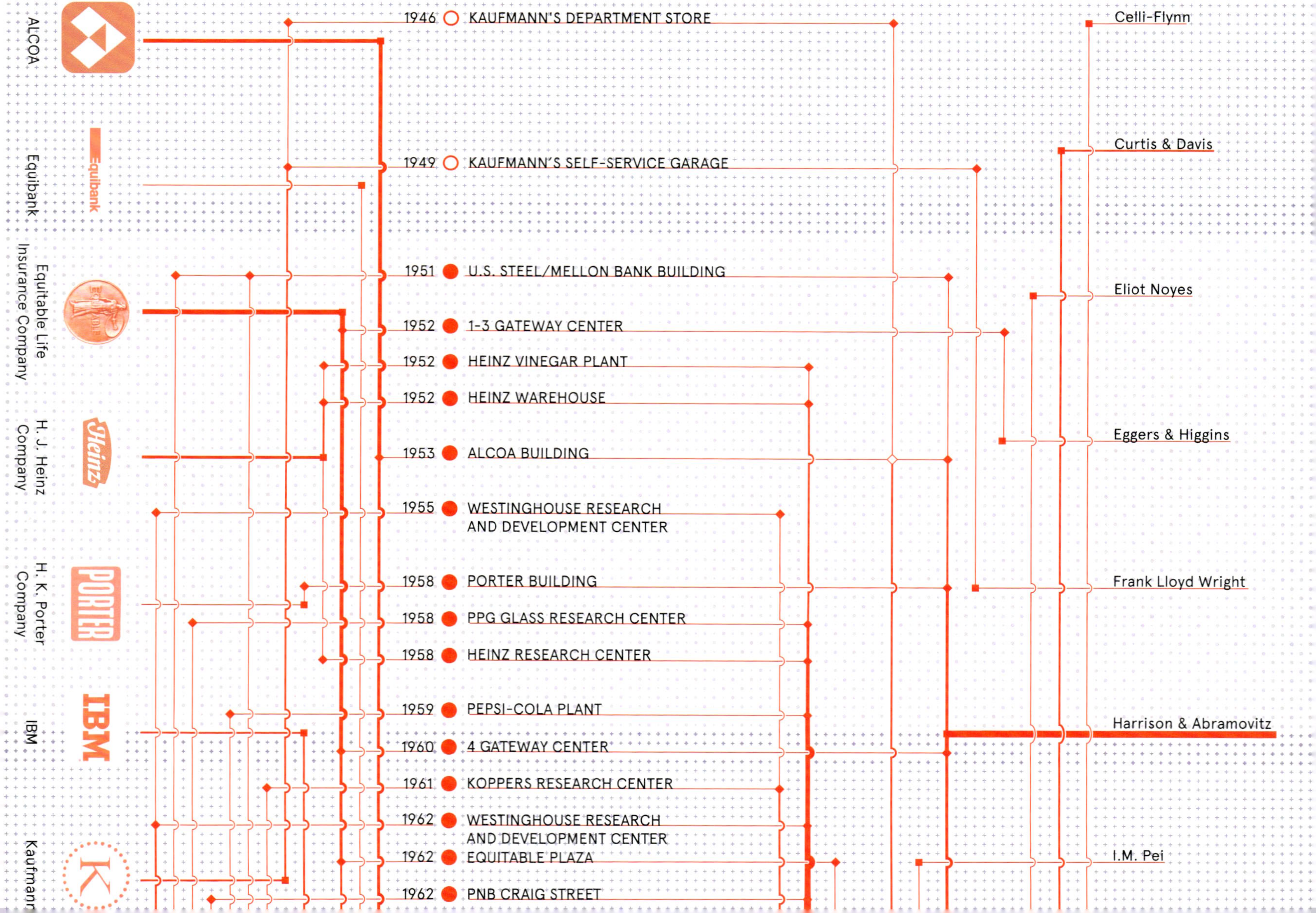

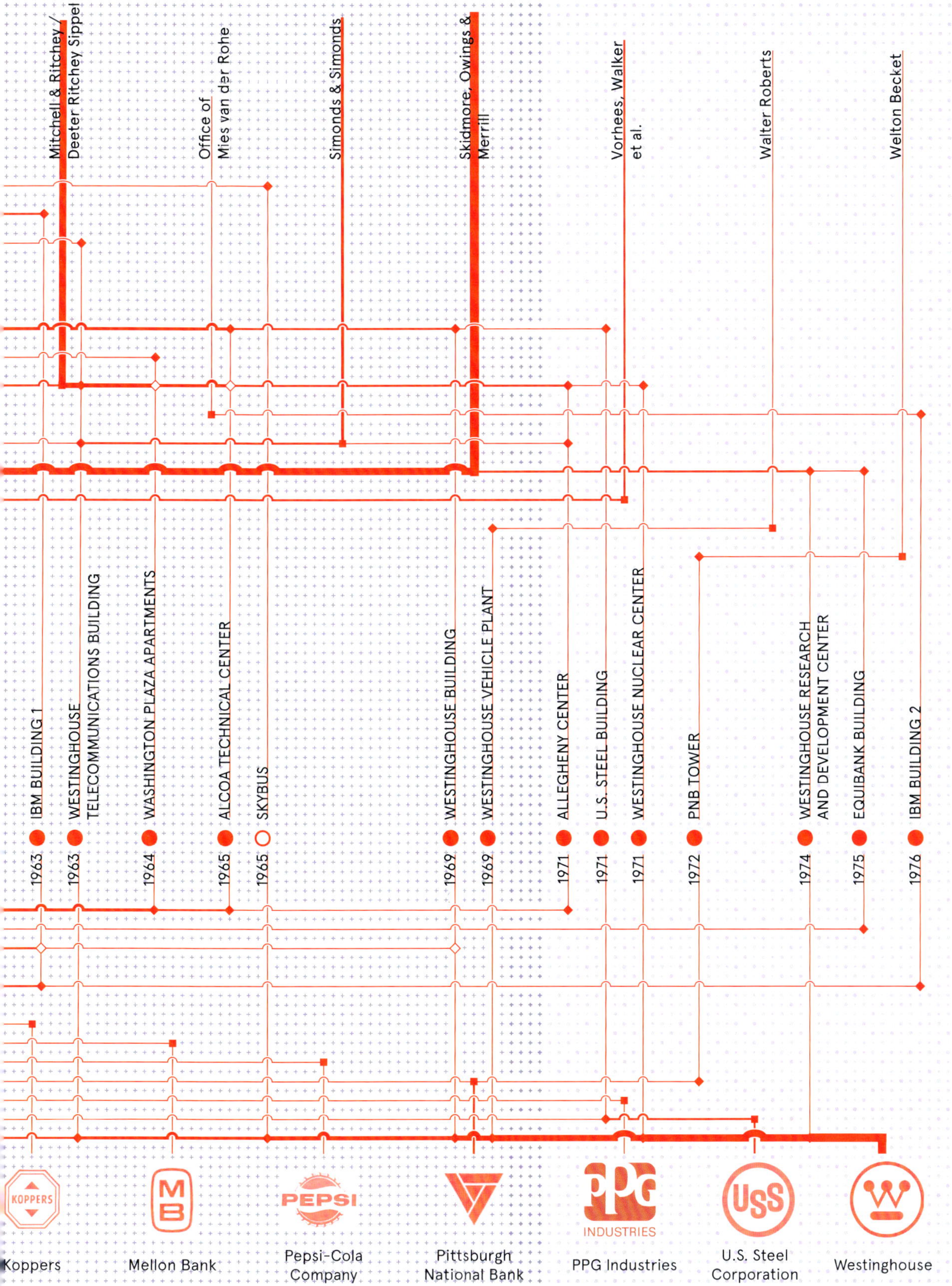

Mitchell & Ritchey/
Deeter Ritchey Sippel
Office of
Mies van der Rohe
Simonds & Simonds
Skidmore, Owings &
Merrill
Vorhees, Walker
et al.
Walter Roberts
Welton Becket
1963 IBM BUILDING 1
1963 WESTINGHOUSE TELECOMMUNICATIONS BUILDING
1964 WASHINGTON PLAZA APARTMENTS
1965 ALCOA TECHNICAL CENTER
1965 SKYBUS
1969 WESTINGHOUSE BUILDING
1969 WESTINGHOUSE VEHICLE PLANT
1971 ALLEGHENY CENTER
1971 U.S. STEEL BUILDING
1971 WESTINGHOUSE NUCLEAR CENTER
1972 PNB TOWER
1974 WESTINGHOUSE RESEARCH AND DEVELOPMENT CENTER
1975 EQUIBANK BUILDING
1976 IBM BUILDING 2
Koppers
Mellon Bank
Pepsi-Cola Company
Pittsburgh National Bank
PPG Industries
U.S. Steel Corporation
Westinghouse

Imagining Modern Pittsburgh

Media

The staging of the Renaissance took place not just in the city's changing spaces but across a rich array of media through which politicians, developers, designers, critics, and citizens alike sought to imagine a modern Pittsburgh in formation. Visionary projections and pragmatic planning documents charted possible directions for the city, while promotional materials advertised the benefits of development. Architectural representations offered depictions of buildings and landscapes in the making, serving as powerful instruments for construction and imagination. Professional journals and magazines brought Pittsburgh's reinvention to national audiences as part of broader discussions on the postwar American city. Newspapers offered venues for presenting and discussing the impacts of urban renewal on the city's communities, revealing the often conflicting actors and agendas that shaped Pittsburgh's transformation. All of these artifacts record how the Renaissance was invented, publicized, and received, tracing conflicting as well as shared visions for the future of the city.

01
Visionary Documents

Two early promotional booklets anticipated the ambitious scope of urban transformation in the remaking of Pittsburgh in the years immediately after World War II. *Pittsburgh in Progress* (1947) was sponsored by Edgar J. Kaufmann, the department-store magnate whose patronage of modern architecture in Pittsburgh included the commissioning of Frank Lloyd Wright's Point Park proposals following Wright's design of his weekend home, Fallingwater. Produced and illustrated by the design firm of Mitchell and Ritchey, *Pittsburgh in Progress* offered a visionary timeline of Pittsburgh's development, from the geology of its "prehistorical background" all the way to its distant future. The brochure features dramatic space-age renderings of a city populated by modernist high-rises set within acres of green space and serviced by amenities including a monorail system, aircraft landing fields, and large civic centers for sports, leisure, and entertainment. Organized by proposed development area, its sections largely predicted the major sites of urban renewal in Pittsburgh over the next three decades, including the Lower Hill (featuring an early version of the future Civic Arena), Point Park, the Northside (later Allegheny Center), and Panther Hollow in Oakland. In comparing the multiple projects sponsored by Kaufmann and their impact on the city, Martin Aurand has written that *Pittsburgh in Progress* "was, it turned out, a far more important vision for Pittsburgh than Frank Lloyd Wright's celebrated Point projects."[1] While "Wright's plans would have spectacularly transformed Pittsburgh's Point," Aurand notes, they lacked civic support; in contrast, "The Mitchell and Ritchey plan significantly reshaped the city."[2]

Published in the same year as Kaufmann's report, *Pittsburgh: Challenge and Response* (1947) outlined the aims of the Allegheny Conference on Community Development, a coalition of business and civic leaders chaired by Richard King Mellon that was dedicated to the city's large-scale renewal through the "united community action" of governmental, corporate, and public interests.[3] As its title suggests, the pamphlet is organized around a series of pressing urban "challenges"—including smoke, blight, housing, garbage, pollution, boredom, traffic congestion, and floods—following each with a comprehensive response through which the city would enact "a full sweep toward the future."[4] These responses described many of the large-scale urban initiatives that would be spearheaded by the Allegheny Conference in the years to come, including smoke abatement and flood control efforts, the development of Point Park, the construction of new housing in neighborhoods throughout the city, and the reengineering of the region's traffic patterns from the Golden Triangle to the interstate highway system.

1 Martin Aurand, *The Spectator and the Topographical City* (Pittsburgh: University of Pittsburgh Press, 2006), 57.
2 Ibid.
3 Allegheny Conference on Community Development, *Pittsburgh: Challenge and Response* (1947), 1.
4 Ibid., 3.

PITTSBURGH in PROGRESS
presented by KAUFMANN'S

Covers of two promotional booklets key to the Pittsburgh Renaissance, *Pittsburgh in Progress*, 1947, and *Pittsburgh: Challenge and Response*, 1947.

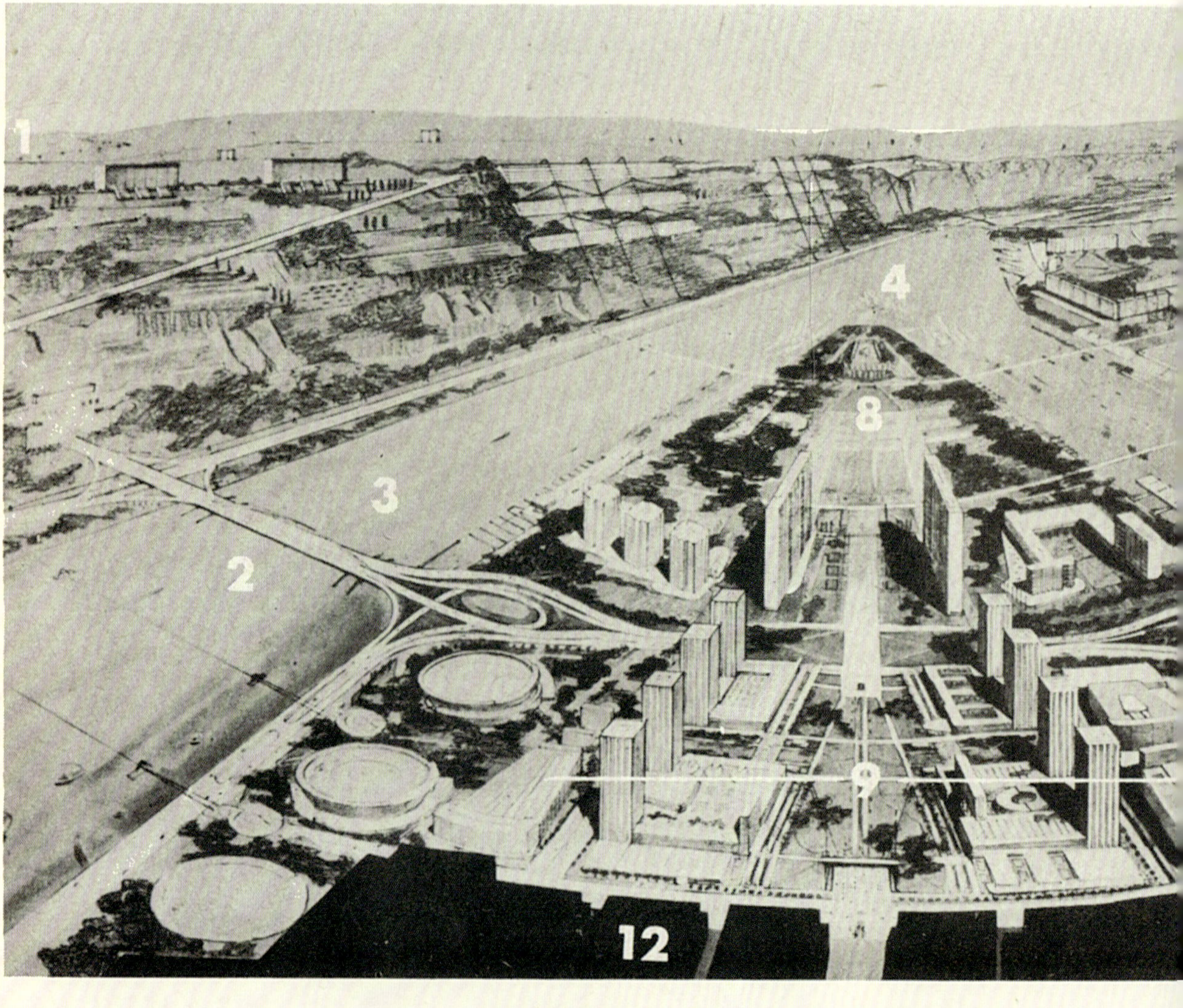
1
4
8
3
2
9
12

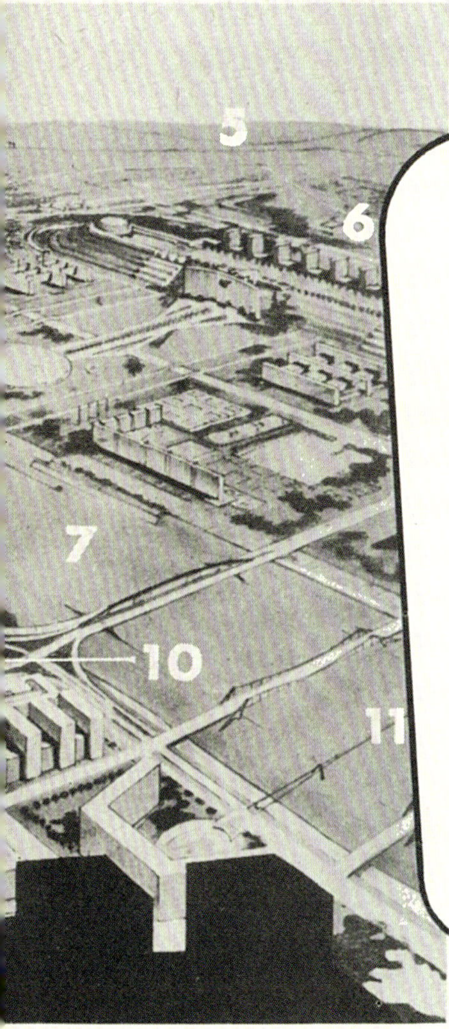

1. The South Side Development
2. Liberty Bridge
3. Monongahela River
4. Ohio River
5. The Northside Development
6. Municipal Group
7. Allegheny River
8. Point Park
9. Commercial Group
10. Point Interchange
11. Monorail Transportation
12. The Point Development

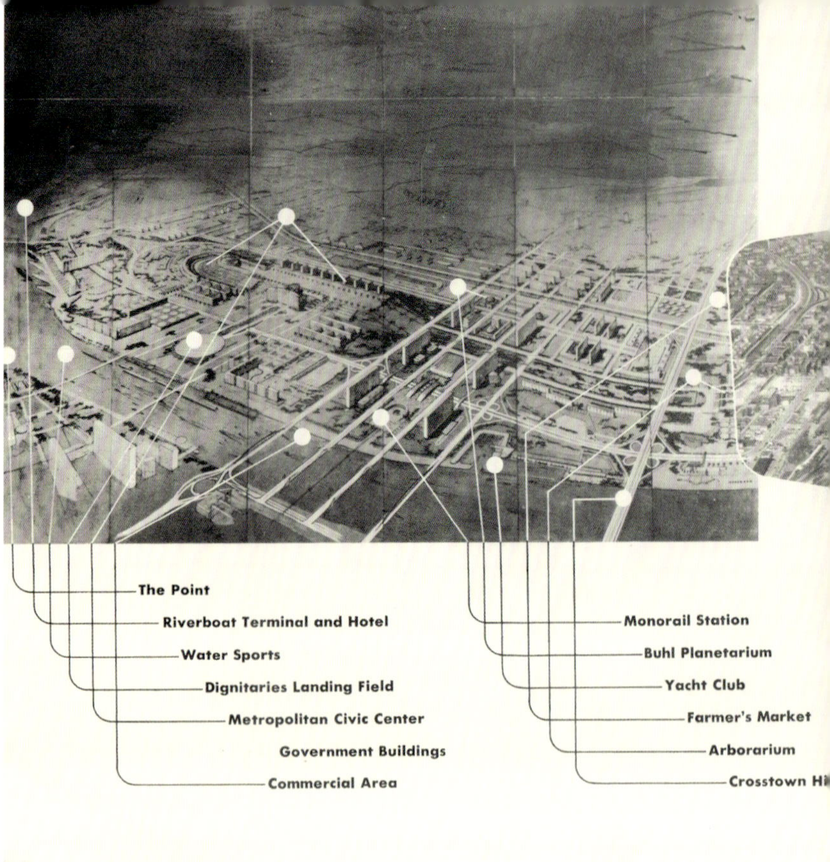
The Point
Riverboat Terminal and Hotel
Water Sports
Dignitaries Landing Field
Metropolitan Civic Center
Government Buildings
Commercial Area
Monorail Station
Buhl Planetarium
Yacht Club
Farmer's Market
Arborarium
Crosstown Hi

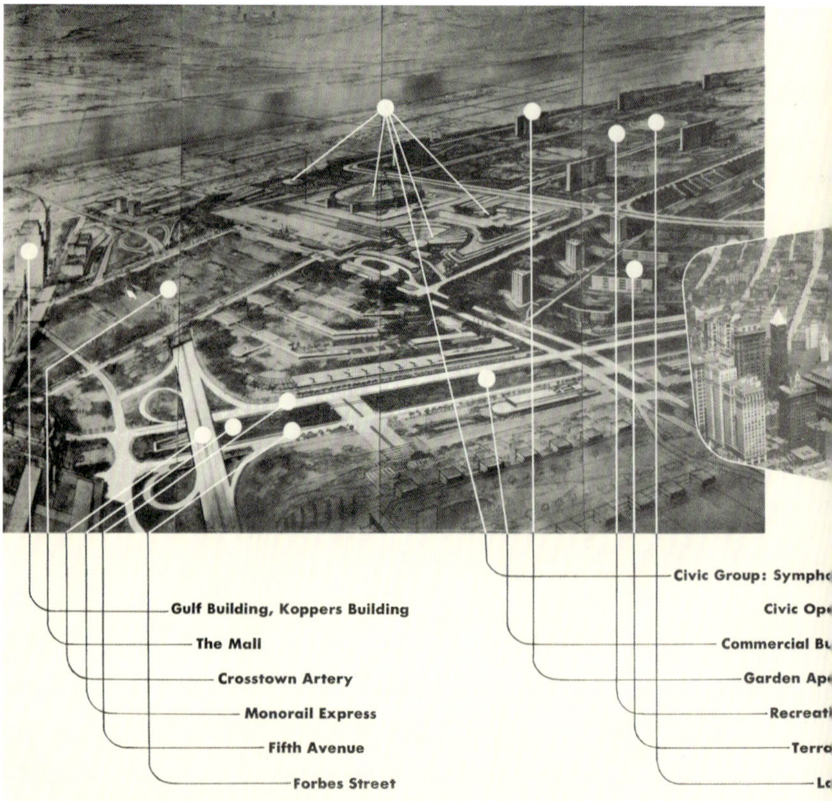
Gulf Building, Koppers Building
The Mall
Crosstown Artery
Monorail Express
Fifth Avenue
Forbes Street
Civic Group: Symph
Civic Op
Commercial Bu
Garden Ap
Recreat
Terra
L

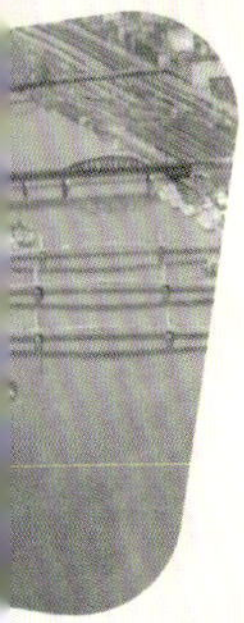

7

NORTH SIDE

This redevelopment can be a forecast not a fairy tale . . transforming Pittsburgh from a dark city to a wondrously beautiful park city . . if we truly wish to make it so.

Familiar old Allegheny has had a change of face, too, as the Point Park of the downtown triangle faces a North Side stage for river-made fun. Tiers of grandstand seats line the water front, offering a breeze swept view of water sports, boat races, diving exhibitions, and aquacades. Farther north, the wide sand of a bathing beach gleams in our smoke-freed sunshine.

Directly in back of the grandstands lies the central landing field. Two pedestrian traffic bridges lead from this field to Point Park. Surrounding the landing field is the Monument Hill area. Here stand the government buildings and other structures fulfilling our dreams for a metropolitan civic center.

Where the Ohio begins is the site of the Eastern Riverboat terminal and hotel. To this point, travelers from New England and northeastern United States will come to make pleasant river trips on palatial inland ships. Down the Ohio and north to Duluth . . to the Lakes in summer . . and in the winter, south to the Mississippi, to New Orleans and the Gulf. Pittsburgh, eastern terminal of the greatest waterway in the United States, tomorrow can become the grand Central Station of Riverboat travel.

Accessible from downtown over the Sixth, Seventh, and Ninth Street bridges is the commercial area of the North Side with its stores and towering apartment buildings. In the center of the commercial area, is the site of the underground monorail station of the transportation system connecting all points in the Pittsburgh of tomorrow.

To the north spreads a magnificent arborarium. Still farther north, behind the arborarium and across the monorail line spreads an ultra modern farmer's market . . bringing the vegetable gardens and orchards of nearby farm lands into the kitchens of North Side's apartment houses.

6

LOWER HILL

. . Another wonder of redevelopment that may be achieved by sustained, determined civic aspiration. A matter of years . . few or many as you yourself choose to make it.

Grant Street, with the Federal building, figures prominently in this neighborhood, connecting with the wide through-traffic boulevard that enters the city from the North and South sides. Familiar landmarks remain in the County Court House and its neighboring City-County office building, Hotel William Penn, the little German Lutheran Church, and the tall twins—the Koppers building and Gulf building. But the motly mixture of houses, storerooms and factories of the present have disappeared.

The natural green that starts at the Point sweeps up through downtown. The business section occupies a compact area. And a civic and cultural center has been built.

The trio of buildings at the left center of the broad, green Mall includes a large, circular exhibition hall where sporting events, conventions, and industrial exhibits are conducted; a symphony hall; and an open-air amphitheater where future seasons of civic light opera will be presented. This amphitheater is built with a roof of flexible segments that open fan-like to protect spectators from changes in the weather. Around these three main buildings other civic-interest buildings will complete Pittsburgh's cultural center.

Now, too, Pittsburgh has near-town apartments . . terraced garden apartments overlooking old Fifth Avenue and Forbes Street. The area between these streets is a sweeping parkway of natural green along which speeds the monorail, connecting the business, civic, and residential districts.

·ts Arena, Open-Air
and Cultural Center

rs

·Iousing

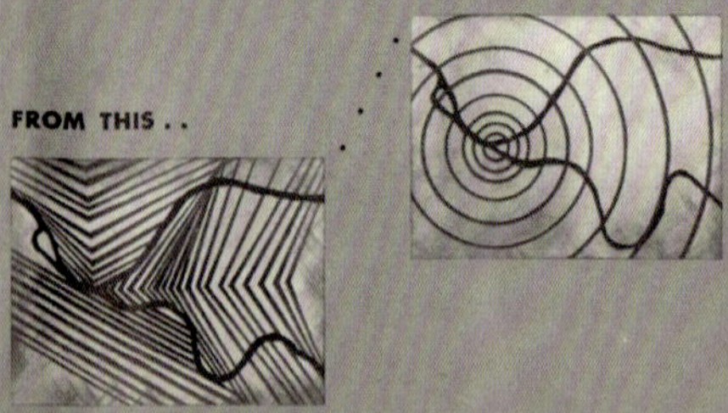

Decongestion of Blight Areas

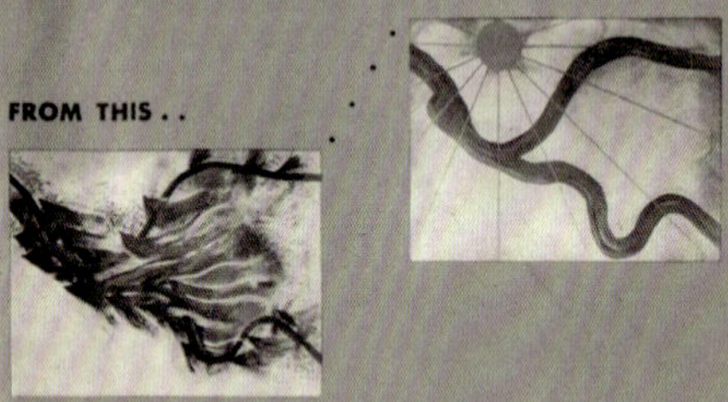

Depollution of Air and Water

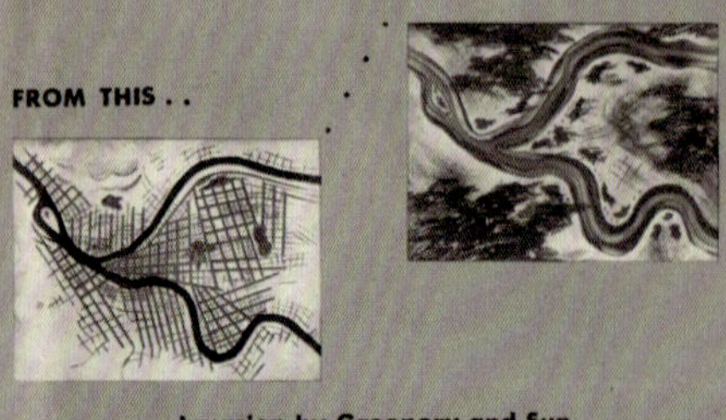

Invasion by Greenery and Sun

THE PARK CITY

The future city will grow and change by plan and foresight and not by chance and hazard. It may have tall buildings so more space will be available for playgrounds, parks, schools, sports, and homes. Communities within the city will be built around their business, civic, and educational centers. The city will be made up of many of these partner-communities connected to major business and industrial areas, parkways and rapid transportation.

Decongestion . . the old city wilderness will be cleared way. New pioneers will have cleansed and opened the land for living areas of noble proportions. The citizens of the Park City will know it as they know their homes and yards and they will be as proud of their city as they are of their house and garden.

Invasion by greenery . . the clear sky, clean air, pure water, green leaf and open vista of life in nature will displace the dusty, dry, and crowded city. Nature will be as much a part of the city as it is of the country. And Pittsburgh, with its naturally dramatic setting, will then offer panoramas of unmatched beauty.

Depollution of air and water . . until present sources of energy are displaced by atomic or other more advanced ones, effort will be made to remove smoke and gases by techno-chemical means. Relocation of heavy and smoke-bearing industry in the east and south sections of the city, away from the direction of prevailing winds, will clear the city of smoke. The planned sewage disposal plant will free the rivers of pollution.

HAPPIER LIVING THROUGH PLANNING

Tomorrow's communities will be completely planned and integrated to provide pleasant living, work and play within walking distance for everyone; all communities will be closely linked by adequate means of transportation and communication.

Traffic hazards will be eliminated. All vehicle traffic will be separated from walkways. A start in this direction is already underway in the Penn Lincoln Parkway. The western extension of the East West Parkway will follow. Such parkways are freeways. They will be amply wide and will provide for through express traffic as well as inter-connection with local arteries of traffic.

Parking problems will disappear with the magic of Park City. Already contemplated are plans for providing adequate parking in the Golden Triangle. It will be possible for workers, shoppers, and theater-goers to store their cars readily and free the streets for easier flow of traffic. Mass transportation will be efficient and attractive.

The heart of each community will be the social, religious, administrative and shopping center. The schools of tomorrow will allow students to enjoy the benefit of fresh air while they study. Ideal working conditions will be provided in well-planned shops and plants set in the spacious and verdant landscape.

A major new development for Pittsburgh will be a tremendous expansion in the use of the rivers for educational and recreational purposes. There will be Ohio River Tours . . connecting with the Great Lakes northward . . with New Orleans through Natchez and Mobile southward . . a *new* inland waterway at the very front door of our future communities.

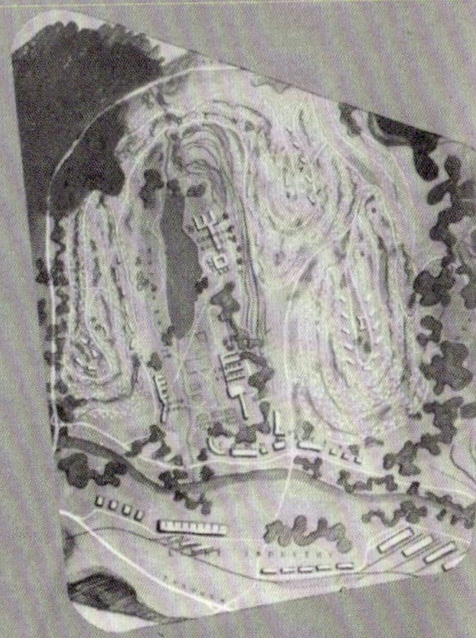

Typical Planned Community of the Future

Schools Nestled in Nature

Integrated Recreation Areas

Highways by-pass Communities

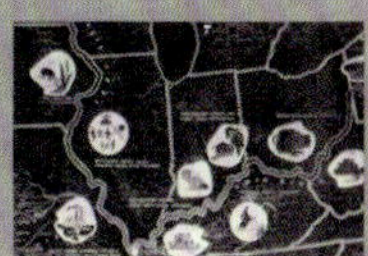

River Development Tours

smoke

Domestic Stokers . . . Stokers and new-type smokeless stoves find the Pittsburgh market brisk as smoke control moves ahead

Gasification . . . (*Left*) Most significant development in the coal industry since bituminous coal replaced charcoal in making steel!

The Pittsburgh Consolidation Coal Company and the Standard Oil Company of New Jersey have announced that they will soon build their first plants to turn coal into gasoline and fuel gas. This supply will make Pittsburgh's smoke control program easy, because the plants will be in the city's metropolitan area.

Still more important, the new process assures the future of a basic industry in the Pittsburgh region's economy.

THE RESPONSE

control Pittsburgh and Allegheny County are on the way to smoke control. The answer is to stop smoke at the source. If you don't make smoke in your fire, there can't be smoke in the air.

The mechanisms: smokeless fuels, and mechanical firing equipment that won't allow any fuel to smoke.

The method: the force of law, backed by intense public sentiment.

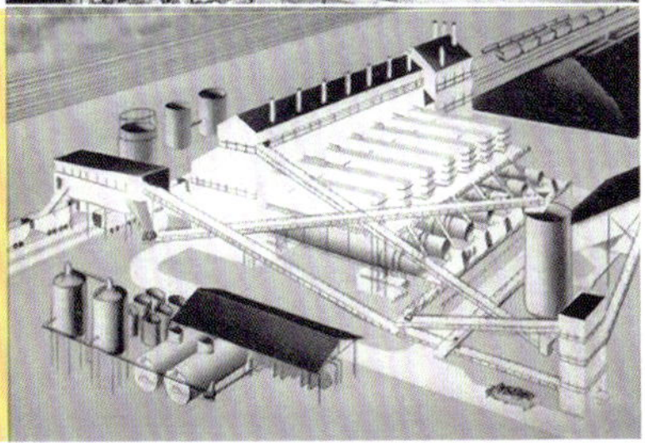

Cleaner Surroundings . . . There will be millions of dollars in savings in a smokeless Pittsburgh when the cleaning, laundry, and decorating bills are added up. More important still, life will be brighter all around.

Coal Processing Plant . . . (*Left*) Smokeless fuels for the Pittsburgh market will pour from this new $3,000,000 plant in 1948.

● **ACTION:** **Dense smoke from any source will be a sign of lawbreaking when the city's smoke control ordinance goes into full effect on October 1, 1947. The ordinance outlaws nuisance smoke.**

Because smoke doesn't recognize a city line, county-wide smoke control is essential in metropolitan Allegheny County. Through the pioneering efforts of the United Smoke Council of the Conference, the 1947 Legislature gave the County Commissioners the legal right to outlaw smoke—from railroads as well as from the household chimney.

A county-wide ordinance is in the making. The Commissioners have appointed a director of their smoke control program and a Citizens' Advisory Committee to help achieve control.

New Diesels . . . To meet the law, the district's railroads are turning to Diesel locomotives. Diesel-powered switching engines are taking over the city freight-yard work. Before many years have passed, smokeless locomotives may run on powdered Pittsburgh coal instead of oil.

Cleaner Homes . . . (*Above*) The lady of the house is the strongest advocate of smoke control. Her work will be reduced. Her leisure time will increase.

5

"Pittsburgh is the test of industrialism everywhere to renew itself, to rebuild upon the gritty ruins of the past a society more equitable, more spacious, more in the human scale."

"FORTUNE" February 1947

PITTSBURGH has accepted the challenge

A Great Industrial Region increases its productivity and develops its human values.

blight

THE RESPONSE

triangle redevelopment

American cities grow old from the heart out. Pittsburgh has been no exception. Decay at its core has been pronounced.

The city was born at the junction of its rivers at the Point. Now it will be reborn there, as a plan of redevelopment takes place.

● **ACTION:** A Point Park is in the making where the rivers meet. The state, recognizing the importance of the site, has already acquired more than half of the properties in the park area.

With the park assured for Pittsburgh, it becomes possible for public and private enterprise to unite in redeveloping the 23 acres adjoining its borders. The Pittsburgh Redevelopment Authority, created late in 1946, is already armed with a Planning Commission declaration of blight, which gives it power of eminent domain for the area.

Insurance companies are surveying the 23-acre redevelopment area, where a combined commercial and apartment district is being studied.

The Federal Works Agency has made $250,000 available to the city for further planning of the project.

The State Highway Department has authorized the preliminary engineering surveys for the Point Park traffic interchange and a new Point Bridge as part of the Penn-Lincoln Parkway.

Point Park Study . . . *Right:* One of the views of Point Park as shown in the unofficial study prepared by the Pittsburgh Regional Planning Association and presented to the Allegheny Conference.

7

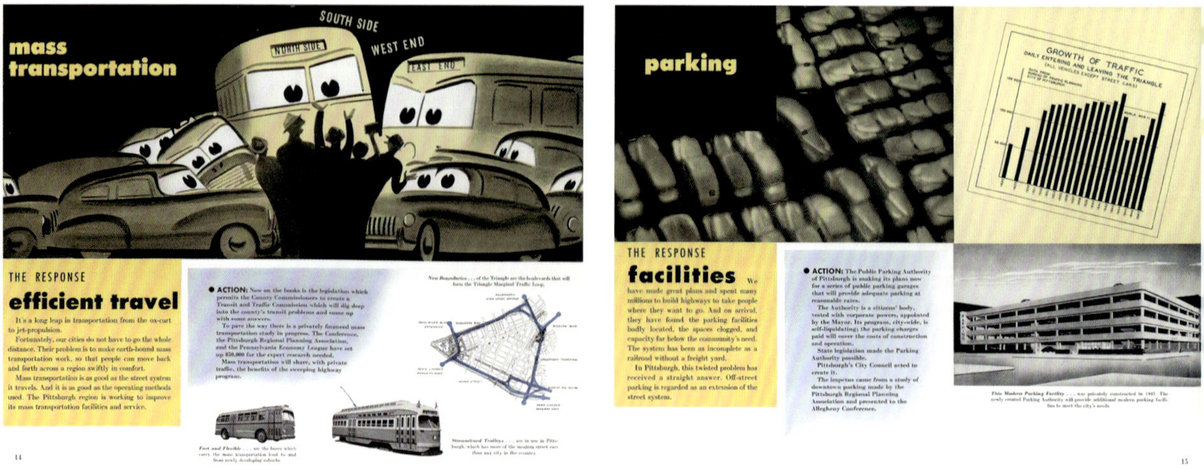

mass transportation

THE RESPONSE

efficient travel

It's a long leap in transportation from the ox-cart to jet-propulsion.

Fortunately, our cities do not have to go the whole distance. Their problem is to make earth-bound mass transportation work, so that people can move back and forth across a region swiftly in comfort.

Mass transportation is as good as the street system it travels. And it is as good as the operating methods used. The Pittsburgh region is working to improve its mass transportation facilities and service.

● **ACTION:** Now on the books is the legislation which permits the County Commissioners to create a Transit and Traffic Commission which will dig deep into the county's transit problems and come up with some answers.

To pave the way there is a privately financed mass transportation study in progress. The Conference, the Pittsburgh Regional Planning Association, and the Pennsylvania Economy League have set up $50,000 for the expert research needed.

Mass transportation will share, with private traffic, the benefits of the sweeping highway program.

New Boundaries . . . of the Triangle are the boulevards that will form the Triangle Marginal Traffic Loop.

Fast and Flexible . . . are the buses which carry the mass transportation load to and from newly developing suburbs.

Streamlined Trolleys . . . are in use in Pittsburgh, which has more of the modern street cars than any city in the country.

14

parking

THE RESPONSE

facilities

We have made great plans and spent many millions to build highways to take people where they want to go. And on arrival, they have found the parking facilities badly located, the spaces clogged, and capacity far below the community's need. The system has been as incomplete as a railroad without a freight yard.

In Pittsburgh, this twisted problem has received a straight answer. Off-street parking is regarded as an extension of the street system.

● **ACTION:** The Public Parking Authority of Pittsburgh is making its plans now for a series of public parking garages that will provide adequate parking at reasonable rates.

The Authority is a citizens' body, vested with corporate powers, appointed by the Mayor. Its program, city-wide, is self-liquidating; the parking charges paid will cover the costs of construction and operation.

State legislation made the Parking Authority possible.

Pittsburgh's City Council acted to create it.

The impetus came from a study of downtown parking made by the Pittsburgh Regional Planning Association and presented to the Allegheny Conference.

This Modern Parking Facility . . . was privately constructed in 1947. The newly created Parking Authority will provide additional modern parking facilities to meet the city's needs.

15

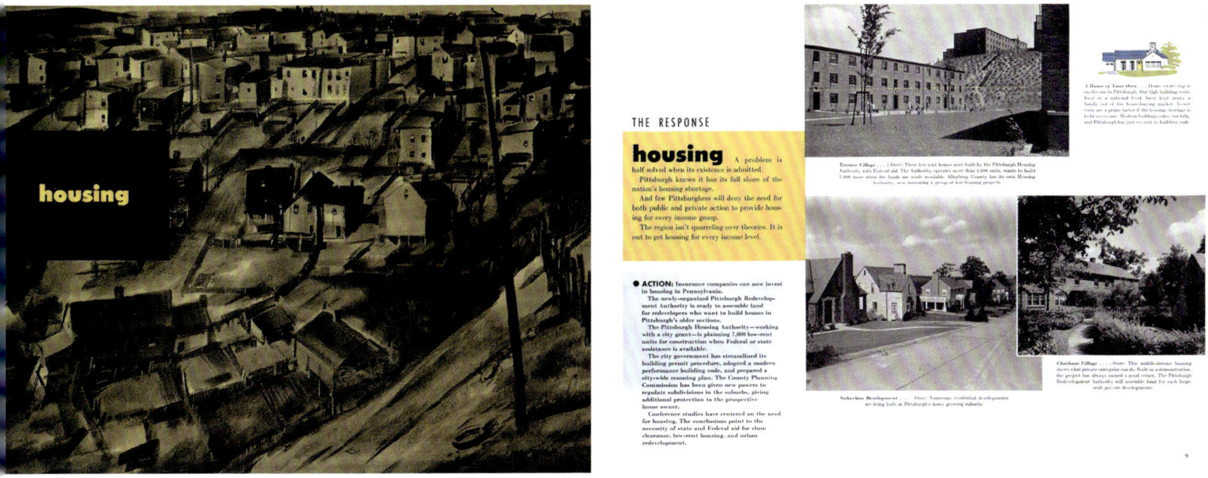

THE RESPONSE

housing A problem is half solved when its existence is admitted.

Pittsburgh knows it has its full share of the nation's housing shortage.

And few Pittsburghers will deny the need for both public and private action to provide housing for every income group.

The region isn't quarreling over theories. It is out to get housing for every income level.

● **ACTION:** Insurance companies can now invest in housing in Pennsylvania.

The newly-organized Pittsburgh Redevelopment Authority is ready to assemble land for redevelopers who want to build homes in Pittsburgh's older sections.

The Pittsburgh Housing Authority—working with a city grant—is planning 7,000 low-rent units for construction when Federal or state assistance is available.

The city government has streamlined its building permit procedure, adopted a modern performance building code, and prepared a city-wide rezoning plan. The County Planning Commission has been given new powers to regulate subdivisions in the suburbs, giving additional protection to the prospective home owner.

Conference studies have centered on the need for housing. The conclusions point to the necessity of state and Federal aid for slum clearance, low-rent housing, and urban redevelopment.

Terrace Village . . . (Above) These low-rent homes were built by the Pittsburgh Housing Authority with Federal aid. The Authority operates more than 5,000 units, wants to build 7,000 more when the funds are made available. Allegheny County has its own Housing Authority, now managing a group of war-housing projects.

A Home of Your Own . . . Home ownership is on the rise in Pittsburgh. But high building costs, fixed at a national level, have kept many a family out of the home-buying market. Lower costs are a prime factor if the housing shortage is to be overcome. Modern building codes can help, and Pittsburgh has just revised its building code.

Suburban Development . . . (Above) Numerous residential developments are being built in Pittsburgh's many growing suburbs.

Chatham Village . . . (Above) This middle-income housing shows what private enterprise can do. Built as a demonstration, the project has always earned a good return. The Pittsburgh Redevelopment Authority will assemble land for such large-scale private developments.

9

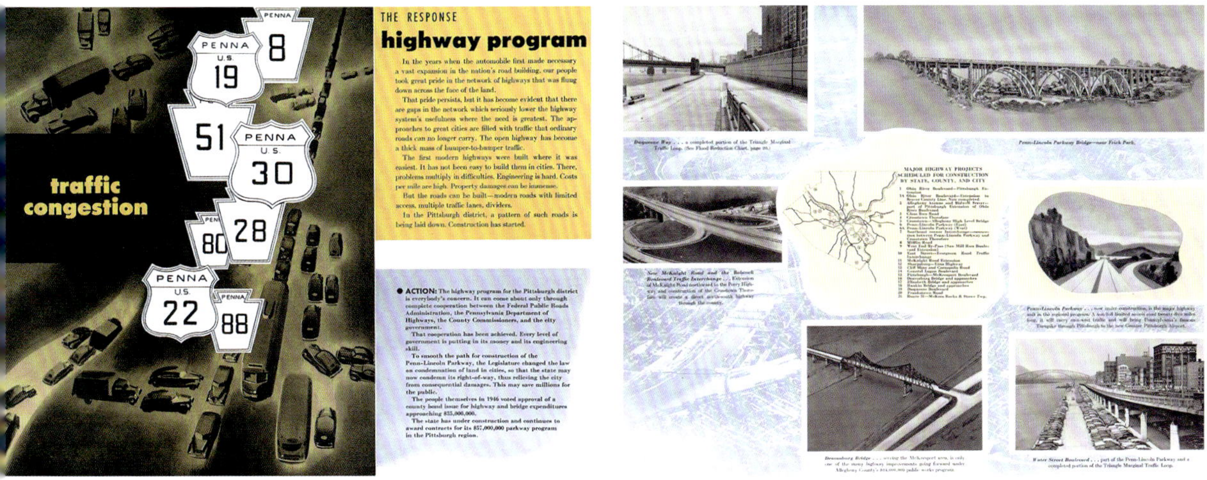

THE RESPONSE

highway program

In the years when the automobile first made necessary a vast expansion in the nation's road building, our people took great pride in the network of highways that was flung down across the face of the land.

That pride persists, but it has become evident that there are gaps in the network which seriously lower the highway system's usefulness where the need is greatest. The approaches to great cities are filled with traffic that ordinary roads can no longer carry. The open highway has become a thick mass of bumper-to-bumper traffic.

The first modern highways were built where it was easiest. It has not been easy to build them in cities. There, problems multiply in difficulties. Engineering is hard. Costs per mile are high. Property damages can be immense.

But the roads can be built—modern roads with limited access, multiple traffic lanes, dividers.

In the Pittsburgh district, a pattern of such roads is being laid down. Construction has started.

● **ACTION:** The highway program for the Pittsburgh district is everybody's concern. It can come about only through complete cooperation between the Federal Public Roads Administration, the Pennsylvania Department of Highways, the County Commissioners, and the city government.

That cooperation has been achieved. Every level of government is putting in its money and its engineering skill.

To smooth the path for construction of the Penn-Lincoln Parkway, the Legislature changed the law on condemnation of land in cities, so that the state may now condemn its right-of-way, thus relieving the city from consequential damages. This may save millions for the public.

The people themselves in 1946 voted approval of a county bond issue for highway and bridge expenditures approaching $35,000,000.

The state has under construction and continues to award contracts for its $57,000,000 parkway program in the Pittsburgh region.

Duquesne Way . . . a completed portion of the Triangle Marginal Traffic Loop. (See Flood Reduction Chart, page 20.)

Penn-Lincoln Parkway Bridge—near Frick Park.

MAJOR HIGHWAY PROJECTS SCHEDULED FOR CONSTRUCTION BY STATE, COUNTY, AND CITY

Pittsburgh is the test of industrialism everywhere to renew itself, to rebuild upon the gritty ruins of the past a society more equitable, more spacious, more in the human scale.

—*Fortune*, February 1947, quoted in *Pittsburgh: Challenge and Response*, 1947.

Betterment of the Region through United Action

What is the Allegheny Conference?

In a troubled world, postwar planning is an ironic phrase, with a bitter savor. In the Pittsburgh region, through united community action, planning is speeding ahead to accomplishment.

The Allegheny Conference was formed in the war years to achieve such unity of action. It is a citizens' non-profit organization, enlisting the full strength and best talents of industry, public administration, education, finance, science, and the agencies of public opinion. Its one objective is to develop the material and human resources of the region where the Conference works, and to make secure its future. It is founded on a fresh concept of modern community life—the concept of people living together in productive enterprise, rewarded in terms of work and enjoyment.

The Conference does not impose.................. It unites!

It approaches a region's problems through the expert agencies at work—the State, City, and County governments, the Pittsburgh Regional Planning Association, the Pennsylvania Economy League, the Pittsburgh Chamber of Commerce, the Federation of Social Agencies, and the Civic Club. Where no qualified agency exists, the Conference deals directly with the problem to be met.

Long-range planning is rescued from futility by long-range action!

PUBLIC ADMINISTRATION COOPERATES

"The Allegheny Conference can recommend. It cannot enact. For the exercise of the power of government, a community must look to its elected officials who are given the responsibility of legislation and administration.

"The civic program for this region can go forward only with the help of the people's representatives. That help has come unstintingly from Governor Duff, from Mayor Lawrence, and from County Commissioners Kane, Rankin, and Herron.

"Party differences have been submerged in community betterment. Legislative bodies such as the General Assembly and the Pittsburgh City Council have created the implements of progress.

"As citizens, we have cause to be grateful.

"Courageous and capable public administration is essential to public progress."

Edward R. Weidlein
Chairman, Allegheny Conference on Community Development

PUBLIC AND CIVIC UNITY

● "As Governor of Pennsylvania, I am greatly pleased by the vigorous drive in progress to vitalize the whole activities of the Pittsburgh area.

"The Allegheny Conference program is wonderful and an example for the entire state.

"You have asked the Commonwealth to give you tools to work with. We have tried to do so and will be right with you in your total program."

James H. Duff
Governor, Commonwealth of Pennsylvania

● "I have very often said that I became Mayor of Pittsburgh at a most fortunate time. We are making the decisions now that are critical for the future of our city. In making them, we have a united community to support us. With that measure of support, in which the Conference takes a leading place, anything good that is planned for Pittsburgh cannot fail to succeed."

David L. Lawrence
Mayor, City of Pittsburgh

● "The County Commissioners have supported the Conference program from its very beginning. We believe that the fulfillment of the Conference program is essential to the future development of Allegheny County.

"The County government is the nearest thing to a regional government that exists. To develop fully the resources of a region that is more populous and far more productive than many states, we need cooperation at every level of government.

"The County Commissioners have been working toward that end, and appreciate sincerely the suggestions and recommendations of the Conference at all times."

John J. Kane
Chairman, Board of Commissioners of Allegheny County

● "The Pittsburgh Regional Planning Association is proud to be a part of the combined operation which will give us a better community.

"Great achievements have been made. But the greatest of them—the one which makes the others possible—is the teamwork we have developed. Political differences, sectional competition, and old rivalries have been submerged in a common program for the good of all."

Richard K. Mellon
President, Pittsburgh Regional Planning Association

● "The Federation of Social Agencies is gratified at the emphasis placed on human values in the Conference program. As its President, I can testify to the fruitful results of our work together. Physical resources and human resources are complementary and inseparable. I am proud that we are developing both!"

H. J. Heinz II
President, Federation of Social Agencies

● "Very frankly and quite proudly, the Pittsburgh Chamber of Commerce speaks for business in the Pittsburgh district. We know that the broad interests of business and the vital interests of the community are identical. The Conference program is welcomed by our officers and members."

William B. McFall
President, Pittsburgh Chamber of Commerce

● "The success of the Conference program is necessarily dependent upon creating sound economic conditions which in turn depend on effective governmental, administrative and fiscal policies.

"As an organization whose sole purpose is the improvement of local public administration and finance, the Pennsylvania Economy League will continue to work with the Conference and elected public officials to help them achieve our community program."

M. D. Howell
Chairman, Executive Committee, Western Division
Pennsylvania Economy League

● "We will have as much industrial expansion and attract as many new industries to this region as we can justify with economic facts. Industry will locate where productivity is high, where markets are close, where raw materials are convenient.

"These are direct material factors. There is also a powerful indirect attraction which comes when a city is known as a good place in which to live. In making Pittsburgh a better place in which to live, we are making it a better place in which to work, both for management and labor."

Pressly H. McCance
President, Pittsburgh Civic-Business Council

. Non-Partisan Legislative
rogram Brings Benefits
) the Whole Community

IE Pittsburgh district does not hang suspended in a vacuum.
s part of a state and part of a nation. The state capital and the
ional government can either erect roadblocks or spread carpets
the progress of any city.
'hrough determined and well-planned action, a united com-
nity can secure the legislation that will remove the blocks and
ır the road ahead. The record of the 1947 legislative session on
bills that helped the Pittsburgh region is an example of such
nmunity success.
'he development of a comprehensive civic program for the
tsburgh district revealed broad gaps in the powers granted local
ernment by the Commonwealth of Pennsylvania.

was to bridge these gaps that enabling acts were drafted under
sponsorship of the Conference and its cooperating organizations.
ders of both political parties, city and county officials, and the
slative delegation from Allegheny County shared in the con-
ences that shaped the legislation and arranged for its introduction
he General Assembly.
'he whole program was tagged "The Pittsburgh Package."
ctually, the program benefits the entire county.
'he legislation has varied purposes but a uniform theme. It is
igned to help a community attack and solve its own problems
its own ingenuity and from its own resources.

GHT measures were introduced by joint action of Republican
Democratic sponsors. Two bills, with direct effects on the
's governmental and fiscal structure, were introduced by
nocrats with pledges of organized Republican support.
'wo of the bills, low on the priority list, died in committee.
'he eight vital bills survived all legislative hazards.

WERFULLY supported by public opinion in Allegheny County,
y won final passage by overwhelming votes. Approved by the
ernor—who was their vigorous champion—they are now
ruments of progress in the hands of the people of the Pittsburgh
rict.
n addition, the legislative session and its 1945 predecessor
lt with other urban problems on a state-wide basis. The legal
ers needed to promote blight elimination, insurance invest-
nt in housing, stream purification, and the construction of free-
ing parkways were extended and strengthened. State funds
e voted for planning a Port Authority program for Pittsburgh's
nd waterways.

its passage of these bills, the Pennsylvania Legislature gave
ll-speed-ahead signal to the community program.

WHAT IS ACCOMPLISHED!

● SMOKE

A county-wide smoke program is assured, as railroads are brought under the county's regulatory powers.

The vote:

House: Yes 198—No 0

Senate: Yes 35—No 4

See page 5

● BLIGHT

The Pittsburgh Redevelopment Authority is organized to promote the rebuilding of blighted areas, under the Redevelopment Acts of 1945.

The vote on the major Act was:

House: Yes 203—No 0

Senate: Yes 49—No 0

See page 7

● HOUSING

Insurance companies are permitted to invest in real estate and housing in Pennsylvania, under Insurance Act Amendments of 1947.

The vote on the amendments was:

House: Yes 193—No 11

Senate: Yes 34—No 5

Allegheny County's Planning Commission can control subdivision plans in growing suburban communities.

The vote:

House: Yes 191—No 0

Senate: Yes 50—No 0

See page 9

● REFUSE

Allegheny County is permitted to build incinerators and other disposal facilities for the use of the county's 129 municipalities.

The vote:

House: Yes 196—No 2

Senate: Yes 39—No 0

See page 11

● POLLUTION

The Allegheny County Sanitary Authority is organized to purify the rivers, under the Municipal Authorities Act of 1945.

The vote on the Act was:

House: Yes 194—No 1

Senate: Yes 48—No 0

See page 11

● RECREATION

The city is given a Parks and Recreation Department, emphasizing the importance of public recreation in modern urban living.

The vote:

House: Yes 201—No 0

Senate: Yes 48—No 0

See page 13

● MASS TRANSPORTATION

The county government is enabled to create a Transit and Traffic Commission to study mass transportation.

The vote:

House: Yes 201—No 0

Senate: Yes 50—No 0

See page 14

● PARKING

Pittsburgh is allowed to establish a Public Parking Authority to construct and operate parking facilities for the people.

The vote:

House: Yes 186—No 4

Senate: Yes 45—No 4

See page 15

● HIGHWAYS

The Penn-Lincoln Parkway is speeded, as government is freed from the burden of consequential damages in building express roads in Pittsburgh.

The vote:

House: Yes 191—No 0

Senate: Yes 50—No 0

See page 16

● AVIATION

In the 1946 People's Bond Issue $6,000,000 was earmarked for county aviation improvements.

The vote:

Yes 123,135 No 57,124

See page 19

● PORT OF PITTSBURGH

A river-rail-truck terminal for the Port of Pittsburgh is being surveyed under a grant of $100,000, made possible by Act No. 413 of 1945.

The vote on the Act was:

House: Yes 202—No 0

Senate: Yes 37—No 0

See page 21

● PUBLIC FINANCE

Pittsburgh and its suburbs now can broaden their tax base beyond real estate tax levies.

The vote:

House: Yes 144—No 51

Senate: Yes 45—No 5

See page 24

02
Planning and Promotion

In parallel with the visionary and often fantastical images of modernity promoted by Kaufmann and the Allegheny Conference on Community Development were more pragmatically-oriented documents through which public and private agencies sought to effect more concrete plans for Pittsburgh's neighborhoods and infrastructures. In 1939, Robert Moses, the notorious "master builder" of New York City, was hired to produce one such report as an outside "diagnostician" by condiment king Howard Heinz for the Pittsburgh Regional Planning Association.[1] Unlike privately commissioned schemes of similar magnitude like Wright's Point Park proposal, Moses's *Pittsburgh Arterial Plan* (1939) had a wide-reaching impact on the city's downtown and road network. The 26-page report targeted both the snarled traffic in the Triangle and the concurrent political roadblocks of "overlapping jurisdictions" and "personalities involved" that had prevented its resolution.[2] The *Arterial Plan* proposed a new highway encircling the Point, allowed the land cleared at its center to be used for lush public parks and a monumental obelisk. Although even by Moses's own account the proposal included "little that was new," it highlighted a foundational period of Pittsburgh planning—before the formal beginning of the "Renaissance"—in which civic power was consolidated into private-public coalitions to put large-scale infrastructural plans on the table. Documents like *Pittsburgh Perceived: A Critical Review of Form, Features and Feasibilities of the Prodigious City* (1963), published by Department of City Planning, demonstrated the immense scope of such ambitions in proposing a massive structure that would serve at once as highway, bridge, and megabuilding for offices and apartments.

As the Renaissance took shape, Pittsburgh's altered its commercial core dramatically through the complete redevelopment of the Point and the more strategic acupuncture of new construction in the Golden Triangle. These changes did not occur overnight;

twenty years of intense construction marked the period between the completion of One Gateway Center (1952) and the second U.S. Steel Building (1971). Brochures commemorating the major buildings built in these decades, like *Aluminum on the Skyline* (1953) for Alcoa and *Equitable Builds a Gateway* (c. 1972), touted the distinctiveness of these new additions to the city's modern skyline, each marking a milestone in the gradual development of a modern corporate office district as the primary engine of urban transformation. On a different register, the *Make It Pittsburgh!* brochure (c. 1961), an advertisement for the Civic Arena as a new possibility for national conferences, attempted to persuade both locals and out-of-towners of that project's value. Similarly, *From Blueprint to Reality* (1968) celebrated both the construction of the Civic Arena and the development that its planners envisioned would surround it.

In contrast to such corporate self-promotion, other documents argued for the broader social and economic impact of large-scale urban developments through which, as the business magazine *Fortune* sought to convey, Pittsburgh might serve as "the test of industrialism everywhere to renew itself, to rebuild upon the gritty ruins of the past a society more equitable, more spacious, more in the human scale."[3] *Allegheny Center* (1967), produced by Deeter Ritchey Sippel, reflected the character of an ambitious and complex neighborhood project that required the production of multiple documents for both disciplinary and non-disciplinary audiences in order to gain support. The publication contained photographs of built work as well as architectural drawings and models, suggesting that it was completed in the later stages of the project and was intended to be read primarily by architects and planners, rather than by the neighborhood's future inhabitants.

An even more ambitious proposal that garnered national attention at its release was publicized in these years by the Oakland Corporation, a short-lived consortium of six non-profits led by the University of Pittsburgh (1961–65) entrusted with the development of a massive new center that would attract a portion of the country's rapidly expanding scientific and research industries.[4] Shortly after its founding, the Oakland Corporation hired the architects Harrison & Abramovitz to design the expansive "Panther Hollow Research Park," making use of the ravine that divided Carnegie Tech from the University of Pittsburgh to create a multi-level megastructure that would house more than 10,000 daytime occupants. Unveiled as "the greatest cultural complex, probably in the world," Harrison & Abramovitz' 18-million-square-foot proposal included spaces for research, medical facilities, and education.[5] The dramatic images in *Prospectus for Panther Hollow: The 21st Century City* (1963) show a new extension of Schenley Park extending across the gulch, allowing trains and cars to pass below unseen.

1 Robert Moses, *Arterial Plan for Pittsburgh* (1939), 1.
2 Ibid.
3 "Pittsburgh's New Powers," *Fortune* 35, no. 2 (February 1947): 187.
4 See Patrick Vitale, "Cradle of the Creative Class: Reinventing the Figure of the Scientist in Cold War Pittsburgh," *Annals of the American Association of Geographers* 106, no. 6 (2016), 1378-96.
5 William Faust, "Panther Hollow Project," *The Pittsburgh Press*, November 24, 1963, 7.

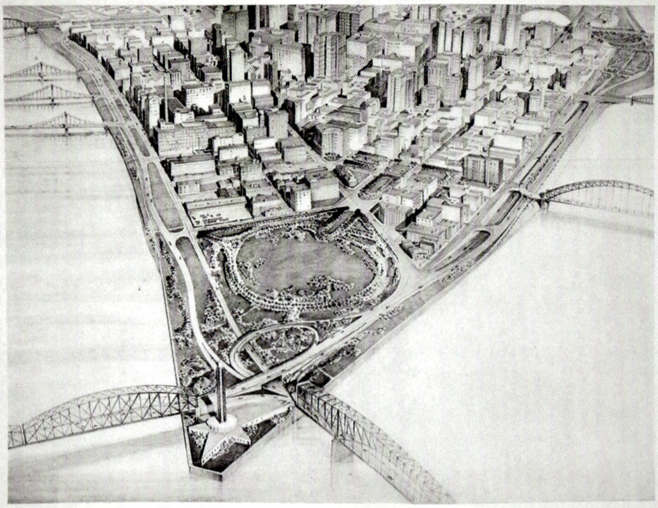

POINT PARK

EXHIBIT E

PROPOSED SHAFT AT POINT

A student of city growth who cannot see ahead more than ten years is a fool, but one who claims to be able to plan for a century is usually an impractical visionary.

Robert Moses, 1939

152b 152c

Any bridge which conveys local traffic from one side of the valley to the other can be designed to support offices or apartments, thereby providing several services simultaneously. The accommodation can be suspended from the principal beams supported from the valley bottom anchored upon high ground.

Patrick Horsbrugh, 1963

JAMES C. ARMSTRONG, JR.
REGISTERED ARCHITECT
337 SOUTH WINEBIDDLE AVE.
PITTSBURGH 24, PENNSYLVANIA
Aluminum
on the Skyline

FOUR GATEWAY CENTER
A new dimension for Pittsburgh's famed business location

The Great Space Adventure.
Join it.
U. S. Steel Building
600 Grant St.
Pittsburgh
Enjoy them all:
The location
The neighbors
The comfort
The security
The flexibility
The modular design
The movable walls
The lighting
The colors
The indoor parking
The shops
The banking service
The restaurants
The view
The Space Men
John W. Galbreath & Co. Realtors
U. S. Steel Building
600 Grant Street
Pittsburgh, Pa.
15219
Call
Ross Ford
or Jim Dawson
391-8950

No one had ever attempted the stamping of aluminum panels of this great size.

‹ *Aluminum on the Skyline*, 1953

Wide open and sky high, with miles of southwestern Pennsylvania to gaze at...

‹ *The Space Men*, 1972

Pittsburgh is now second only to New York in office space built since the end of World War II—and all of its postwar buildings enjoy either 100% or near 100% occupancy.

› *Equitable Builds a Gateway*, c.1972

Although Pittsburgh has gained national and international recognition for its spectacular redevelopment program, the city remains seriously handicapped from a civic standpoint by the absence of a major, all-purpose auditorium.

Auditorium: From Blueprint to Reality, 1968

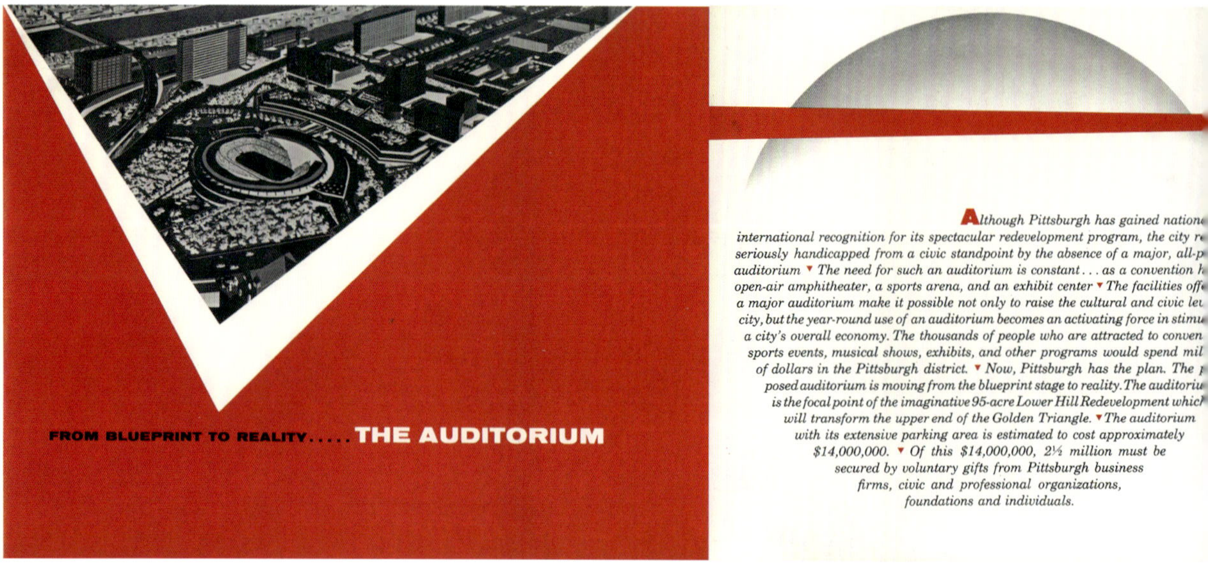

FROM BLUEPRINT TO REALITY..... THE AUDITORIUM

Although Pittsburgh has gained nation
international recognition for its spectacular redevelopment program, the city r
seriously handicapped from a civic standpoint by the absence of a major, all-p
auditorium ▾ The need for such an auditorium is constant . . . as a convention
open-air amphitheater, a sports arena, and an exhibit center ▾ The facilities off
a major auditorium make it possible not only to raise the cultural and civic le
city, but the year-round use of an auditorium becomes an activating force in stimu
a city's overall economy. The thousands of people who are attracted to conven
sports events, musical shows, exhibits, and other programs would spend mil
of dollars in the Pittsburgh district. ▾ Now, Pittsburgh has the plan. The
posed auditorium is moving from the blueprint stage to reality. The auditori
is the focal point of the imaginative 95-acre Lower Hill Redevelopment whic
will transform the upper end of the Golden Triangle. ▾ The auditorium
with its extensive parking area is estimated to cost approximately
$14,000,000. ▾ Of this $14,000,000, 2½ million must be
secured by voluntary gifts from Pittsburgh business
firms, civic and professional organizations,
foundations and individuals.

MAKE IT PITTSBURGH!

. . . For your CONVENTION, EXPOSITION, MEETING, EVENT

CIVIC ARENA and EXHIBIT HALL

THE LOWER HILL REDEVELOPMENT

The Auditorium will form the nucleus of the Lower Hill Redevelopment which will transform 95.4 acres of blighted area at the upper end of the Triangle into another modern showplace of civic planning.

The Auditorium, including the Mall and the parking area, will occupy about 20 acres.

Completion of the Lower Hill Redevelopment . . . including the Auditorium, the Mall, the commercial structures, the parking area . . . is scheduled for 1959.

Property acquisition began in March 1956.

The Lower Hill Redevelopment in its entirety is the responsibility of the Urban Redevelopment Authority of Pittsburgh in cooperation with the Housing Authority of the City of Pittsburgh, the Public Auditorium Authority of Pittsburgh and Allegheny County, the Allegheny Conference on Community Development, the Commonwealth of Pennsylvania, and the Federal Housing and Home Finance Agency.

The Lower Hill Redevelopment will be an important junction point of the Crosstown Thorofare which will be linked with the Penn-Lincoln Parkway and other major traffic arteries.

Planning authorities feel the Auditorium will foster the growth of additional hotels, shops, restaurants, etc.

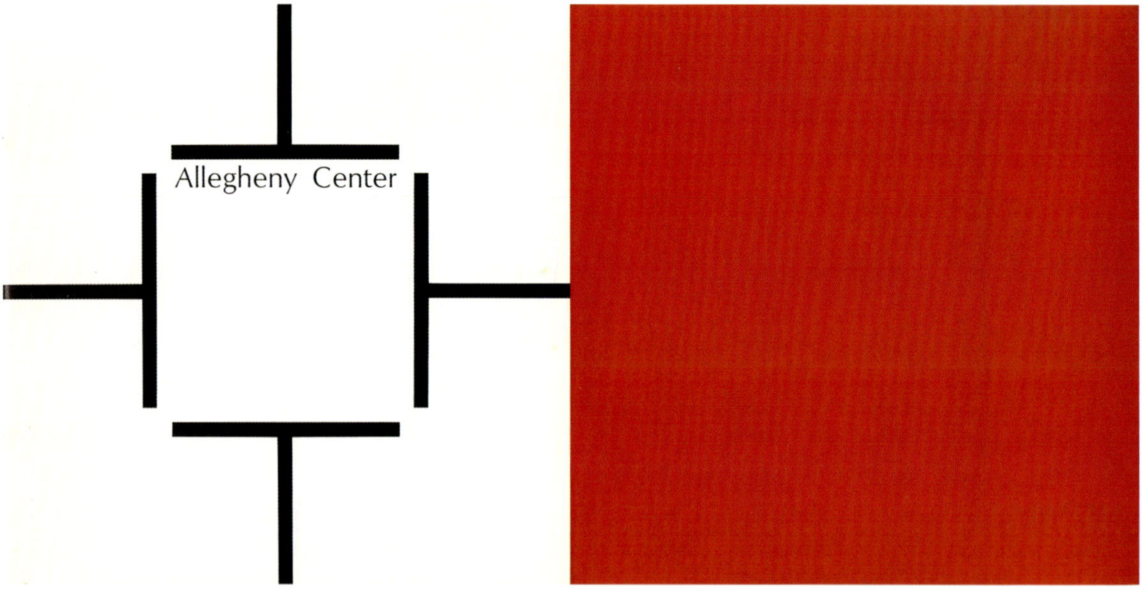

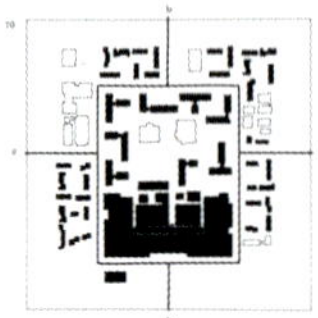

Form

The Design Form of Allegheny Center is explained with the section drawings and a recent photograph of completed work. The tower of existing Carnegie Library and Auditorium is the dominant visual focal point which was maintained by placing height restrictions on the nearby apartment buildings and the office building. The public square in front of the planetarium is recessed slightly below the surrounding ground level to emphasize the space. Townhouses on the periphery of Allegheny Center have been made the lowest scale of building in order to better relate physically and functionally to the adjacent park. The front of Allegheny Center, facing the city, contains the shopping complex which in turn contains three levels of underground parking within the natural fall of the topography.

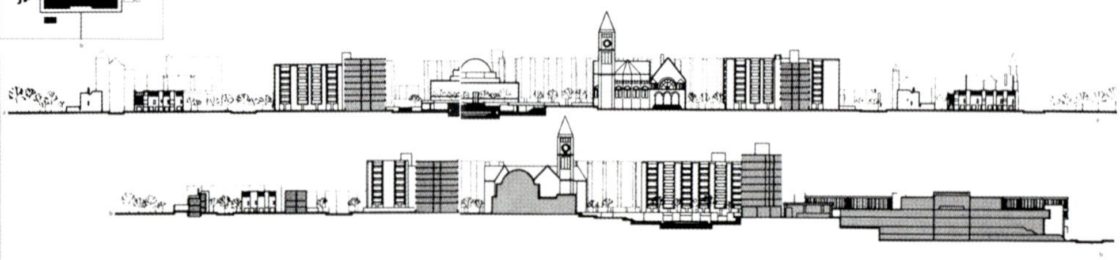

This is the story of an idea and how that idea became an architectural reality in Allegheny Center, a totally planned community within the City of Pittsburgh.

Allegheny Center, 1967

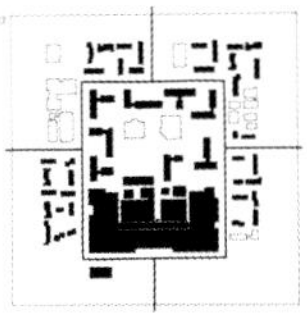

Final Plan

The Evolution of the design for Allegheny Center is completed here with the final site plan and architectural model.

This represents a completely planned and functionally balanced community across the river from Pittsburgh's Golden Triangle. The design integrates residential and business areas and the public amenities to serve them. The Center will contain 1150 apartment units and 220 townhouses accommodating a permanent population of over 4000 persons. Intermingled with the residential community are four churches, two schools, a hospital, a public library-auditorium and a planetarium. Adjacent to the Center are the aviary and a 100-acre park.

A new office building containing 140,000 square feet of space is being provided as well as an entirely new shopping complex of 750,000 square feet containing two department stores, a food market, variety store, 60 specialty shops, and parking for 2800 cars. Other commercial spaces are being included on the ground floors of the apartment buildings around the public square.

These enterprises add a working population of over 2300 to the resident population. Because of its nearly center-city location, three-quarter million people reside within five miles of Allegheny Center and have immediate access by public and private transportation.

After the initial planning and design work for the public agencies, Deeter Ritchey Sippel served as Architects for the private developer of Allegheny Center. The final design shown here represents a 60-million-dollar investment. The next few pages describe the buildings.

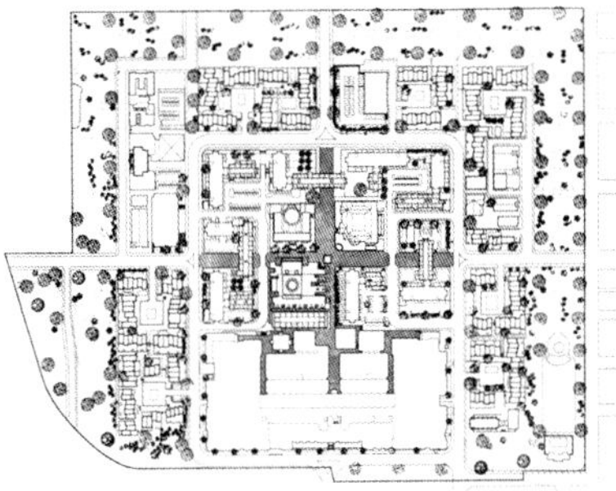

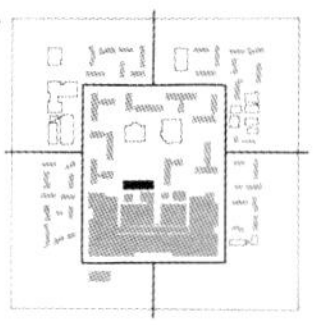

Office Building

The most dominant new structure in Allegheny Center is the office building. It faces the public square on one side and is adjacent to the Commercial Complex. Major pedestrian ways are located on all sides. The building is 8 stories in height, which recognizes the height limitation established to keep Carnegie Library tower the tallest form around the public square. A large 24 x 24 foot structural bay was used in this design in order to minimize the number of interior columns and allow for economical use of 88% of the rental space per floor. Each floor contains 17,000 square feet. The building is air conditioned throughout.

The curtain wall features the first use of a thin-wall aluminum casting, 1/8-inch thick, which frames 9-foot-square glass windows. Such large glass areas afford exciting views of the landscape. These flush-surfaced exterior walls also dramatically reflect other buildings around the public square.

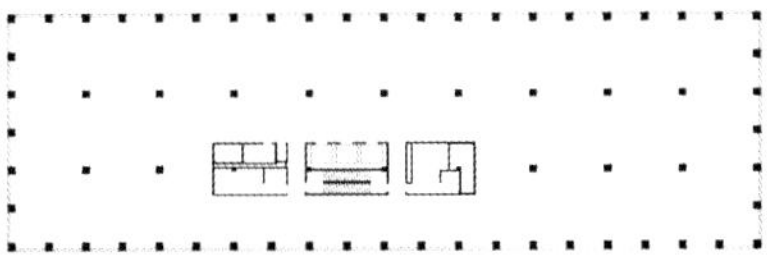

What OakCorp proposes to do, in summary, is to take an ugly useless ravine located in an immensely valuable area and transform it into a research complex which will serve as a focal point of a great cultural-educational-scientific center, and by doing so lift Pittsburgh into first rank among world cities

Prospectus for Panther Hollow: The 21st Century City, 1963

This is an urban area

First phase of Panther Hollow project will be built in a ravine between Carnegie Institute of Technology (right foreground) and Carnegie Institute (left background) and serve to unify Oakland educational complex. University of Pittsburgh campus is immediately adjacent to and behind Carnegie Institute.

OAKLAND CORPORATION

4008 FIFTH AVENUE • SUITE 804 • PITTSBURGH 13, PENNSYLVANIA

Proximity of educational and scientific institutions to new Panther Hollow research park is dramatized in this photo of scale model of project. Inspecting model are principals of the Oakland Corporation, Fred Smith (left), President, and Dr. Edward H. Litchfield, OakCorp Chairman and Chancellor of the University of Pittsburgh.

03
Practice and Polemics

Pittsburgh-based planners, architects, and landscape architects were actively engaged not only in postwar design but also in its discourse. Beyond the documents that explained essential planning choices and their consequences to decision-makers (including city officials, civic leaders, and private developers), these designers worked through an array of media to sway public opinion regarding these urban transformations. Through their writing in journals, magazines, and monographs, they encouraged, defended, or criticized what occurred during this period of growth. These arguments were supplemented through independent publications and exhibitions, op-eds in newspapers, and publications produced through various professional and educational organizations.

Most notable among these professional venues was the journal the *Charette*, at the time a local architectural publication of extremely high quality and reach. Launched by the Pittsburgh Architectural Club in February 1920, in the following five decades of its existence the *Charette* evolved to become the unique chronicle of a changing city. While it began as a short newsletter for announcements of the Club's Christmas parties and other social events, the journal gained steam during the Depression as a venue for architectural discourse in Pittsburgh even as building commissions faded away. By the time of urban renewal after World War II, the *Charette* had transformed into a sleek magazine with bold, full-color covers, documenting three projects in each issue and filled with advertising targeted at architects and designers. As a professional journal sponsored in this period by the AIA Pittsburgh Chapter and the Pennsylvania Society of Architects, the *Charette* was never strongly political. Yet it was often unparalleled in its coverage of regional architecture, particularly of projects overlooked by national outfits.

In addition to professional publications of such work, the architects of the Renaissance were often invested in broader polemics about the nature of modern architecture and its meaning in Pittsburgh. Primary among these figures was Tasso Katselas, perhaps Pittsburgh's most prolific modernist, whose oeuvre in these decades extended to airports, jails, university buildings, multi-family housing complexes, and single-family homes. He wrote and published his thoughts in self-published monographs like *Tasso Katselas Architect Planner* (1969), which intersperses his essays with drawings and photographs of his work. Katselas's writings reveal a thoughtful and humanistic approach to design that contradicts the stereotype of the modernist's preoccupation with a building's form at the expense of those who use it or the context in which it sits.

The city's museums and universities provided additional venues for architects to promote and reflect upon their work and on the transformation of Pittsburgh as a whole. In the mid-1960s, the Carnegie Museum of Art held an exhibit by Paul Schweikher, then head of the School of Architecture at Carnegie Institute of Technology (later Carnegie Mellon University), of work by professors and practitioners who taught at the school. The accompanying catalog, *Buildings By Pedagogs* (1965), served as a showcase for modern architecture, by then well-entrenched under Schweikher's tenure, displaying a variety of approaches from Schweikher's robust concrete structures to rural housing by Robert Taylor that seemed to disappear into the western Pennsylvania landscape, to an elegant glass and steel suburban church by John Pehkrin.

Other publications, produced by designers who were also educators, suggested a critique of standard views of modernism. A textbook by landscape architect John O. Simonds, *Landscape Architecture: The Shaping of Man's Natural Environment*, questioned the supremacy of architectural form. First published in 1961, this volume quickly became a standard introduction to the discipline for students of landscape architecture. In a different vein, *Our Way Manifesto* (1972), by architect Troy West, insisted on citizen participation in the redevelopment of the Lower Hill, a radical polemic at the time of its writing. Saul Alinsky's notions of community engagement in planning processes were just beginning to take hold in Pittsburgh, and West's innovative methods for working with communities in the Hill District, recorded in the *Manifesto*, stood at the forefront of the movement toward participatory frameworks for development. Such efforts were preceded by more anonymous documents like *Official Oakland Planning Roadmap* (c. 1968), which contested Pitt's controversial plans to expand through the removal of Forbes Field, home of the Pittsburgh Pirates since 1909, in favor of a new university complex. The unknown authors of the Roadmap provided a tongue-in-cheek guide to development in Oakland that revealed both a deep knowledge of the planning processes involved and a suspicion of authority.

The CHARETTE

Editor
C. RONAL WOODS
2422 Koppers Building
At. 2543

Business Manager
PHILIPS B. BOWN
2422 Koppers Building
At. 2543

Advertising Manager
JOHN GROSSMAN - Ce. 5200

AUGUST · 1937
VOL. XVII No. 8

a little Journal of Rejuvenation
Published every month by the
Pittsburgh Architectural Club, Inc.

Impressions and Reflections

*PART II

JAMES A. MITCHELL — DAHLEN K. RITCHEY

IT is true that the influence of Academism has been vast and its disciples have lost themselves in limitless efforts to recapture the spirit of past ages. They have sought Architecture on paper. Draughtmanship, technique, and sentimental romanticism have been their chief vehicles.

They have sought to clothe structures of complicated and multiple functions necessary to modern living in garments of Greek and Gothic prototypes.

Science has developed; The field of Mathematics has been broadened and many new theories have grown into axioms; Industry has grown and exerts tremendous influence upon society.

Yet, notwithstanding all this progress that of necessity alters and lends new color to living and life, Academism would still force the throttle upon us.

We should "build in style", or we should "adapt style".

As a result the world has been blighted with much that is no more than loathsome caricaturing of the past. Civic centers have been relegated to the devices and pranks of clever counterfeiters. Railroads have their termini in Roman Baths, Scientific Institutes have been housed in Greek Temples, and the Egyptian Temples that once hid the morbid mysteries of shrouded priests today serve the public as amusement centers.

Is it a wonder, then, that there appeared a reaction to all this?

Men like Sullivan, Wagner, Hoffman, and Wright rebelled at Traditionalism and by individual efforts achieved the foundation of a living Architecture.

In a world seething with unrest there appeared many enthusiasts that followed in the wake of these fore-runners, and with the growth of the movement the desire to break away completely from tradition and to be different has presented a greater danger than the copying of the styles.

Monstrosities have reared their heads everywhere: The block and the cube have become the fad, and all in all, it seems that a vast number of the so-called Modernists have dreamed themselves senseless into conceiving nightmares.

*This is the second of two articles, the first having appeared in last month's issue.

The facility of gaining publicity by styling one's self a Modernist has been readily perceived by cheap propagandists and they have not failed in fully exploiting it.

One will find any number who over night will give one "the world's most streamlined Garage", or the world's most "modern peanut stand". They'll convert a monument into a rocketing machine armature so that it may be modern, or they'll perch a flop-house on a turn-table to follow the rays of the sun.

To them the trade is tricks and stunts.

They build with glass and veneer with celophane.

They seem to thrive on revolting rebukes to reason's concepts.

They will not build a house on firm ground—They would rather hang it with cables down steep ravines.

They will seize upon the various principles of construction and will stunt them into stunning people by their abrupt exposé.

One may say that the result of the movement for Modernism has been one of reaction. Opposed to the over elaboration of the styles we find the stark and stolid blankness of the modern surfaces. In contrast to the massive wall construction of the past we find the ephemeral curtain walls. As a departure from the false screening of construction we find the almost naked appearance of the steel construction.

The Modernists feel that construction should be expressed, and expression to them means unlimited exposure. They find beauty in the skeleton.

They feel that function should be expressed in facade as well as in plan.

The lesser and more numerous of them have devised wondrous and extremely complicated structures that are full of affection. This too is no more than a reaction to Academism.

A great many of them have aligned themselves with extreme philosophies and try to penetrate nature and life through intellect rather than reasoning them by spiritually motivated and emotionally guided observation, and the result has been a conscious striving for abstraction and a condemnation of the inequalities of society by bluntly elaborating on the grotesque that borders on the ugly and degenerate.

The fact that all these developments of Modernism have arrived as a reaction to Academism brings home the point that a change is needed.

It is true that rebellion is usually violent and at times will repel logic in whose behalf it is sponsored. This truth finds its parallel in the movement for modern Architecture. In it there are many that are neither thoroughly trained nor highly endowed. But there are some from whose work we may profit by study. They are imbued with a sincere desire for true and noble expression.

Certainly the Architecture of our time should not reflect a conscious striving for innovation, nor should it be no more than a mirror of the works of the past.

Every age has a culture and consciousness. Its Architecture usually reflects the aspirations of its people. It is the pool into which have drained the rivulets of all its endeavours and accomplishments.

This age, too, has its own particular consciousness, and it must be given the opportunity for expression.

In the works of Saarinen, Tengbom, and Ostberg we find much that belongs to our age.

From Wagner 'til now, there hasn't been enough time to develop an arrived expression that may be called a style.

We shall not be able to say that we have a modern style until Architects cease to condemn all that is modern, or all that belongs to the past.

When at some future date we shall have been freed from the shackles of Academism, and when we thoroughly become immersed in the problems and situations that surround us, and are a part of us, them we may justly speak of a new style.

Editor's Note:

This article and the preceding one in last month's issue contain much food for serious thought. They constitute a sincere effort to discuss a very touchy but never-the-less a most important problem in the hope of arriving at a clearer understanding and better approach to modern architecture.

It is hoped that there will be other honest and frank discussions by those who may wish to set forth their conception of this problem, which in the main is—*does architecture as practiced today express the spirit of our time?*

Use these pages as the "town-hall meeting" for your ideas and thoughts—*send them in!*

TASSO
KATSELAS
ARCHITECT
PLANNER

Questions must be asked about any design decisions made purely in the name of order.

Tasso Katselas, 1968

Memphis 1968

"There is no easy way of imparting a sense of architecture. I am firmly convinced that very little is grasped from slides and conversation. Instead, each of you must probe for relevance because every project has its own approach—its own special problems—its own necessary strategy of execution. There is also, of course, constant danger in words; too much has been said and written about architecture—planning—urban design—too much talking by too many and I begin to wonder what one dares to say—dares to offer—dares to be misunderstood about."

"If there were some way we could transfer images there would be no problem—this sort of communication is fantastic because vision is a mode of thinking. We look, we see, we perceive. It is one of the authentic delights in life when one senses this focusing of power and thought.
I find safety in images if they remain personal, they cause me trouble when I reduce them to any type of graphic analysis or when I attempt to explain them in words. Indeed I sometimes contemplate a world where no words are spoken, but a transfer of images is possible where senses remain lively and the mind attentive and alert. Spoken words murder imagery."

"What I hope to achieve through design is a spatial complex that improves with and because of use—like the muscles in our body. If this realization is not evident from what you hear, please remember words, not deeds are to blame. Before presenting my project, I must, however, run the risk of words to establish a methododogy for looking at architecture because each of us is so bound up by what he is doing that he tends to insulate himself and I wonder how can we live—work—create with the anxiety of not really comprehending the thinking of others. It seems sensible to pause to evaluate an approach to a design problem—to ask some reasonable and penetrating questions."

"Initial questions must be asked about the architect as a man. Elementary analysis reveals man as a rational animal, body and soul, matter and spirit—a polarity with a resulting tension far more dramatic and puzzling than most of us care to think about. Matter is stable but spirit in its essence is art—creativity—restless movement—freedom."

"Spirit, however, must operate in matter—in us, and sometimes by choice, sometimes by necessity, accomodates itself to the demands of matter—a seepage occurs. Spirit gets tired and stiff—repeats itself—seeks stability. Patterns and habits evolve and as they repeat themselves, effortlessly almost unconsciously, fall into a silent tragedy where the creative act begins to bear a frightening resemblance to a conditioned reflex; apply the proper stimulus and out comes the trained response—the standard solution. Fixed design attitudes result where rhythm becomes repetition; order—uniformity; beauty—fashion; love—sympathy."

"Questions must be asked about any design decisions made purely in the name of order. If there is a program and a definite progression of internal space, the building can have dimension and be specific. When the user moves from office to auditorium, to dark room, to stair, should something happen to recognize these events? Should there be a reflection within the total architectural vocabulary? Should this articulation generate a kind of physical and visual rhythm constantly apprehended by the user and, thus, enhance total function where form becomes specific process? If this is true of individual buildings, it must, of necessity, be expanded, building to building, block to block—each unit effecting the other. Instead today we have no activity pattern suggested—no living form. One feels in our cities a series of separate anonymous volumes. Buildings must reach out to create interrelations and tensions—a rhythmic latent interaction. An architecture of participation. An architecture of discovered patterns. The result could be a more permanent and stable form that demands human use to justify its existence. There can be no effortless instruments of living. We dare not settle comfortably into the contours of biological life. An architect's decision cannot bear the frightening resemblance to a conditioned reflex. This is the antithesis of reason. The baffling of opportunity."

"Questions must be asked about how most of us go about our work. We name our problems—school; shopping center; apartment. These names define standard objects before we start. This is a prevalent ancient beaux art attitude based on tenets of composition with a limited narrow creative range that hinders the necessary sense of connectivity to all outside forces. The results fill our cities with meaningless enclosures devoid of any life and empty of authentic first hand experiences."

"Questions must be asked about our architecture—has it become uncreative like a manufactured product. Architecture must be created and the difference betwen creative and other productive work is this: A product like a shoe is put together from pieces of material following existing methods—patterns. It makes something out of something else. A creation makes something out of nothing; something out of nothing more than the need to explore and express within a dynamic form the use spaces of life."

"Our problem is this, exactly how to understand dynamic form over static form and thus gain insight to life's required spaces. A fusion of this form with others recognizing changes, needs, process, establishes relation to relation until an undeniable rhythm is born—this is effortless, almost natural, when the completion of one distinct event appears as the beginning of another. This jubilant dimension results in living form whose very permanence is really a pattern of continual change and growth; its elements are not independent parts—nothing can be whole and still be subdivided—but interrelated, interdependent centers of activity held together by rhythmic sequence. A process that is characteristic of all life."

"My hope is that somehow we combine practical wisdom and philosophy with our art. The architect's job must be redefined as taking care of the living. Men are difficult, troublesome creatures, but valuable. The creative care of man is an artful and beautiful task. The arts and skills of the architect, the creation and inspiration of which he is capable, must be brought fully into life as consequential beauty. We can no longer pretend the living moment is unreal and only the future actual. Only people at low levels of awareness do not look, see, perceive."

"The Architect, must be involved totally in the character of the activity where use limits, yet, provokes, develops and chooses content. This is where our magic lies—the ability to choose content. Choice is significantly the act of recognition—composition—design. Architecture is the fact and effect of such activity."

"Design is an activity whose content is anticipated in space. Design is determined space—through it, architecture has the power to structure environment. Architecture is declaring—it anticipates without boundaries or necessary conclusions of activity.
Intent to create, to build, is necessary yet, it is finally what an architect makes that is significant. If his perception is intensive, the result might become architecture born from the processes of life to support intrinsic movement that will continually verify its authenticity. Like the muscles in our body, our projects should improve with use and as artists we must never forget the most important muscle is the heart."

17

13

Many architects are teachers whether they profess it or not, but often those who profess it are thought of as teachers only.

Paul Schweikher, 1965

19

21

COMMUNITY

Design Associates 2012 Wylie Avenue Pittsburgh 15219 (412) 232-3118

THESE HOUSES ARE OUR RESPONSE TO LARGE SCALE CITY PLANNING

THEY ARE AN ATTEMPT TO SAVE PITTSBURGH OUR CITY

A CITY THAT COULD GO EITHER WAY ———— THE WAY AS POINTED OUT BY SOME OF ITS EARLY MIDDLE PLANNERS TOWARD BROAD MALLS SWEEPING TRAFFIC CIRCLES LARGE CLEARENCES DEVELOPERS DREAMS A LARGE PLACE IN THE CORPORATE IMAGE OF SOMETHING THAT DOESNT EAT SLEEP OR MAKE LOVE HERE BUT RATHER GROWS HERE IN THE SOULLESSLY MECHANISTIC TERMS OF PROFIT AND GROWTH OUR PITTSBURGH HAS BEEN RAPED NOT LOVED ITS RECENT SPACES AND BUILDINGS HAVE ONLY ABSTRACT DETAILS OF LIFE PARKS THAT CLOSE AT NIGHT NEAR DOORS GUARDED BY DOORMEN WHOSE ONLY WELCOMING GESTURE IS A KEEPOUT WALLS AND FENCES MADE BY FRIENDS RENDERED ENEMIES AFRAID TO USE AND LOVE OUR CITY

A CITY THAT COULD GO EITHER WAY ———— A CITY THAT RECOGNIZES THAT ALL ITS SPACES ALL ITS PLACES HAVE ALREADY BEEN CARVED OUT AND WHAT IS LEFT IS TO FIND A WAY TO FILL THESE PLACES AND SPACES IN WITH SO MANY SMALL MULTI COLORED MARBLES THAT NEVER LOSE THE HUMAN BEING PITTSBURGH

PITTSBU PITTS BURGH PITTSBURGH

Form must take its shape from the planned experience, rather than the experience from the preconceived form.

⌄ John Ormsbee Simonds, 1961

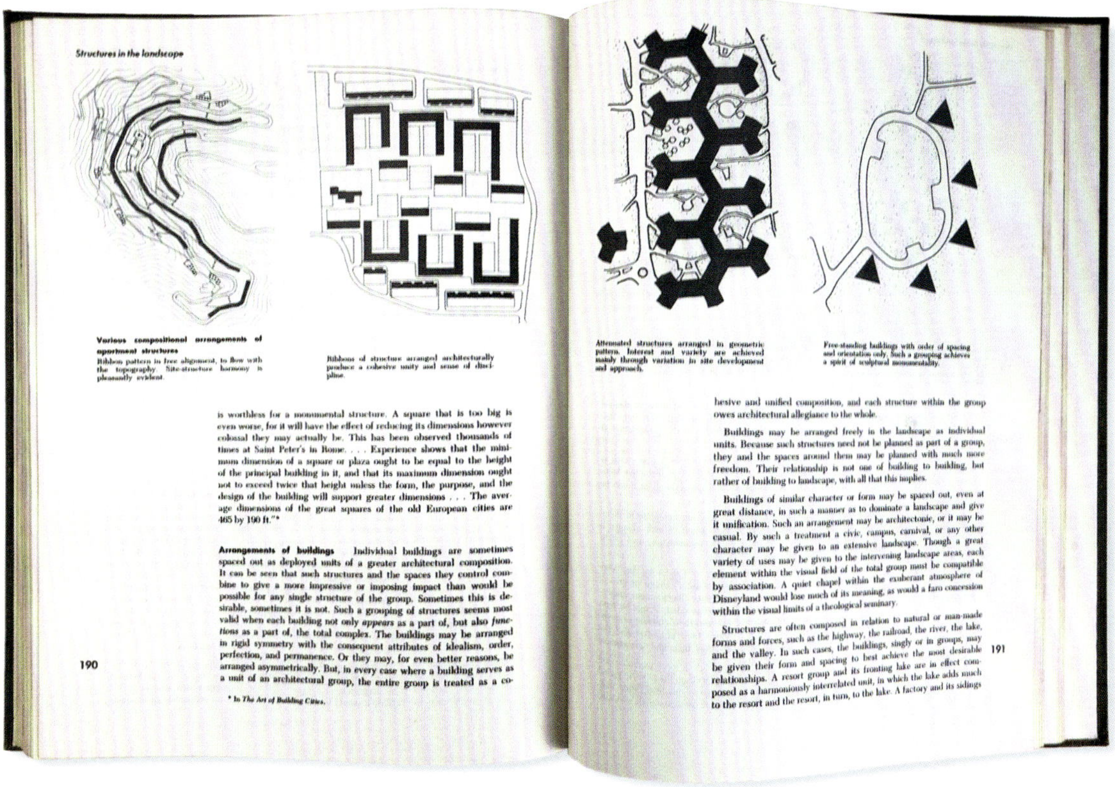
Structures in the landscape

Various compositional arrangements of apartment structures
Ribbon pattern in free alignment, to flow with the topography. Site-structure harmony is pleasantly evident.

Ribbons of structure arranged architecturally produce a cohesive unity and sense of discipline.

Attenuated structures arranged in geometric pattern. Interest and variety are achieved mainly through variation in site development and approach.

Free-standing buildings with order of spacing and orientation only. Such a grouping achieves a spirit of sculptural monumentality.

is worthless for a monumental structure. A square that is too big is even worse, for it will have the effect of reducing its dimensions however colossal they may actually be. This has been observed thousands of times at Saint Peter's in Rome. . . . Experience shows that the minimum dimension of a square or plaza ought to be equal to the height of the principal building in it, and that its maximum dimension ought not to exceed twice that height unless the form, the purpose, and the design of the building will support greater dimensions . . . The average dimensions of the great squares of the old European cities are 465 by 190 ft."*

Arrangements of buildings Individual buildings are sometimes spaced out as deployed units of a greater architectural composition. It can be seen that such structures and the spaces they control combine to give a more impressive or imposing impact than would be possible for any single structure of the group. Sometimes this is desirable, sometimes it is not. Such a grouping of structures seems most valid when each building not only *appears* as a part of, but also *functions* as a part of, the total complex. The buildings may be arranged in rigid symmetry with the consequent attributes of idealism, order, perfection, and permanence. Or they may, for even better reasons, be arranged asymmetrically. But, in every case where a building serves as a unit of an architectural group, the entire group is treated as a cohesive and unified composition, and each structure within the group owes architectural allegiance to the whole.

* In *The Art of Building Cities*.

190

Buildings may be arranged freely in the landscape as individual units. Because such structures need not be planned as part of a group, they and the spaces around them may be planned with much more freedom. Their relationship is not one of building to building, but rather of building to landscape, with all that this implies.

Buildings of similar character or form may be spaced out, even at great distance, in such a manner as to dominate a landscape and give it unification. Such an arrangement may be architectonic, or it may be casual. By such a treatment a civic, campus, carnival, or any other character may be given to an extensive landscape. Though a great variety of uses may be given to the intervening landscape areas, each element within the visual field of the total group must be compatible by association. A quiet chapel within the exuberant atmosphere of Disneyland would lose much of its meaning, as would a faro concession within the visual limits of a theological seminary.

Structures are often composed in relation to natural or man-made forms and forces, such as the highway, the railroad, the river, the lake, and the valley. In such cases, the buildings, singly or in groups, may be given their form and spacing to best achieve the most desirable relationships. A resort group and its fronting lake are in effect composed as a harmoniously interrelated unit, in which the lake adds much to the resort and the resort, in turn, to the lake. A factory and its sidings

191

These houses are our response to large-scale city planning. They are an attempt to save Pittsburgh our city.

‹ Troy West, 1972

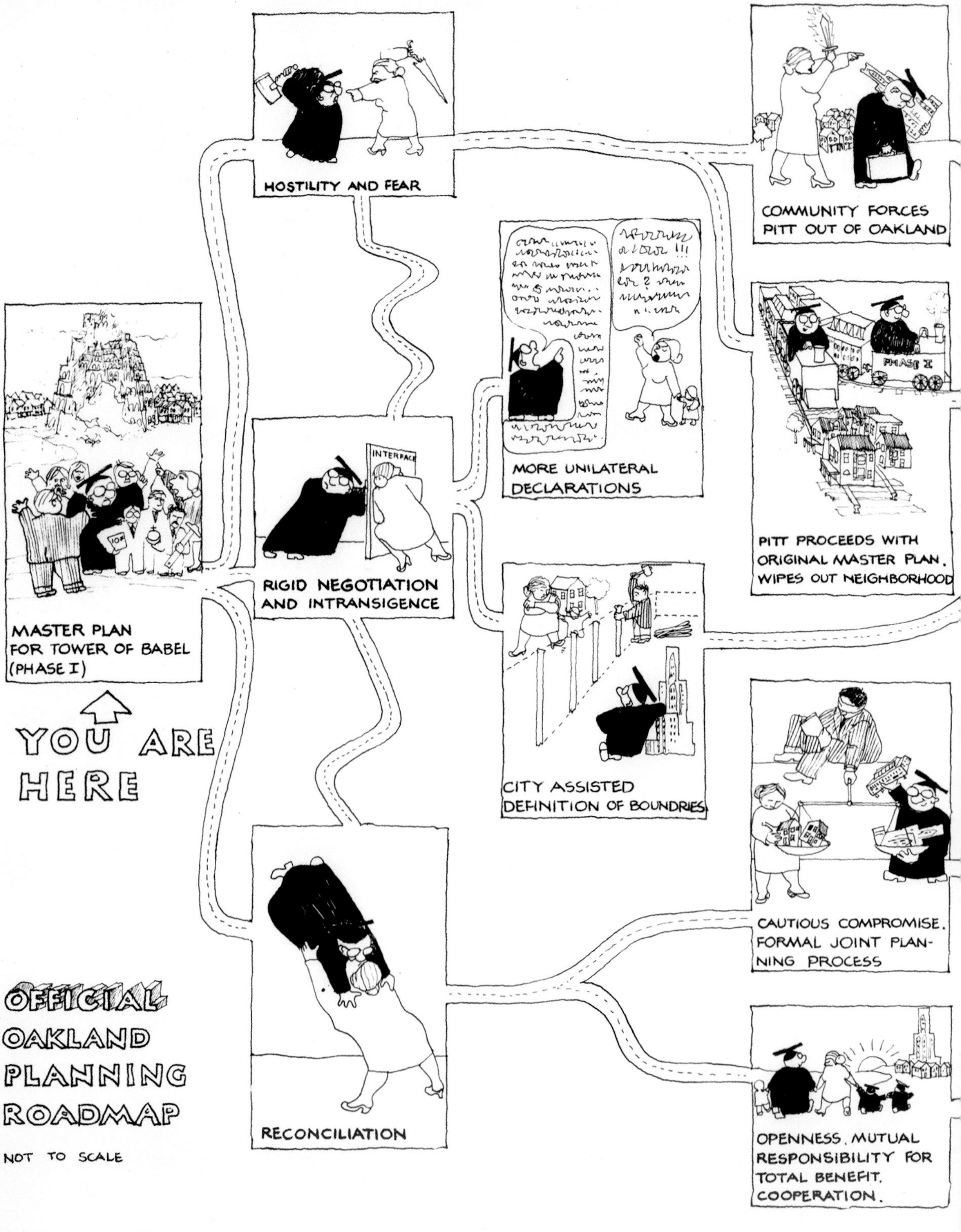

HOSTILITY AND FEAR
COMMUNITY FORCES PITT OUT OF OAKLAND
MORE UNILATERAL DECLARATIONS
PITT PROCEEDS WITH ORIGINAL MASTER PLAN. WIPES OUT NEIGHBORHOOD
INTERFACE
RIGID NEGOTIATION AND INTRANSIGENCE
MASTER PLAN FOR TOWER OF BABEL (PHASE I)
CITY ASSISTED DEFINITION OF BOUNDRIES
YOU ARE HERE
CAUTIOUS COMPROMISE. FORMAL JOINT PLANNING PROCESS
RECONCILIATION
OPENNESS. MUTUAL RESPONSIBILITY FOR TOTAL BENEFIT. COOPERATION.
OFFICIAL OAKLAND PLANNING ROADMAP
NOT TO SCALE

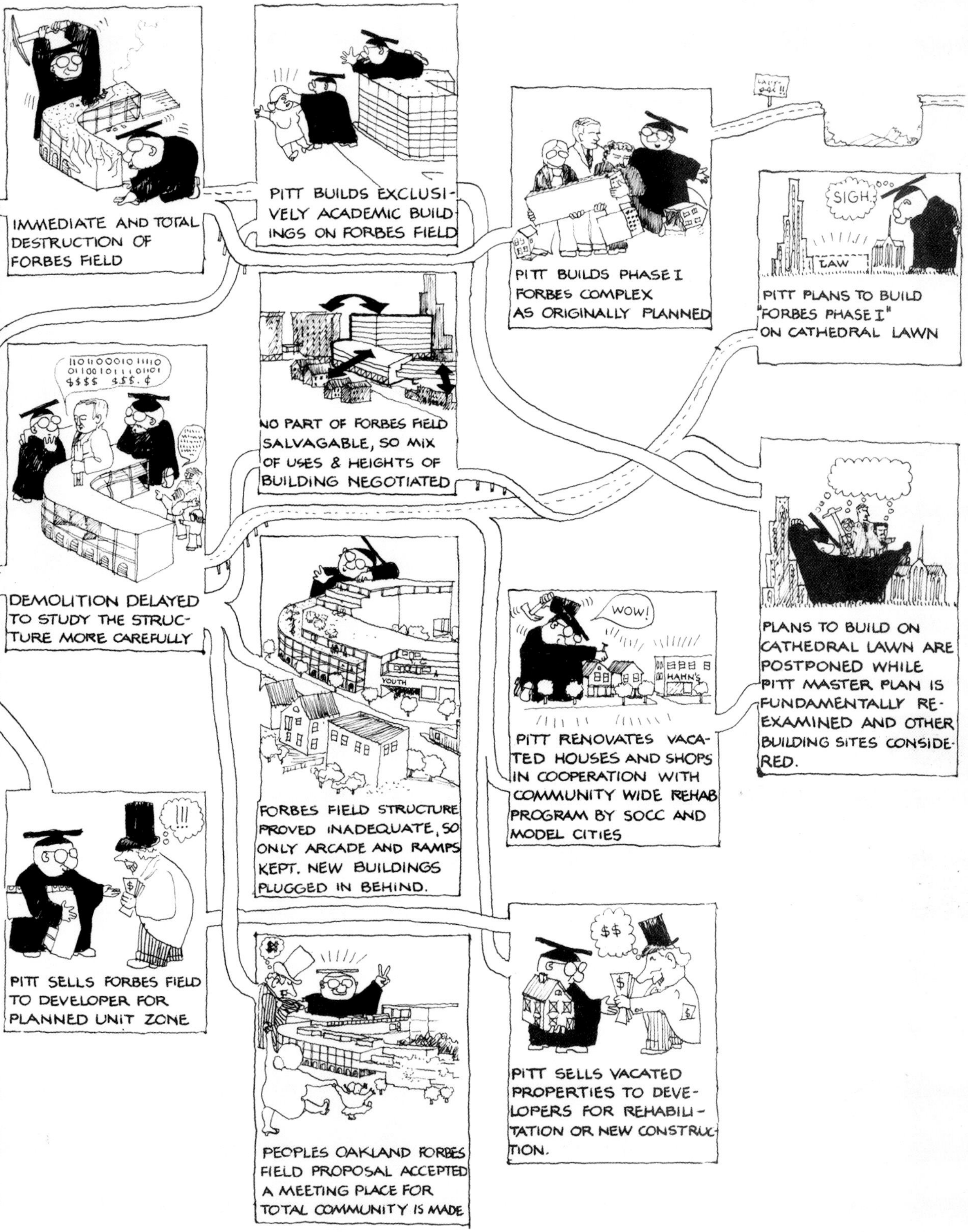
IMMEDIATE AND TOTAL DESTRUCTION OF FORBES FIELD
PITT BUILDS EXCLUSIVELY ACADEMIC BUILDINGS ON FORBES FIELD
PITT BUILDS PHASE I FORBES COMPLEX AS ORIGINALLY PLANNED
SIGH.
LAW
PITT PLANS TO BUILD "FORBES PHASE I" ON CATHEDRAL LAWN
$$$$ $$$.¢
DEMOLITION DELAYED TO STUDY THE STRUCTURE MORE CAREFULLY
NO PART OF FORBES FIELD SALVAGABLE, SO MIX OF USES & HEIGHTS OF BUILDING NEGOTIATED
PLANS TO BUILD ON CATHEDRAL LAWN ARE POSTPONED WHILE PITT MASTER PLAN IS FUNDAMENTALLY RE-EXAMINED AND OTHER BUILDING SITES CONSIDERED.
YOUTH
WOW!
HAHN'S
PITT RENOVATES VACATED HOUSES AND SHOPS IN COOPERATION WITH COMMUNITY WIDE REHAB PROGRAM BY SOCC AND MODEL CITIES
!!!
PITT SELLS FORBES FIELD TO DEVELOPER FOR PLANNED UNIT ZONE
FORBES FIELD STRUCTURE PROVED INADEQUATE, SO ONLY ARCADE AND RAMPS KEPT. NEW BUILDINGS PLUGGED IN BEHIND.
$$
PITT SELLS VACATED PROPERTIES TO DEVELOPERS FOR REHABILITATION OR NEW CONSTRUCTION.
PEOPLES OAKLAND FORBES FIELD PROPOSAL ACCEPTED A MEETING PLACE FOR TOTAL COMMUNITY IS MADE

04 Architectural Tools

The radical transformations of the Renaissance were made concrete through speculative visualizations that sought to make legible the city's modernizing efforts. Representations produced by architects and designers underlay nearly all of the media through which postwar urban development in Pittsburgh was anticipated and promoted. Planning reports, marketing brochures, professional journals, trade magazines, and newspaper articles all mobilized the visual media through which designers tested their ideas and projected the futures they envisioned for Pittsburgh, including plans, sketches, perspective views, renderings, diagrams, and architectural models.

Visualizations by designers varied widely from speculation to marketing to construction, depending on the intended audience and the temporal and physical scope of each proposal. Orthographic drawings and construction documents were produced as instruments for communicating with contractors and clients, providing detailed instructions for projects to be built. Tenant layouts of the Alcoa Building (1953) reflected Harrison & Abramovitz's sophisticated planning of the building's floors to service a range of industrial companies, while elevations codified the intricate design details of the world's first aluminum stamped panel facade. Mitchell & Ritchey's site plan of Allegheny Center (1963–73) described its attachment to the reorganized system of expressways that surrounded it as well as its relationship to anticipated development along the Allegheny River and to Allegheny General Hospital to the north.

In contrast to such technical specifications, visionary drawings sought to convey new possibilities for rethinking the physical and economic structure of the Pittsburgh's districts. Architects employed drawings and models to imagine dramatic, large-scale infrastructures for urban and social transformation. In 1947, Frank Lloyd Wright began a two-year experiment to reimagine the Point at the behest of his patron, Edgar J. Kaufmann. Wright's dramatic aerial views conveyed a synthetic scheme that was a microcosm of Pittsburgh's postwar architectural dreams, encompassing an exhibition hall, a sports arena, and a performing arts center within a gargantuan structure of spiraling ramps and parking levels. Sections and models of Troy West's scheme for Our Way alley revealed a project that was no less ambitious in its conception, organizing housing in two long blocks as an armature for shelter, food production, and community development. Plan drawings of Harrison & Abramovitz's scheme for Panther Hollow made evident the project's massive scale, spanning the ravine that divided Oakland's major cultural and educational institutions with a horizontal mat of scientific, business, and research facilities.

Model photographs offered a powerful means through which the imagined reality of new urban districts could be presented as *fait accompli*, as if already existing. A large-scale model of Panther Hollow provided an accessible way for non-disciplinary audiences to visualize the full extents of the proposal, appearing in brochures published by the Oakland Corporation surrounded by the project's protagonists as they gestured toward its future realization. A model of Skidmore, Owings & Merrill's cultural center for the Lower Hill, photographed by Ezra Stoller, showed a scheme reminiscent of Lincoln Center in New York City in its combination of a symphony hall, museum, and apartment building around a large civic plaza. Scale figures, trees, landscaping, and sun shadows all heightened the photorealism of the city's anticipated (though never built) acropolis-to-be.

In-house draftsmen and professional renderers, often trained as architects, were frequently commissioned by designers to create seductive views that would convey their design intentions to clients. Numerous projects for Pittsburgh were visualized by Helmut Jacoby, the most internationally prominent architectural renderer of the era, following his commissions by Curtis & Davis and others to produce renderings of their projects in other cities including Washington, D.C. and Los Angeles.[1] In his pencil and ink views of Curtis & Davis's IBM headquarters and Deeter Ritchey Sippel's Allegheny Mall (both drawn in 1961), Jacoby strove not for strict realism but to create a "distilled reality" designed to heighten their architectural and urban qualities to the fullest extent.[2] Addison Young, a Pittsburgh native who spent seven years working for Deeter Ritchey Sippel as a renderer and modelmaker before establishing an independent practice specializing in design presentations, offered a more atmospheric aerial perspective of DRS's Allegheny Center Mall, set against the painterly backdrop of downtown and the Lower Hill. Robert Schwartz, a New York-based renderer who worked for firms including Emery Roth & Sons and I. M. Pei & Associates, created intricate cutaway views of Harrison & Abramovitz's Panther Hollow scheme, working in tempera to create strong contrasts in value that were equally legible in color and in black and white.[3]

Other visualizations worked across media to assemble multiple visions for the city into synthetic images of neighborhoods after their intended transformation. SOM's proposal for the Lower Hill formed one part of the city's plans for the neighborhood, which also included I. M. Pei & Associates' Washington Plaza Apartments on an adjacent site. A composite photomontage, of unknown authorship, combined an aerial photograph with renderings and model photographs of varying perspectives to show these independent schemes together. In the end, this image served as a memento for both the unbuilt cultural center and the city's ambitions for the Pei & Associates project, of which only one tower slab of an anticipated three was ultimately constructed.

1 Renderings by Jacoby for a federal building in Washington, D.C. (1959) and a school in Los Angeles (1959) by Curtis & Davis are listed in Helge Bofinger, "Helmut Jacoby. List of Architectural Drawings 1956–2000," in Bofinger and Wolfgang Voigt, ed., *Helmut Jacoby: Master of Architectural Drawing* (Tübingen: Wasmuth, 2002), 181.
2 Helge Bofinger, "Helmut Jacoby—Master of Architectural Drawing," in *Helmut Jacoby: Master of Architectural Drawing*, 11.
3 See "Robert Schwarz," in Minor Bishop, ed., *Architectural Renderings by Winners of the Burch Burdette Long Memorial Prize* (New York: Architectural League of New York, 1965), 64–67.

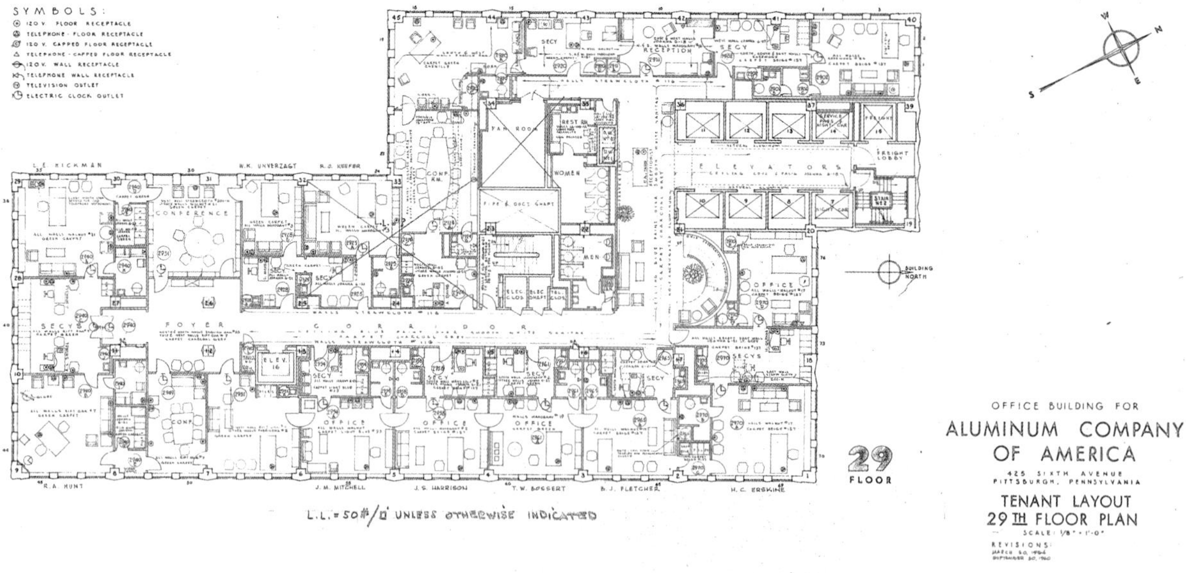
SYMBOLS:
120 V. FLOOR RECEPTACLE
TELEPHONE - FLOOR RECEPTACLE
120 V. CAPPED FLOOR RECEPTACLE
TELEPHONE - CAPPED FLOOR RECEPTACLE
120 V. WALL RECEPTACLE
TELEPHONE WALL RECEPTACLE
TELEVISION OUTLET
ELECTRIC CLOCK OUTLET
CONFERENCE
FOYER
CORRIDOR
RECEPTION
ELEVATORS
FREIGHT LOBBY
WOMEN
MEN
OFFICE
SECY
CONF.
COMP. RM.
FAN ROOM
BUILDING NORTH
29 FLOOR
L.L. = 50#/□' UNLESS OTHERWISE INDICATED
OFFICE BUILDING FOR
ALUMINUM COMPANY OF AMERICA
425 SIXTH AVENUE
PITTSBURGH, PENNSYLVANIA
TENANT LAYOUT
29 TH FLOOR PLAN
SCALE: 1/8" = 1'-0"

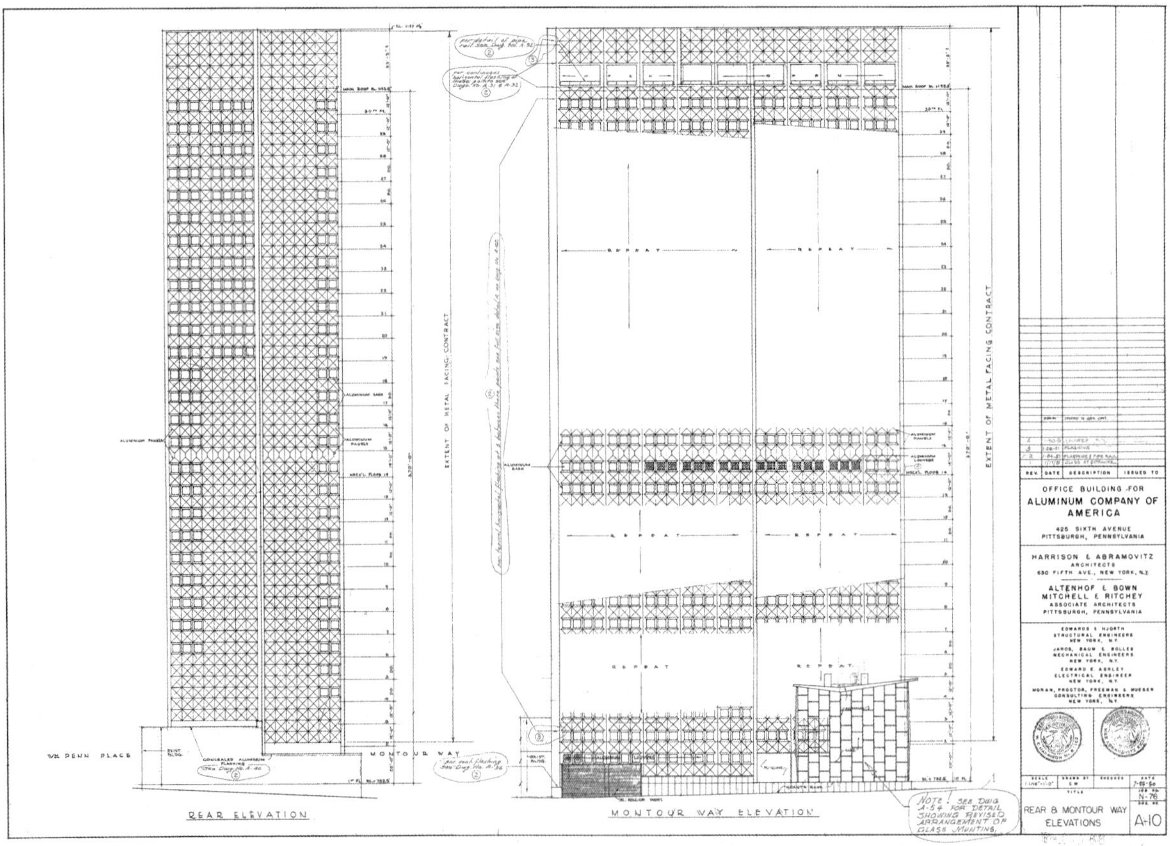
EXTENT OF METAL FACING CONTRACT
REPEAT
MONTOUR WAY
REAR ELEVATION
MONTOUR WAY ELEVATION
Note! See Dwg A-54 for detail showing revised arrangement of glass muntins.
OFFICE BUILDING FOR
ALUMINUM COMPANY OF AMERICA
425 SIXTH AVENUE
PITTSBURGH, PENNSYLVANIA
HARRISON & ABRAMOVITZ
ARCHITECTS
630 FIFTH AVE., NEW YORK, N.Y.
ALTENHOF & BOWN
MITCHELL & RITCHEY
ASSOCIATE ARCHITECTS
PITTSBURGH, PENNSYLVANIA
REAR & MONTOUR WAY ELEVATIONS
A-10

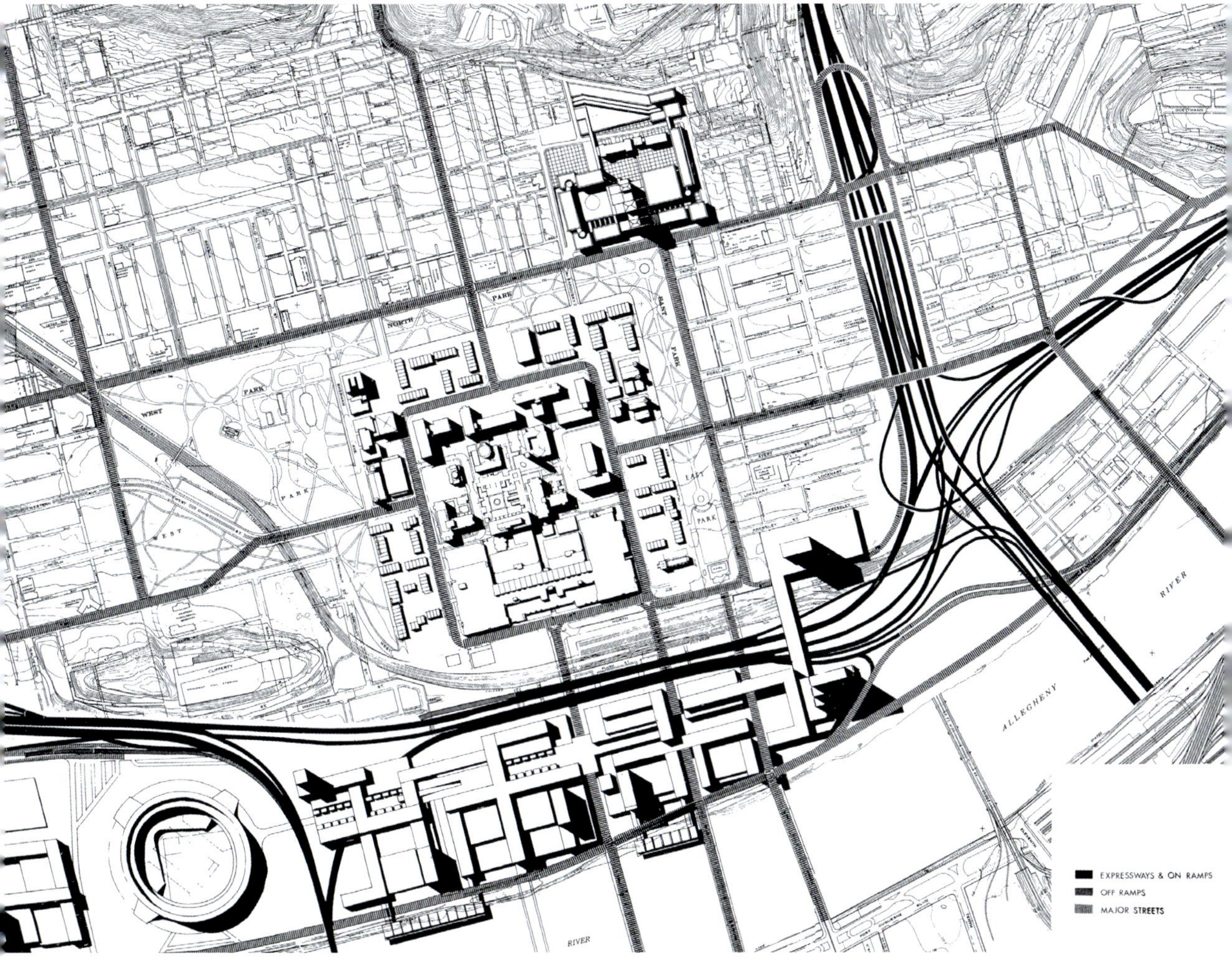

^ **Allegheny General Hospital, long range architectural development, overall plan**, Deeter Ritchey Sippel, May 15, 1970.

< **Office Building for Aluminum Company of America (Alcoa), tenant layout, 29th floor plan**, Harrison & Abramovitz, September 30, 1950.

⌜ **Office Building for Aluminum Company of America (Alcoa), rear & Montour Way elevations**, Harrison & Abramovitz, July 25, 1950.

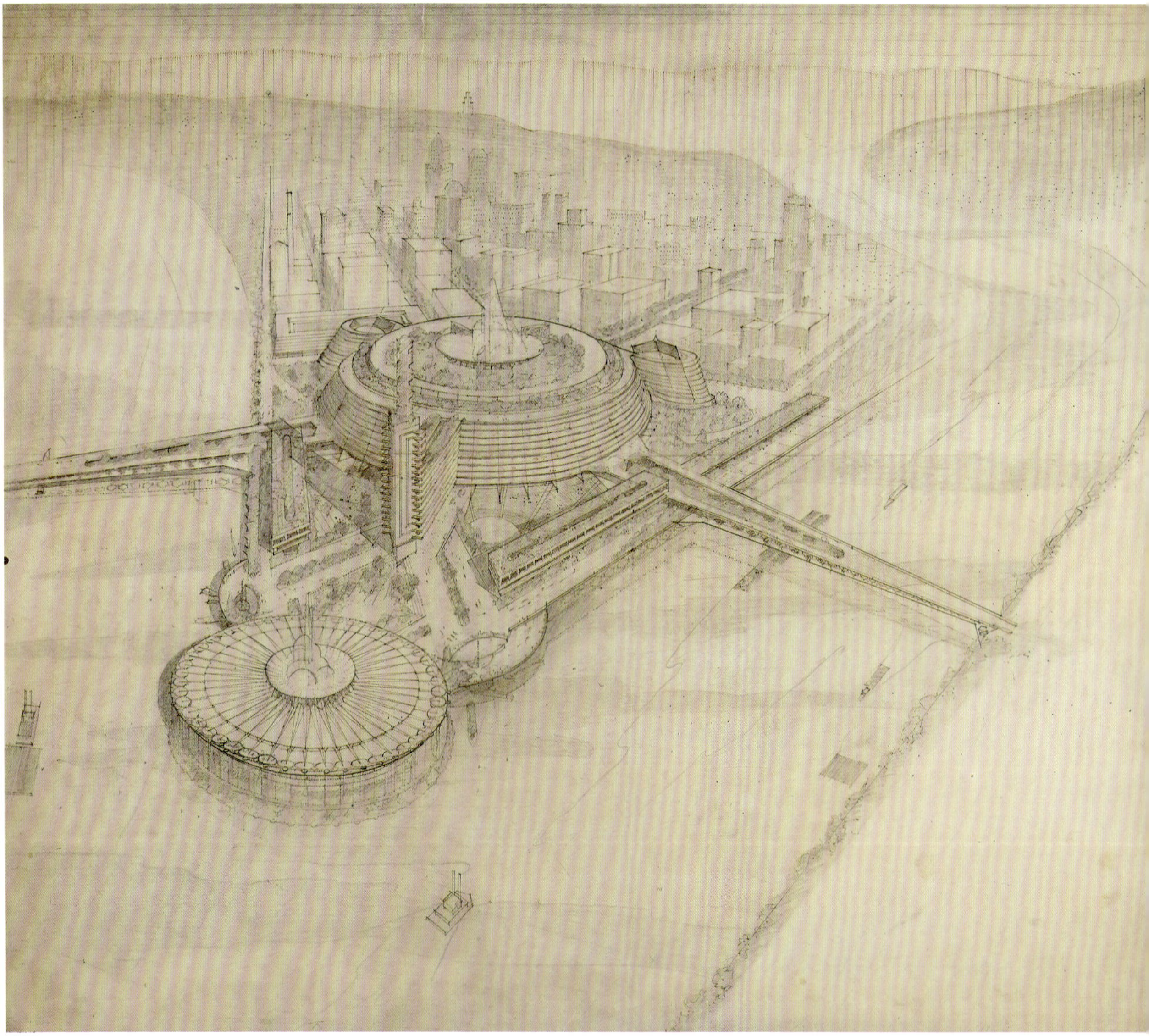

Point Park Civic Center (first scheme), aerial view,
Frank Lloyd Wright, 1947.

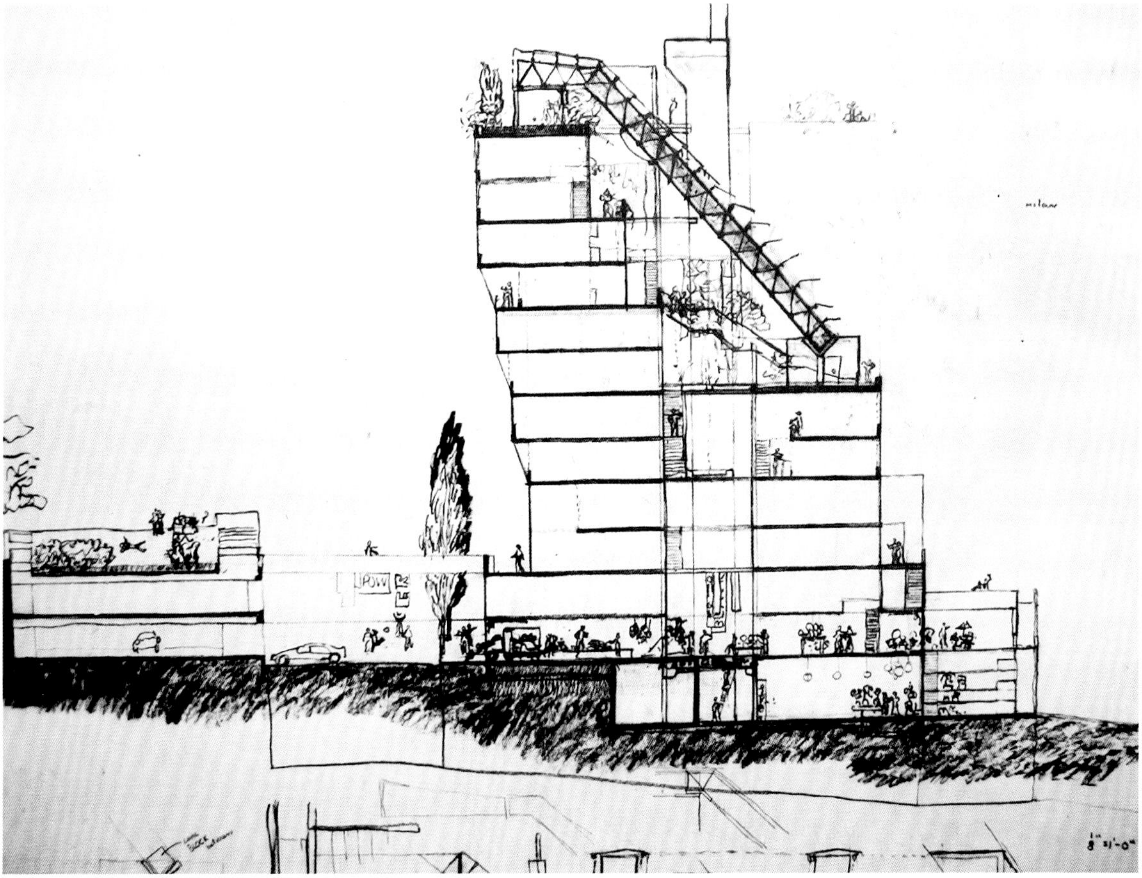

Our Way, section and model, Community Design Associates, 1971.

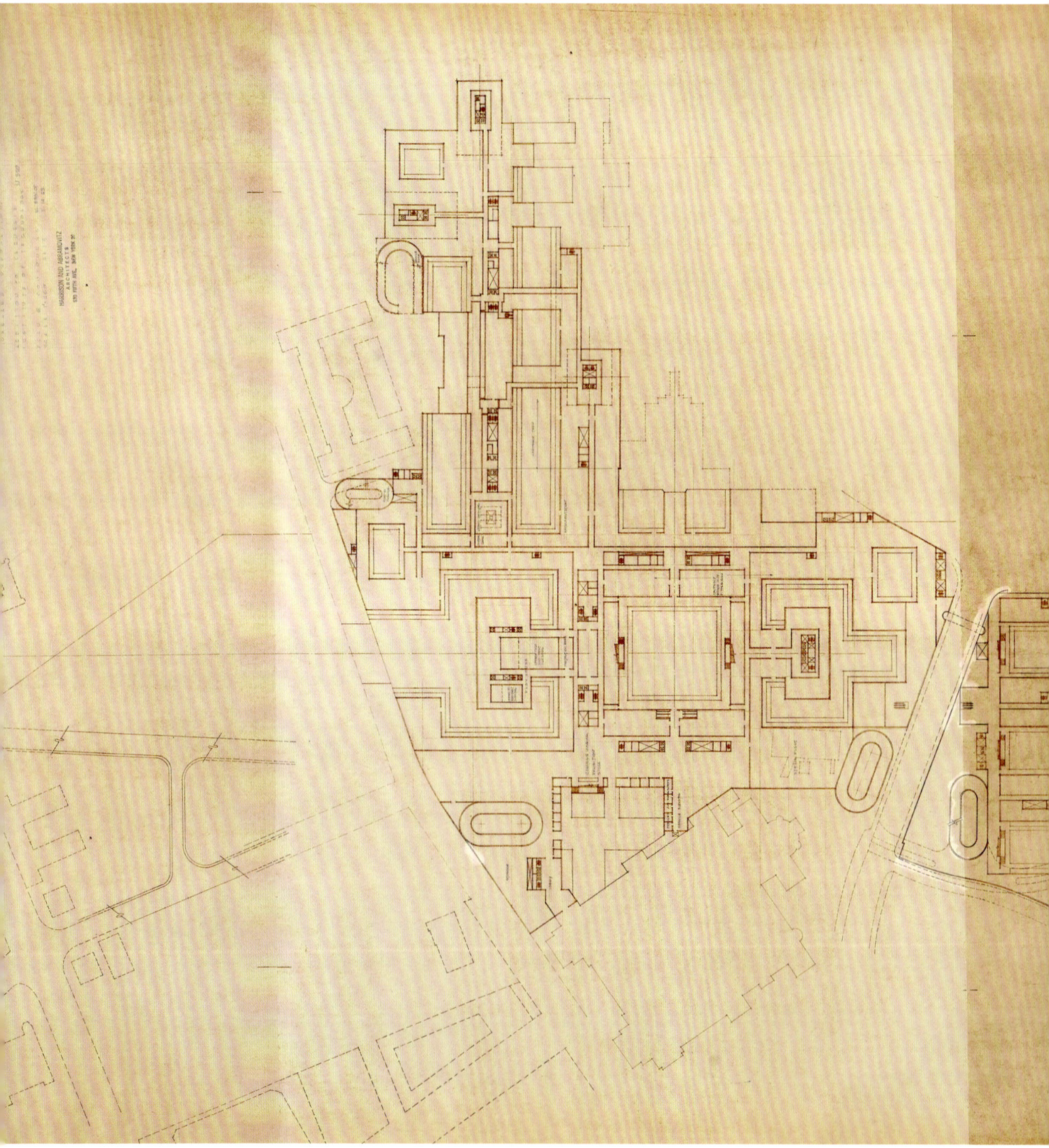

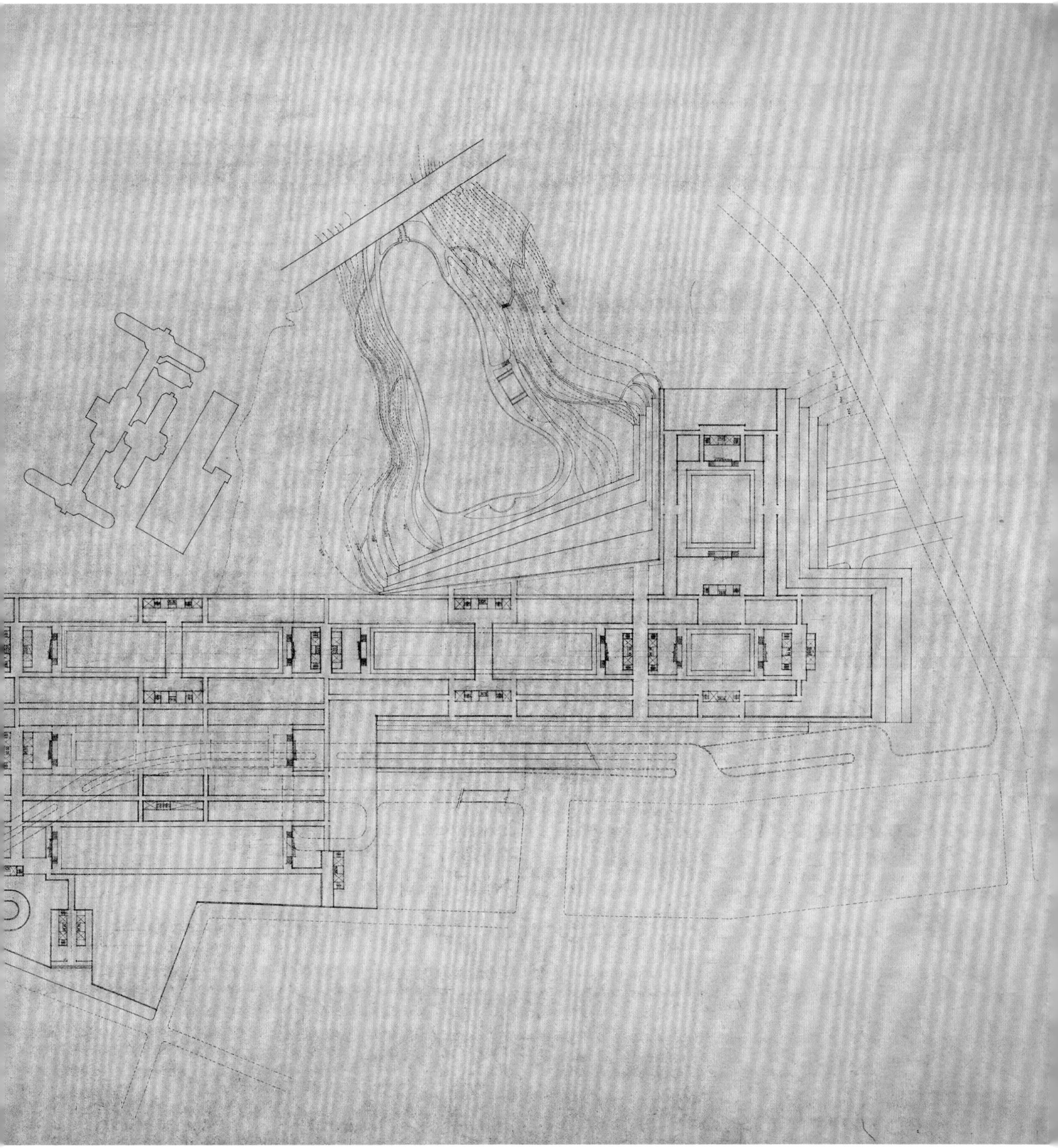

Oakland Research Park (Panther Hollow Project), plan at concourse, Harrison & Abramovitz, c. 1963.

BOULEVARD OF THE ALLIES

< **Oakland Research Park (Panther Hollow Project), model**, Harrison & Abramovitz, c. 1963.

^ **Pittsburgh Art Center, model,** Skidmore, Owings & Merrill, 1966.

> **Portal Bridge at Point State Park, model,** Skidmore ,Owings & Merrill, 1963.

^ **Allegheny Center Commercial Complex, model**, Deeter Ritchey Sippel, c. 1963.

< **Lower Hill Cultural Center, Urban Redevelopment Area No. 3, revised scheme, aerial perspective**, Mitchell & Ritchey, 1953.

> **IBM Building, exterior perspective,** Helmut Jacoby for Curtis & Davis, 1961.

IBM

Westinghouse Building, exterior perspective, Harrison & Abramovitz, n.d.

Allegheny Center Commercial Complex, commercial area including "bazaar," Helmut Jacoby for Deeter Ritchey Sippel, c. 1962.

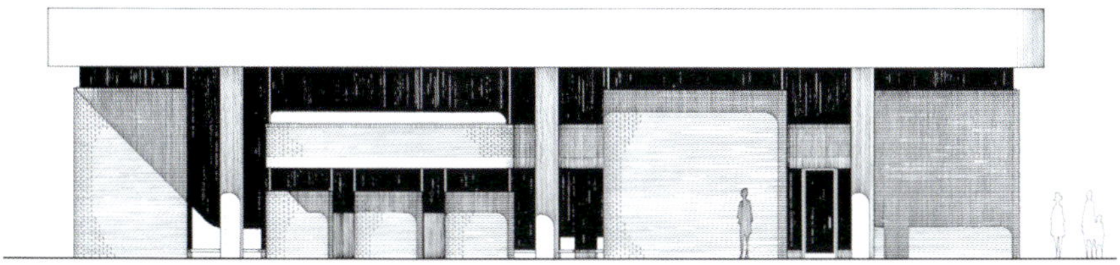

EAST ELEVATION

^ **Allegheny Center Commercial Complex, exterior perspective of the mall**, Addison Young for Deeter Ritchey Sippel, c. 1964.

⌐ **Pittsburgh National Bank Allegheny Center Office, east elevation,** Deeter Ritchey Sippel, n.d.

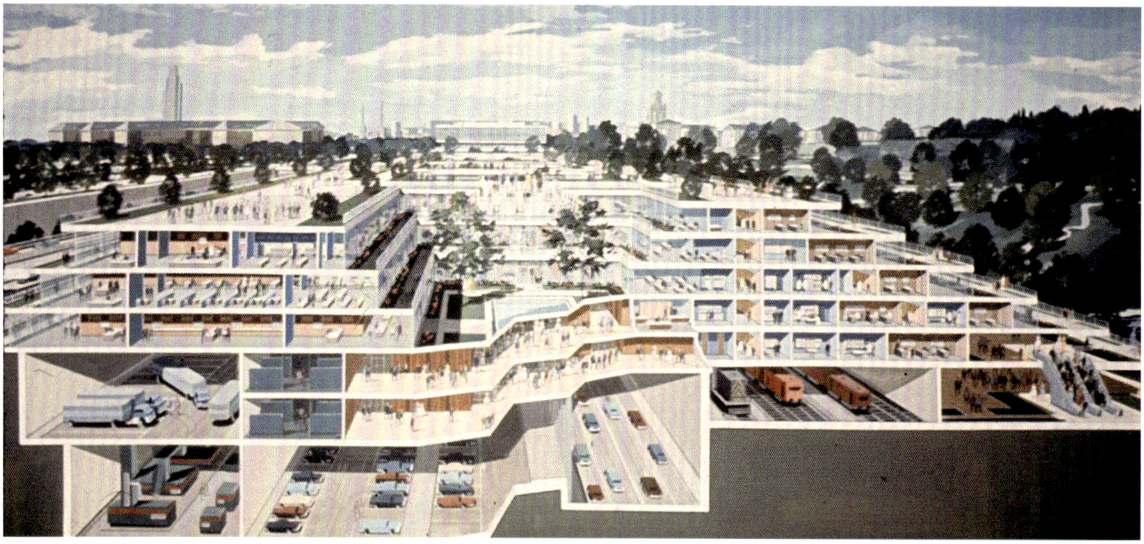

⌜ **Oakland Research Park (Panther Hollow Project), sectional perspective**, Robert Schwartz for Harrison & Abramovitz, c. 1963.

< **Oakland Research Park (Panther Hollow Project), aerial perspective**, Robert Schwartz for Harrison & Abramovitz, c. 1963.

^ **Oakland Research Park (Panther Hollow Project), aerial cutaway perspective**, Robert Schwartz for Harrison & Abramovitz, c. 1963.

^ **East Liberty Pedestrian Mall, aerial perspective**, Simonds and Simonds, 1963–72.

^ **Lower Hill, aerial composite including proposed Pittsburgh Center for the Arts,** Skidmore, Owings & Merrill, **and Washington Plaza Apartments,** I. M. Pei & Associates, from an Alcoa advertisment, c. 1965.

» **Community Map, Hill District,** Community Design Associates & Troy West, 1971.

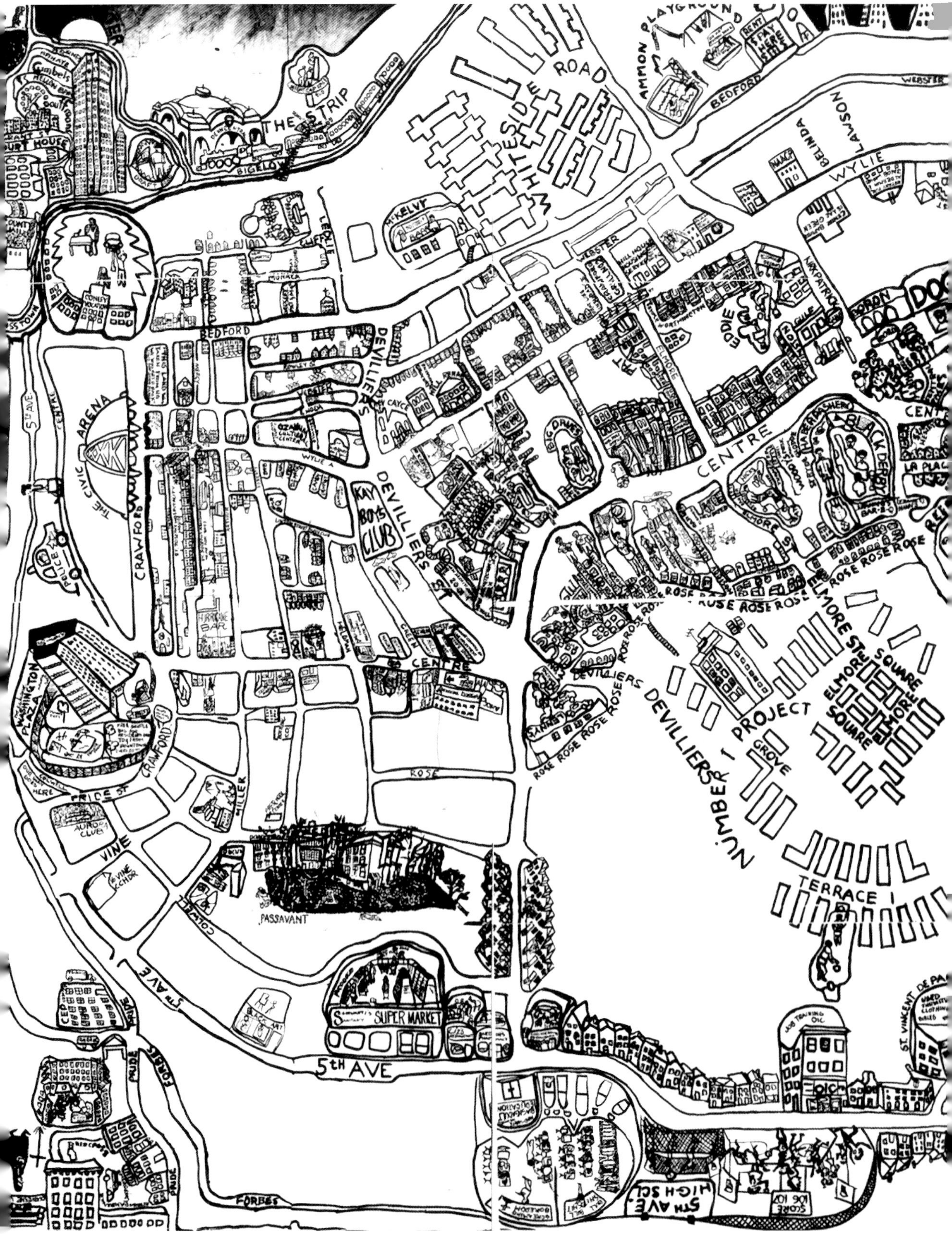
THE STRIP
BIGELOW
WHITESIDE ROAD
AMMON PLAYGROUND
BEDFORD
WEBSTER
LAWSON
BELINDA
WYLIE
McKELVY
LEDLIE
COURT HOUSE
THE CIVIC ARENA
CRAWFORD
5TH AVE
CENTRE
DEVILLIERS ST
KAY BOYS CLUB
OZANAM CULTURAL CENTER
HURRICANE BAR
MILLER
ELMORE
EDDIE
BLACK DERBY
ROSE ROSE ROSE
ELMORE ST SQUARE
NUMBER 1 PROJECT
GROVE
TERRACE I
WASHINGTON PLAZA
PRIDE ST
AURORA CLUB
VINE
POLICE
PASSAVANT
SUPER MARKET
5TH AVE
COLWELL
PRIDE
FORBES
JOB TRAINING OIC
ST. VINCENT DE PAUL
5TH AVE HIGH SCL

WEBSTER
WYLIE
CENTRE
PLEASANT GROVE
HERRON HILL
JUNIOR HIGH
CLARISSA
ADELADE
VETERANS ADMINISTRATION HOSPITAL
ROBINSON COURT
PITT STADIUM
BIGELOW
SCHENLEY HIGH
SPORT FIELD
CENTRE
GAS
BURROWS ST
WADSWORTH ST
NUMBER 2 PROJECT
WHITRIDGE ST
TERRACE 2
BENTLEY DRIVE
KIRKPATRICK
ROBINSON ST.
DAY CARE CENTER
CHILDRENS HOSP.
FORBES AVE
5TH AVE
A&P
FOOD STORES
JUVENILE COURT
FISH
J+L STEEL
MAGEE HOSPITAL

05
Press

During the principal decades of the Renaissance, the mainstream press played a crucial role as public documentarians, promoters, and critics of Pittsburgh's urban renewal efforts. Each of the city's major newspapers offered a particular editorial lens through which to view ongoing processes of development, reflecting positions that catered to differing constituencies, political and business interests, and public and professional audiences. Articles in the *Pittsburgh Post-Gazette*, the *Pittsburgh Press*, and the *Pittsburgh Sun-Telegraph* largely represented the viewpoints and debates occurring within the establishment, while the *Pittsburgh Courier* served as a primary voice for the impact of urban renewal on communities of color. In 1961, for example, the *Post-Gazette* covered the grand opening of the Civic Arena as built evidence of "A Dream Fulfilled" and a "Symbol of City's Progress"; in contrast, the *Courier* warned that "'Jim Crow' Hovers Over Civic Arena," pointing to civil rights concerns in the transformation of the Lower Hill.[1] The differences between these newspapers extended beyond the text and headlines to encompass the selection of photographers, advertising, and political cartoons. Yet despite their often opposed positions, no newspaper remained exclusively for or against urban renewal projects in these decades. The *Courier*, for example, was a vocal early advocate for the city's intervention in the Lower Hill, only later to become its harshest critic.

In shaping public opinion about the transformations taking place in Pittsburgh, these press venues also served as primary vehicles for photography and other forms of media through which the city's development was recorded and made legible to its inhabitants. Local Pittsburgh newspapers ran daily coverage on both the groundbreaking ceremonies and the protests that accompanied new construction, in the process making household names of the local photographers, like Charles "Teenie" Harris, who captured these events in the city's metamorphosis. These publications also revealed traces of the Allegheny Conference's coordinated public relations campaign in these years, including the widespread use of images from the Pittsburgh Photographic Library, a collection paid for and curated by the Conference itself.

At the same time, Pittsburgh's renewal garnered national attention in popular magazines such as *Time*, *Fortune*, and *Collier's*. While often obscuring or ignoring the social and political nuances that were laid bare in local newspaper coverage, long-form articles in these national magazines, often lavishly illustrated with drawings and renderings, surveyed the policies and economics of the city's "Thrilling Civic Renaissance" and profiled its postwar movers and shakers, such as Richard King Mellon.[2] In parallel, nationally prominent professional journals and trade magazines like *Architectural Forum* and *Progressive Architecture* provided venues for architects and planners to promote built projects and unbuilt speculations that revealed subtle and at times competing articulations for the postwar city.

1 Mel Seidenberg, "City's Public Auditorium Now is a Dream Fulfilled," *Pittsbugh Post-Gazette*, September 17, 1961. "Ceremony to Open Auditorium," *Pittsburgh Press*, September 17, 1961. "Jim Crow Hovers Over Civic Arena," *Pittsburgh Courier*, September 23, 1961.
2 Herbert Kubly, "Pittsburgh," *Holiday*, March 1959, 80.

PITTSBURGH POST-GAZETTE
January 24, 1934
Ideal Housing Believed Possible if Pittsburgh Enforces Slum Laws
Federal funds may be obtained to aid program, will provide homes for low-income groups, not unemployed

PITTSBURGH COURIER
July 8, 1939
New Homes Sought For Dispossessed Tenants
Slum dwellers caught in crux of housing lack... Huts of squalor to be changed to models of modernity by PHA

PITTSBURGH COURIER
March 30, 1946
Leaders Condemn Poor Housing In District Area

PITTSBURGH COURIER
April 6, 1946
Shocking Housing Conditions Exposed In Drive

PITTSBURGH COURIER
April 27, 1946
Picture Story of Hill District's Bad Housing Conditions

Picture Story of Hill District's Bad Housing Conditions

Political Picture

HEADLINE PICTURES

SECOND NEWS SECTION

Passing Parade

PITTSBURGH COURIER
May 16, 1946
Immediate Action On Housing Evils
Mayor, council promise reforms armed with a graphic, factual report on flagrant and widespread evils of housing conditions in the Third and Fifth Wards, the Social Action Committee of the Hill District Peoples' Forum forced Mayor David L. Lawrence and City Council to sit up and take notice during two dynamite-packed hearings Wednesday afternoon. Mayor Lawrence promised "immediate action"; Council members said they would "do everything in their power" to relieve the shocking dwelling situations of which they were "already fully aware."

PITTSBURGH PRESS
November 8, 1946
Vast Building Plan Hinted Near New Park At Point

PITTSBURGH PRESS
November 8, 1946
Bigger Than Rockefeller Center! – Vast Home, Business Building Plan Hinted Near New Point Park
New York firm interested in project; State acquires land for memorial

Pittsburgh may have a new residential and commercial development near The Point which would be larger in area, than Rockefeller Center.

That possibility was revealed yesterday at a meeting of The Point Park Committee of the Allegheny Conference on Community Development.

Also disclosed was the fact that the State now has bought 12 of the 31 parcels of property which must be acquired, along with extensive Pennsylvania Railroad holdings, to create the 36-acre memorial park at The Point.

Project Hailed

Tentative plans under discussion would place apartment buildings on the Allegheny River side of the area and office buildings on the Monongahela side.

PITTSBURGH PRESS

October 30, 1947

Giant Center for Sports, Conventions Proposed for Pittsburgh of Tomorrow

'Face-lifting' urged for Hill

Like something conceived by Norman Bel Geddes for a World of Tomorrow is the plan for reconstruction of the Lower Hill District, made public by the Pittsburgh Regional Planning Assn. at its annual dinner last night.

Let us assume that the plan becomes a reality, just as it was drawn up, and follow a visitor to one of the first conventions in the new Pittsburgh Center.

Alighting from a train at Pennsylvania Station, he would get on a moving stairway which would take him up the hill flanking Bigelow Blvd. At the top of the hill he would enter a big hotel, and register for the duration of the convention… He would find a great auditorium, shaped like a covered bowl on the inside, with seats for 18,000 persons.

Backed by Chamber of Commerce

Built of steel, aluminum, glass, and concrete, the whole project was regarded as a monument to the Pittsburgh district's industries as well as to the enterprise of Pittsburgh's civic leaders.

The Pittsburgh Center will not be built as planned, of course. The Pittsburgh Regional Planning Assn. which drew up the plans, regards them as a starting point for discussions.

But the Pittsburgh Chamber of Commerce, which asked that the study be made, is all but for a civic auditorium.

The design that the Regional Planning Assn. made several years ago for the new Point Park is being given consideration. And the planning group's suggested solution for the parking problem in the Triangle has resulted in the formation of the Pittsburgh Parking Authority to do the job.

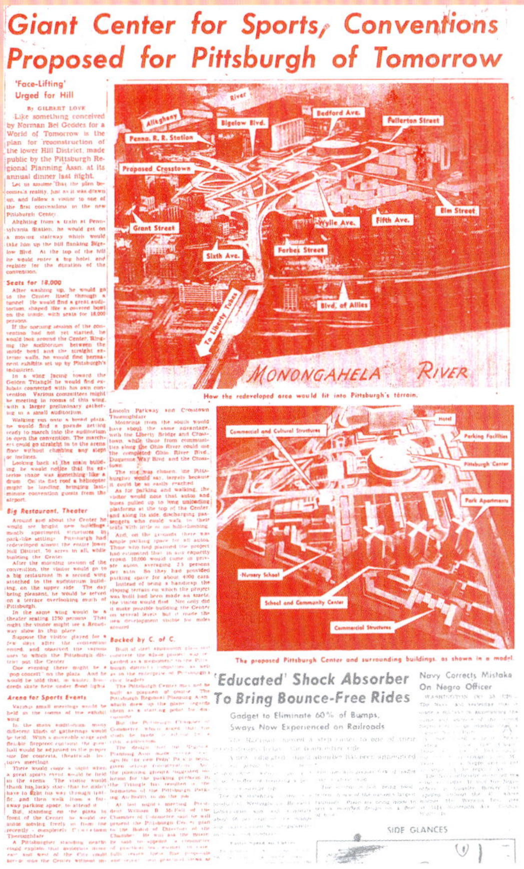

PITTSBURGH POST GAZETTE
October 17, 1949
Pittsburgh Sets Pace In State's Growth
In Pennsylvania Week...
Pittsburgh will play a starring role in Pennsylvania Week, which begins today and ends next Monday, on the birthdate of William Penn. This city, which is attracting nation-wide attention with its face lifting program, is a natural hotspot of interest in any observance carrying the slogan, "It's Your Pennsylvania - Keep It Growing." With some of the new building projects already underway, others contracted for and still more of them definitely out of the dream stage. Pittsburgh may be forgiven for some extra boasting during this week when 10,000,000 Pennsylvanians will be talking about and hearing about their state.

The celebration is designed to spotlight the state's industrial diversity, historical greatness and unlimited facilities for continued business and cultural expansion. Allegheny county will salute the Commonwealth with numerous displays in stores, banks, hotels, and office buildings and with open houses and special movies. Churches will emphasize Pennsylvania's religious traditions. Schools will have special programs. Carnegie Museum will show an exhibit covering every phase of Pittsburgh's building, civic and cultural expansion program.

Carnegie Institute Founder's Day on Wednesday will relate in part to Pennsylvania Week. A visit from Governor James H. Duff and Commerce Secretary Theodore Roosevelt III Thursday also will be highlights.

PITTSBURGH COURIER
January 22, 1950
Story Of Pittsburgh's Boom
Any Pittsburgher more than 10 years old can remember the days when this town's only nickname was "Smoky City." Yet recently a national magazine listed it as having made "more progress than any other city in America."

How come?

First, Pittsburgh cleaned up...

And after the war, Pittsburgh decided to sell itself to the nation, rolled up its sleeves to bring in new industries, expand those already here, improve the roads, knock out the possibility of floods, stop steam pollution.

PITTSBURGH COURIER
April 22, 1950
Is The Hill District Doomed?
BY PAUL L. JONES (FIRST IN A SERIES)
The shadow of redevelopment hangs over the Hill District; home to some 35,000 of the Negroes of Pittsburgh. Within the next few years, the run-down shacks, the rough streets, the rampant rackets that now characterize this ghetto will join the other memories that once justified the description of Pittsburgh as "Hell with the lid lifted."

Molding a new Hill will take place under the direction of the Urban Redevelopment Authority, one of the agencies set up to stem the blight, deterioration and abandonment of other parts of the city.

Part of what must be done to make Pittsburgh an attractive place in which to live, work and play in the middle of the twentieth century is already under way.

Out along East Carson Street on the Southside are many boarded up dwellings, once the homes of people who lived in the shadows of the Jones and Laughlin steel mills. Here the Urban Redevelopment Authority is assembling a tract of land on which J&L will erect a large new mill.

Downtown near the Point the way is being cleared for the erection of three new office buildings that will replace the deteriorating eyesore that is now the Lower Triangle. The Urban Redevelopment Authority closed this deal in a fanfare of publicity a few weeks ago.

Next target of this gigantic munificent rebuilding program is the Hill. Because of the large number of people who live here, the impact of this phase of the program will be much greater. It will affect profoundly the lives of everyone who lives on the Hill. Yet there seems to be little realization of how much present patterns of living will be changed.

In a meeting where John P. Robin, executive director of the Urban Redevelopment Authority, spelled out the broad plans for the bank and a shopping center.

Between this kind of salve for the continuing ills of the Hill, and the deep surgery that Mr, Robin projects, is a tremendous gulf in awareness of the needs of the area.

This series is an attempt to help bridge that gulf. In these articles we will try to tell why urban redevelopment is necessary, what powers the agency has, and how it stands to affect the lives of everyone now living or working in the Hill.

To understand why the Hill is to be redeveloped leads far afield. City planning and urban finance can become mazes that are sometimes bewildering to specialists in these fields. The key fact is that cities, like people, have patterns of growth, use and aging. In this process there must be constant maintenance of municipal well-being. Cities must be places where people enjoy living and working and playing.

Meeting these standards isn't something that just happens. Into it must go planning, foresight and intelligent action. Otherwise, a city finds itself dying.

Civic Heads Plan

Civic leaders, business men and city officials got together on plans to rehabilitate Pittsburgh to eliminate the blighted areas and to enable the city to meet the demands of the postwar years. Out of this cooperation has come the Sanitary Authority, Smoke Control, the Parking Authority and the Urban Redevelopment Authority.

Urban Redevelopment Authority

In 1945, the State Legislature passed the law under which the Pittsburgh Urban Redevelopment Authority was set up. The state agreed that neither regulation nor private enterprise was able to deal effectively with the problem of broken down cities.

PITTSBURGH PRESS
April 29, 1950

City Of Pittsburgh's Housing For Negroes: Is The Hill District Doomed?

BY PAUL L. JONES

Second in a Series on "Housing"

When Jack Robin says that present living patterns in the Hill are "undesirable, unacceptable, and unendurable," just what does he mean? Is he simply slurring life there?

Is he seeking to justify redevelopment with a slogan? Or does his statement give a measured evaluation of the way Negroes actually live in the Hill?

This is Hill Housing

First, let's take a look at what exists at present.

In the Hill area bounded by Tunnel Street on the West, Fifth Avenue on the south, Bigelow Boulevard on the north, and Heron Avenue on the east, there are approximately 11,500 dwelling units.

More than 6,000 of these are sub-standard, that is have major structural defects, or lack adequate sanitary facilities such as a bathroom or hot and cold running water.

Public Housing

Another 3,000 are public housing units in Bedford Dwellings and Terrace Village. These low-rent developments have been almost for ten years an oasis of decent conditions in housing on the Hill.

In these projects, those whose income was low enough to be eligible have had better housing than those who theoretically could pay going rent.

2,500 Decent Units

That leaves 2,500 units in the whole Hill area which meet minimum requirements for decent housing. This is in terms of buildings alone, leaving out of consideration such an important item as the kind of neighborhood the good structure is in.

In other words, five our of seven houses in the Hill - those occupied by white as well as colored - are definitely below par.

SATURDAY, MAY 6, 1950 THE PITTSBURGH

'Hill Housing Future, What Will It Mean?'

By PAUL L. JONES
(Third in a Series on "Housing")

To redevelop the Hill is an intricate job that will require the cooperation and skill of many agencies and individuals.

There are many headaches involved, some of which have been fully anticipated at this time.

... Tunnel and Webster fit into the general scheme. If private developers can be found, there will be more such apartments on the edge of the downtown area.

NEW APARTMENTS AND PARKWAYS

The Crosstown Parkway will carry traffic around the southern and eastern peripheries of the downtown sector. To provide room for its roadway, approaches will clear away some of the congested lower Hill.

This project is still on the drawing boards, but is scheduled to get started within the next two years.

PARKING REMEDIES

Parking has long been one of the plagues of the downtown area. The garages planned by the Parking Authority are designed primarily for short-term use, for shoppers and businessmen coming into town for a few hours.

There is little intention of providing inexpensive all-day parking facilities within the downtown proper.

All-day facilities will be set up in part of the cleared lower Hill.

Thus the traffic burden of the narrow downtown streets will be eased and the pattern of parking all day on the edge of the city ...

... ready developed a fourth of the units at Bedford Dwellings and Terrace Village are more than 25 per cent of the units on the Hill.

These homes in the Hill projects provide more decent housing, by U. S. Public Health standards, than is available in all the rest of the Hill below Herron Avenue.

PAST SLUM CLEARANCE

The Terrace Village development is a dramatic example of how public housing can be used to reclaim land and remake a portion of the city.

Where 800 families once lived in squalor and filth on old Goat, Gazzam and Ruch Hills, a $3,000,000 grading and filling job has provided the site where 2,700 families now live in open and healthy surroundings.

ELIGIBLE FOR ...

PITTSBURGH COURIER
May 6, 1950
Hill Housing Future, What Will It Mean? Is The Hill District Doomed?

PITTSBURGH COURIER
May 13, 1950
Housing Upheavals, How To Meet Them? Is The Hill District Doomed?

PITTSBURGH POST-GAZETTE
May 13, 1950
Calls City Hopeless Architecturally
Point Park Wrong To Wright
"Pig-Piling," name for skyscrapers, rapped by pundit in lecture here
Pittsburgh's Point Park project is just a continuation of the "pig-pile" school of architecture.

At least, that is the way it looks to architecture pundit Frank Lloyd Wright, who spoke last night at Carnegie Lecture Hall in Carnegie Institute's "Interior Designer Speaks" series.

At a press conference at the William Penn Hotel yesterday morning, Mr Wright continued his personal feud with Pittsburgh which he has long considered hopeless architecturally.

"The trouble is," he went on, "that the connection between architecture and civilization is not understood. Architecture is the foundation of civilization."

Calls City Hopeless Architecturally

Point Park Wrong to Wright

'Pig-Piling,' Name for Skyscrapers, Rapped by Pundit in Lecture Here

By JAMES W. ROSS

Post-Gazette Staff Writer

Pittsburgh's Point Park project is just a continuation of the "pig-pile" school of architecture.

At least, that's the way it looks to architectural pundit Frank Lloyd Wright, who spoke last night at Carnegie Lecture Hall in Carnegie Institute's "Interior Designer Speaks" series.

At a press conference at the William Penn Hotel yesterday morning, Mr Wright continued his personal feud with Pittsburgh, which he has long considered hopeless architecturally.

He's Not Impressed

Despite the progress which it represents to a lot of Pittsburghers, Mr Wright is not impressed with the Point Park program. "It's just a continuation of the pig-piling process," he said. "And we've got to stop pig-piling."

Pig-piling is his own catchy but not too precise term for sky-

In getting at this foundation, Mr. Wright sees structure as the important factor. As structure is to the body, so it is to building, he claims.

"We've never succeeded in humanizing building," he pointed out. "We're living in something washed up on the shore. Architecture is coming alive again—in South America, Mexico, Italy—but always elsewhere more than here."

In a way that he didn't fully explain, Mr Wright blames our present architectural "chaos" on Capital, Mellon Institute and the new Mellon-U. S. Steel Building

FRANK LLOYD WRIGHT

Has feud with city

PITTSBURGH PRESS
Plans For Big Municipal Area Unveiled In Hill Slum Clearance
Hill auditorium for civic opera, sports first phase of 106-acre face-lifting

PITTSBURGH POST-GAZETTE
February 27, 1953
New Cultural Center Planned For Lower Hill

PITTSBURGH POST-GAZETTE
June 30, 1953
Cinderella City
Ridiculed, scorned and snubbed for over a century and a half, Pittsburgh throws off her pall to become the "City of Tomorrow"
Even though she was always respected for her strength and admired for her talents, she was scorned, snubbed, profaned, reproached, ridiculed. They said she was dirty, ill-kept, devoid of beauty.

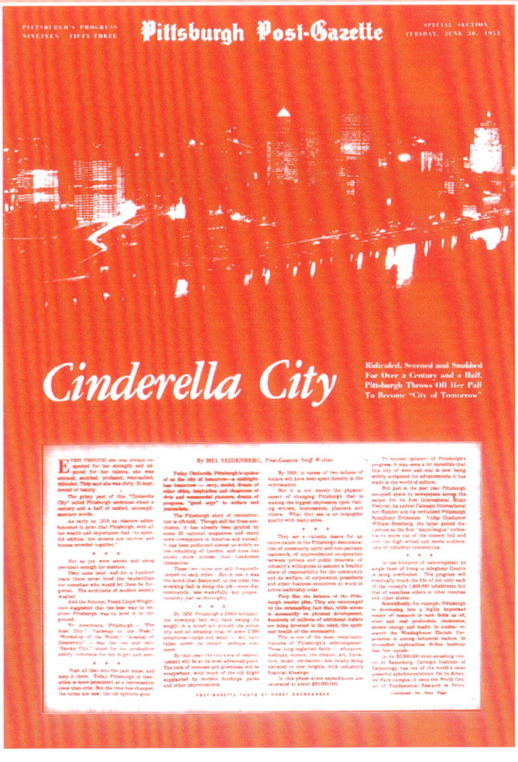

PITTSBURGH'S PROGRESS NINETEEN FIFTY-THREE

Pittsburgh Post-Gazette

SPECIAL SECTION TUESDAY, JUNE 30, 1953

Cinderella City

Ridiculed, Scorned and Snubbed For Over a Century and a Half, Pittsburgh Throws Off Her Pall To Become "City of Tomorrow"

By MEL SEIDENBERG, Post-Gazette Staff Writer

EVEN THOUGH she was always respected for her strength and admired for her talents, she was scorned, snubbed, profaned, reproached, ridiculed. They said she was dirty, ill-kept, devoid of beauty.

The grimy past of this "Cinderella City" called Pittsburgh embraces about a century and a half of unkind, uncomplimentary words.

Today Cinderella Pittsburgh is spoken of as the city of tomorrow—a midnightless tomorrow — envy, model, dream of other cities, inspiration and classroom of civic and commercial planners, dream of progress, "good copy" to writers and journalists.

Not as yet were smoke and smog prevalent enough for mention.

They came later, and for a hundred years there never lived the vaudevillian nor comedian who let them be forgotten. The architects of modern society laughed.

And the futurist, Frank Lloyd Wright, once suggested that the best way to improve Pittsburgh was to level it to the ground.

To Americans, Pittsburgh - "The Steel City," "Gateway to the West," "Workshop of the World," "Arsenal of Democracy" - was the once and only "Smoky City," noted for her productive ability, notorious for her blight and soot.

Push all that in the past tense, and keep it there. Today Pittsburgh in transition is more prominent as a conversation piece than ever. But the tone has changed, the terms are new, the old epithets gone.

PITTSBURGH POST-GAZETTE
June 30, 1953
Many Join Forces To Alter Face Of Pittsburgh
Cinderella City feels the touch of Magic

PITTSBURGH POST-GAZETTE
June 30, 1953
New Pittsburgh Was Born in The Minds of Bold Men
Birth of a Plan — The Allegheny Conference

PITTSBURGH POST-GAZETTE
June 30, 1953
Urban Development Proves A Miracle Of Faith
Dreams make the stone that rebuild a city

PITTSBURGH POST-GAZETTE
June 30, 1953
Triplet Skyscrapers Attest Soundness Of Vision
Gateway — Proof of the redeployment pudding

PITTSBURGH POST-GAZETTE
June 30, 1953
We Grew Up Here
A new Pittsburgh!

PITTSBURGH POST-GAZETTE
June 30, 1953
Point Park Looks To The Future
Where history was made

Fairy Godmother's Wand Poised Over Lower Hill

Golden Triangle Will Soon Break Its Barriers

New Buildings in Progress at PCW

PENNSYLVANIA COLLEGE FOR WOMEN

Insulations

Now We Can Serve You Even Better!

BELTS

HOSE

CONSOLIDATED RUBBER CORPORATION

THE REPUBLIC RUBBER of Pittsburgh

OPALO

"How much is that city in the window?"

PEOPLES FIRST NATIONAL BANK & TRUST COMPANY

PITTSBURGH POST-GAZETTE
June 30, 1953
Golden Triangle Will Soon Break Its Barriers
Fairy Godmother's wand poised over Lower Hill
"How much is that city in the window?"
Generations of work...the genius and sweat and savings of millions of Pittsburghers past and present have gone into the modern metropolis centered in the Golden Triangle. It means so much to Pittsburghers that upwards of $2,000,000,000 has been spent in a huge redevelopment program to keep it one of America's great cities.

It's a tremendous community effort and, from the very start, Peoples First has been happy to take active part in it. In addition to modernizing and expanding our own facilities, we have extended credit to assist in the development of many Pittsburgh companies, large and small. And business, generally, in the Pittsburgh area benefitted from the 56,465 loans we made last year for purchase of autos, appliances, home modernization and other personal needs.

After all, banking is essentially a community enterprise. Strong, progressive communities and strong, progressive banks work hand in hand. And Peoples First is proud to be working and growing with the most progressive city in America.

PITTSBURGH POST-GAZETTE
June 30, 1953
Hopes Of Thousands Rose With Dust Of Rubble
Men must work - - and Pittsburgh meets the test

PITTSBURGH POST-GAZETTE
As Health Is Wealth, Wealth Is Also Health
June 30, 1953
Medical center becomes a reality

PITTSBURGH POST-GAZETTE
Our Colleges Answer Yearning For Knowledge
June 30, 1953
Reading maketh a full man ...
PROGRESSIVE CAMPUS This architect's sketch shares what Duquesne University's $13,000,000 campus will look like when the Blufftop school finishes the building program. Present structures are (a) the Administration Building erected in 1884, (B) the faculty's new Community House, and (C) Canevin Hall, The new buildings, in order of their priority, are, 91) dormitories for men and women students, (2) Hall of Law and Finance, (3) Mellon Hall, (4) addition to library, (5) general classroom building, (6) Student Union, and (7) Field House. The future site of the remodeled school will fit in a rectangle formed by a 96-acre tract bounded on the east by Mercy Hospital, the west by the edge of the Bluff, between Locust and Bluff Streets.

PITTSBURGH POST-GAZETTE
November 26, 1953
Alcoa Marks 65th Birthday
Born in back-street shop
Original output 9 tons a year

PITTSBURGH POST-GAZETTE
July 23, 1955
Mayor Signs 'Contract' For Hill Development
Action to appraise, purchase properties expected this Fall

Mayor David L. Lawrence signed the co-operation agreement between the Urban Redevelopment Authority and the city of Pittsburgh last Thursday, thus giving city approval to the Lower Hill redevelopment program. Authority to enter into the agreement was given by City Council July 12.

Thus the way was cleared for the Pittsburgh Urban Redevelopment Authority to submit its plans to the Philadelphia regional office of the Federal Housing and Home Finance Agency for approval, and to undertake negotiations for a loan and grant from the Federal Government to carry out the redevelopment plan.

1. Complete contract with Federal Government between now and Aug. 1.
2. Final property appraisals to be made in August and September, 1955
3. Acquisitions of properties to start Oct. 1, 1955
4. Some demolition to start Oct. 1, 1955.
5. Long range completion of project, five to since years and finished by 1960.
6. Acquisition of properties will require three years plus.
7. Relocation of families will require four years plus.
8. The Civic Light Opera outdoor stadium should be ready by 1958

PITTSBURGH COURIER
Word on Lower Hill: 'Say Goodbye Next Spring'
August 27, 1955
Residents, old landmarks must bow to Progress

PITTSBURGH PRESS
October 11, 1955
38 Men And A Model

Its a rare occasion when so many business executives, civic leaders, clergymen and educators get together. And it is more rare when a photograph of the men is made.

But these 38 Pittsburghers met recently as the "Pittsburgh Progress" general committee. They got together to talk over ways to keep Pittsburgh's name before the country and the world now that the bicentennial year is nearing its end. In other words, they want the Renaissance here to continue and they want to make other cities constantly aware of it.

They are seated behind a model of the Civic Auditorium, now a building in the Lower Hill. It

August 27, 1955 THE PITTSBURGH COURIER Page 3

Word on Lower Hill: 'Say Goodbye Next Spring'

Residents, Old Landmarks Must Bow to Progress

By GEORGE BARBOUR

(See Pictures on Page 15)

For every gain there's a loss, and that's the gist of the story on the Lower Hill District redevelopment project.

Besides the many Third Ward homes, there also are other endeared friends of the residents, and the city in general. They are the various institutions which in the past have responded wholeheartedly to the needs of the scores of tenants in the area.

"There's no cause for alarm; but starting next spring, "goodbyes" will be in order for the historic landmarks and places many have known as "home."

Many months or even years may pass before the headache balls topple the last surviving landmark into a heap of masonry and twisted steel, but the machinery of Pittsburgh progress—the Urban Redevelopment Authority—is already being lubricated to swing into action.

The mechanics in this project, are highly skilled planners, who day-in and day-out over the past five years have formulated the plans and are now "Zeroing" the some 1,000 pages of plans, thirty maps, and ideas

Fifth Avenue to Sixth Avenue intersection.

Modern buildings are to be constructed on all of the area with the exception of the Epiphany Roman Catholic Church property.

The re-developers, the persons who will build anew, fall into three categories—public, such as the Arena Authority; commercial, erecting business establishments; and residential, who will build high-rent, luxury apartments.

With the exception of land for public improvement, other property will be sold by bids.

CLOSE SCRUTINY

EDWARD C. DILLINGHAM

... with Aircon Company

Registration

GOP Faces Election Problems

By JOHN L. CLARK

To be successful, Republican candidates for election Nov. 8 must overcome a Democratic registration of better than 140,000.

Who's Who In Labor

By HAROLD L. KEITH

Police Break Up Fight

East End police say that Leon Mickens, 31, of 343 Prince Street and Thomas Walker, 37, of 648 Larimer Avenue were engaged in a fight in Abe's Bar, 6325 Frankstown Avenue, Saturday night. They were arrested and booked on disorderly conduct charges.

5 Star Studded Days and Nights of

is the big talking point in "Pittsburgh Progress" at the moment.

PITTSBURGH POST-GAZETTE
April 14, 1960
3 Architectural Experts Criticize Point Buildings
2 Teachers, Editor Say Visual Planning Is Ignored, Insist Gateways 1, 2, 3 Are Already Dated
Chateau St. Renewal Plan Pushed
City, Authority Promise Residents, Businesses Action
Pittsburgh is no longer the Smoky City, but three authorities on architecture have a new name for us:

Pittsburgh - the No. 1 city in the world that missed the boat!

"Any time an architect gives a lecture and starts to talk about a city that missed the boat he refers to Pittsburgh," said Paul M. Rudolph, 41, crew-cut, youthful looking chairman of Yale University Department of Architecture.

If words were bombs, the shining array of new buildings at the Point would have been demolished yesterday by Mr Rudolph and two contemporaries: Joseph Hazen, managing editor of Architectural Forum, and Paul Schweikher, chairman of the Department of Architecture at Carnegie Tech.

PITTSBURGH POST-GAZETTE
April 14, 1960
Experts Rap Point Buildings, Claim They're Out Of Date
Not competing with you, Pitt man tells merchants... Vieh tries to mollify Oaklanders, cries 'unfair' to recent criticisms
Manchester redeveloping plan pushed, Council, Authority promise Residents, businesses action
"There has been a lot of economic thought given to the Point and Lower Hill, even social thought. The Big trouble, as far as architects go, is that there is no visual planning...

The Urban Redevelopment Authority and the Allegheny Conference are full of men trained in industry... It's like having a football team made up of all halfbacks." (Schweikher)

"The Point is a big success commercially, but with planning and vision it could have been a greater success." (Hazen)

"We've built an obsolescence..." (Rudolph)

The buildings at the Point will have short lives because their forms are chaotic," Mr. Schweikher forecasts.

PITTSBURGH PRESS
May 19, 1961
Allegheny Center... Renaissance On The North Side

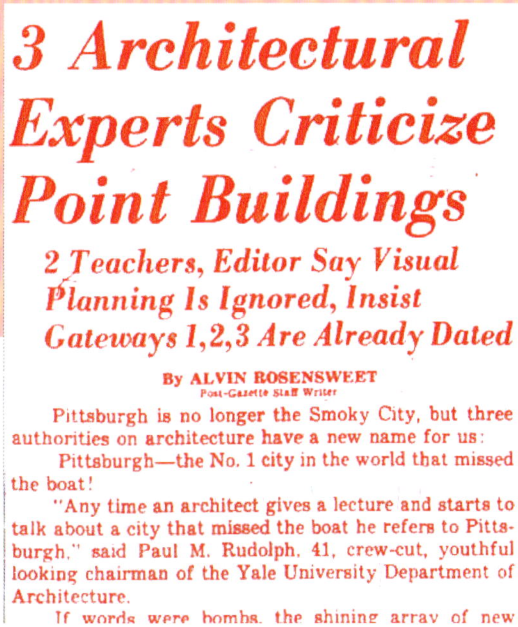

3 Architectural Experts Criticize Point Buildings

2 Teachers, Editor Say Visual Planning Is Ignored, Insist Gateways 1,2,3 Are Already Dated

By ALVIN ROSENSWEET
Post-Gazette Staff Writer

Pittsburgh is no longer the Smoky City, but three authorities on architecture have a new name for us:

Pittsburgh—the No. 1 city in the world that missed the boat!

"Any time an architect gives a lecture and starts to talk about a city that missed the boat he refers to Pittsburgh," said Paul M. Rudolph, 41, crew-cut, youthful looking chairman of the Yale University Department of Architecture.

If words were bombs, the shining array of new

PITTSBURGH PRESS

October 11, 1955

38 Men And A Model

PITTSBURGH PRESS
July 2, 1961
What You Think About Downtown Wanted For Triangle Master Plan
Planners going to people for ideas
Folks asked what's good and/or bad
Few knew much about Point Park

PITTSBURGH COURIER
November 5, 1961
Landlords Bow In Housing Bias Fight
Kaufmann's next NAACP picket target

PITTSBURGH COURIER
November 5, 1961
'HELP US!' Urban Renewal "DP's" Plead
EDITOR'S NOTE: While Pittsburgh (The Renaissance City) proudly displays its renovation of the Golden Triangle, highlighted by the $55 million Civic Arena, to its many citizens and visitors, and maps magnificent plans for urban renewal, it has "swept under the rug" its "drags of human misery" - those displaced persons, a majority of whom are Negroes, who either have not been relocated or unable to find suitable housing on their own. Crack Courier reporter, Phyl Garland, has gone behind the scenes to interview and write about these "Prisoners of the Ghetto" and their vicious "jailers." This is the first in a series of articles which the Courier offers its readers...

...In a decaying structure beyond the edge of the Golden Triangle, an aged roomer dozes before a window over looking the "Renaissance City." The feeble, late afternoon sunlight, filtered through a dirt-dimed paned of glass, touches the dark slope of his forehead...

...They used to live in the Lower Hill, but "Progress" came to that area and they had to get out. They used to live in the sprawling Manchester area of the North Side, but now many of them have to "get out" of there too. Most of them still live in scattered, run-down sections of Pittsburgh.

How long they will remain where they are is indefinite, for a new force has come to influence the uneven pattern of their lives.

For Pittsburgh has been undergoing a drastic face-lifting process, during the past few years. It is called Urban Redevelopment.

With a broad stroke of a steam shovel, it sweeps away the fetid dwellings of the down-and-out, leaving only the human debris.

PITTSBURGH POST-GAZETTE
November 21, 1961
Oakland Of 1980 Unveiled
Pitt to play football in Northside stadium

PITTSBURGH POST-GAZETTE
November 21, 1961
Oakland Unveils 1980 Blueprint
Plans call for huge college-health center

Tripling of floor space for academic use by Pitt, Tech and Mr. Mercy College to serve, by 1980, a total of nearly 28,000 students, 22,000 of them at Pitt.

About four times more space than now for hospitals, medical offices and related actives… Approximately $50 million worth of urban renewal…Total clearance of some 50 acres for development of 3,000 to 4,000 new dwelling units…Altogether, the plan proposes 6,200 additional parking spaces for Oakland.

PITTSBURGH POST-GAZETTE
October 2, 1961
Another $22,000,000 Baby

PITTSBURGH POST-GAZETTE
May 5, 1961
Northside Renewal Program Okayed
Kansas City firm, Alcoa offers funds, authority accepts two proposals for Allegheny Center
Allegheny Center moves into city's changing patterns

PITTSBURGH POST-GAZETTE
January 16, 1965
Citizens Unveil Plan For Solvent Folks To Renew, Remain On Hill

PITTSBURGH COURIER
August 7, 1965
Does Urban Renewal Mean Negro Removal?

PITTSBURGH POST-GAZETTE
October 2, 1968
Pitt Drafts Masterplan For 40,000
Cathedral will serve as core of sprawling campus

SECOND SECTION **Pittsburgh Post-Gazette** WEDNESDAY, OCTOBER 2, 1968

CATHEDRAL WILL SERVE AS CORE OF SPRAWLING CAMPUS

Pitt Drafts Master Plan for 40,000

A master plan unveiled for the University of Pittsburgh yesterday visualized the Oakland campus as a consolidated academic core for 40,000 students with the towering Cathedral of Learning as a focal point.

The plan was conceived by the Pittsburgh architectural firm of Deeter Ritchey Sippel for the state Department of Properties and Supplies. The 14-volume plan was two years in the making.

The bulk of the proposal concerned the development of the Forbes Field area which the university already owns.

Other Facilities Later

Immediately upon completion of the municipal stadium on the Northside in 1970, the Forbes Field area will provide a site for the schools of education and social sciences, the graduate school of library and information sciences and the school of law.

Later, other facilities will be added, including the humanities, the graduate school of business, the graduate school of social work, the graduate school of public and international affairs and a new undergraduate library.

These schools now occupy space in scattered locations.

Deeter Ritchey Sippel recommended low, continuous inter-connected buildings achieved by consolidating building programs that would create a close proximity between teaching facilities and faculty offices.

New Dormitories Planned

The firm said this concept would encourage a high degree of utilization, flexibility, expansion potential and interaction between education disciplines.

The plan calls for new dormitory facilities on the upper hill and in the lower campus facing Schenley Park and connected directly to the new Forbes complex.

The master plan visualizes the use of an escalator to link the upper hill housing development with the lower campus.

The design also proposes an increase in the number of off-street parking places by constructing a three-level 1,530 car garage beneath the Schenley Park Plaza and return of the plaza to pedestrian use.

Master Recommendations

The master plan also made these recommendations:

►Construct bridges across Forbes Avenue to free students of having to cross through traffic.

►Close off several streets, including Bigelow Boulevard, Bouquet and Sennott Streets and Pennant Place in the Forbes Field area.

►Use new buildings for multi-school purposes instead of using one building for one school.

►Co-ordinate classes so that a student is never more than 10 minutes away from his class on foot.

Initial plans call for some 1.5 million square feet of new space—three times more than what is now in the Cathedral of Learning.

Much of the plan came from suggestions from students and faculty members.

Pitt's Future Look?

Model of new buildings in master plan shows existing buildings intermingled with new ones to be built in Forbes Field complex. Carnegie Institute (lower left), circular dormitories (upper right), Cathedral of Learning (right) and Hillman Library (near center), will be joined by facilities for Pitt's schools of education and social sciences, school of law, and graduate schools on what is now Forbes Field. The architectural firm of Deeter Richey Sipple prepared this model.

Suggestion Experts to Meet

About 1,100 suggestion administrators will meet here next week.

Suggestion administrators protect the interests of suggesters and satisfy the goals of management as the middle link between the communication of an idea from the suggester to management.

They will convene at the Hilton Hotel Monday through Wednesday for the 20th international conference of the National Association of Suggestion Systems.

The keynote address, "Countdown for Tomorrow," will be given by Dr. John H. Furbay, of Trans World Airlines, Inc.

Sessions also will be held in such fields as manufacturing, marketing, services, transportation, and government.

The East Liberty project, biggest ever tackled here, is about 80 per cent complete. This is one of the pedestrian malls.

Federal Agency Has $37 Million Stake in Renewal

East Liberty 'Rebirth' Spotlighted

THE U.S. DEPARTMENT of Housing and Urban Development (HUD) is proud of East Liberty.

The agency has dumped nearly $37 million into the vast urban renewal project there and HUD officials feel the grants have helped East Liberty to "regain its reputation as a self-contained, cosmopolitan community on the east end of Pittsburgh."

The renewal of the 254-acre project is about 80 per cent complete. It will provide over $20 million worth of new construction when it's finished, along with 1,500 new dwellings, extensive residential rehabiliation and three pedestrian shopping malls.

HUD points out that East Liberty is a "first" for Pittsburgh in several ways.

★ ★ ★

THE EAST LIBERTY project is the biggest ever tackled here as well as the first to put emphasis on rehabilitation. Only 48 per cent of the area has been cleared.

It is by far the most complex of 18 separate urban renewal projects undertaken by the Pittsburgh Urban Redevelopment Authority (URA).

East Liberty business leaders called for the project in 1956 as a means of revitalizing the community of East Liberty. The following year, the city received assurance of financial support from the Housing and Home Finance Agency—the predecessor of HUD.

Eight years of progress has followed in the areas of housing, rehabilitation, commercial development and site improvement.

★ ★ ★

NEARLY 40 ACRES of renewal land have been sold or committed for new residential development. A total of 1,231 new dwellings are complete or under construction. Of these, 469 are designed for families of low and moderate income, the latter being financed through the Federal Housing Administration's below-market-interest rate program, permitting families whose incomes are too high for public housing to find rental housing within their means.

Also under construction is a development sponsored by the Harriet Tubman Guild, a Negro women's organization. The project is the city's first under the Rent Supplement program.

On completion, the housing supply will be about 30 per cent larger than it was before the beginning of renewal.

The area's total population is expected to increase well over its 1958 level of roughly 8,500 persons, despite the relocation of over 800 families to other areas of the city.

Some 597 of a total 1,113 dwellings in East Liberty have been renovated by owners to meet renewal standards. Another 268 were under rehabilitation last fall.

★ ★ ★

PRIVATE INVESTMENT in residential rehabilitation has reached $713,882. Over $65,000 worth of residential rehabilitation has been made possible by FHA insured loans and HUD's rehabilitation loan and grant programs.

Almost 20 acres of land in the East Liberty area have been sold or committed for new private commercial development.

Approximately $4 million in private capital has been expended for commercial development and an additional $3 million in private funds has been invested for modernization and expansion of retail shops, service and office facilities, and commercial rehabilitation. Altogether, 23 firms have rehabilitated or are in the process of renovating their properties.

Main portions of East Liberty's major business arteries are being converted into three inter-connecting pedestrian shopping malls, at a total cost in public funds of about $700,000.

Already in service, and recently the scene of a successful arts and music festival, is the Broad Street Mall which offers a variety of landscaping, patio areas with benches, canopies, kiosks, fountains, and other such attractions.

Expected to rival the Broad Street Mall in interest and inducements to shoppers are the Penn and Highland Malls, both of which are still under construction.

★ ★ ★

WHILE ALL AUTO traffic, except emergency and maintenance vehicles, is to be prohibited, the Penn and Highland Malls will remain open to public buses operating on center lanes especially designed for these or other types of public transit vehicles.

By 1970, nearly $13.7 million in public funds will have been expended for malls, parks, parking lots, new streets, sewers, water lines, lighting, traffic control, signs and other site improvements.

Throughout most of the community, overhead wiring and cables are being put underground.

Progress in East Liberty, according to HUD, can be measured in many ways. As the community assesses its progress over the last decade, consideration must be given to the way all sectors of the community have united to meet the area's needs, officials said.

– Post-Gazette Photos by Morris Berman

Even play areas were planned to blend with surroundings.

PITTSBURGH POST-GAZETTE
February 1, 1969
East Liberty 'Rebirth' Spotlighted
Federal Agency has $37 million stake in renewal
The U.S. Department of Housing and Urban Development (HUD) is proud of East Liberty.

The agency has dumped $37 million into the vast urban renewal project there and HUD officials feel the grants have helped East Liberty to "regain its reputation as a self-contained, cosmopolitan community on the east end of Pittsburgh."

The renewal of the 254-acre project is about 80 per cent complete. It will provide over $20 million worth of new construction when it's finished, along with 1,500 new dwellings, extensive residential rehabilitation and three pedestrian shopping malls.

HUD points out that East Liberty is a "first" for Pittsburgh in several ways.

The East Liberty project is the biggest ever tackled here was well as the first to put emphasis on rehabilitation. Only 48 per cent of the area has been cleared.

PITTSBURGH POST-GAZETTE
August 29, 1969
Workers Fight Job Shutdowns
We want to work! We need our pay!" 100 trade unionists shout Downtown: Talks in progress on blacks' demands

PITTSBURGH PRESS
November 23, 1969
Another Renaissance... East Liberty Takes On A New Look
Pittsburgh's first outdoor malls renovate 254 acres

PITTSBURGH PRESS
November 23, 1969
The New Look Of East Liberty

PITTSBURGH PRESS
January 26, 1969
2001 Fixing Up Hill, Its People
Construction supplants heroin

PITTSBURGH PRESS
February 7, 1971
Hill District Map Has A 'Heart'
To put heart into a map of a community, forget proportion. Like a child, make what is important very large, and what isn't - well, squeeze that into as small a space as possible.

That's what Pittsburgh architect Troy West and Community Design Associates did when commissioned to draw a map of the Hill District to be used in urban renewal.

The rightness of this approach has been proven. That map won a citation in the recent 18th annual design awards competition sponsored by Progressive Architecture.

He Cares About Hill
Perhaps the map has heart because Troy West really cares about the Hill District and its people. He has been involved with the Hill District for years and maintains his office there.

"I have been working up here for seven years for citizens' groups" West said. "About three

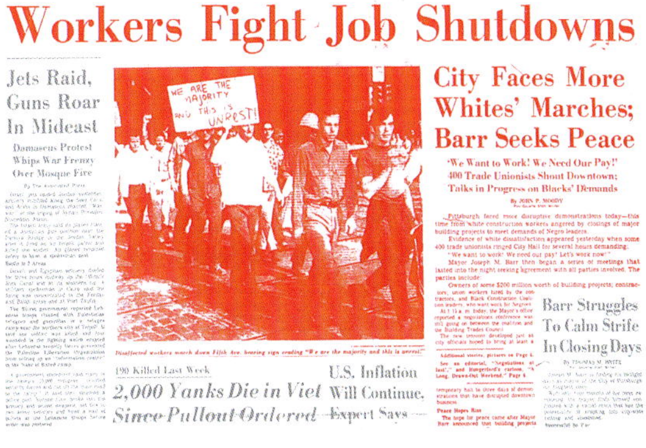

Workers Fight Job Shutdowns

Jets Raid, Guns Roar In Mideast

Damascus Protest Whips War Frenzy Over Mosque Fire

City Faces More Whites' Marches; Barr Seeks Peace

'We Want to Work! We Need Our Pay!' 400 Trade Unionists Shout Downtown; Talks in Progress on Blacks' Demands

By JOHN P. MOODY

Pittsburgh faced more disruptive demonstrations today—this time from white construction workers angered by closings of major building projects to meet demands of Negro leaders.

Evidence of white dissatisfaction appeared yesterday when some 400 trade unionists ringed City Hall for several hours demanding:

"We want to work! We need our pay! Let's work now!"

Mayor Joseph M. Barr then began a series of meetings that lasted into the night seeking agreement with all parties involved. The parties include:

Owners of some $200 million worth of building projects; contractors, union workers hired by the contractors, and Black Construction Coalition leaders, who want work for Negroes.

Barr Struggles To Calm Strife In Closing Days

Disaffected workers march down Fifth Ave. bearing sign reading "We are the majority and this is unrest!"

190 Killed Last Week

2,000 Yanks Die in Viet Since Pullout Ordered

U.S. Inflation Will Continue, Expert Says

years ago, the architectural design class I was teaching at Carnegie Mellon University (CMU) set up a Hill classroom. Also, we keep going by a fee-generating project with organizations like Community Action Pittsburgh and Benjamin Banneker Homes."

"The map project was done for the Department of Transportation in Washington which was interested in solving transportation problems in five cities, including Pittsburgh," West went on, "The Hill District was recognized as a district which might have special seeds and problems."

To find out what should loom large on a map with a heart, ask the people who live there. Then incorporate what they say, unrealistically if necessary, into the picture.

On the 25' × 40' prize map, for example, a building labeled the Aura Club, in reality a small place, is a quarter the size of the Washington Plaza Apartments, a high-rise building which is on the border of the Hill District...

Many People Play Role
The area in Fifth Avenue where Fifth Avenue High School is located has a drawing of an oversized basketball court complete with players, and next to it an indistinct classroom labeled "Screaming Boredom."

Many people were part of the map-making project. Two Hill District citizens, Cornelius Brown and Ed Woodall, were hired to give advice and information.

Chuck Culbertson, a young architect, took pictures and acted as information co-ordinator. Douglas Cooper, an architectural graduate of CMU who had done studies and worked out techniques for this type of map, was job captain on the design. Jay Greenfield, a psychologist who assists the firm to design buildings that fit human needs, helped...

The hope of the mapmakers was to give a sense of community to the people who live on the Hill by presenting an overall picture of the streets, buildings, empty lots which make up their home area...

How does the map fulfill its makers' hopes?
One day this week it was spread out on the floor of the big room at the Frederic Ozanam Cultural Center. Wylie Avenue Sister Marcella Mary from the school where the center is located brought some of her third-graders to see the map...

...Where's Elmore Square, one little boy kept asking plaintively until he found his street. Standing firmly on this spot he then directed a friend to his right. "Over there," he pointed, "there's Junilla Street. That's where you live."

Two little girls stood close to Sister Marcella as she showed them the school building on the map. One boy decided a park was a place to rest, so he stretched out stop a green area. Another girl walked carefully between the lines which designated Forbes Avenue, as if out for a stroll on the street.

At least for these children, the map held all the fascination its designers hoped for.

The Pittsburgh Press
for and about Women
Sunday, Feb. 7, 1971

Prize-winning map made by Community Design Associates is set against stark reality of photograph of area.

Hill District Map Has A 'Heart'

By SYLVIA SACHS

To put heart into a map of a community, forget proportion. Like a child, make what is important very large, and what isn't — well, squeeze that into as small a space as possible.

That's what Pittsburgh architect Troy **West and Community** Design Associates did **when commissioned** to draw a map of the Hill District to be used in urban renewal.

The rightness of this approach has been proven. The map won a citation in the recent 18th annual design awards competition sponsored by Progressive Architecture.

He Cares About Hill

Perhaps the map has heart because Troy West really cares about the Hill District and its people. He has been involved with the Hill for years and maintains his office there.

"I have been working up here for seven years for citizens' groups," West said. "About three years ago, the architectural design class I was teaching at Carnegie-Mellon University (CMU) set up a Hill classroom. Also, we keep going by fee-generating projects with organizations like Community Action Pittsburgh and Benjamin Banneker Homes.

"The map project was done for the Department of Transportation in Washington which was interested in solving transportation problems in five cities, including Pittsburgh," West went on. "The Hill District was recognized as a district which might have special needs and problems."

To find out what should loom large on a map with a heart, ask the people who live there. Then incorporate what they say, unrealistically if necessary, into the picture.

On the 25'x40' prize map, for example, a building labeled the Aurora Club, in reality a small place, is a quarter the size of the Washington Plaza Apartments, a high-rise building which is on the border of the Hill District. One tree is drawn near the apartment house with a sign, "Private Tree."

Many People Play Role

The area on Fifth Avenue where Fifth Avenue High School is located has a drawing of an oversized basketball court complete with players, and next to it an indistinct classroom labeled "Screaming Boredom."

Sisters' Park is a pleasant area of green in one corner of the map. All Pro Chicken, the Black Derby (an eating place), Connelly Vocational School, stand out in other sections.

Many people were part of the map-making project. Two Hill District citizens, Cornelius Brown and Ed Woodall, were hired to give advice and information.

Chuck Culbertson, a young architect, took pictures and acted as information co-ordinator. Douglas Cooper, an architectural graduate of CMU who had done studies and worked out techniques for this type of map, was job captain on the design. Jay Greenfield, a psychologist who assists the firm to design buildings that fit human needs, helped.

And a poet much admired in the district, Charles Williams, contributed inspiration with his poetry and creative ideas.

The hope of the mapmakers was to give a sense of community to the people who live on the Hill by presenting an overall picture of the streets, buildings, empty lots which make up their home area.

Seeing it all as a rather attractive exercise in design, a map to relate to and feel at home with, should arouse local pride, they reasoned. With this in mind, the map has been submitted to Model Cities with the designers' suggestion that small replicas be printed on cards and given to Hill residents.

How does the map fulfill its makers' hopes?

One day this week it was spread out on the floor of the big room at the Frederic Ozanam Cultural Center, Wylie Avenue. Sister Marcella Mary from the school where the center is located brought some of her third-graders to see the map.

Told they could take off their shoes and run over the map looking for their home or a favorite place, the children were entranced.

Where's Elmore Square, one little boy kept asking plaintively until he found his street. Standing firmly on this spot he then directed a friend to his right. "Over there," he pointed, "there's Junilla Street. That's where you live."

Two little girls stood close to Sister Marcella as she showed them the school building on the map. One boy decided a park was a place to rest, so he stretched out atop a green area. Another girl walked carefully between the lines which designated Forbes Avenue, as if out for a stroll on the street.

At least for these children, the map held all the fascination its designers had hoped for.

Third-grader resting "at home."

Architect Troy West has been working with citizens' groups in the Hill District for seven years. He explains one of his projects in the picture at left to Chuck Dial, seated.

—Press Photos by Edwin Morgan

"Can you find your house?" is the name of the game, above.

Three little girls from school enjoy map, left.

The Pittsburgh Press

Sunday, December 13, 1953

Pittsburgh's Renaissance

1936–1953

The Story of Sixteen Years of Progress

75 Years of Christian Education in Pittsburgh

DUQUESNE UNIVERSITY

Men Behind the Renaissance

Robertson
Galbestos
is the ONLY protected metal roofing and siding that resists weather and corrosion alike!

OPEN HEARTHS
For the City that Steel Built

LUMBER for Industrial Users

How Pittsburgh Did the Job

Electricity Powers Pittsburgh
GATEWAY TO OPPORTUNITY AND PROGRESS

DUQUESNE LIGHT COMPANY

EDWIN BELL COOPERAGE COMPANY

Blight of Years Ended
Smoke Victory Key To City's Renaissance

Progress at Copperweld
TODAY'S BIG Copperweld FAMILY
OVER 4,500 EMPLOYEES
STEEL DIVISION
WIRE AND CABLE DIVISION
OHIO SEAMLESS TUBE DIVISION
FINE WIRE DIVISION
FLEXO
COPPERWELD STEEL COMPANY
GROWING WITH PITTSBURGH FOR 38 YEARS!

Gateway Center for the NEW CONCEPT IN BUSINESS LIVING

These Buildings Were Built to Build Your Business!

Owned and Operated by The Equitable Life Assurance Society of the United States

Old Point Gets New Look
40 Buildings Came Down For Gateway

Air Brakes?
YES! but hundreds of other products, too

Westinghouse Air Brake COMPANY

ARCHITECTURAL FORUM
November 1949
Pittsburgh Renascent
The biggest real estate and building in the U.S. today is Pittsburgh.

Five years ago, Pittsburgh was a soot-covered relic of a great age two generations past.

Yet today there is more progress evident in Pittsburgh than in any other city in America.... Almost daily, Pittsburghers read of new plans to make their town a better place to live in, and everywhere there is evidence of how fast these plans are being turned into reality Specifically: Something drastic and affective, usually to the tune of many millions of dollars, is being done about Pittsburgh's floods, about Pittsburgh's river pollution, about Pittsburgh's parking problem, about Pittsburgh's airport, and about Pittsburgh's parks.

Pittsburgh is getting something like $130 million worth of new expressways to end its highway congestion and preserve Pittsburgh's position as the great shopping center of all the way from Johnstown to Youngstown. Pittsburgh is getting a marvelous plastic umbrella to pull up over the crowds at its open air light operas in case of rain, and Pittsburgh's children are getting a wonderful children's zoo with the aquarium inside the body of a whale and the mouse house inside a piece of cheese.

The old industries are spending close to a billion dollars for new or modernized Pittsburgh plant. U.S. Steel, Westinghouse, and Alcoa, instead of moving away, have decided to concentrate still more of their headquarters' operations in Pittsburgh. In the heart of the Golden Triangle, Pittsburgh is erecting the two smartest new skyscrapers in the country (see page 66), and at the tip of the Triangle Pittsburgh is pioneering the concept of an office building redevelopment whose sponsors promise to outdo Rockefeller Center - of a development whose nine cross-shaped towers will each be set in a two-acre park.

Pittsburgh's smoke is becoming a thing of the past. A new city smoke ordinance is being enforced to make Pittsburgh's air as clear as the air of New York, Chicago or Boston; and, as the smog cleared away, people could see for the first time in two generations that Pittsburgh with its hills and rivers, has perhaps the most beautiful location between the Alleghenies and the Rockies.

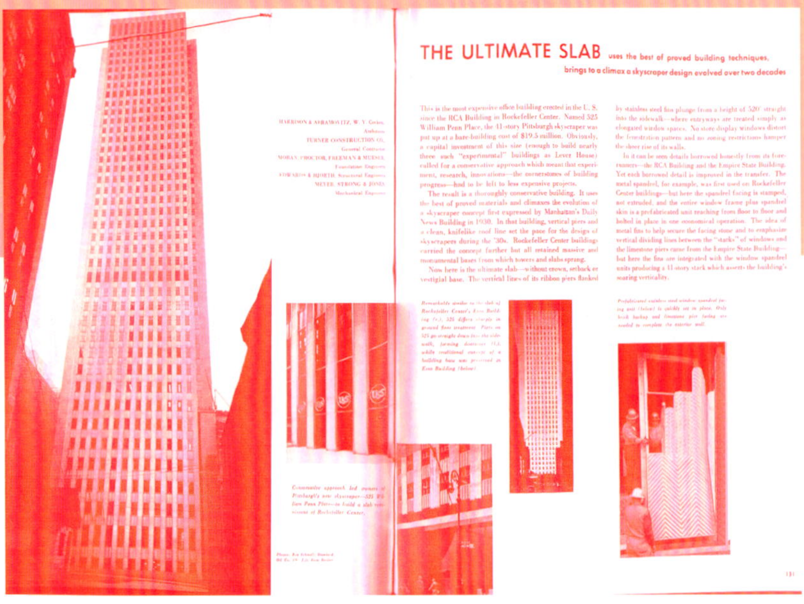

HARRISON & ABRAMOVITZ, W. Y. Cocken, Architects
TURNER CONSTRUCTION CO., General Contractor
MORAN, PROCTOR, FREEMAN & MUESER, Foundation Engineers
EDWARDS & HJORTH, Structural Engineers
MEYER, STRONG & JONES, Mechanical Engineers

THE ULTIMATE SLAB uses the best of proved building techniques, brings to a climax a skyscraper design evolved over two decades

This is the most expensive office building erected in the U. S. since the RCA Building in Rockefeller Center. Named 525 William Penn Place, the 41-story Pittsburgh skyscraper was put up at a bare-building cost of $19.5 million. Obviously, a capital investment of this size (enough to build nearly three such "experimental" buildings as Lever House) called for a conservative approach which meant that experiment, research, innovations—the cornerstones of building progress—had to be left to less expensive projects.

The result is a thoroughly conservative building. It uses the best of proved materials and climaxes the evolution of a skyscraper concept first expressed by Manhattan's Daily News Building in 1930. In that building, vertical piers and a clean, knifelike roof line set the pace for the design of skyscrapers during the '30s. Rockefeller Center buildings carried the concept further but all retained massive and monumental bases from which towers and slabs sprang.

Now here is the ultimate slab—without crown, setback or vestigial base. The vertical lines of its ribbon piers flanked by stainless steel fins plunge from a height of 520' straight into the sidewalk—where entryways are treated simply as elongated window spaces. No store display windows distort the fenestration pattern and no zoning restrictions hamper the sheer rise of its walls.

In it can be seen details borrowed honestly from its forerunners—the RCA Building and the Empire State Building. Yet each borrowed detail is improved in the transfer. The metal spandrel, for example, was first used on Rockefeller Center buildings—but here the spandrel facing is stamped, not extruded, and the entire window frame plus spandrel skin is a prefabricated unit reaching from floor to floor and bolted in place in one economical operation. The idea of metal fins to help secure the facing stone and to emphasize vertical dividing lines between the "stacks" of windows and the limestone piers came from the Empire State Building—but here the fins are integrated with the window spandrel units producing a 41-story stack which asserts the building's soaring verticality.

Remarkably similar to the slab of Rockefeller Center's Esso Building (r.), 525 differs sharply in ground floor treatment. Piers on 525 go straight down to the sidewalk, forming doorways (l.), while traditional concept of a building base was preserved in Esso Building (below).

Prefabricated stainless steel window spandrel facing unit (below) is quickly set in place. Only brick backup and limestone pier facing are needed to complete the exterior wall.

ARCHITECTURAL FORUM
April 1952
The Ultimate Slab Uses The Best Of Proved Building Techniques
THE ULTIMATE SLAB uses the best of proved building techniques, brings to a climax a skyscraper evolved over two decades

SHOWCASE FOR STEEL

Keynote of the building's extensive use of steel is the lobby. Is it, chromium stainless steel sheathes irregularly shaped exposed beams and columns. A black-painted steel pan ceiling conceals pinhole lighting which is reflected from the white terrazzo floor. High level lighting prevails in the elevator lobbies where most of the ceiling consists of fluorescents concealed behind plastic pans. Here again, walls are finished with stainless steel as are elevator doors and cabs.

ARCHITECTURAL FORUM
April 1952
The Curtain Wall Comes of Age

After a decade of research and experiment, the metal-faced curtain wall has emerged from the test tube to enclose four of the largest postwar buildings: the aluminum-clad Alcoa headquarters and the steel-clad trio of office towers sponsored by Equitable Life—both in Pittsburgh.

Unlike anything ever used before, these metal skins offer certain distinct advantages over masonry. Besides having the properties of masonry (structural adequacy, insulation, fire resistance and flexibility) they are thin in cross section, light in weight, and, because they are built of large panels with relatively few joints, they are quickly erected, highly resistant to rain and moisture penetration and easy to maintain.

ENGINEERING NEWS RECORD
April 24, 1952
An Urban Redevelopment Dream Is Coming True In Pittsburgh
As Pittsburgh's redevelopment dream comes true… Order out of disorder

ARCHITECTURAL FORUM
December 1953
Office Towers In A Park…Gateway Center, The Eken-Dowling Equitable Life Slum Clearance Redevelopment
Le Corbusier made this prophetic sketch in 1922 now, at last…

OFFICE TOWERS IN A PARK

Gateway's disappointing buildings half conceal the four important ideas they contribute to planning and building:

1. Site planning - the major accomplished above (demonstrated that Le Corbusier's "Ville Radieuse" - the concept of office towers in a park - made sense in terms of city planning), plus a fine scheme of traffic separation and of parking.

2. Office planning. A bold affirmation in

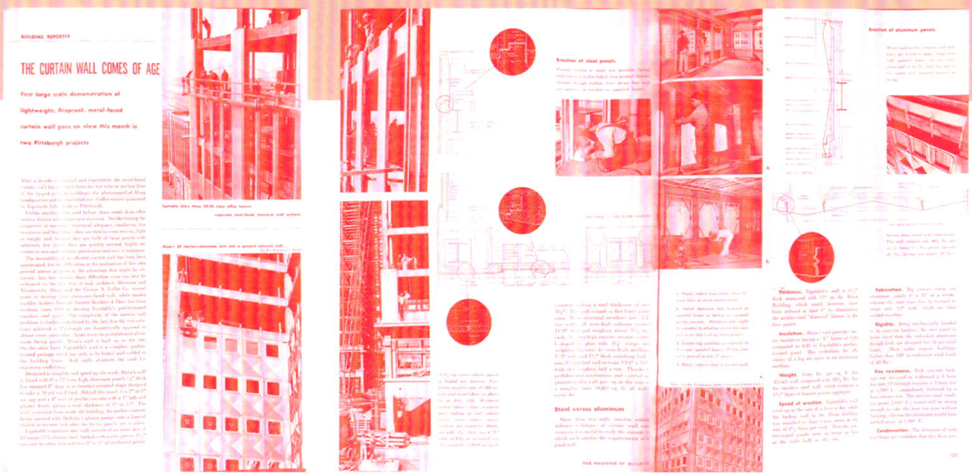

BUILDING REPORTER

THE CURTAIN WALL COMES OF AGE

First large scale demonstration of lightweight, fireproof, metal-faced curtain wall goes on view this month in two Pittsburgh projects

favor of building only prime space within 24' of a window, at a time when most buildings are taking advantage of air conditioning and artificial lighting to put a high price on bulk space. The decision to build only prime space explains the much-debated cruciform plan.
3. Prefabrication and metal facing. Really two techniques carried out at large scale: 1) prefabrication of the complete exterior wall (and not just the skin); and 2) the use of stainless steel facing for the first time in major U.S. construction.
4. Windows. The development of a big, handsome, completely reversible, single-pane window hat will cut cleaning costs - and was cheaper to start with than a conventional double-hung unit.
The story on these pages describes in detail each of these four major ideas. And, on p. 117 FORUM's editorial chairman frankly discusses some of the controversial issues raised by Gateway and by the manner in which it was designed.

SITE: auto traffic stays outside the Center... so pedestrians can walk in the park
OFFICES: every floor has 13,500 sq. ft. (net)... yet every desk is near a window
WALL: steel panels backed with perlite were bolted together to form complete outside walls for tall buildings
WINDOWS: cheaper than conventional double-hungs, Gateway's reversible windows are handsome, slim-edged and big

Architecture: stepchild or fashioner of cities?
The sad thing about Gateway is that its architecture is not up to genuine poetry of its ideas; and this at the precise moment when architecture as an art is ready as it has not been for 50 years to deal with just such a problem as making the civic center the crown and focus of urban life.

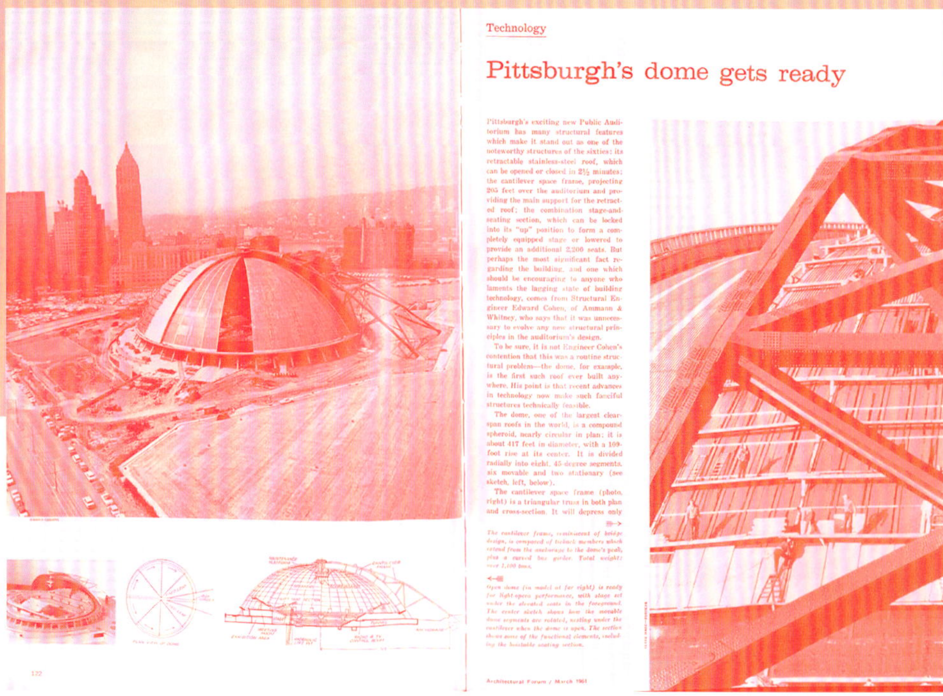

Technology

Pittsburgh's dome gets ready

Pittsburgh's exciting new Public Auditorium has many structural features which make it stand out as one of the noteworthy structures of the sixties: its retractable stainless-steel roof, which can be opened or closed in 2½ minutes; the cantilever space frame, projecting 205 feet over the auditorium and providing the main support for the retracted roof; the combination stage-and-seating section, which can be locked into its "up" position to form a completely equipped stage or lowered to provide an additional 2,200 seats. But perhaps the most significant fact regarding the building, and one which should be encouraging to anyone who laments the lagging state of building technology, comes from Structural Engineer Edward Cohen, of Ammann & Whitney, who says that it was unnecessary to evolve any new structural principles in the auditorium's design.

To be sure, it is not Engineer Cohen's contention that this was a routine structural problem—the dome, for example, is the first such roof ever built anywhere. His point is that recent advances in technology now make such fanciful structures technically feasible.

The dome, one of the largest clear-span roofs in the world, is a compound spheroid, nearly circular in plan; it is about 417 feet in diameter, with a 109-foot rise at its center. It is divided radially into eight, 45-degree segments, six movable and two stationary (see sketch, left, below).

The cantilever space frame (photo, right) is a triangular truss in both plan and cross-section. It will depress only

The cantilever frame, reminiscent of bridge design, is composed of ... members which extend from the anchorage to the dome's peak, plus a curved box girder. Total weight: over 1,100 tons.

Open dome (in model at far right) is ready for light-opera performance, with stage set under the elevated seats in the foreground. The center sketch shows how the movable dome segments are rotated, nesting under the cantilever when the dome is open. The section shows some of the functional elements, including the hoistable seating section.

122

Architectural Forum / March 1961

L'ARCHITECTURE D'AUJOURD'HUI
December 1953
Building De L'Alcoa, Pittsburgh, Pennsylvania

LIGHT METAL AGE
April 1953
Aluminum -- 234,000 Sq. Ft. Of Stamping -- A Production Feat

LANDSCAPE ARCHITECTURE
July 1956
From Fort Pitt To Point Park: A Turning Point In The Physical Planning Of Pittsburgh

ARCHITECTURAL FORUM
February 1957
Projects Without Plans
Pittsburgh, long considered the Mecca of urban renewal, may have cleared smoked and erected a lot of buildings, but its lack of comprehensive plan is blocking a sustained renaissance.
Many wistful glances have been cast at Pittsburgh's civic progress by other cities struggling with the problems of urban redevelopment. But on closer inspection the methods that got this progress started don't look so good for the long haul that is still ahead. Neither do the architectural results thus far.

Highways without egress
Buildings without parking
A city without residents
Public spaces without the public
A boom without a masterplan

ARCHITECTURAL RECORD
February 1957
An Open Place At The Heart Of A City
Perhaps no American city has ever so much needed and, latterly, so much deserved a garden at its heart. This bright mosaic of water and terrazzo and green growth is giving back to the people of Pittsburgh something of their long-lost hill and river heritage.

Here is the light and open, the cool and almost quite space so often urged by planners and so seldom reclaimed from downtown congestion.
Here, too is a foreground for the buildings that surround the Square; for the new Alcoa building; for the buildings on east and west whose axial symmetries have so long awaited this vista;

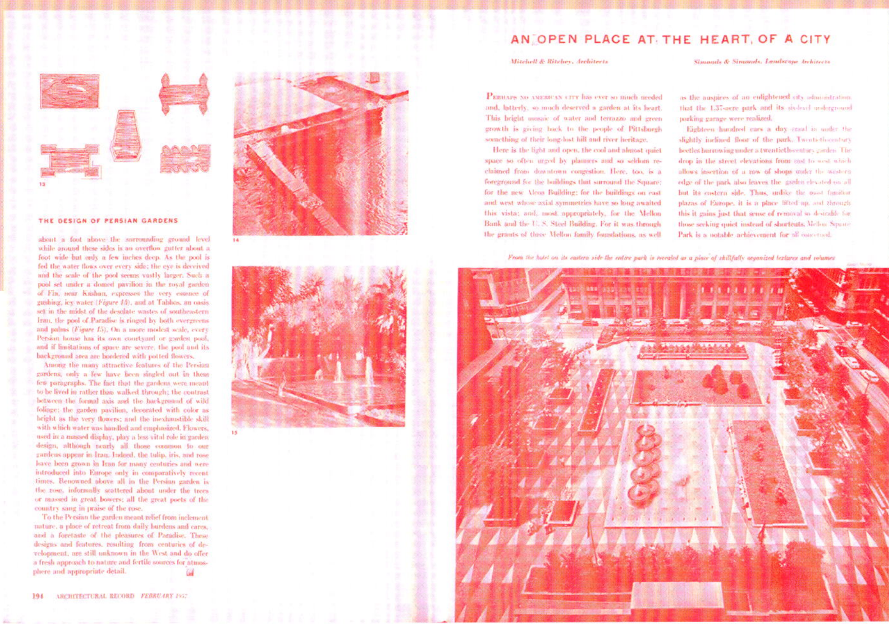
13

THE DESIGN OF PERSIAN GARDENS

about a foot above the surrounding ground level while around these sides is an overflow gutter about a foot wide but only a few inches deep. As the pool is fed the water flows over every side; the eye is deceived and the scale of the pool seems vastly larger. Such a pool set under a domed pavilion in the royal garden of Fin, near Kashan, expresses the very essence of gushing, icy water (*Figure 14*), and at Tabbas, an oasis set in the midst of the desolate wastes of southeastern Iran, the pool of Paradise is ringed by both evergreens and palms (*Figure 15*). On a more modest scale, every Persian house has its own courtyard or garden pool, and if limitations of space are severe, the pool and its background area are bordered with potted flowers.

Among the many attractive features of the Persian gardens, only a few have been singled out in these few paragraphs. The fact that the gardens were meant to be lived in rather than walked through; the contrast between the formal axis and the background of wild foliage; the garden pavilion, decorated with color as bright as the very flowers; and the inexhaustible skill with which water was handled and emphasized. Flowers, used in a massed display, play a less vital role in garden design, although nearly all those common to our gardens appear in Iran. Indeed, the tulip, iris, and rose have been grown in Iran for many centuries and were introduced into Europe only in comparatively recent times. Renowned above all in the Persian garden is the rose, informally scattered about under the trees or massed in great bowers; all the great poets of the country sang in praise of the rose.

To the Persian the garden meant relief from inclement nature, a place of retreat from daily burdens and cares, and a foretaste of the pleasures of Paradise. These designs and features, resulting from centuries of development, are still unknown in the West and do offer a fresh approach to nature and fertile sources for atmosphere and appropriate detail.

14

15

194 ARCHITECTURAL RECORD *FEBRUARY 1957*

AN OPEN PLACE AT THE HEART OF A CITY

Mitchell & Ritchey, Architects *Simonds & Simonds, Landscape Architects*

PERHAPS NO AMERICAN CITY has ever so much needed and, latterly, so much deserved a garden at its heart. This bright mosaic of water and terrazzo and green growth is giving back to the people of Pittsburgh something of their long-lost hill and river heritage.

Here is the light and open, the cool and almost quiet space so often urged by planners and so seldom reclaimed from downtown congestion. Here, too, is a foreground for the buildings that surround the Square; for the new Alcoa Building; for the buildings on east and west whose axial symmetries have so long awaited this vista; and, most appropriately, for the Mellon Bank and the U. S. Steel Building. For it was through the grants of three Mellon family foundations, as well as the auspices of an enlightened city administration that the 1.37-acre park and its six-level underground parking garage were realized.

Eighteen hundred cars a day crawl in under the slightly inclined floor of the park. Twentieth-century beetles burrowing under a twentieth-century garden. The drop in the street elevations from east to west which allows insertion of a row of shops under the western edge of the park also leaves the garden elevated on all but its eastern side. Thus, unlike the most familiar plazas of Europe, it is a place lifted up, and through this it gains just that sense of removal so desirable for those seeking quiet instead of shortcuts. Mellon Square Park is a notable achievement for all concerned.

From the hotel on its eastern side the entire park is revealed as a place of skillfully organized textures and volumes and, most appropriately, for the Mellon Bank and the U.S. Steel Building.

LANDSCAPE ARCHITECTURE
July 1958
Mellon Square: An Oasis In An Asphalt Desert
We live in The Age of The City. Few persons remain untouched by the fantastic growth of cities and their problems. Never was there greater challenge, never a greater opportunity for the professional architect. Thus the Editors of this Quarterly welcome to these pages a variety of authors whose views and proposals for 'Creating a Livable City' should offer clear guidelines to those who are planning tomorrow's landscape.

ARCHITECTURAL FORUM
June 1960
Some Progress In Pittsburgh
Perhaps more than any other urban renewal project in the U.S., the long-watched development of Pittsburgh's "Golden Triangle" has stood as a symbol of What Could Be Done. This idea of clearing a whole slum at the confluence of two rivers, and turning it into a shining new city-in-a-park, has fired the imagination of civic leaders elsewhere, as well as proving of immense promotional value to Pittsburgh itself. Sadly, however, no amount of stirring talk can dispel the feeling that Pittsburgh's mighty Point, brilliant in its first concept, has turned out to be pretty much of an architecture flop.

...Out of a disappointing collection of buildings, the new gold-tinted Hilton hotel steps forward to make a point.

ARCHITECTURAL FORUM
March 1961
Pittsburgh's Dome Gets Ready

ARCHITECTURAL RECORD
November 1961
Pittsburgh's Retractable Dome Now In Operation
Over 15 years ago architects Mitchell and Ritchey proposed that Pittsburgh build a civic auditorium with a retractable roof. Their idea which seemed far-fetched to many has at last been realized and Pittsburghers began to enjoy their indoor-outdoor arena this fall.

LANDSCAPE ARCHITECTURE
October 1962
Equitable Plaza, Pittsburgh

PROGRESSIVE ARCHITECTURE
January 1966
PA 13th Annual Design Awards Program: Award: Lower Hill Development For the Citizens Committee For District Renewal, Pittsburgh, Pennsylvania

A citizen-sponsored urban renewal scheme which the jury praised as creating a bold and imaginative image of the city, in the tradition of futurist urban architecture.

ARCHITECTURAL RECORD
April 1967
United States Steel Office Building, Pittsburgh, PA
Pittsburgh Skyscraper Achieves Breakthrough In Steel Fireproofing

CIVIL ENGINEERING ACSE
April 1970
U.S. Steel Headquarters Building

ENGINEERING NEWS RECORD
July 1970
Three Story Buildings Stacked In Triangular Frame
Big Steel stacks many buildings in one frame

ARCHITECTURAL RECORD
July 1971
Should Pittsburgh Save Forbes Field?
Seldom is it possible in the super-scale world of university planning and architecture to examine two alternative professional proposals for the same site. Seldom are the two schemes as bold and innovative as there; seldom do they spring from social premises so far apart. In effect the problems the University of Pittsburgh faces are problems faced by institutions all over the country which are trying to expand into communities that suddenly refuse to give way. Such conflicts can be resolved through reasoned public discussion, as in Pittsburgh; especially when architects are ready to explore and present viable alternatives.

INDUSTRIAL DESIGN
December 1971
Tripleheader
U.S. Steel's new headquarters presents three faces to the Pittsburgh skyline, and it may be the biggest thing to hit the town since the Pirates.

ARCHITECTURAL FORUM
December 1971
Big Steel Spike
The U.S. Steel Building is a symbol of both an industry and a city
From the outset, planning involved an "innovations committee," in close touch with the corporation product, engineering, and construction divisions. The architects were brought into the process at the same time as the engineers, the building managers, and the contractor (who worked on a negotiated bid basis). The structural innovations can be attributed largely to Engineers Skilling, Helle, Christianson & Robertson, whose structural audacity can also been seen in New York's World Trade Center and the Federal Reserve Bank of Minneapolis.

IN SOLEMN SILHOUETTE, Richard King Mellon, head of Pittsburgh's patriarchal clan and guardian of its $8,500,000,000 holdings, poses at the window of his office. The sharpness of his profile matches that of the view—the Gateway Center development on the site of an old commercial slum.

IN OPEN SUNLIGHT, a portion of Pittsb Golden Triangle basks in a dramatic bath o such as it never knew when the city lived ur perpetual industrial smog. Here the renas started—a county-wide schedule of improve that will cost a staggering $2,760,000,000

PITTSBURGH

The city that quick-changed from unbelievable ugliness to shining beauty in less than half a generation

by Herbert Kubly

PHOTOGRAPHS BY BURT GLINN

• The plane flying west followed the glistening silver ribbon of the Monongahela below. I noted the air was pure and bright. We descended gently, toward forested hills so green it was like coming down on County Limerick. We glided over the runway toward a new five-decker terminal, modern and hygienic as a biscuit factory. Waving from the observation platform was my long-time friend, Mary Shaw Marohnic.

My visit to America's traditionally most ill-favored city was a kind of homecoming, like a man returning to make peace with his people. I am a Wisconsin native, but I am often tempted, when asked where I was born, to reply, "Pittsburgh." It would be an untruth truer than true, for spiritually I was born here. I was an unfledged college graduate when I came to Pittsburgh for my first job, as a newspaper reporter, and stayed five years. Since then I have lived in many other cities but I have never learned to know one so well, nor to love and hate one so much. Now I was returning for a birthday—Pittsburgh's two hundredth—and to see for myself the renaissance that was turning the old "Mellon Patch" into "Mellon's Miracle."

For me, Mary Shaw symbolizes Pittsburgh. She is a large, hearty woman descended from pioneer families, the English Irwins and the Irish Shaws, both of which have streets named after them. She married a first-generation Croatian whose family came with the great tide of Eastern European laborers to the mills and mines. "The blood was running thin in my group," she says, "and those Slavs had such straight backs." She is an artist who paints the hills and mills, the rivers and buildings of her city with relentless affection. One summer vacation she sent her son to work in a mill. "No young man has a right to live in Pittsburgh without at least once making steel," she told him. "I want you to understand your roots."

As she drove me over a new parkway toward the city, I remembered, too vividly for pleasure, my first arrival from a Wisconsin farm. Awe and panic were my emotions then, as the train clicked up the black, malodorous canyon of the Ohio River and creaked over a trestle into the old brown station. A doctor at home had warned me of evils that stalk youths in cities, so I went straight from the train to a room at the Y.M.C.A.—around the corner from roaring Diamond Street (now Forbes Avenue), a casbah of low bars, burlesque and girls. In the morning I reported for work on the police beat of the *Sun-Telegraph*, and met assistant city editor William "Fuzzy" Pfarr, a mercurial old-timer with a robust allergy to college men.

One evening that first week I saw an explosion of flames in the night sky and ran to a phone to report a very big fire. "Gee whiz, thanks," said Pfarr, after I'd explained where the blaze seemed to be. "Hop a cab and get right over there." I raced to my first big story—and found that the volcano in the sky was a Jones and Laughlin blast furnace. Pittsburgh in those days was a sooty Klondike of blackened buildings over which a pillar of smoke hung by day and a pillar of fire by night. The "Golden Triangle," named for its concentration of banks, was golden only to those few who amassed their gold under its clouds. To the rest it was, in words attributed to Charles Dickens, "Hell with the lid lifted."

I thought sadly how Fuzzy Pfarr, like many of my other *Sun-Tele* colleagues, was dead. The road rolled down green hills into a dark valley of cinders and piled-up railroad cars. We wove our way through a tangle of bridges under which lean, unpainted houses reached into air and light like thin yellow plants growing in a

Continued on Page 83

05

Photography

Perhaps the most striking and omnipresent medium for Pittsburgh's transformation in these years was the camera lens, wielded by professionals, amateurs, locals, and visitors alike to register unique stories of the changing city. Civic institutions marshalled the power of photography to create positive images of Pittsburgh's transformation for a national audience, while corporations and private clients commissioned photographers to promote buildings, objects, products, and public spaces. Through these images, the modern city was imagined through the fleeting expressions of passersby, the sweat of workers, or an unexpected reflection of a neighboring building in a new facade.

Local press and studio photographers documented the faces and streetscapes of urban renewal and its often contentious reception by the public, significantly including its impact on the city's communities of color. Chief among these chroniclers was Charles "Teenie" Harris, a prolific photographer who captured nuanced views of African-American life in Pittsburgh. Born in the city's Lower Hill district, Harris documented the city's civil rights decades and the tumultuous changes of urban renewal. In his work as a photojournalist for the *Pittsburgh Courier*, Harris was part of the newspaper's early efforts to highlight housing problems in the Lower Hill through visual essays on substandard properties and tenant protests. In later years, when his contemporaries at other newspapers continued to focus on urban dilapidation and poverty, Harris's images offered a counter-narrative through his documentation of the richness of culture and community life in so-called "blighted" neighborhoods.

In the same years, the *Pittsburgh Post-Gazette* and the *Pittsburgh Press* employed photojournalists whose prolific black-and-white images told compelling visual stories about the city's transformation. Paul Slantis, like Harris a native Pittsburgher, amassed a diverse collection of images for the *Post-Gazette* over a career that spanned five decades. His photographs—including unique views of the subterranean construction of Mellon Square and public appearances by eminent politicians like Mayor David Lawrence—often went beyond the traditionally glossy views of a transformed city, revealing the frequently rough road that led there.

In 1950, the Allegheny Conference on Community Development funded and commissioned the Pittsburgh Photographic Library (PPL), an ambitious effort to comprehensively document the "Renaissance" underway in the city. Roy Stryker, who had been responsible for commissioning poignant images of American life as the Information Director for the U.S. Farm Security Administration during the Great Depression, was hired to lead the project. Headquartered at the University of Pittsburgh, Stryker oversaw a team of photographers including Harold Corsini, James Blair, and Clyde "Red" Hare that systematically documented the city's changing neighborhoods, amassing over 18,000 images of Pittsburgh between 1950 and 1952. Styker was clear about the primary role of photography in both documenting and imagining the modern in Pittsburgh:

> No other city has ever attempted to make such a use of photography, and I think it significant that the camera—itself an offspring of modern technology—should be considered to have a real function in a great industrial center which is beginning to examine itself critically and carefully planning for the future.[1]

The broad ambitions of the PPL project, however, belied conflicts among its photographers about how best to represent the city's ongoing transformation. For example, Hare, a young photographer who began his career at the PPL at the age of 23, recalled that Stryker would reject images by the team that he felt did not adequately capture "social responsibility." Hare's later images juxtaposed the remains of demolished buildings with the gleaming architecture of the new city, and he spoke of sneaking into the PPL office at night to erase Stryker's "kill" marks on his photographs.[2] Stryker's social motivations ultimately diverged from the Allegheny Conference's demand for "progress pictures," and he left the project after only two years as its director.

Beginning at the turn of the twentieth century, Brady Stewart Studio (BSS) served as the local commercial photography studio in the Steel City. Brady Wilson Stewart, a native Pittsburgher, opened his business on Liberty Ave in 1920 and soon became a fixture at local events, regularly greeted by politicians such as Mayor Lawrence. Under the leadership of his son, Brady Stewart Jr., and later his grandsons Brady and Mike, the studio amassed an archive of the city's history over seven decades through wide-ranging commissions of commercial products, advertisements, and architectural documentation. The BSS collection also represents the perspectives of local photographers whose side ventures included regular trips to Mt. Washington—providing a timeline of annual images of the changing Pittsburgh skyline—and photographs of daily life, including church services, philanthropic events, and street activity in new suburban communities.

W. Eugene Smith arrived in Pittsburgh in 1955, shortly after ending his stormy fifteen-year tenure as a photographer for *Life* magazine. Known for his often contentious relationships with magazine editors and others who commissioned his work, Smith arrived in the city looking for professional and artistic redemption against the backdrop of a city that was itself undergoing profound change. Smith had been hired by Stefan Lorant to produce a specially commissioned body of photographs for the voluminous *Pittsburgh: Story of an American City* (1964), an imprint of the Allegheny Conference on Community Development. Yet Smith soon went far beyond Lorant's assignment, immersing himself deeply within the industrial and urban life of the city. A Guggenheim grant in 1956 further expanded the scope of what he termed his "Pittsburgh Project," ultimately producing over 17,000 images. Smith's powerful, often haunting photographs captured both melancholy and extraordinary beauty in Pittsburgh's streets and factories, testament to a personal struggle to discover the city's essential character through photographs that might form "a part of the teaming into the teeming whole that is the city."[3]

Joining the iconic designers of the mid-twentieth century was a roster of architectural photographers, famous in their own right, who sought to elevate the buildings they documented to the status of modernist masterworks. Ezra Stoller and Joseph Molitor were among those commissioned most frequently to photograph significant new architecture in Pittsburgh. Both were trained as architects, which influenced their unique ability to capture buildings with a striking singularity of vision. Stoller developed sustained relationships with the architects and firms whose work he helped make famous, including Harrison & Abramovitz and Gordon Bunshaft of Skidmore, Owings & Merrill (SOM). The U.S. Steel Building, Four Gateway Center, and SOM's unbuilt proposal for the Pittsburgh Center for the Arts were among the Pittsburgh projects "Stollerized" through the photographer's lens. Molitor, who practiced as a designer for twelve years before turning to photography, also had a client list that constituted a Who's Who of mid-century U.S. architects. In Pittsburgh, Molitor's photographs captured the unique qualities of the IBM Building by Curtis and Davis, highlighting its sleek interiors and innovative diagrid facade of diamond-shaped panels.

1 Roy Stryker in a letter quoted in "The Pittsburgh Photographic Library." Info-Ren.org. info-ren.org/projects/btul/exhibit/photog13.html. Accessed June 17, 2015.

2 Constance Schulz and Steven Plattner, eds. *Witness to the Fifties The Pittsburgh Photographic Library, 1950–1953* (Pittsburgh: University of Pittsburgh Press, 1999). 12

3 As quoted in Jeremy Lybarger "Doomed to Pittsburgh: W. Eugene Smith in the City of Steel," BeltMag.com beltmag.com/doomed-to-pittsburgh-w-eugene-smith-in-the-city-of-steel/. Accessed June 16, 2015.

Members of Pittsburgh Housing Authority and politicians pulling rope attached to pillar of dilapidated house, with workers on porch, porch roof, and roof, Kirkpatrick Street, Hill District,
Charles "Teenie" Harris, 1951.

‹ **Boy holding a sign inscribed "Give to all, all at once, jobs,"** Charles "Teenie" Harris, 1961–70.

⌄ **Protesters, including Rev. Bill Powell, James McCoy, Mal Goode, and Byrd Brown**, Charles "Teenie" Harris, October 1961.

Lynette May, Gerri Walker, Shirley Jenkins, and Alberta Thompson hitting golf balls at Washington Plaza putting field, with Civic Arena in the background, Charles "Teenie" Harris, August 1969.

› **Plans for Downtown Renaissance**, Paul Slantis, 1950.

⌄ **Construction of Mellon Square Park**, Paul Slantis, 1954–55.

˅ **Mellon Square Dedication**, Paul Slantis, October 18, 1955.

‹ **City Council Chamber, City Council Building,**
W. Eugene Smith, 1955–57.

Self-Portrait, Pittsburgh, W. Eugene Smith, 1955–56.

Industry: Riveters at Work on Steel Framework of New Building at Gateway Center, Clyde Hare, 1951.

Downtown: Mellon Park Site before Demolition, Clyde Hare, 1952.

Downtown Street Scene: U.S. Steel-Mellon Building William Penn Way, Clyde Hare, 1953.

USS
USS
USS
USS

Demolition of Old Buildings and Gateway Center Construction, Clyde Hare, 1951.

^ **Allegheny Conference on Community Development Meeting at the Duquesne Club,**
Clyde Hare, 1951.

Brady Stewart Studio on location for Morton Frozen Pies at Gateway Center in downtown Pittsburgh,
Brady Stewart Studio Inc., 1957.

Easter services in Civic Arena,
Brady Stewart Studio Inc., 1963.

^ **LeMont Restaurant,**
Brady Stewart Studio Inc., 1962.

> **Mellon Square,**
Brady Stewart Studio Inc., 1955.

^ **Aerial view of Pittsburgh and the Gateway Towers construction,** Brady Stewart Studio Inc., 1964.

> **View of the Christmas promotion at Horne's department store in downtown Pittsburgh,** Brady Stewart Studio Inc., 1962.

⌄ **View of the first Light Up Night in Pittsburgh,** Brady Stewart Studio Inc., 1960.

< **March on MLK Jr. National Day of Mourning,** Charles R. Martin, April 7, 1968.

^ **March on MLK Jr. National Day of Mourning,** Charles R. Martin, April 7, 1968.

> **Aerial view of Oakland,** Aerial Photographs, 1930.

Point State Park Bridge, photographer unknown, 1935–80.

United States Steel-Mellon Building during construction, Shrader Studios, Inc., 1949-50.

Alcoa Building under construction, Newman-Schmidt Studios, November 15, 1951.

˅ **Aerial view of Allegheny Center**,
A. Church Photographers,
September 26, 1968.

Pittsburgh Hilton Hotel under construction, Altwater & Brothers Photographers, April 1, 1959.

‹ **Golden Triangle's Transformation**, George L. Bower, July 21, 1954.

⌄ **Allegheny Conference on Community Development Display**, photographer unknown, September 16, 1949.

^ **Lower Hill District Clearance near Completion**, John R. Shrader, August 1957.

< **New Townhouses under Construction**, Paul Russell Photography, 1935–1980.

Crosstown Boulevard,
James McClain,
November 23, 1964.

> **Two Allegheny Center**, Alcoa - Public Relations Department, April 1971.

⌄ **Allegheny Center Public Square**, Balthazar Korab, 1935–80.

^ **Fountain at Point State Park looking toward the North Side,** photographer unknown, 1974.

> **Pennley Park Apartments,** photographer unknown, 1935–80.

< **Aerial view of the Lower Hill**, photographer unknown, n.d.

‹ **View from the back of the Public Auditorium**, photographer unknown, October 11, 1960.

˅ **Gateway Center under construction**, Harold Corsini, 1947–52.

› **Four Gateway Center, exterior, facade, from below**, Ezra Stoller, 1961.

MELLON BANK
EXIT ONLY
GROGSHOP

‹ **Westinghouse Tower, exterior, main entrance**, Ezra Stoller, 1971.

⌄ **Four Gateway Center, exterior, view of plaza from above**, Ezra Stoller, 1961.

» **U.S. Steel Tower, exterior, glasswork, detail**, Ezra Stoller, 1971.

⋙ **U.S. Steel Tower, exterior, facade**, Ezra Stoller, 1970.

< **IBM Building Pittsburgh**, Joseph Molitor, 1969.

^ **Civic Auditorium**, Joseph Molitor, 1961.

> **Mellon Square Park, night view of shops**, Joseph Molitor, 1956.

>> **IBM Building, front elevation**, Joseph Molitor, 1969.

IBM

CONTRACTING ENGINEERS
IBM

Pittsburgh Projects

Sites

A compilation of built, unbuilt, proposed, and demolished projects provides a rich history of the city's transformation during the past century. When overlaid with traces of what was and what might have been, a map of Pittsburgh reveals that the concentration of the era's efforts was localized to six areas of the city. In each of these neighborhoods, differing circumstances and constraints resulted in urban interventions that varied widely in their methods of planning and execution, as well as in their perceived success or failure.

The building texts in this section were written by Adam Himes, Phillip Denny, Martin Aurand, and Rami el Samahy.

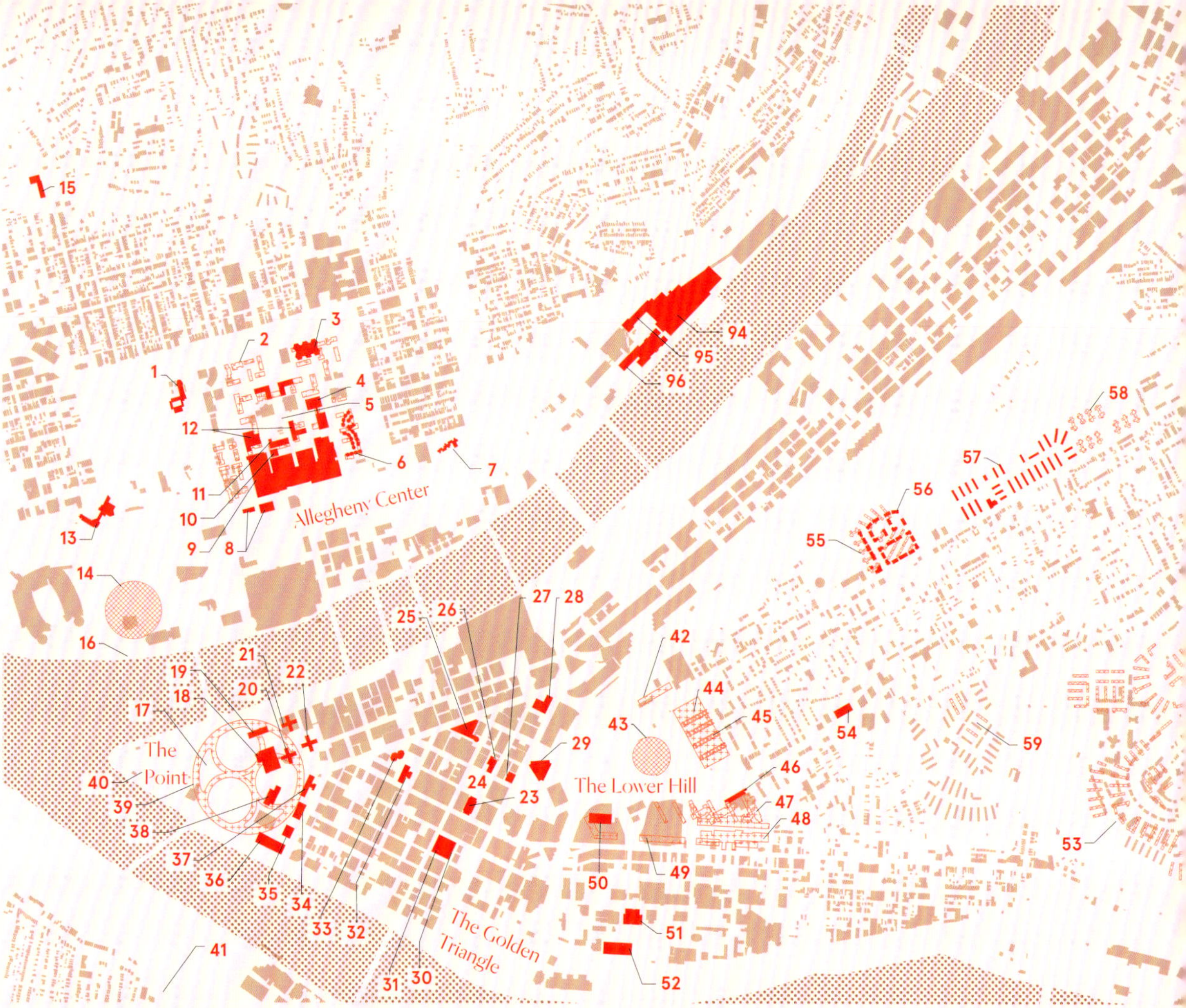

1 **Aviary Conservatory** 1969 Simonds and Simonds
2 **Allegheny Center Masterplan** 1966 Deeter Ritchey Sippel
3 **Martin Luther King Jr Elementary School** 1973 Liff, Justh and Chetlin
4 **East Commons Professional Building** 1976 Office of Mies van der Rohe
5 **Allegheny Public Square** 1966 William Breger
6 **Allegheny Commons East** 1974 Tasso Katselas
7 **Pressley Street High Rise** 1970 Tasso Katselas
8 **Central Heating and Cooling Plant** 1966 Deeter Ritchey Sippel
9 **Allegheny Center Commercial Complex** 1965 Deeter Ritchey Sippel
10 **Pittsburgh National Bank** 1966 Skidmore, Owings & Merrill
11 **One Allegheny Center** 1966 Deeter Ritchey Sippel
12 **Three Seven Eight and Ten Allegheny Center Apartments** 1967, 71, 73 Deeter Ritchey Sippel
13 **CCAC Allegheny Campus** 1973 Tasso Katselas
14 **Three Rivers Stadium** 1970 Deeter Ritchey Sippel
15 **Columbus School** 1967 Curry & Martin
16 **Riverfront Park** 1971 Deeter Ritchey Sippel
17 **Portal Bridge** 1963 Charles & Edward Stotz
18 **Wyndham Grand Hotel** 1959 William B. Tabler
19 **Gateway Towers** 1964 Emery Roth & Sons
20 **Three Gateway Center** 1952 Eggers & Higgins
21 **One Gateway Center** 1952 Eggers & Higgins
22 **Two Gateway Center** 1952 Eggers & Higgins
23 **525 William Penn Place** 1951 Harrison & Abramovitz
24 **Mellon Square** 1955 Simonds and Simonds
25 **Smithfield Liberty Garage** 1965 Altenhof & Brown
26 **Alcoa Building** 1953 Harrison & Abramovitz
27 **Porter Building** 1958 Harrison & Abramovitz
28 **Federal Building** 1964 Altenhof & Brown
29 **U.S. Steel Building** 1971 Harrison, Abramovitz & Abbe
30 **Kaufmann's Self-Service Garage** 1949 Frank Lloyd Wright
31 **Kaufmann's Department Store** 1946 Mitchell & Ritchey
32 **PNB Tower** 1972 Welton Becket
33 **Equibank Building** 1975 SOM
34 **Bell Telephone Building** 1957 Dowler & Dowler
35 **IBM Building** 1963 Curtis & Davi
36 **Westinghouse Building** 1969 Harrison & Abramovitz
37 **Four Gateway Center** 1960 Harrison & Abramovitz
38 **State Office Building** 1957 Altenhof & Brown
39 **Point Park Civic Center** 1947/194 Frank Lloyd Wright
40 **Point State Park** 1974 Ralph Griswold et al.
41 **Grandview Avenue Overlooks** 1968 Ralph Griswold et al.
42 **Lower Hill Cultural Center Master Plan** 1953 Mitchell & Ritchey
43 **Civic Arena** 1961 Mitchell & Ritchey, Simonds and Simonds
44 **Center for the Arts** 1966 Skidmore, Owings & Merrill
45 **Lower Hill Development** 1968 Citizens Committee for Hill District Renewal, Troy West
46 **Washington Plaza Apartments** 1964 I. M. Pei & Associates

Washington Plaza Master Plan 1964 I. M. Pei & Associates
Our Way Housing 1971 Community Design Associates
Lower Hill Cultural Center Master Plan 1953 Mitchell & Ritchey
Chatham Center 1966 William Lescaze
Duquesne Union 1967 Paul Schweikher
R.K. Mellon Hall of Science 1968 Ludwig Mies van der Rohe
Terrace Village 1941
Hill House Center 1973 Walter Roberts
Bedford Dwellings 1940
Bedford Dwellings Additions 1954
Bedford Dwellings 1940
Bedford Dwellings 1940
Terrace Village 1941
Trees Hall 1965 Deeter Ritchey Sippel
Panther Hollow Project 1963 Harrison & Abramovitz

62 **Forbes Field Alternate Plan** 1972 Community Design Associates
63 **Forbes Complex Master Plan** 1968 Deeter Ritchey Sippel
64 **Posvar Hall** 1978 Celli-Flynn & Associates, Johnstone Newcomer & Valentour, Campbell Green Cunzolo
65 **Barco Law Building** 1976 B. Kenneth Johnstone et al.
66 **Lawrence Hall** 1968 B. Kenneth Johnstone et al.
67 **Tower Residence Halls** 1963 Deeter Ritchey Sippel
68 **M.L. Benedum Hall** 1971 Deeter Ritchey Sippel
69 **Learning Research and Development Center** 1974 Harrison & Abramovitz
70 **Hillman Library** 1968 Celli-Flynn & Associates
71 **Sarah Mellon Scaife Gallery** 1974 Edward Larrabee Barnes
72 **Information Sciences Building** 1965 Tasso Katselas

73 **PNB Craig Street** 1962 SOM
74 **Graphic Arts Technical Center** 1965 WTW
75 **Wean Hall** 1971 Deeter Ritchey Sippel
76 **Fine Arts Complex** 1970 Paul Schweikher
77 **Warner Hall** 1966 Charles Luckman
78 **Fraternity Quadrangle** 1970 Curry & Martin
79 **Skibo Building** 1960 Lawrie & Green
80 **Donner Hall** 1954 Mitchell & Ritchey
81 **Graduate School of Industrial Administration** 1952 B. Kenneth Johnstone et al.
82 **Hunt Library** 1961 Lawrie & Green
83 **J.K. Mellon Library** 1973 B. Kenneth Johnstone et al.
84 **Squirrel Hill Library** 1972 Liff Justh & Chetlin

85 **East Mall Residential Tower Apartments** 1971 Tasso Katselas
86 **Penn Plaza Apartments** 1967 Tasso Katselas
87 **Pennley Park** 1965 Tasso Katselas
88 **Friendship Plaza Building** 1966 Howard But and Hill
89 **Carnegie Library of Pittsburgh** 1968 Liff Justh & Chetlin
90 **East Liberty Pedestrian Mall** 1969 Simonds and Simonds
91 **Penn Circle Tower Apartments** 1971 Tasso Katselas
92 **Liberty Park Apartments** 1971 Tasso Katselas
93 **Reizenstein School** 1975 Walter Roberts
94 **Heinz Warehouse** 1952 Skidmore, Owings & Merrill
95 **Heinz Vinegar Plant** 1952 Skidmore, Owings & Merrill
96 **Riley Research Center** 1958 Skidmore, Owings & Merrill

[W]hen the air was cleared and the black ugly confusion of the Point was revealed in full sunlight, a civic shudder shook the citizens... A complete new life, urban reincarnation, was the only hope. This was the challenge—a drastic challenge requiring equally drastic measures.

Ralph Griswold

Landscape architect and superintendent of the Pittsburgh Bureau of Parks, 1956

THE POINT

The aptly named Point, where Pittsburgh was founded and the Monongahela and the Allegheny Rivers converge to form the Ohio River, developed into a major node in the city's industrial network. By the 1930s, however, pollution, abandoned railroad structures, underused warehouses, dilapidated housing, and periodic flooding had brought the Point to a state of disrepair, and it soon became a focus for government and business-led redevelopment efforts.

Following a number of studies, including two bold designs by Frank Lloyd Wright and a Robert Moses plan that placed the Point at the center of an automobile-driven metropolis, civic leaders proposed Point State Park and Gateway Center. The former, a state-designated 36-acre parcel, was designed by an impressive group of local, national, and international landscape architects, architects, and engineers, including Ralph Griswold and Skidmore, Owings & Merrill's Gordon Bunshaft. Point State Park, which opened in 1974, features an iconic fountain at the Point's tip.

To the east of the park, Equitable Life, a New York-based insurance company that was committed to large-scale investment in Pittsburgh, developed twenty-three acres of land. Gateway Center became a commercial and high-end residential development that epitomized modern life through its architecture, landscape, and planning. Its distinctive modernist buildings included three cruciform towers, the IBM Building with its "diagrid" facade of diamond-shaped panels, and the massive Westinghouse Building. Gateway Center was considered a huge success, and became a model for urban renewal throughout the nation. The Point's revitalization embodied hopes for a competitive business climate for Pittsburgh and increased employment in the city center, and the potential spread of this growth to other parts of the city.

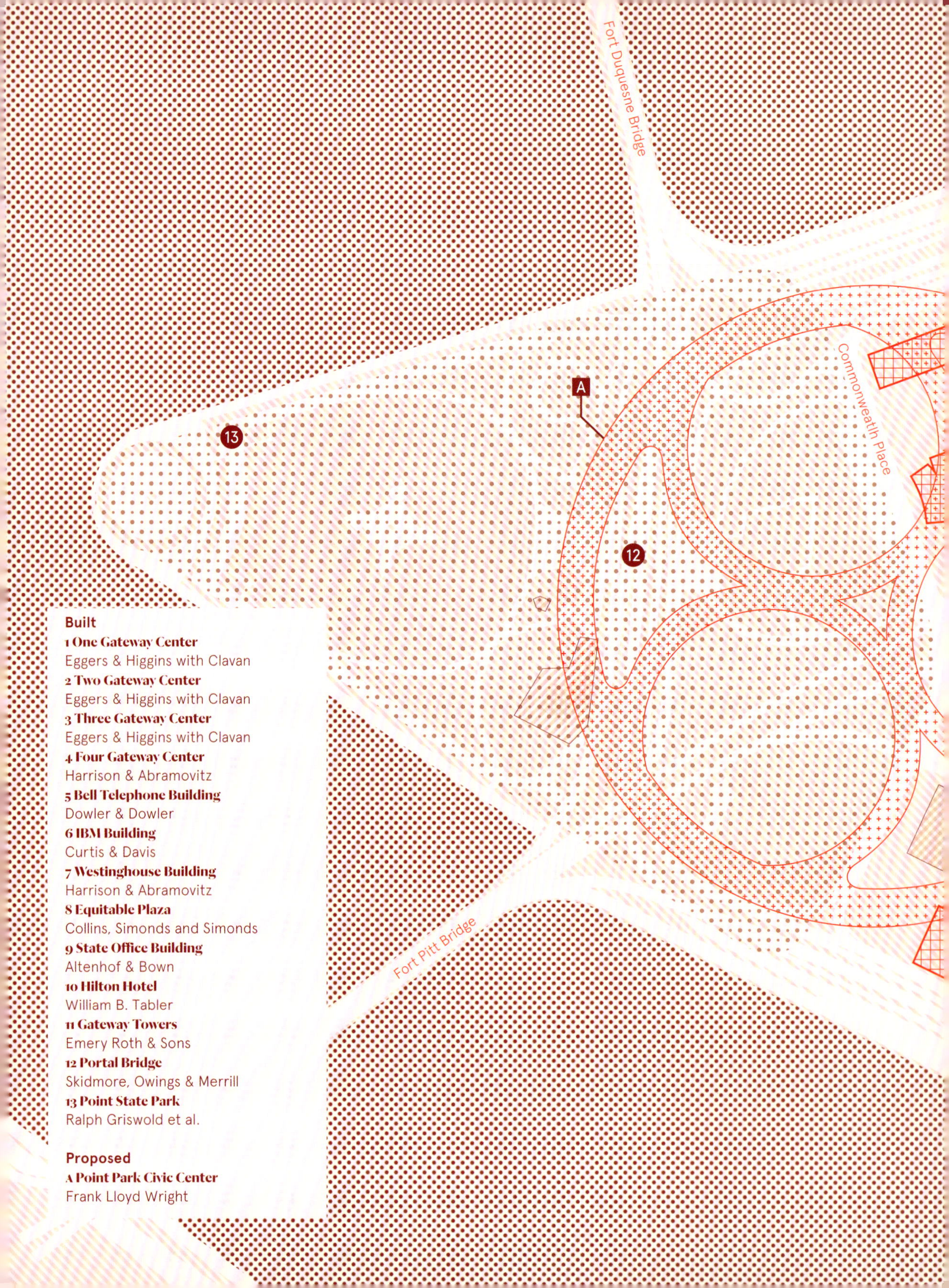

Built

1 One Gateway Center
Eggers & Higgins with Clavan
2 Two Gateway Center
Eggers & Higgins with Clavan
3 Three Gateway Center
Eggers & Higgins with Clavan
4 Four Gateway Center
Harrison & Abramovitz
5 Bell Telephone Building
Dowler & Dowler
6 IBM Building
Curtis & Davis
7 Westinghouse Building
Harrison & Abramovitz
8 Equitable Plaza
Collins, Simonds and Simonds
9 State Office Building
Altenhof & Bown
10 Hilton Hotel
William B. Tabler
11 Gateway Towers
Emery Roth & Sons
12 Portal Bridge
Skidmore, Owings & Merrill
13 Point State Park
Ralph Griswold et al.

Proposed

A Point Park Civic Center
Frank Lloyd Wright

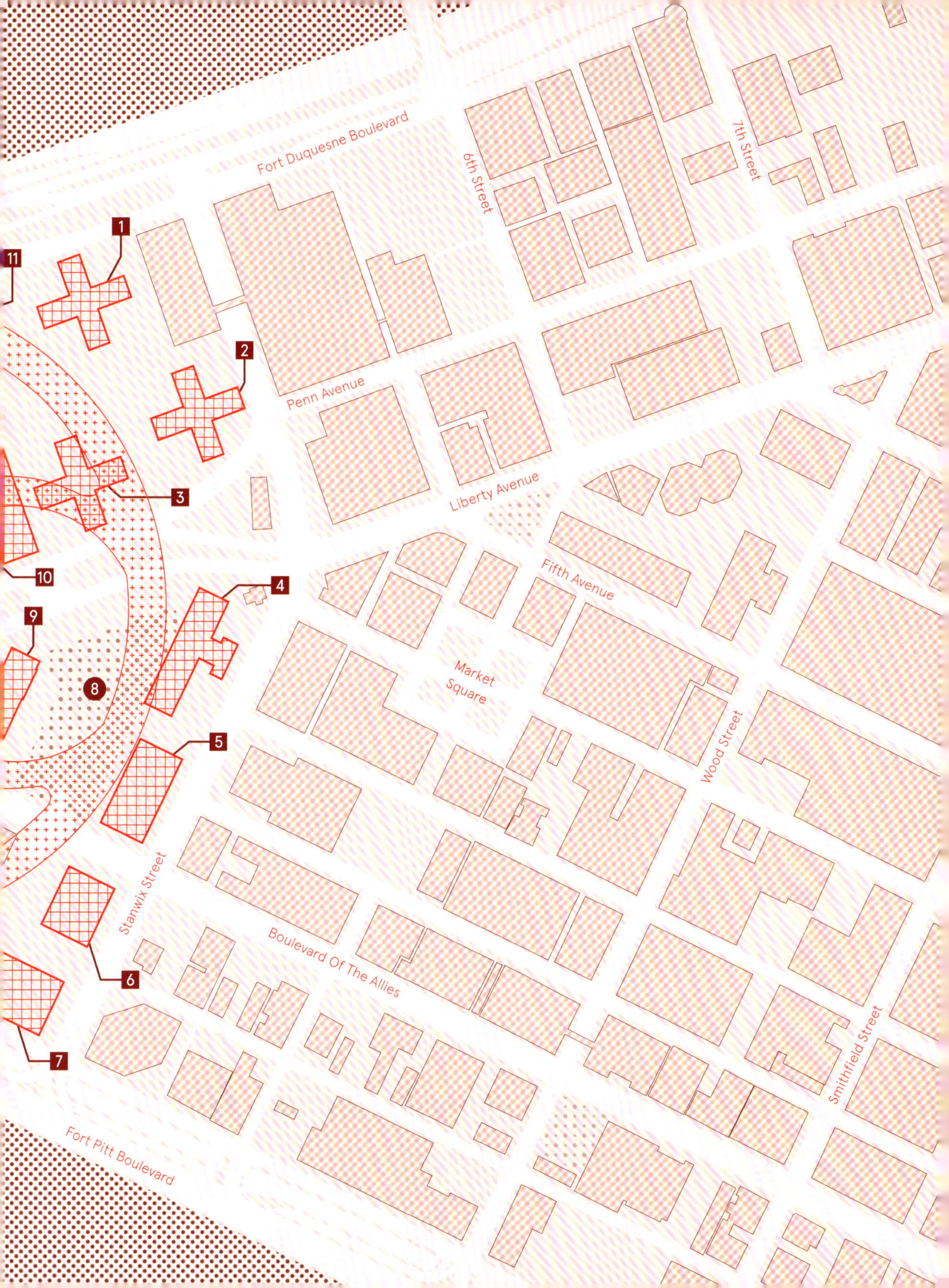

Fort Duquesne Boulevard
6th Street
7th Street
Penn Avenue
Liberty Avenue
Fifth Avenue
Market Square
Wood Street
Stanwix Street
Boulevard Of The Allies
Smithfield Street
Fort Pitt Boulevard
1
2
3
4
5
6
7
8
9
10
11

THE POINT

Point Park Civic Center

Frank Lloyd Wright, 1947, 1948

In 1946, at Edgar J. Kaufmann's behest, the City of Pittsburgh commissioned Frank Lloyd Wright to design a civic center at the Point that would incorporate plans to restore the colonial-era forts and address concerns about vehicular congestion. Wright did neither, responding instead with a proposal for a massive concrete spiral wrapped around an agglomeration of an opera house, planetarium, exhibition hall, and sports arena, and topped by a giant park and fountain. The structure was to be over 1,000 feet in diameter. To travel between each of its fifteen levels would have required a 4.5-mile circumnavigation through ramps lined with shops and parking. Two triple-decked river bridges—separating trucks from cars with pedestrians on top—would be cantilevered from the concrete spiral. A 500-foot tower would jut out toward a second circular building at the tip of the Point, with a semi-submerged aquarium, an insectarium, an openable amphitheater for the Civic Light Opera, and another rooftop fountain.

Dubbed by Wright the "Point Park Coney Island in Automobile Scale," it was a paean to vehicular infatuation, but utterly failed to meet the client's expectations and was both structurally dubious and wildly beyond budget. Sent back to the drafting board, Wright returned in 1948 with a "simplified" scheme featuring a central 100-foot tower, which supported two cable-stayed bridges. The giant spiral ramp was eliminated, but its footprint remained as a parking podium for the tower and surrounding parkland. The project was canceled soon after.

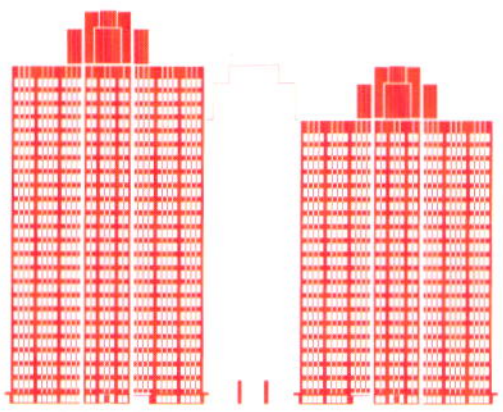

1, 2 & 3 Gateway Center

Eggers & Higgins with Irwin Clavan, 1952

Thirty years after Le Corbusier's radical proposal for sixty-story cruciform towers for the Ville Contemporaine, three similar towers (albeit at a third of the scale) were realized in Pittsburgh's Gateway Center through the banal agencies of real estate values and construction efficiencies. Though credited to architects Eggers & Higgins and Irwin Clavan, neither they nor any other architect were consulted on the project for the first twenty-nine months of its development; the cruciform plan, column spacing, floor-to-floor heights, and fenestration were all determined beforehand by a combination of real estate developers and building and construction managers. The architects were tasked with deciding the orientation, grouping, heights, and material palette of the towers as well as their relationship to parking and ground-level retail.

Though nine nearly identical towers were originally proposed in 1947, only three were realized—one twenty-four-story tower and two twenty-story towers. They were the first buildings to be clad in a chromium-stainless steel skin, intended to symbolize the Steel City at the newly prominent Point. This skin and the entire exterior wall system were prefabricated into panels, allowing the buildings to be erected at a rate of one floor a day. The towers were generously spread across a six-acre public garden designed by landscape architects Clarke & Rapuano. Criticized for its retrograde formal axes and central fountain, the park's geometry evokes the colonial-era King's Gardens that once occupied the site adjacent to Fort Pitt.

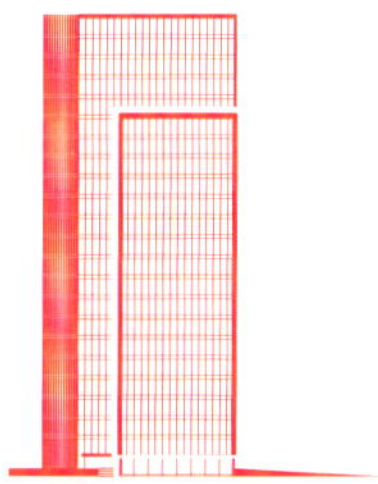

4 Gateway Center

Harrison & Abramovitz, 1960

Though commissioned by the Equitable Life Assurance Society, this addition to the Gateway Center eschews the cruciform plan of the company's original three office towers. Designed by Max Abramovitz, the twenty-two-story building is separated into two parts: an office slab clad in green-tinted glass and a service tower clad in opaque stainless steel. The separation of elevators and restrooms into the service tower freed the entirety of the slab's floor space for offices. The green glazing is complemented by stainless steel mullions that run the full height of the building, accentuating its verticality. The folded stainless steel cladding of the service tower echoes this upward thrust.

Like its predecessors, 1, 2, & 3 Gateway Center, 4 Gateway Center stands in a public park-like environment, which Equitable believed to be good for business and a generator of goodwill. Equitable Plaza, a modernist urban plaza with geometrically patterned hardscape and highly irregular planting beds, is a striking landscape setting for a modern office tower. Like their earlier design for Mellon Square, landscape architects Collins, Simonds and Simonds designed Equitable Plaza to conceal an underground parking garage.

Portal Bridge

Charles Stotz, Gordon Bunshaft for Skidmore, Owings & Merrill, 1963

In 1953 engineer George Richardson and his team determined that a network of freeways would conjoin in an elevated passage across the new Point State Park; but they did not resolve the design of an underpass needed to facilitate pedestrian access through the park. Architect and historian Charles Stotz and his brother, engineer Edward Stotz Jr., were called on to design this connection because of their involvement with the excavation and preservation of Fort Pitt and the development of the park. Henry J. Heinz II suggested that the Stotzes collaborate with Gordon Bunshaft, of Skidmore, Owings & Merrill, who was designing a research center for his factory at the time.

Bunshaft proposed a long, low arch, which was developed into the Portal Bridge, a succession of three curved concrete vaults spanning 182 feet and perfectly framing a view of the great fountain that was built at the Point. The low-slung arch required an innovative structural approach: four massive concrete blocks were buried at each end of the portal to handle the extreme spring loads, and each pair of opposing blocks was tied together by seventy-five steel cables buried beneath the passageway. The area beneath the arch was filled with a shallow reflecting pool traversed by a low footbridge at its center. Because the water would need to be drained in winter, stones were laid on the bottom of the pool in a "fish-scale" pattern. Fluted light vessels at the pool's edges light the vaults above.

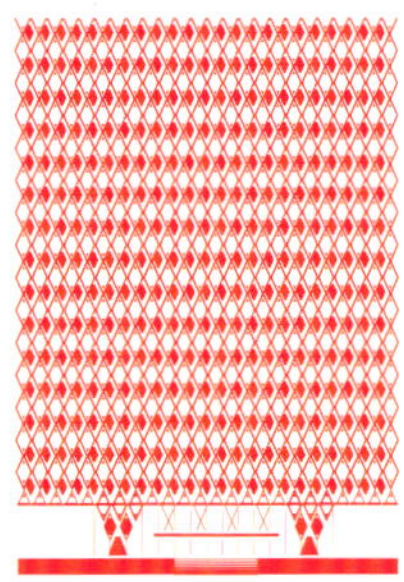

IBM Building

Curtis & Davis, 1963

Formerly the IBM Building, and now fittingly the headquarters of the United Steelworkers, this gem of a building beautifully expresses the structural potential of steel. Each exterior wall is composed of a diamond grid of steel infilled with alternating bands of opaque and transparent glass. Five varieties of steel are used to accommodate differing loads, which are brought to the ground via two concrete pylons on each side of the building. The structural facades free the interior from all vertical supports except the central core, eliminating 200 tons of steel when compared to typical frame construction. This approach met IBM's desire for flexible office space in the six floors it leased from the Equitable Life Assurance Company (the building being the fifth in the latter company's Gateway Center development). The regular grid also enabled the prefabrication of large portions of the facades off-site, simplifying on-site construction.

Here and elsewhere, IBM cultivated a modernist architectural image under the leadership of designer Eliot Noyes. Curtis & Davis, a noted modernist architectural firm from New Orleans, designed the Pittsburgh building. Structural engineer Leslie E. Robertson, of Worthington, Skilling, Helle & Jackson, designed the exoskeleton, a technical precursor of his designs for the World Trade Center in New York City and Pittsburgh's U.S. Steel Tower.

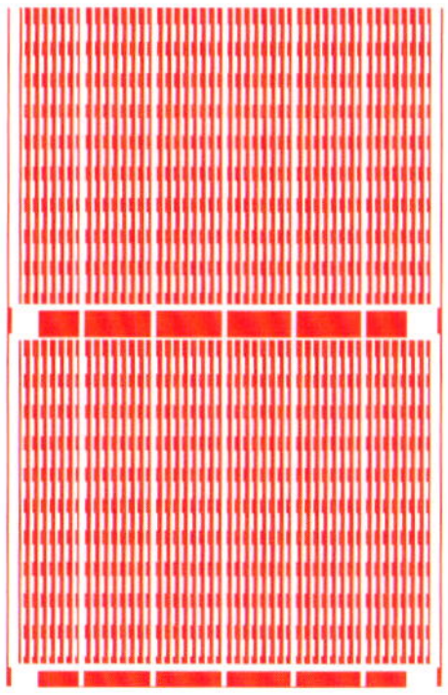

Stanwix Street

Harrison & Abramovitz, 1969

When this tower opened in 1969, it signaled the completion of the Gateway Center and two decades of urban redevelopment in the Golden Triangle. It was also a signal element of design consultant Eliot Noyes's efforts to update the Westinghouse Electric Corporation and its image.

Noyes hired Max Abramovitz to design the first all-electric skyscraper, showcasing the Westinghouse corporate product much as Harrison & Abramovitz's Alcoa Building showcased aluminum and their U.S. Steel Tower showcased steel. Extensively engineered with an eye towards energy efficiency, the tower employed a number of innovative new systems such as pumping water through its light fixtures to absorb excess heat, which could then be used to warm the building when removed via a heat exchanger.

The building is raised on a riverside podium. Its simple massing, clad in dark bronze anodized aluminum, cuts an imposing figure on the skyline. The lobby is recessed beneath an office block, which is topped by a recessed mechanical floor and a second office block of nearly identical proportions to the first. Structural steel columns, partially embedded in the exterior wall, span both recesses and emphasize the verticality of the twenty-three-story building. A large black cube, faced with Paul Rand's new Westinghouse logo stood outside.

Let them multiply, there is no sky in the world which needs scraping more than that which arches over the Iron City.

Pittsburgh Bulletin, 1959

THE GOLDEN TRIANGLE

Pittsburgh's downtown Golden Triangle is in some respects the most visible aspect of the effort to reshape the city during the Renaissance era. Lead by civic and corporate leaders, this effort included a series of new towers that served as the corporate headquarters for Pittsburgh-based companies and showcased the materials that led to these companies' successes.

Among these are the Alcoa Building and two U.S. Steel buildings, each designed by Harrison & Abramovitz, then the architects of choice for corporate America. The Alcoa Building used aluminum in new and innovative ways, from the cladding to the insulation to the wiring and plumbing. The second U.S. Steel Building is an architectural masterpiece that evokes not just the client in its bold use of material but the entire city in a formal resolution that celebrates the Triangle's two grids.

Nearby, the modernist landscape of Mellon Square offered the city a fascinating new prototype: the underground garage disguised as a plaza.

A number of other architecturally notable parking garages were built during this period. Each celebrated the automobile—sometimes with dramatic gestures—and endeavored to provide efficient means of visiting the Golden Triangle by car.

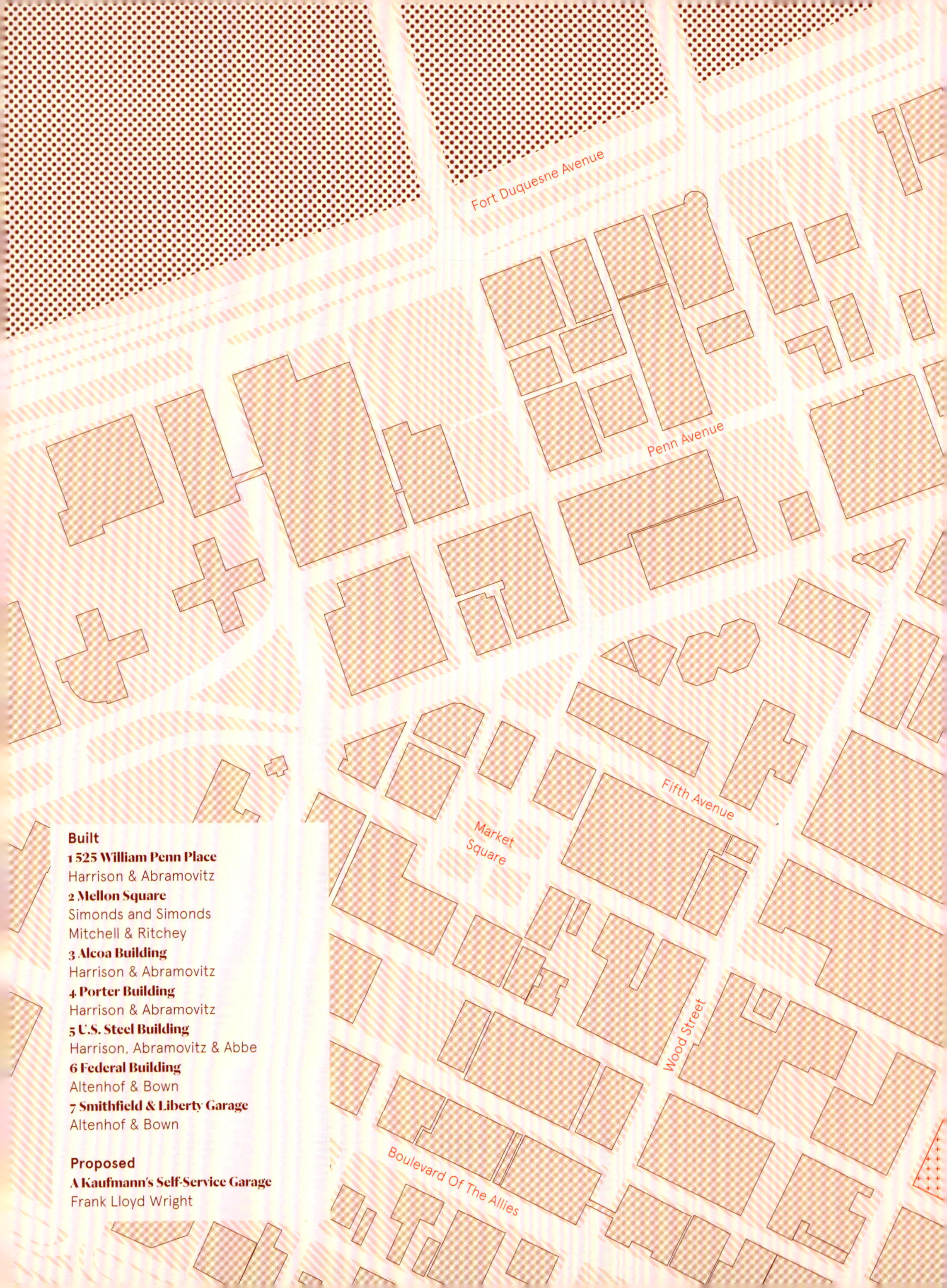
Fort Duquesne Avenue
Penn Avenue
Fifth Avenue
Market Square
Wood Street
Boulevard Of The Allies
Built
1 525 William Penn Place
Harrison & Abramovitz
2 Mellon Square
Simonds and Simonds
Mitchell & Ritchey
3 Alcoa Building
Harrison & Abramovitz
4 Porter Building
Harrison & Abramovitz
5 U.S. Steel Building
Harrison, Abramovitz & Abbe
6 Federal Building
Altenhof & Bown
7 Smithfield & Liberty Garage
Altenhof & Bown
Proposed
A Kaufmann's Self-Service Garage
Frank Lloyd Wright

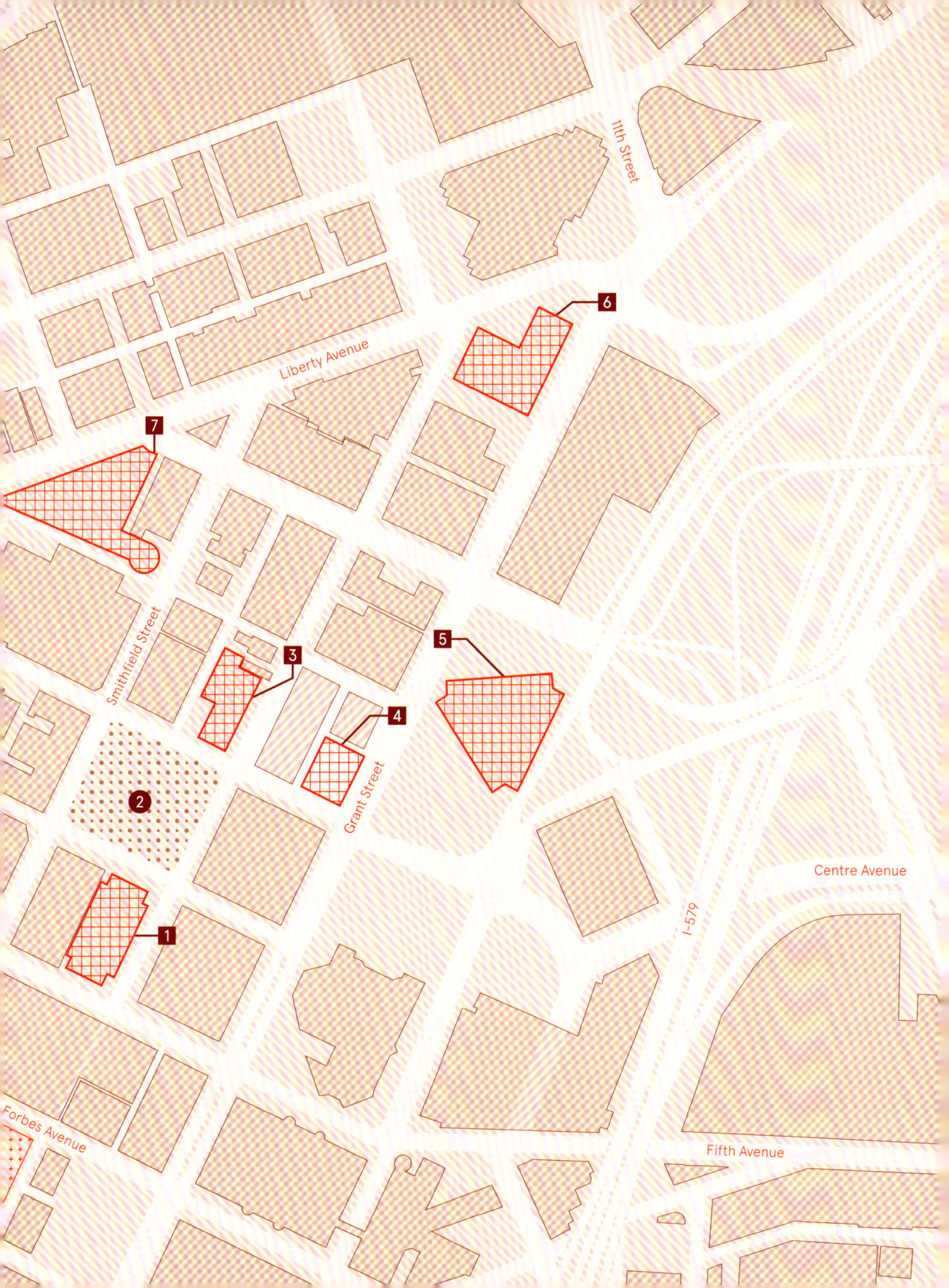

11th Street
6
Liberty Avenue
7
5
3
4
Smithfield Street
2
Grant Street
Centre Avenue
1
I-579
Forbes Avenue
Fifth Avenue

THE GOLDEN TRIANGLE

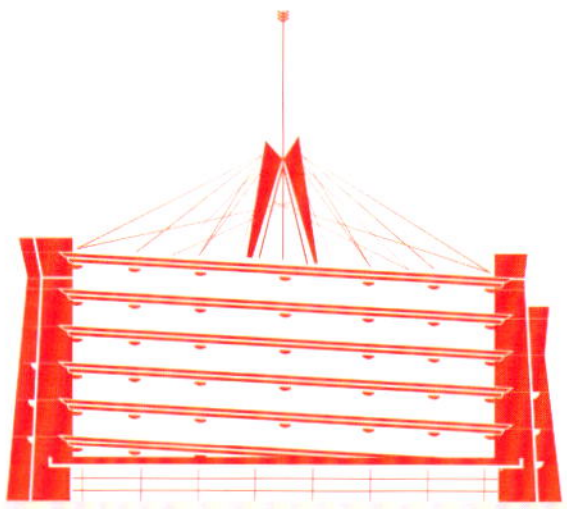

Kaufmann's Self-Service Garage

Frank Lloyd Wright, 1949

Following the rejection of Frank Lloyd Wright's designs for the Point Park Civic Center, Edgar J. Kaufmann commissioned the architect to design a public parking garage adjacent to his department store in downtown Pittsburgh, the same site of Kaufmann's first attempt to engage Wright—for a planetarium—fifteen years before. The garage was to be "self-service," a novel concept at the time, where drivers parked their own cars. Structural and functional concerns shelved the project, though it was briefly revived a few years later for a site next to the Carnegie Institute in Oakland.

One of Wright's many explorations of the spiral, the design called for six tiers of concentric reinforced concrete ramps revolving about a central void for ventilation. A descending ramp open to the exterior wrapped two ascending ramps flanked by parking, which in turn enveloped an inner pedestrian spiral overlooking the fountain at the bottom of the shaft. The ramps were suspended from steel cables attached to four concrete piers at the garage's center, enabling the parking areas to be column-free. Four massive pylons stabilized the structure from the exterior. Direct access to retail space was provided through a basement while a sixth-floor bridge led to the store's office level. Shops were proposed for the building's Smithfield Street frontage.

Alcoa Building

Harrison & Abramovitz, 1953

The 30-story tower was built as an experimental showcase of the construction applications of its namesake's product: aluminum. The first building to be clad in stamped aluminum panels, it also served as a test case for aluminum wiring, plumbing, and a combination acoustic ceiling panel and radiant heating and cooling system; even the venetian blinds were made of aluminum. Though designed for the mundane purposes of lightweight economy and ease of assembly, and to demonstrate the insulative and fireproofing capabilities of an aluminum envelope, the building's facades achieve a high level of refinement. They are punctuated by round-cornered aluminum-frame windows that pivot 360 degrees to allow for cleaning from the interior. As a final demonstration of aluminum's light weight, the entirety of the four-story glass entry vestibule hangs from two cantilevered girders.

Harrison & Abramovitz were tasked with studying the use of aluminum in building in 1945. They designed an aluminum-faced low-rise office building for Alcoa in Davenport, Iowa, completed in 1949, as a trial run of sorts for the Pittsburgh tower. Alcoa was looking towards a site in Manhattan for the latter; but Richard King Mellon persuaded the company to remain in Pittsburgh by offering Alcoa a prime downtown site and proposing an adjacent garage topped by a public plaza, which became Mellon Square. The square offers excellent views to and from the tower. Alcoa relocated to the Alcoa Corporate Center on the North Shore in 2001. The building then became home to government entities, regional nonprofits and small start-up companies; in 2015, it was converted into residential apartments.

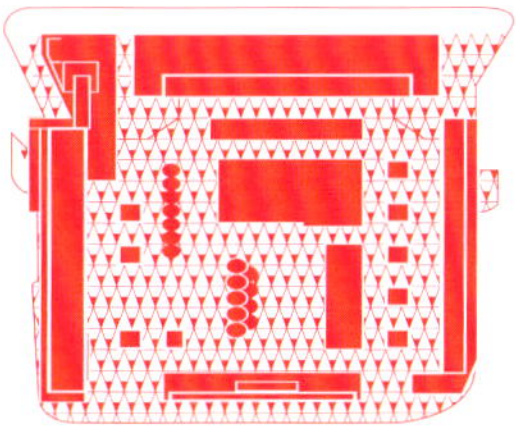

Mellon Square

Simond & Simonds,
Mitchell & Ritchey, 1955

Since its completion in 1955, Mellon Square has offered a popular respite from the tight streets and tall buildings of Pittsburgh's Golden Triangle. A garage that was initially proposed for the site was trumped by Richard King Mellon's vision of a car park beneath a public plaza, inspired in equal parts by his admiration for San Francisco's Union Square and his desire to keep Alcoa from relocating its headquarters to New York. To secure both the site and Alcoa, a trio of Mellon foundations funded purchase of the property. Construction began as the adjacent Alcoa and U.S. Steel-Mellon towers neared completion. Not coincidentally, the plaza secured excellent views of and from the two Mellon-funded projects.

Mellon Square covers six levels of parking on a sloping full block site. There is a level of retail space on its western edge. The change in elevation and peripheral plantings seclude the plaza from the busy surrounding streets. The asymmetrical landscape plan by Simonds and Simonds placed taller plantings at the edges, to heighten this effect, while nine large bronze fountains occupy the center. A series of equally sizable basins cascades alongside a stairway at the square's southwest corner. The composition is unified by terrazzo paving, featuring a triangular motif evocative of the Golden Triangle or a series of Ms for the Mellon family. The Pittsburgh Parks Conservancy restored Mellon Square in 2014.

Smithfield Liberty Garage

Altenhof & Bown 1965

The Smithfield-Liberty Garage consists mostly of a triangular enclosure of parking levels that faces Liberty Avenue; but it is best known for the protruding spiral exit ramp that seems to nose out over Smithfield Street. By dint of a combination of site, form, and context, the ramp is surprisingly visible as one walks along Smithfield and is immediately noticeable along Strawberry Way. At a distance, the spiral's recessed support arches disappear, giving the impression that the ramp and each of its seven discs are floating. The ramp's unadorned poured-in-place concrete contrasts with the brick facade the garage presents to Liberty Avenue such that they appear as two separate buildings rather than a single garage. This disjunction heightens the sculptural, object-like quality of the spiral.

The garage was designed by the firm of Altenhof & Bown, who have a number of other modernist projects to their credit. In 2004, Pfaffmann + Associates were commissioned to redesign the garage's wayfinding, most prominently adding a nine-story marquee to the Liberty Avenue entry.

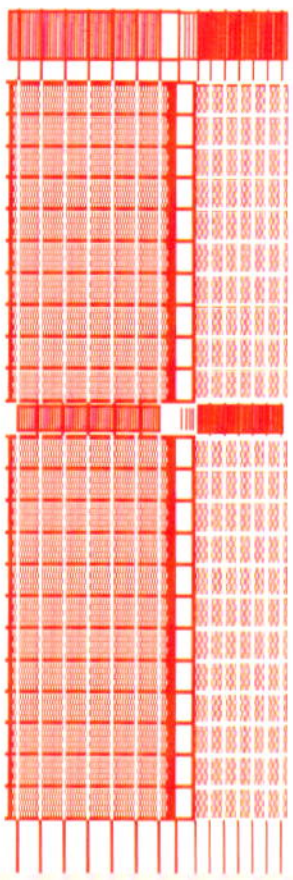

U.S. Steel Tower

Harrison, Abramovitz & Abbe, 1971

The U.S. Steel Tower is the quintessential architectural manifestation of modern Pittsburgh. It is an honest expression at a monumental scale of little-explored structural possibilities in the city's most well-known export: steel. Even its triangular plan echoes the geography of the Golden Triangle. Measuring 841 feet above ground, it is the apex of the Pittsburgh skyline and one of the few buildings to peer over the surrounding plateau.

Unlike its staid predecessor headquarters at Mellon Square, this tower is an innovative showcase of steel representing years of research and development, not unlike Harrison & Abramovitz's use of aluminum in the Alcoa Building. Beginning in 1965, Max Abramovitz worked with the U.S. Steel Innovations Committee and engineers Worthington, Skilling, Helle, Robertson to develop the tower's unique structural system. The building envelope consists of Cor-Ten steel panels that snap into place, requiring no bolts or welding. Six structural columns, fireproofed with a water-based solution containing antifreeze and anticorrosive agents that circulates through their hollow cores, are offset nearly three feet from each facade. The columns are connected to a cantilevered floor slab every three stories. The extended slabs connect to the building's core and in turn support two stories each, effectively making a stack of linked three-story buildings. A space frame "hat," comprising the top two stories, stabilizes the tower against strong winds. The notched corners of the otherwise triangular plan further reduce wind loads and double the number of corner offices.

Mayor Lawrence… always said that Pittsburgh, if it's going to survive in the long run, has to be a big league city. We have to have major league ball teams, major league symphonies, major league governments; and to do that we have to have major league stadiums and major league symphony halls.

Robert Pease

Executive Director of the Urban Redevelopment Authority, 1971

LOWER HILL

City planners had eyed the redevelopment of the Lower Hill as early as 1939 with Robert Moses's *Pittsburgh Arterial Plan*, which advocated clearing the area in order to develop a more efficient highway system and new housing. The site was the commercial, institutional, and cultural heart of the city's African American community; yet it was characterized by overcrowding, poor sanitation, absentee landlords, and property values that were falling faster than anywhere else in the city.

Beginning in 1953, local architects Mitchell & Ritchey developed a master plan for Pittsburgh's "Cultural Acropolis." In 1956, with backing from several civic leaders and foundations, significant federal funding, and some community support, a large swath of land was cleared for the construction of the Civic Arena, displacing thousands of residents and hundreds of businesses. Claiming the largest dome in the world at the time of its construction, the Arena was originally intended as an all-purpose facility, including a home for the Civic Light Opera and local sports teams. Because its acoustics proved incompatible with musical theater, it remained primarily a sports venue.

Subsequent plans to add the equally ambitious Pittsburgh Center for the Arts, designed by Skidmore, Owings & Merrill (SOM), and Washington Plaza, a three-tower luxury housing project designed by I. M. Pei & Associates, did not receive the same support. Displacement and failed relocation efforts left the local community deeply distrustful of further development, while a lack of consensus among civic leaders combined with a slow market for high-end housing in the area. Only one of Pei's three towers was completed, and the SOM project was scrapped completely. The grand project stalled, and the Civic Arena was left stranded in a sea of parking lots for more than sixty years. With the demolition of the Arena completed in 2012, the midcentury dream of a cultural district adjacent to downtown was finally put to rest.

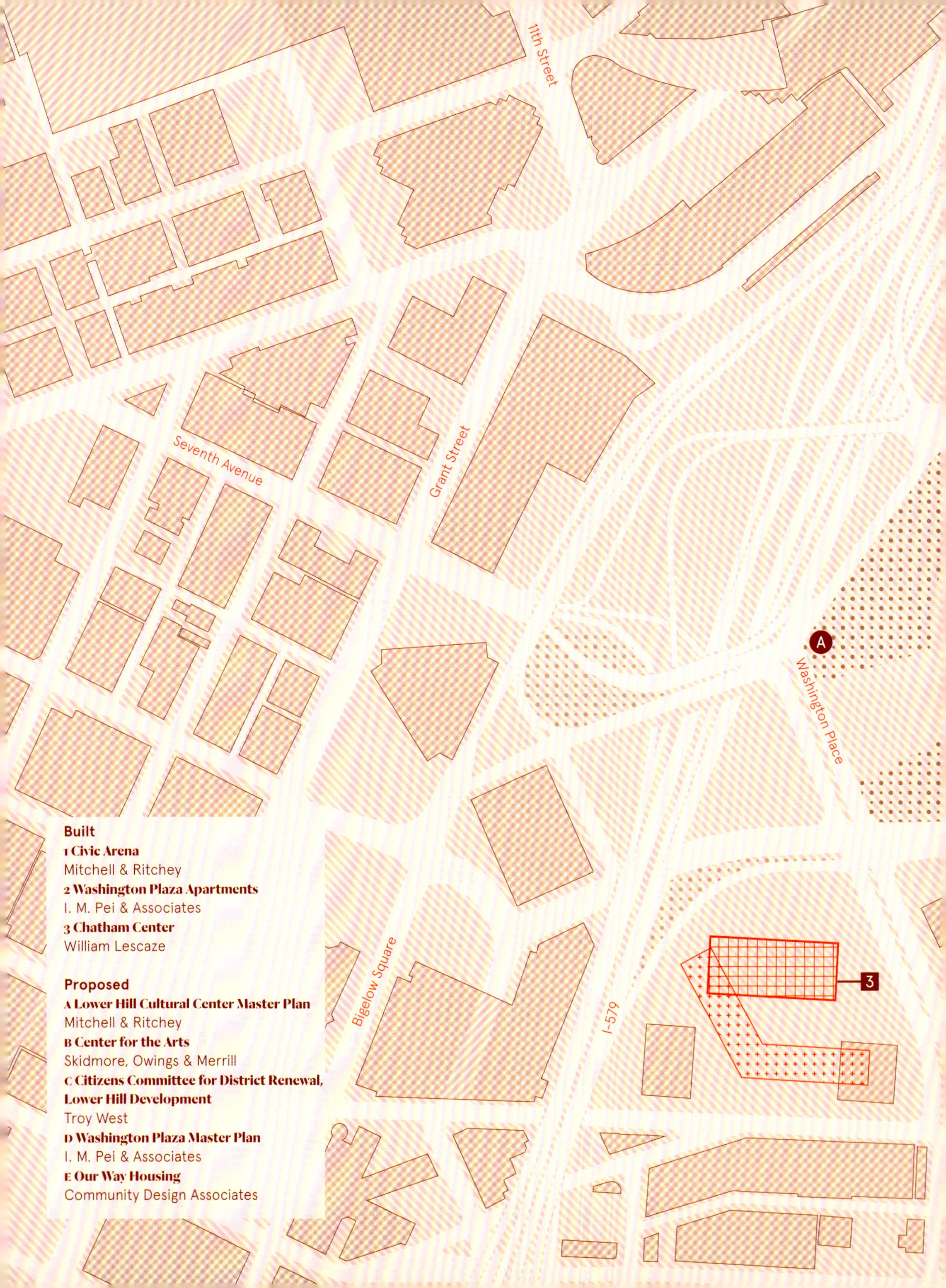

Built

1 Civic Arena
Mitchell & Ritchey

2 Washington Plaza Apartments
I. M. Pei & Associates

3 Chatham Center
William Lescaze

Proposed

A Lower Hill Cultural Center Master Plan
Mitchell & Ritchey

B Center for the Arts
Skidmore, Owings & Merrill

C Citizens Committee for District Renewal, Lower Hill Development
Troy West

D Washington Plaza Master Plan
I. M. Pei & Associates

E Our Way Housing
Community Design Associates

Bedford Avenue
Webster Avenue
Wylie Avenue
B
D
C
1
D
2
entre Avenue
Crawford Street
D
E
Fifth Avenue

LOWER HILL

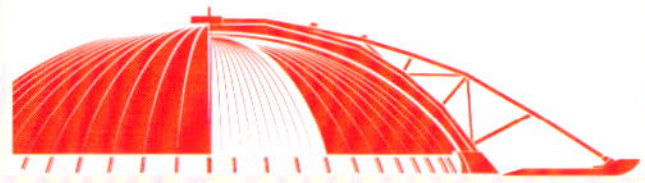

Civic Arena

Mitchell & Ritchey, 1961

The Civic Arena dominated Pittsburgh's Hill neighborhood for half a century. Initiated by Edgar J. Kaufmann, the department store magnate and patron of legendary residences by Richard Neutra and Frank Lloyd Wright, the arena was initially intended to serve as a venue for the Pittsburgh Civic Light Opera, though it was never well-suited for this purpose. Mitchell & Ritchey, the premier architects of the so-called Pittsburgh Renaissance, designed the structure. James Mitchell was the lead designer, and took out a patent on an early soft-shelled version of the design. After many compromises, the final design featured a massive stainless steel dome, supported by a single cantilevered arm, which provided a clear span across the diameter of the building and was the world's first retractable roof over a major venue. A complex, automated system allowed for the roof to be opened in under three minutes.

Site clearance for the Lower Hill Cultural Center, including the arena, controversially displaced over 8,000 residents and hundreds of small businesses. Yet the Center's planned apartments, a Symphony Hall, and other facilities remained almost totally unrealized. Variously referred to as the The Auditorium, the Civic Auditorium, the Civic Arena, the Mellon Arena, and more colloquially as the Igloo, referencing its shape and latter-day role as the home of the Pittsburgh Penguins hockey team, the arena hosted an extraordinary number of concerts, sporting events, and distinguished visitors. Truly one-of-a-kind, the building's demolition in 2012 was controversial as well.

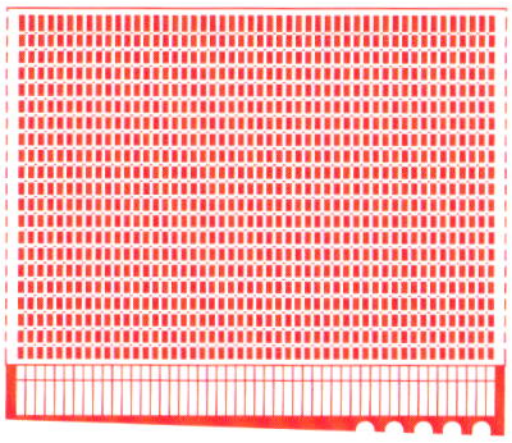

Washington Plaza Apartments

I. M. Pei & Associates, 1964

Today a solitary sentinel near the bottom of the Hill, this high-rise was originally intended to be one of a trio of apartment buildings bracketing communal plazas in Mitchell & Ritchey's Lower Hill Development plan. Upon this building's completion in 1964, tenants were slow to move in, possibly prompting the decision to not construct the remaining buildings. The lone twenty-four-story high-rise is a long concrete slab intersected perpendicularly by an additional mass of apartments on its southern face. The apartments are raised over a recessed ground level and the entire building rests on a plinth of parking.

I. M. Pei & Associates' involvement with the project was a product of Pei's long-term relationship with developer William Zeckendorf, represented here by Webb & Knapp, Inc. Zeckendorf's interest was largely assumed by an Alcoa subsidiary, Alcoa Properties Inc., before construction; but Pei remained on board. The building is a lesser-known sibling of Pei-designed residential towers in New York, Philadelphia, and Boston. With the failure to complete this project and much of the development plan, and with the demolition of the Civic Arena that once stood nearby, this building is the only remaining remnant of Pittsburgh's highly ambitious and disruptive postwar schemes for the Lower Hill.

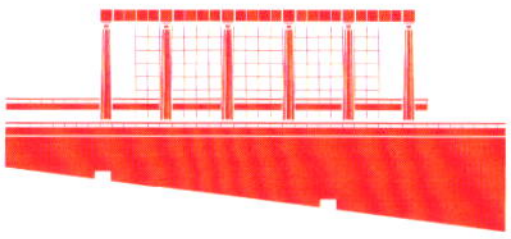

Pittsburgh Center for the Arts

Skidmore, Owings & Merrill, 1966

Following the success of Gateway Center and other projects in the Golden Triangle, Pittsburgh's civic leaders and businessmen set their sights on the renewal of the Lower Hill. In an attempt to redefine it as the city's "cultural Acropolis," a large swath of land was cleared for construction, displacing thousands of mainly African American residents and hundreds of businesses. The Civic Arena was the first project built on the site. Soon after, plans developed for a Center for the Arts, including a new Museum of Art, relocated from the Carnegie Institute in Oakland, and a new symphony hall, to be built immediately behind the Civic Arena. When the Howard Heinz Foundation contributed $8 million to fund the symphony hall, it became the dominant programmatic element. Skidmore, Owings & Merrill [SOM] were hired to design the project, with Gordon Bunshaft leading the effort.

SOM addressed the sloping site by designing an enormous plinth. The art museum and the symphony hall were placed on top of the plinth, at opposite ends of a landscaped plaza, which afforded dramatic views of downtown. The symphony hall was wrapped in a monumental glass box (100 feet by 300 feet and 75 feet tall) and flanked by oversized travertine-clad columns that supported a waffle slab roof. The three-story art museum was enlivened with a crenelated roof structure.

The project was never realized. The coalition formed to support it eventually fell apart in the face of opposition by Hill residents who were grew increasingly suspicious of the project's intentions and by Oakland institutions who did not want to see the art museum relocated. Heinz eventually chose to invest in establishing a Symphony Hall in a refurbished building downtown. The art museum stayed in Oakland. The Hill waited for decades for the site to be developed.

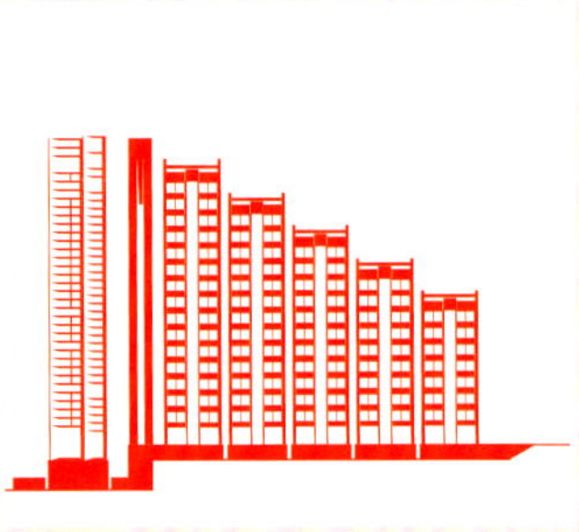

Lower Hill Development

Troy West, 1967

After training with Louis Kahn and Oscar Stonorov, Troy West returned to Pittsburgh to take a teaching position at his alma mater, Carnegie Institute of Technology (now Carnegie Mellon University). His practice, called Community Design Associates and Architecture 2001, was one of the first university-based community design centers in the United States. Drawn to the vibrancy of the Hill neighborhood, he was soon taken under the wing of a group of African American artists who encouraged his work, including painter and activist Ewari Ed Ellis and playwright August Wilson. West's counter-proposals for the Hill and Oakland offered a community-based alternative to the prevailing top-down development patterns, gaining national recognition in the process.

Early in his career, West worked with a community group on the Hill called the Citizens Committee for District Renewal. Together they created an alternative plan for the redevelopment of the Lower Hill, a local reaction to the plans underway by the civic leaders, including SOM's Pittsburgh Center for the Arts and I. M. Pei's Washington Plaza Apartments. West's proposal merged the two programs, combining a cultural plinth with residential towers. The plinth, which negotiated the change in height between the neighborhood and the Civic Auditorium, contained flexible exhibition halls that could be subdivided as needed. Below the exhibition area sat a parking garage for 1,600 cars, while the top of plinth was devoted to playing fields for the neighborhood. Two high-rise and two low-rise residential bar buildings stood above the plinth. The residential elements were organized as double-loaded corridors, with each pair of units articulated as a distinct component in plan. On the low-rise buildings, these components maintained a five-story height throughout, in deference to the adjacent neighborhood scale. On the high-rise, however, these components varied in height, rising from five stories on the neighborhood side to nearly forty stories when facing the Civic Auditorium. Two additional buildings sat closer to the Civic Auditorium: a restaurant and a motel.

The project received national attention with a Progressive Architecture award in 1967, with the jury calling it "the embodiment of a tremendous force, a terrific and kind of tragic vision of the character of life.... a moving and stupendous source sense of what it's like to be here in the vast city." While the project never came to fruition, it is worth noting as an early community-led effort that was both pro-development and distinctively modern in its aesthetic.

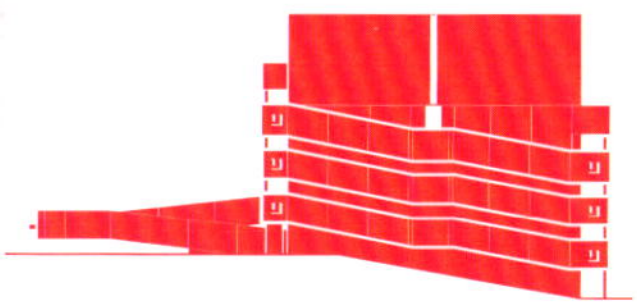

Duquesne University Union

Paul Schweikher, 1967

The Duquesne University Union accommodates dining, student services, and administrative offices for the University. It was designed by Paul Schweikher, a noted modernist architect and one-time head of the Carnegie Tech School of Architecture. The building showcases Schweikher's skill in manipulating massing and materials—here concrete, brick, glass, and wood—as also demonstrated in Pittsburgh projects like the WQED Headquarters and the Knoxville Branch of the Carnegie Library. Constructed in 1967, the Union is contemporaneous with Mies van der Rohe's nearby Richard King Mellon Hall of Science, and the two buildings are based on the same 28-foot module.

The Union's deep concrete frame with recessed glass walls displays a Brutalist vocabulary, while the building's highly regular composition reflects a nearly classical attitude towards design. Cantilevered scissor ramps climb the east and west sides. The most dramatic feature, an extreme cantilevered entrance ramp, was removed from the south facade in the 1990s to enhance the building's "curb appeal," which significantly compromised the power of Schweikher's design. Additions on the north facade are awkward and ill-considered. The wood panels that once alternated among planes of glass have been removed. Today the building reveals its original quality, but is a vestige of its former self.

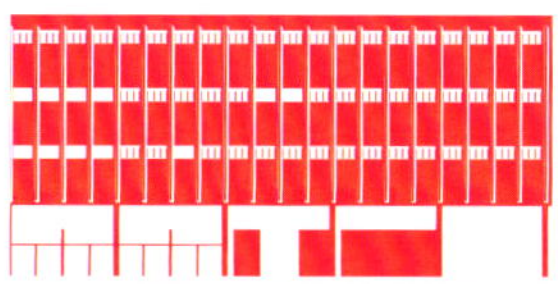

Richard King Mellon Hall of Science

Ludwig Mies van der Rohe, 1968

Perched atop the Bluff overlooking the Monongahela River, the Richard King Mellon Hall of Science stands in close proximity to the Duquesne University Union. That building's architect, Paul Schweikher, facilitated Mies van der Rohe's selection to design Mellon Hall. Mies's building can be seen as the conceptual opposite of the universal space that he pursued at the contemporaneous Neue Nationalgalerie in Berlin. Here planimetric flexibility is largely absent due to the programmatic requirements of the laboratories on the upper three floors. Program also mandated the minimal use of glazing on these levels: floor-to-ceiling glass is reserved for three bays at either end of each floor. Elsewhere, two-thirds of the normally glazed curtain wall is filled with steel panels.

Mellon Hall is framed on a 28-foot grid that creates an arcade around the recessed ground level and is subdivided by I-beams applied to the facades of the upper floors. The redundant beams are signifiers of structure, though the verticality that they reinforce in Mies's skyscrapers is precluded here by the building's long, low massing. Departing from both the rigidity of the steel frame and the ideal of universal space, the ground floor is defined by two curvilinear auditoria, whose curves clearly express their function.

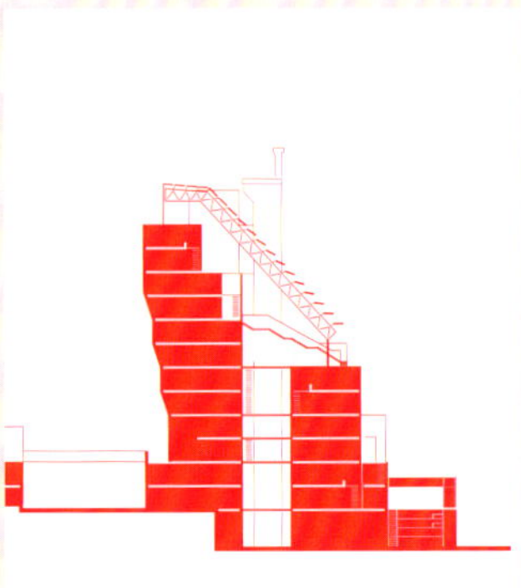

Our Way

Community Design Associates, 1969

Among West's most interesting projects is Our Way, a communal living complex in the Lower Hill, straddling an alley named Our Way. Reminiscent of work by Alison and Peter Smithson or Aldo van Eyck, the project is composed of bar buildings on both sides of the alley. The larger of the two has staggered massing composed of a double-loaded corridor that holds multiple unit types, from studios to duplexes, and public open spaces of various sizes. A superstructure on the upper floors hosts plantings that provide residents with shading and food. A series of elevated walkways connect the housing to a parking structure and a community roof garden.

Though speculative, the project received some serious attention, in part because it was supported by the Hill community. Like most of West's work, Our Way was both a community designed effort and an extremely modern project, a combination almost unthinkable today.

Hill House Center

Walter Roberts Associates, 1973

The Hill House Association was formed in 1964, with the merger of three preexisting agencies, to deliver integrated social services to the Hill District community. The Hill House Center, built in 1972, offered a new image for the organization, and announced that a disadvantaged neighborhood could boast sophisticated modern design. The building is defined by its enormous scale and explicit superstructure of laminated wood. Widely spaced pairs of slanted piers, which rest on exposed steel connectors and trapezoidal concrete feet, carry massive horizontal beams. The piers and beams frame two stories of program spaces. The first story is faced in brick and glass and deeply recessed behind the piers, while the second story is faced in white panels and intersects with the piers. There are narrow ceiling-level horizontal windows throughout. A child care playground occupies polygonal pods outside.

Walter Roberts, Pittsburgh's premier African-American architect of this period, designed the new structure. Roberts placed special emphasis on planning and designing institutional, industrial, and public works structures for the inner city. Newspapers referred to the center as a "'supermarket' social service center" and "ultramodern [version] of the old-fashioned settlement house," and to its construction as a "breakthrough in black capitalism" (a number of African-American contractors also worked on the project). The building was formally renamed the James F. Henry Hill House Center in 2003 after a former executive director of the Association.

This is a very far-reaching proposal. Indeed, I would suspect that it has not been paralleled either in this country, or perhaps, in the world…

Edward Litchfield
Chancellor of the University of Pittsburgh, 1955

OAKLAND

The urban redevelopment of Oakland during this period was driven largely by educational and cultural institutions. Chief among them was the University of Pittsburgh as it transformed itself from a regional to a national university by harnessing the energy of the Pittsburgh Renaissance. Although other Oakland institutions built notable modern buildings and additions, including the Carnegie Museums of Art and Natural History and Carnegie Tech (Carnegie Mellon University after 1967), none rival the University of Pittburgh's scope or scale.

Following World War II, the university spread out along the Forbes Avenue and Fifth Street corridor, a trend that only accelerated with the selection of the ambitious Edward Litchfield as chancellor in 1955. In one of his first acts, he retained Harrison & Abramovitz to consult on Pitt's campus growth. The university quickly committed to twelve major capital projects including the new Hillman Library, Trees Hall (which at the time of completion housed the largest indoor pool in the country), and the Tower Residence Halls (later Litchfield Towers).

When Pitt purchased the land under Forbes Field, the city's disused but venerable baseball stadium, Deeter Ritchey Sippel produced several versions of a new Forbes Complex Master Plan, of which the Forbes Quadrangle (later Posvar Hall) was completed. Troy West's practice Architecture 2001 led an alternative effort to repurpose the stadium structure, transforming it into affordable housing and other uses. Other unrealized visions for Oakland included Harrison & Abramovitz's breathtaking Panther Hollow development. Designed for the Oakland Corporation, a jointly owned, Pitt-dominated consortium of seven institutions, the project proposed a built structure to fill in the entire ravine that sat between Pitt, the Carnegie Museums, and Carnegie Tech. Although soon shelved, it remains a fascinating idea as well as a symbol of the era's optimism.

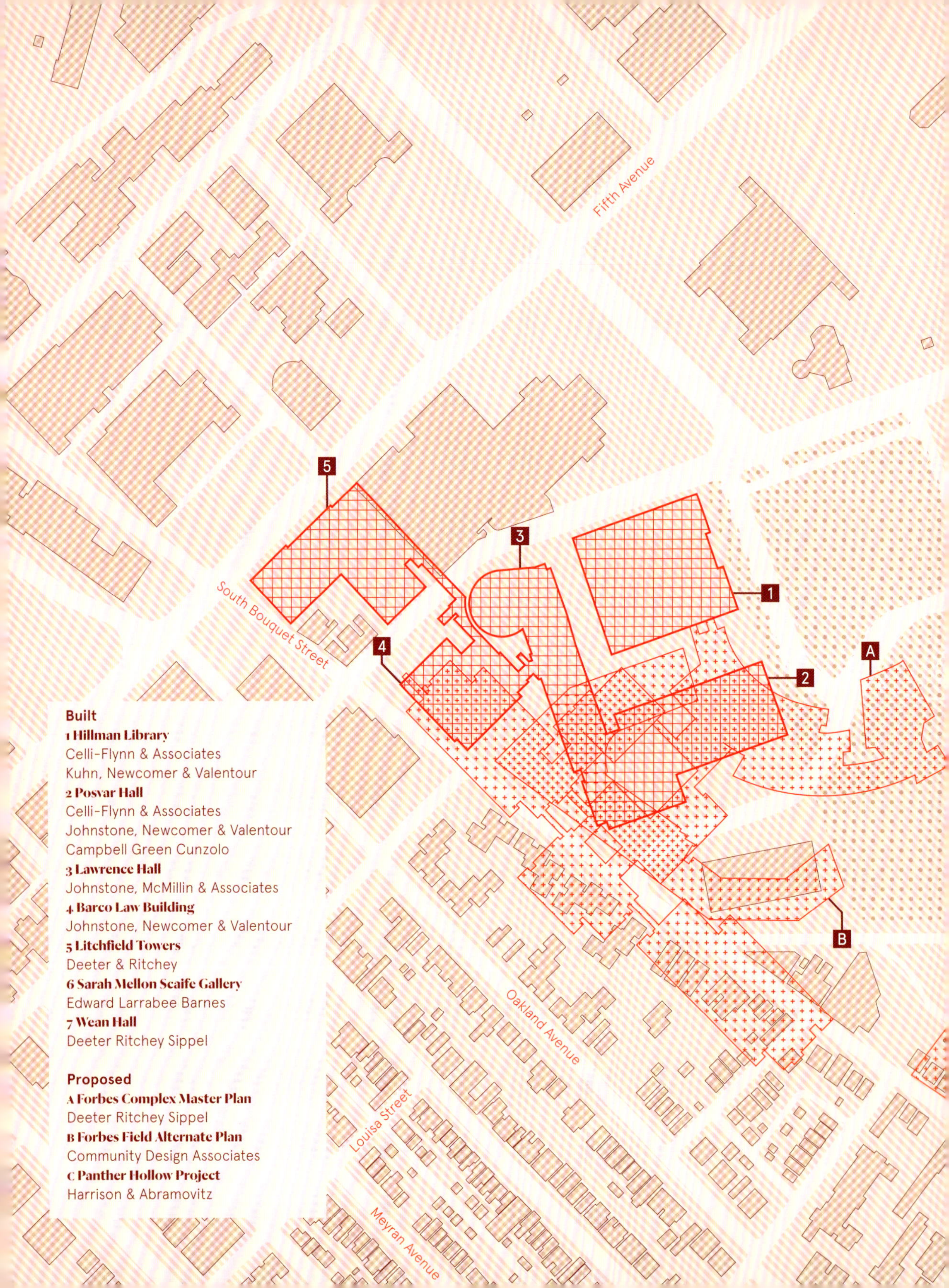
Fifth Avenue
South Bouquet Street
Oakland Avenue
Louisa Street
Meyran Avenue
5
3
1
4
2
A
B
Built
1 Hillman Library
Celli-Flynn & Associates
Kuhn, Newcomer & Valentour
2 Posvar Hall
Celli-Flynn & Associates
Johnstone, Newcomer & Valentour
Campbell Green Cunzolo
3 Lawrence Hall
Johnstone, McMillin & Associates
4 Barco Law Building
Johnstone, Newcomer & Valentour
5 Litchfield Towers
Deeter & Ritchey
6 Sarah Mellon Scaife Gallery
Edward Larrabee Barnes
7 Wean Hall
Deeter Ritchey Sippel
Proposed
A Forbes Complex Master Plan
Deeter Ritchey Sippel
B Forbes Field Alternate Plan
Community Design Associates
C Panther Hollow Project
Harrison & Abramovitz

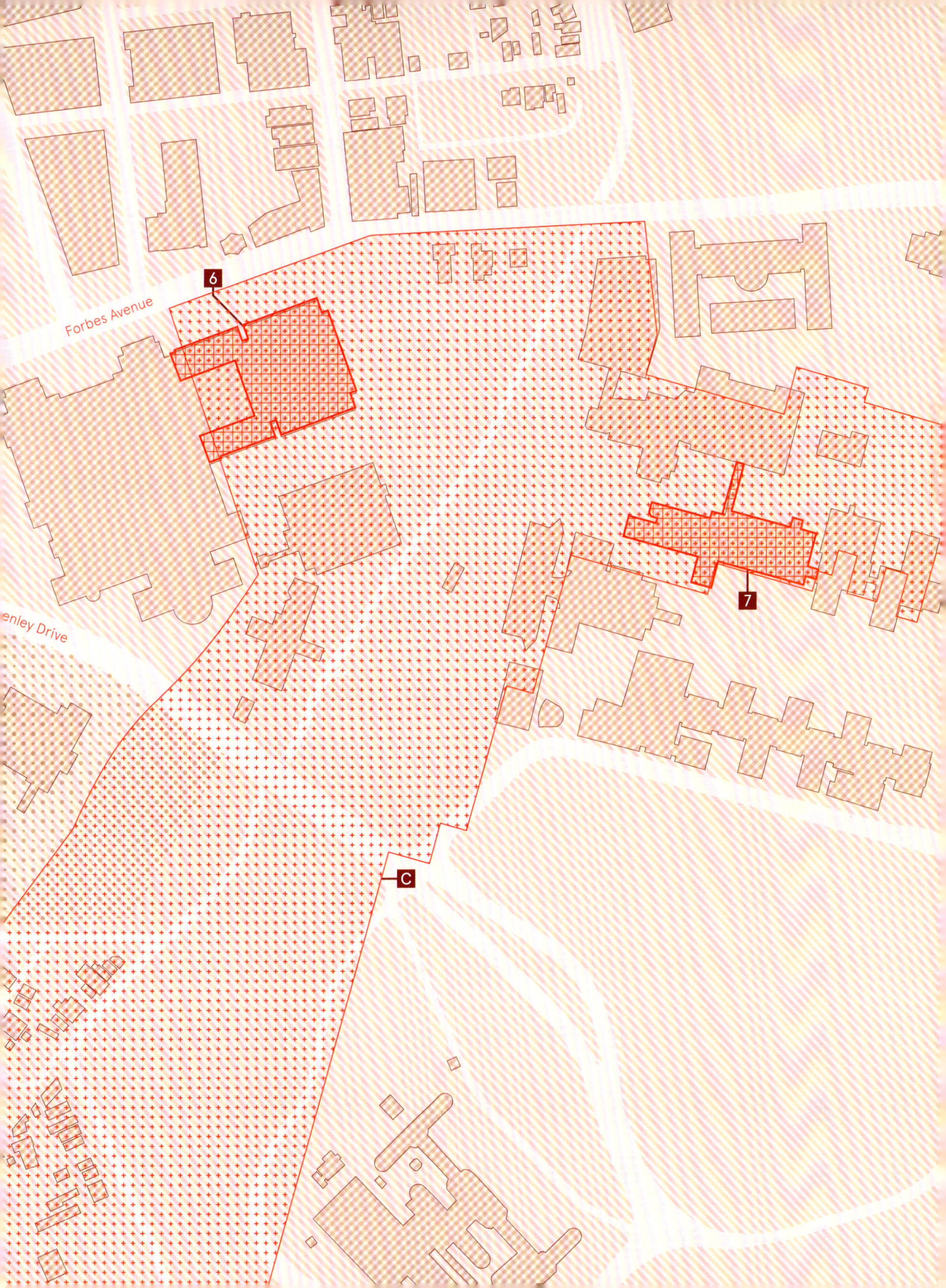

Forbes Avenue
enley Drive
6
7
C

OAKLAND

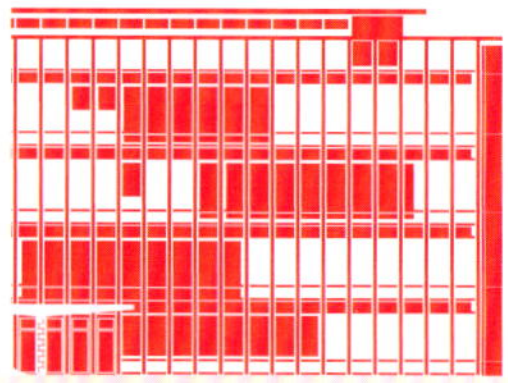

Hunt Library

Lawrie and Green, 1961

Built by the largess of magnate Roy A. Hunt and his wife, Rachel, Hunt Library is an aluminum lantern given pride of place on the Steel King's Carnegie Tech (now Carnegie Mellon University) campus. Indeed, the Hunts stipulated that the opposite end of the new north-south mall—would remain open-ended to assure a good view of the building. Designed by Harrisburg-based architects Lawrie and Green, the library is a sharp departure from other buildings facing Henry Hornbostel's Beaux-Arts campus mall, while it replaced a former World War I-era aeronautics laboratory designed by Green. Aluminum fins march along at regular five-foot intervals on all sides, spaced to the dimensions of the book-shelving system of the interior. A detached canopy compensates for the subsequent lack of entry articulation. The fins allow for continuous glazing from the ground to the fourth story, creating a luminous interior for research and study.

The fifth-story Rachel McMasters Miller Hunt Botanical Library was inset from the building perimeter to make way for a planted rooftop ambulatory that never materialized. Muddling the building's otherwise rigid aesthetic, this penthouse is furnished with an eclectic array of premodern artifacts and capped with an aluminum-clad hipped roof. Visible only at a distance, the roof is obscured from nearer vantage points by a brise soleil and an extension of aluminum fins past the fourth-story roofline.

4600 Fifth Avenue Bank

Skidmore, Owings & Merrill, 1961

Sited at the corner of Fifth Avenue and Craig Street, the normally unassuming branch bank turned into a powerful structural exhibition. Atop only four columns, two massive reinforced concrete beams support twenty-one equally prodigious precast "U" channels that span the width of the site. The construction is frankly expressed: the channels are left open-ended between a thin roof slab and the beams, which in turn celebrate and expose the scale of their steel reinforcement with steel bolt caps more commonly seen in bridge construction. The weighty architectonics of the roof shelters a small parking lot and a delicate Miesian box containing the bank functions.

Litchfield Towers

Deeter & Ritchey, 1963

Otherwise known as the Tower Residence Halls or Men's Dormitories, Litchfield Towers was named for Edward Litchfield, Chancellor of the University of Pittsburgh between 1955 and 1965. The towers exemplify the university's expansive building program under Litchfield's leadership. Three large cylindrical dormitories, built to house male students, are elevated on a podium that spans a slope. The complex is raised slightly above Fifth Avenue to the north, but is raised high above Forbes Avenue to the south. The podium contains a parking garage and dining services. Architects Deeter & Ritchey proposed two additional towers on the opposite side of Forbes Avenue, but these were never built.

The towers are arranged in an L-shaped configuration and range from sixteen to twenty-two stories in height. At their centers are circulation and service cores, while wedge-shaped dorm rooms and lounges ring their peripheries. The towers are constructed of reinforced concrete, clad with precast insulated concrete panels, and are visually subdivided by projecting vertical ribs. Hardscape plazas top the podium where the towers are linked by low glazed lobbies like underscores.

The building, commonly differentiated as A, B, and C, have also been called Ajax, Bab-O, and Comet, nicknamed for commercial cleansing products packaged in cylindrical containers. Tower B has also been called Bon Ami and Bounty. Despite such levity, and decades of use, the cylindrical forms of Litchfield Towers remain a futuristic presence on the University of Pittsburgh campus.

Panther Hollow Project

Harrison & Abramovitz, 1963

Stretching for nearly a mile, and filling a ravine as much as 150 feet deep and 900 feet wide, Max Abramovitz's Panther Hollow Project envisioned a megastructural "research city" linking Oakland's academic and cultural institutions. The massive complex would have filled the hollow to the brim, and expanded Schenley Park with a series of roof terraces and gardens. Only in the first of three phases—between the Forbes Avenue and Schenley Drive bridges—would buildings have risen above ground level. As the megastructure grew from north to south it was to expand from four to seven levels with transit and utilities buried beneath. Terraced courtyards would have provided ample light to the research facilities, commercial areas, and auditoria within. At its southern end, the megastructure was to fan out around Panther Hollow Lake, creating a public "hanging garden."

The megastructure would have integrated services and amenities within itself and supported a series of residential developments in the surrounding area. A complex structural system would have enabled the replacement of portions of the complex so that it could remain up to date. The community consortium driving the project, the Oakland Corporation, was dissolved in 1966, and the project was abandoned due to insufficient investment.

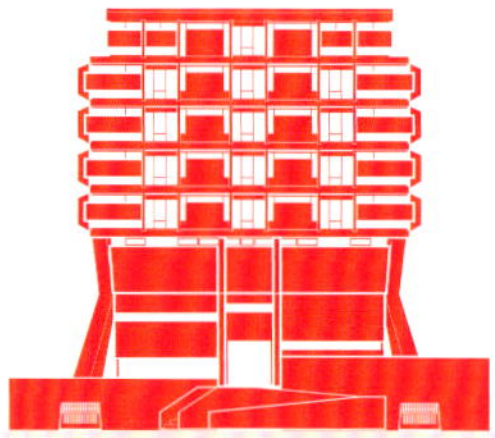

Information Sciences Building

Tasso Katselas, 1965

The striking bent piers of this Brutalist concrete building are the expressive resolution of city setback requirements and competing functional needs. Zoning stipulated that columns be placed within fifteen feet of property lines, if the lower levels were to be used solely for parking, yet required a much more significant setback for the perimeter of the building proper. Each pier negotiates these demands within one structural member: the piers support perimeter beams at the ground- and first-floor ceiling levels, then kink out to meet the exterior walls of the parking podium to avoid occupying potential parking spaces.

Katselas conceived the piers equally as *pilotis* to lift the box-like building above the ground and leave the ground floor largely open. This effect was later diminished when the ground floor was enclosed to house additional interior space. The upper floors are distinguished by high recessed windows that turn the building's corners and by a rhythmic series of vertical concrete fins that shade other windows on the facades. The muscular frame allows for column-free interior spaces, a requirement of the client, the American Institutes for Research in the Behavioral Sciences. The building now houses the University of Pittsburgh's School of Information Sciences.

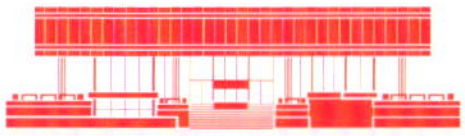

The Graphic Arts Technical Center

Williams Trebilcock Whitehead, 1965

The Graphic Arts Technical Center consolidated the research, educational, and administrative functions of the Graphic Arts Technical Foundation that were previously located in New York and Chicago. In Pittsburgh—halfway between the two—the foundation built the printing industry's first purpose-built structure for research in the graphic arts.

The building is comprised of four levels. Research areas were placed well underground as an economical means of climate control. Massive printing equipment was installed on a floating slab to control vibrations. A level for parking and deliveries acts as a plinth along Forbes Avenue, where the main entry may be accessed via a flight of steps to a bench-lined terrace above the street. The brick and glass entry floor recedes from the perimeter of the plinth and is in turn overhung by the floor above. These two floors contain offices and are joined by a two-story lobby and stair.

The upper story is a highly expressive exercise in exposed precast concrete. A carefully detailed vertical grid wraps the structure and highlights the windows. It intersects with a waffle slab, and its complementary horizontal grid forms the ceiling of the terrace. The slab remains exposed on the interior of the building and organizes the layouts of the upper two floors, where lighting and acoustic panels are integrated into the concrete coffers of the slab.

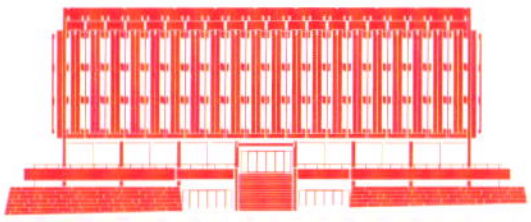

Hillman Library

Celli-Flynn & Associates, 1968

Hillman Library emerged from the University of Pittsburgh's long-gestating plans to erect campus buildings on the west side of Schenley Plaza. Chancellor Edward Litchfield retained Harrison & Abramovitz to consult on campus growth and to make studies for the university's first central library. That firm's 1960 proposal raised the library on a podium. A few years later, with a gift from the Hillman Foundation in hand, the university chose Celli-Flynn to be the library architect. That firm designed a massive five-story building, with four stories raised over a broad podium. This was the first of a grand complex of modern buildings that the university erected in this locale during the late 1960s and early 1970s.

The exposed faces of Hillman Library's podium are canted, and their limestone masonry is rusticated like the walls of the Carnegie Library of Pittsburgh, on the far side of Schenley Plaza. Ground-floor spaces within the podium are lit by a nearly continuous band of clerestory windows. The first floor, a piano nobile of sorts, is surrounded by a terrace, is largely glazed, and is somewhat recessed beneath the limestone-clad stories above. A large portion of the first floor opens vertically to the second, creating expansive over-height spaces within the library. These areas were originally planned as the undergraduate library, with a graduate library on the building's upper floors.

Oriel windows with angled sides, reportedly designed by Max Abramovitz, project rhythmically from the building's facades and house carrels planned for faculty and graduate students. Portions of the interior are finished with polished white granite surfaces and teak furnishings.

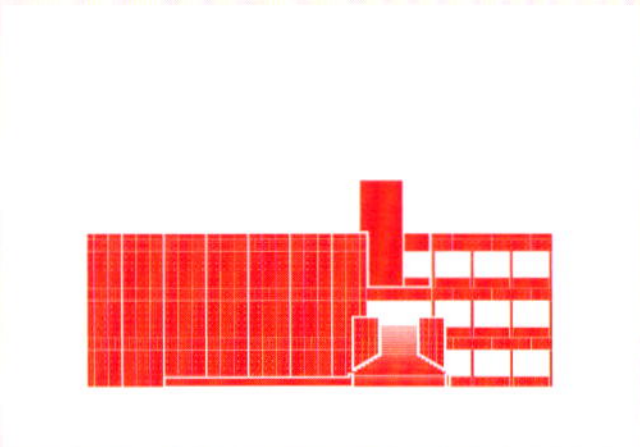

WQED Headquarters

Paul Schweikher, 1970

Paul Schweikher was head of the Department of Architecture at Carnegie Mellon University between 1958 and 1970. One of his last projects was a building for Metropolitan Pittsburgh Educational Television, WQED-WQEX, which has produced *Mister Rogers' Neighborhood* and other notable shows. In an article entitled "The Architecture of Usefulness" Schweikher described architecture as "an ordered relationship of spaces, making a comprehensive whole." At WQED, this approach is expressed in a central circulation spine with studios on one side and office towers on the other. The functional requirements of television studios, such as large spatial volumes and artificial lighting, called for solid monolithic blocks. Alternately, the office towers, the primary spaces of human occupation, have multiple stories and numerous windows. The building's original entryway, an expressive configuration of flaring steps and walls that led to the building's second floor, was removed in the interests of accessibility and controlled access.

Schweikher was highly regarded for his handling of materials. WQED is a building where carefully formed concrete and concrete block dominate outside and in, but are softened by wood detailing. The exterior panel-formed concrete walls exhibit a regular pattern of form tie holes and a mix of receding and protruding joints that create multiple patterns on the otherwise smooth facades.

Wean Hall

Deeter Ritchey Sippel, 1971

The massive Wean Hall is often criticized as a dissonant invader into Palmer & Hornbostel's carefully choreographed Beaux-Arts campus plan. While it is impossible to argue that Wean makes stylistic references to its yellow-brick predecessors, the size and position of its protruding auditorium echoes the repeating wings of the other buildings surrounding the original campus Mall. To avoid capitulating to Beaux-Arts symmetry, the architects only included one such protrusion whereas two would have mirrored the wings of Porter Hall across the lawn. This omission strengthens the visual presence of Wean Hall's main mass, while muddling the convergence of rooflines as intended to be seen from the College of Fine Arts.

Examined independently of its context, Wean Hall is a monument to concrete, not unlike the nearby WQED

Headquarters. Sitting heavily on the Mall at five stories, the building extends down a steep slope on its northern side to present nine stories of exposed concrete. Not surprisingly, it is Pittsburgh's largest building made entirely of these materials (a title previously held by the same architects' Three Rivers Stadium until its demolition in 2001).

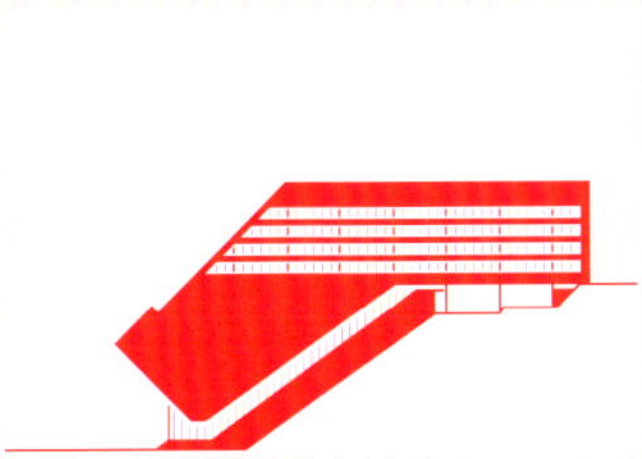

Learning Research & Development Center

Harrison, Abramovitz & Abbe, 1974

Designed by Max Abramovitz, the Learning Research & Development Center (LRDC) is a unique solution to Pittsburgh's difficult topography: rather than go around it or burrow into it, the building glides up a hillside at a 45-degree angle. Its southeastern face echoes this slope, displaying balconies at each successive level. The building reaches the top of one slope approximately halfway up its height and is extruded horizontally to meet the next slope to the north, crossing over streets that circle down the hill.

LRDC was founded in 1963 to advance learning science. The building was conceived in conjunction with Deeter Ritchey Sippel's 1968 University of Pittsburgh master plan, which proposed a residential complex to wrap the upper reaches of the hillside and house 1,300 students. An axial sequence of escalators located within and above the LRDC building would have connected the lower parts of the campus to the residences above. The building's diagonal step-wise massing evokes this, and a diagonal ribbon of windows mirrors the proposed path of an escalator on the building's northeast side, yet they were never installed.

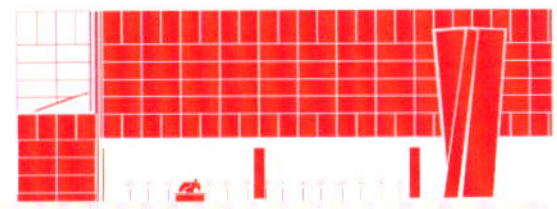

Carnegie Museum of Art

Edward Larrabee Barnes, 1974

When the Carnegie Museum of Art, which once occupied rooms in the Carnegie Institute, built its own attached museum building in 1974, key museum spaces like the Hall of Architecture and Hall of Sculpture remained behind in the older building.

The emerald pearl granite facade was selected to relate to the sooty garb of the earlier institute building; but with the stone of that building cleaned of all traces of industrial Pittsburgh, the art museum appears dusky in turn. A language of large rectangular boxes creates unobtrusive settings for art. A sculpture court, hidden from the front of the building, is rimmed on two sides by expansive glazed walls. Behind the glass, a wide attenuated public stair climbs a wall that was painted by Sol LeWitt in 1985–1986 in two campaigns: *Wall Drawing 450* and *Wall Drawing 493*. The earlier work was installed for the 1985 Carnegie International, as was Richard Serra's *Carnegie*, which shares a plaza in front of the building with Henry Moore's *Reclining Figure*.

Many of us watched with sorrow as the Northside declined in its age and obsolescence took its toll. But a new era is beginning for the Northside.... There is no fountain of youth that keeps our neighborhoods and cities perpetually young and healthy... but we have demonstrated that we have the determination, impatience and all the vitality of youth...

Mayor Joseph Barr

Groundbreaking of Allegheny Center Mall, 1964

ALLEGHENY

The once-prosperous Allegheny City, annexed to Pittsburgh in 1907, featured a civic core with public buildings, a ring of parkland, and an abundance of architecturally rich neighborhoods that would ultimately be preserved and revived. But by the 1950s, the Northside, as it came to be known, experienced high crime rates, traffic congestion, derelict housing, and a population drop of nearly a quarter in a decade.

In response, the city began razing over 500 buildings in the civic core to create the new Allegheny Center, with the support of Alcoa and the federal government. In keeping with the prevailing thinking of the era, thirty-six city blocks were transformed into a new pedestrian super-block surrounded by a one-way, four-lane loop designed to facilitate vehicular traffic. The center included office buildings, mid-rise apartment slabs, townhouses, and a shopping mall with 2,400 parking spaces below. Deeter Ritchey Sippel master planned and designed much of the project. Tasso Katselas added townhouses along the edge (Allegheny Commons East), and the Office of Mies van der Rohe designed an office building (East Commons Professional Building). An international competition chose the design of William Breger, a former employee of Walter Gropius, for the Public Square at the Center's new heart.

Despite some initial success, the plan proved ill-fated. The traffic circle cut off most of the Center's commercial space from pedestrian reach of the surrounding neighborhoods, and it could not compete with the ease of vehicular access offered by suburban shopping centers, despite the new road network and mega-garage. As a result, most of the mall's stores were eventually replaced by back-of-house office space, populated by businesses that did not rely on foot traffic. The housing remains popular to this day, and the public square has been rebuilt along with the surrounding public realm. New owners have injected life into the complex, upgrading systems and bringing new programs and pedestrians back to the area.

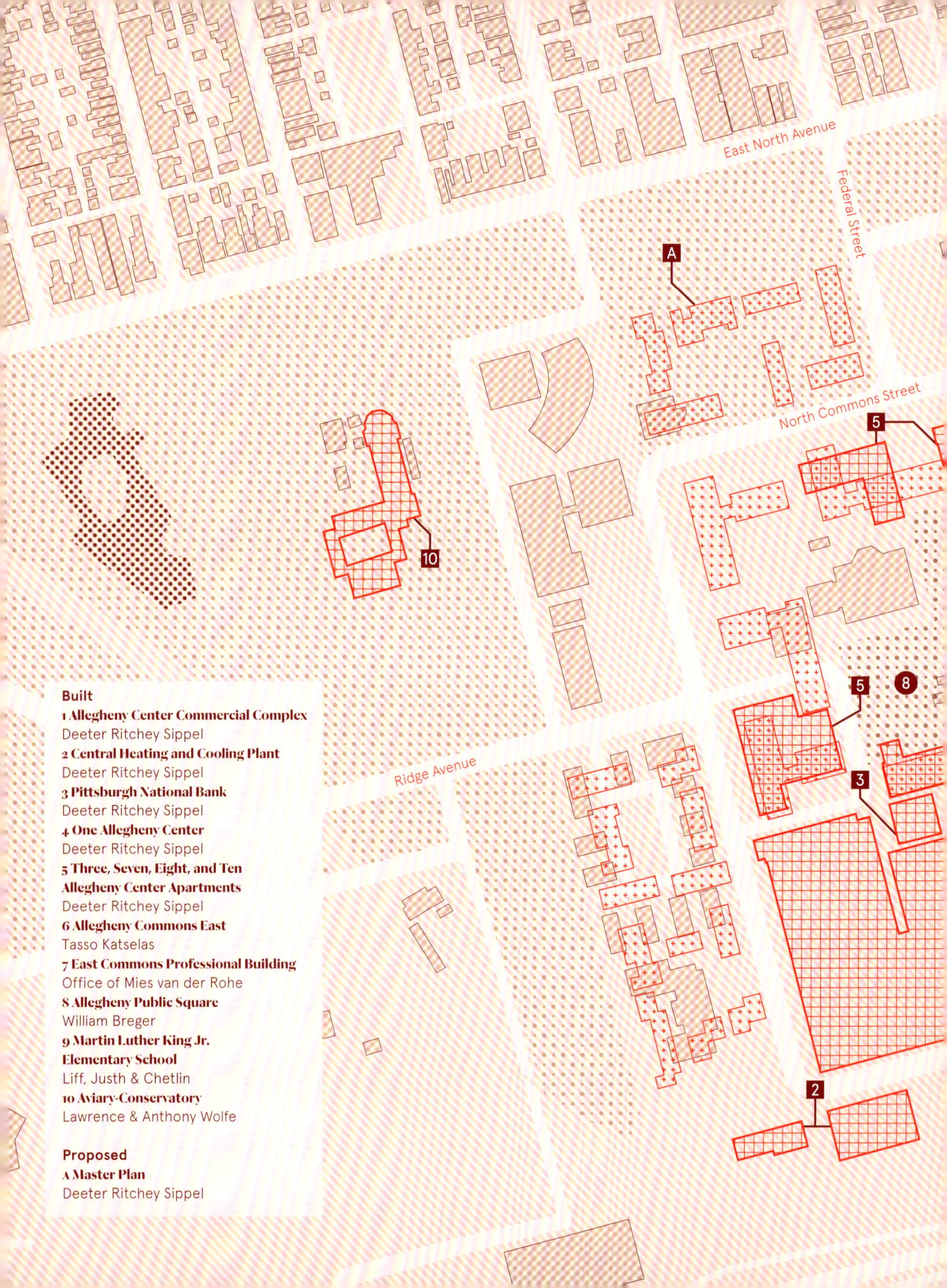
East North Avenue
Federal Street
North Commons Street
Ridge Avenue
A
5
10
5
8
3
2
Built
1 Allegheny Center Commercial Complex
Deeter Ritchey Sippel
2 Central Heating and Cooling Plant
Deeter Ritchey Sippel
3 Pittsburgh National Bank
Deeter Ritchey Sippel
4 One Allegheny Center
Deeter Ritchey Sippel
5 Three, Seven, Eight, and Ten Allegheny Center Apartments
Deeter Ritchey Sippel
6 Allegheny Commons East
Tasso Katselas
7 East Commons Professional Building
Office of Mies van der Rohe
8 Allegheny Public Square
William Breger
9 Martin Luther King Jr. Elementary School
Liff, Justh & Chetlin
10 Aviary-Conservatory
Lawrence & Anthony Wolfe
Proposed
A Master Plan
Deeter Ritchey Sippel

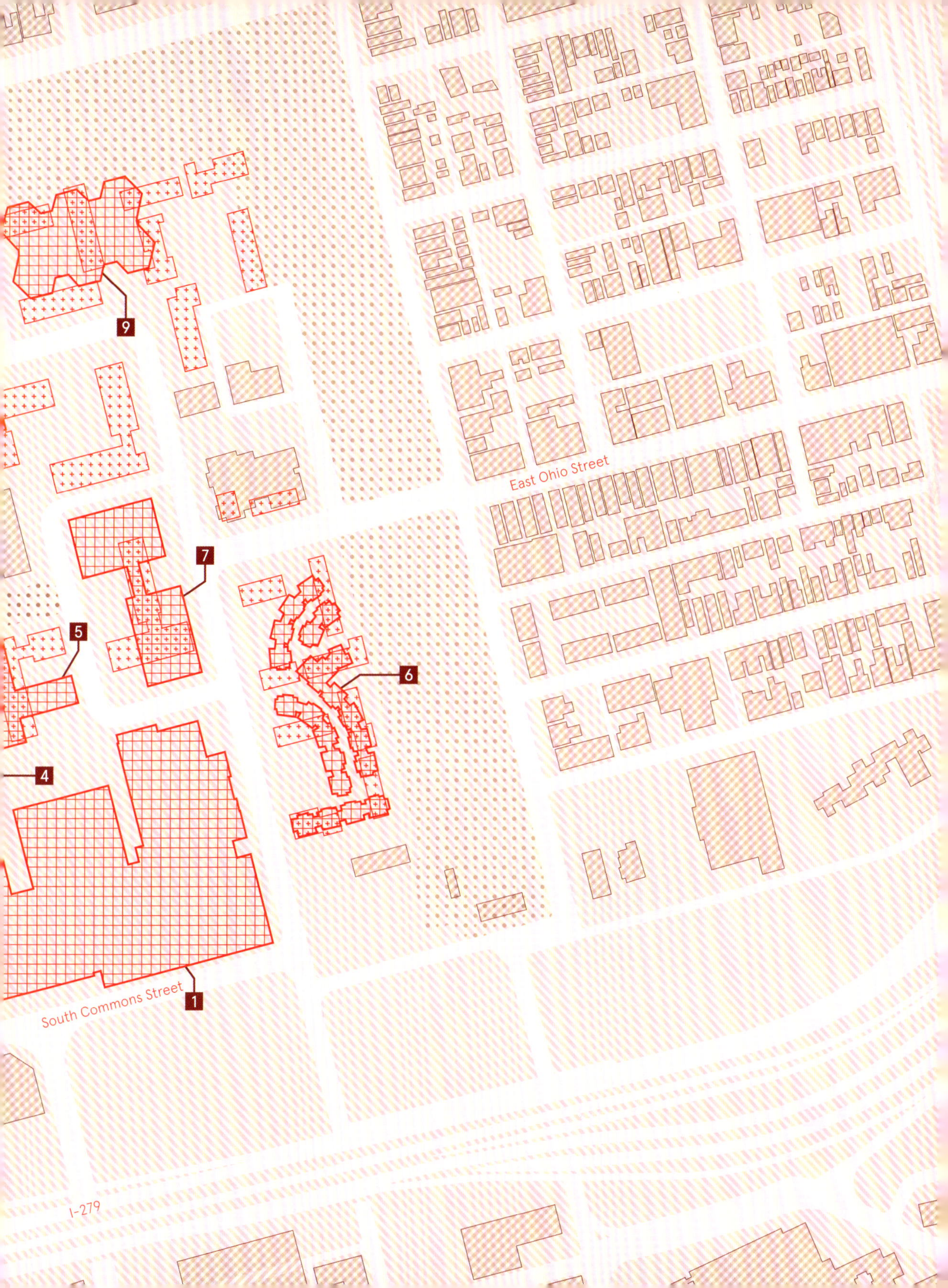

9
7
5
6
4
1
East Ohio Street
South Commons Street
I-279

ALLEGHENY

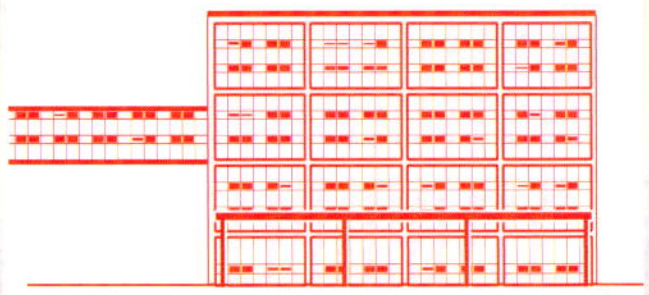

Heinz Vinegar Plant and Warehouse

Gordon Bunshaft for Skidmore, Owings & Merrill, 1952

Upon completion, the dark, glazed vinegar plant and the windowless white-brick warehouse made a striking pair and set a new standard for industrial architecture. Opened not long before Skidmore, Owings & Merrill's seminal Lever House, the vinegar plant used a stock curtain wall system to beautiful effect. A black steel frame was filled with green-blue glass panels that were outlined in aluminum. Red accents boldly enlivened the overall palette. Because no fireproofing was required, the steel was left exposed, enabling any corrosion caused by the vinegar fumes to be detected and remedied. The two buildings were linked by a third-story bridge through which packaged goods could be transferred from the plant to the warehouse via a conveyor along the ceiling. Most of the plant's critical machinery was housed on the upper stories to avoid water damage on the floodplain site. Vinegar tanks and goods intended for imminent transit occupied the ground level of the plant and warehouse, respectively.

The vinegar plant and warehouse are the only buildings that were completed according to SOM's master plan for the H.J. Heinz Company complex. The plant and warehouse have been remodeled in recent years; both are now encased beneath an unfortunate layer of exterior insulation. Though the vinegar plant's beautiful glazing was heat- and glare-resistant, it did little to prevent the infiltration of cold air.

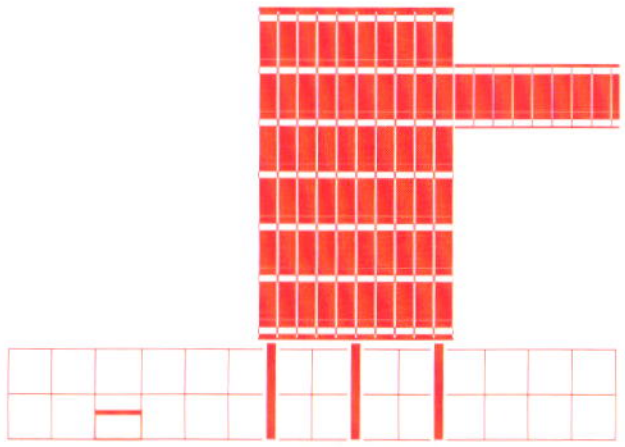

Riley Research Center

Gordon Bunshaft for Skidmore, Owings & Merrill, 1958

SOM's master plan for the H.J. Heinz Company plant called for a research and quality control facility to be the public face of the redeveloped complex. After SOM completed work on a number of factory buildings, Heinz called on the firm to design a more modest research center. Six levels of laboratories and offices are housed in an elegant slab of glass and aluminum raised over a plinth containing the lobby and pilot plant. The building presents a narrow face to the street, and the adjacent buildings block views of its full mass, creating the impression of a tower rather than a slab. In an homage to Mies, designer Gordon Bunshaft heightens this impression by thickening the aluminum mullions to emphasize the building's height. A fifth-floor bridge, which links the executive suite to an older office building, echoes the elevated connections found between production buildings—such as SOM's vinegar plant and warehouse—elsewhere in the complex.

In 1957 Heinz commissioned a monumental painting for the lobby from artist Stuart Davis. *Composition Concrete*, which includes a jumbled "1957" in its lower left corner, a reference to the year and to Heinz's "57 Varieties," now hangs at the Carnegie Museum of Art. The research center is being repurposed like many other buildings in the former Heinz plant complex.

Northside Institutional Church of God in Christ

James A. Mitchell, 1960

Just across the street from Allegheny Commons, this elegant modern church comprises a single rectangular room sheltered by a series of horizontal rounded-arched concrete vaults. The vaults meet the ground via thin concrete columns on the east and west sides of the building. The columns stand slightly in front of curtain walls that wrap the interior on all four sides. The glass and metal curtain walls seem to hang from the vaults, though they are tied to the concrete columns by metal anchors. A free-standing pavilion divides narthex from nave and is topped with a loft that hovers above the congregation. Sunlight streams into the interior through myriad panes of violet glass, an effect that is simultaneously warm and otherworldly.

Designed by James A. Mitchell, a native of Greece, shortly after the demise of his partnership with Dahlen K. Ritchey, this building was built as the Holy Trinity Greek Orthodox Church. It was subsequently expanded with a more utilitarian addition, creating a T-shaped plan. Since 2011 the building has been the home of a Pentecostal congregation. Some of the building's original fittings—including an elegant freestanding screen of stainless-steel crosses that stood before the front facade—were unfortunately removed during the transition in ownership.

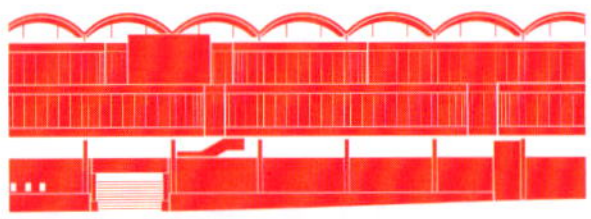

Allegheny Center

Deeter Ritchey Sippel, 1965-1971
Allegheny Center Mall, 1965
Central Heating and Cooling Plant, 1966
One Allegheny Center, 1966
Two Allegheny Center, 1971
Three, Seven, Eight, Ten Allegheny Center, 1967, 1971, 1973

Deeter Ritchey Sippel master planned and designed much of this project, as a response to serious decline of the Northside. They rendered each typology in its own architectural language: the mid-rise residential slabs in brick, the office buildings in flat glass and aluminum panels, the bank in rusticated brick with concrete columns, the heating and cooling plant as a minimalist, glazed box that exposes the inner mechanical works, and the mall in concrete and aluminum panels. The vast size of the mall was somewhat diminished by expressing the parking garage and the commercial complex separately within the concrete structure. A series of barrel vaults that sits atop the structure allows light to enter deep into the interior.

Although Allegheny Center saw some early popularity, it soon fell on hard times. The mall and the sunken plaza were particularly unpopular, the latter converted to office space and data center storage, the former eventually filled in and replaced. Recently acquired by Faros Properties, the new owners have invested in the complex, and, together with neighboring cultural institutions, are breathing new life into an area that lay moribund for decades.

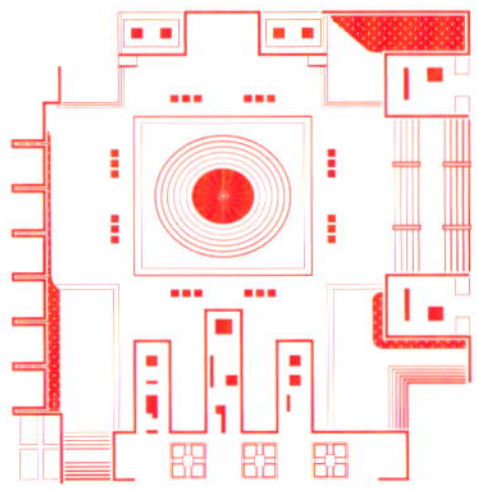

Allegheny Public Square

William Breger, 1967

In October 1963, Mayor David Lawrence launched an international competition for a new public space intended to serve as a centerpiece for the Allegheny Center development. The square was to replace the historic public square of Allegheny City. The competition jury was chaired by Hideo Sasaki, a modernist landscape architect and chair of the Landscape Architecture Department at Harvard. Other members included Henry J. Heinz II; Gordon Bunshaft of Skidmore, Owings & Merrill; and Pittsburgh modernist architect Dahlen K. Ritchey.

Over 300 entries arrived, nearly a quarter from overseas; yet the jury deemed just one entry to be acceptable. "Altogether too many of the submitters felt the need to clutter up the square with kiosks, pavilions, pilons [sic] and other self-conscious architectural and sculptural elements," they wrote. The only design "of high enough quality to receive an award" was submitted by William Breger—a former employee of Walter Gropius and the Chairman of Pratt Institute's School of Architecture—and a team of students, James Terjesen and Warren Winter. They proposed a stark suite of concrete walls, with benches and steps that punctuated a continuous brick-paved surface and created places for walking and sitting around a slightly sunken pool and fountain.

Breger's design was built; but the square was underappreciated and badly neglected over time. In 2007, its neighbor, the Children's Museum of Pittsburgh, organized another competition to usher in its removal, won by Andrea Cochran Landscape Architecture. The new design, known as Buhl Community Park, filled in the sunken pool, softened hard surfaces with plantings, and strengthened connections with the fabric of the city.

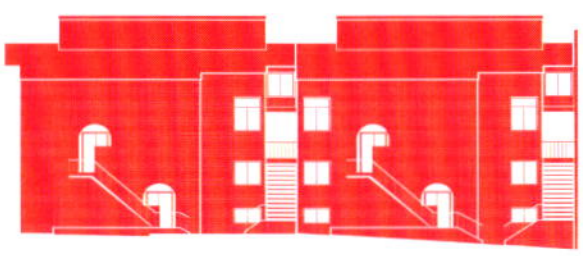

Allegheny Commons East

Tasso Katselas, 1973

This small housing community is an unlikely presence on a site between Allegheny Center, a massive commercial development, and Allegheny Commons, a historic public park. Allegheny Commons East is frequently likened to a village, and architect Tasso Katselas cites Greek hill towns as precedents. In some respects it mirrors Chatham Village with housing units that face central communal spaces and car access from the rear. It was built as low-income housing, but designed with the amenities of a neighborhood.

The community is organized into nineteen distinct apartment blocks, which are configured in curvilinear sequences that snake across the site. The blocks each contain six units, of varying sizes, within more or less cubic brick masses with gabled roofs. Blocks are linked to one another by first-floor breezeways and upper level balconies, which act as hinges when the blocks pivot axially. Exterior stairways, round-arched entrances, and diverse window types further animate the elevations. One additional block contains one-bedroom apartments and community spaces.

A pedestrian street winds through the village. All of the units open onto this street, encouraging social interaction among neighbors.

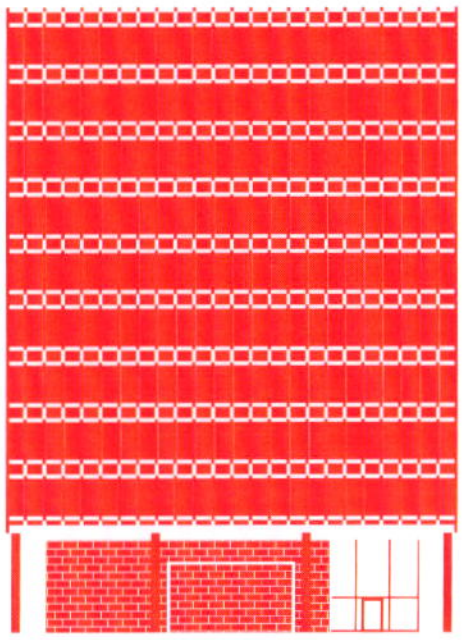

East Commons Professional Building

Bruno Conterato for the Office of Mies van der Rohe, 1976

The East Commons Professional Building, built for the IBM Corporation, was designed by Bruno Conterato on behalf of the Office of Mies van der Rohe. The commission came shortly after Mies and Conterato designed IBM's Chicago headquarters; but the Pittsburgh building was designed after Mies died in 1969. Following a prior succession agreement, the firm operated as "The Office of Mies van der Rohe" for five years, during which time this building was designed. The firm was renamed Fujikawa, Conterato, Lohan & Associates in 1975. When the building was completed in 1976, IBM moved its Pittsburgh office to Allegheny Center from its former building in Gateway Center, now the United Steelworkers Headquarters.

The new project comprised a boxy steel-framed ten-story tower with an accompanying concrete parking garage. A canopied walkway connects the two structures, providing cover on rainy Pittsburgh days. Mies's influence is immediately apparent in the office tower, where an open arcade surrounds the glazed elevator lobby, which is anchored by a brick core. The building's aluminum and glass curtain wall rehashes a familiar Miesian theme, with I-sections attached to the window mullions. Here, however, the finish is white instead of the more common black (as at Duquesne University's Mellon Hall of Science). Thick spandrels display the divisions between stories, creating a rhythmic series of stripes along the building's elevations in tandem with tinted glass.

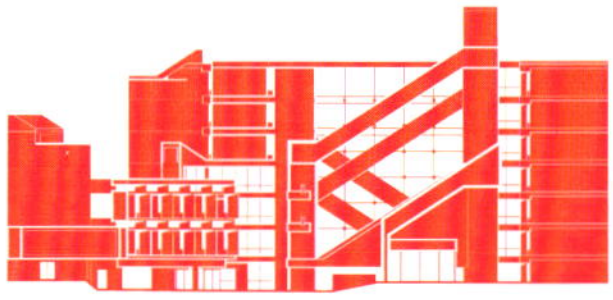

Community College of Allegheny County, Allegheny Campus

Tasso Katselas Associates, 1975

Like much of Tasso Katselas's architecture, the Allegheny Campus of the Community College of Allegheny County (CCAC) has been revered and reviled for its ambitious Brutalist architectural design. CCAC's brick and concrete construction materials, cylindrical pylons, jutting fenestration, and expressive diagonal escalators are trademarks of Katselas' architectural language as demonstrated in key projects such as the Saint Vincent Archabbey Monastery and the later Pittsburgh International Airport. The interiors of the CCAC buildings are marked by weighty forms and occasional soaring spaces while housing a wide variety of educational facilities.

Here Katselas designed interlocking classroom, library, and humanities buildings, and a freestanding physical education building. The cluster of buildings encloses a loosely defined quadrangle at the campus on Monument Hill. Overlooking a web of highways, the campus accommodates the parking needs of a commuter college, while offering some urbane amenities. A sunken outdoor theater sits near the campus entrance on Ridge Avenue, and another opens up from the basement level of the library building. Both recall a key element of another commuter college of the era, Walter Netsch's design for the University of Illinois at Chicago Circle.

I am not in favor of the destruction of automobiles, not even necessarily of the diminution of the automotive population, but I am most definitely in favor of domesticating it, and making it useful to the human race, just as we did with the horse and the cow and various types of poultry...

Victor Gruen

The Heart of Our Cities, The Urban Crisis: Diagnosis and Cure, 1964

EAST LIBERTY

Long considered Pittsburgh's second downtown, East Liberty was the commercial core of the East End, historically a preferred location for the city's upper and middle classes. As those with means increasingly relocated to the suburbs in the postwar era, local merchants and other civic leaders asked the Urban Redevelopment Authority (URA) for assistance in saving East Liberty from through-traffic congestion, a high rate of commercial vacancies, and deteriorating housing stock. In 1960, following its successes with the downtown Renaissance and its challenges with redeveloping the Lower Hill, the URA took on its largest redevelopment project to date with an unprecedented amount of community input. Absorbing Gruen's ideas of reestablishing human-centric social spaces in the face of growing sprawl, through-traffic was diverted via a boulevard looped around the commercial core, with surface parking lots available for those intending to shop. The business corridor was transformed into the East Liberty Pedestrian Mall, designed by landscape architects Simonds and Simonds, with wayfinding and signage by Peter Muller-Munk. Tasso Katselas was tasked to design 1,800 new residential units in a mix of townhouses, mid-rise apartment buildings and towers, including the heroic East Mall Residential Tower that spanned Pennsylvania Avenue.

Built by private developers who benefited from government subsidies for building affordable housing, the new residences changed the demographic of the area, but did nothing to stem the tide of middle-class flight. Many retailers relocated, further contributing to the downward slump. The success of the road loop hinged upon a new highway from East Liberty to downtown, which never materialized, and East Liberty Boulevard became famously known as the "road to nowhere." Today, most of the built plans of this era have been undone. With the formerly malled streets reopened, residential towers demolished, new housing in place, and the loop road gradually reintegrated into the street grid, East Liberty is again looking at revitalization.

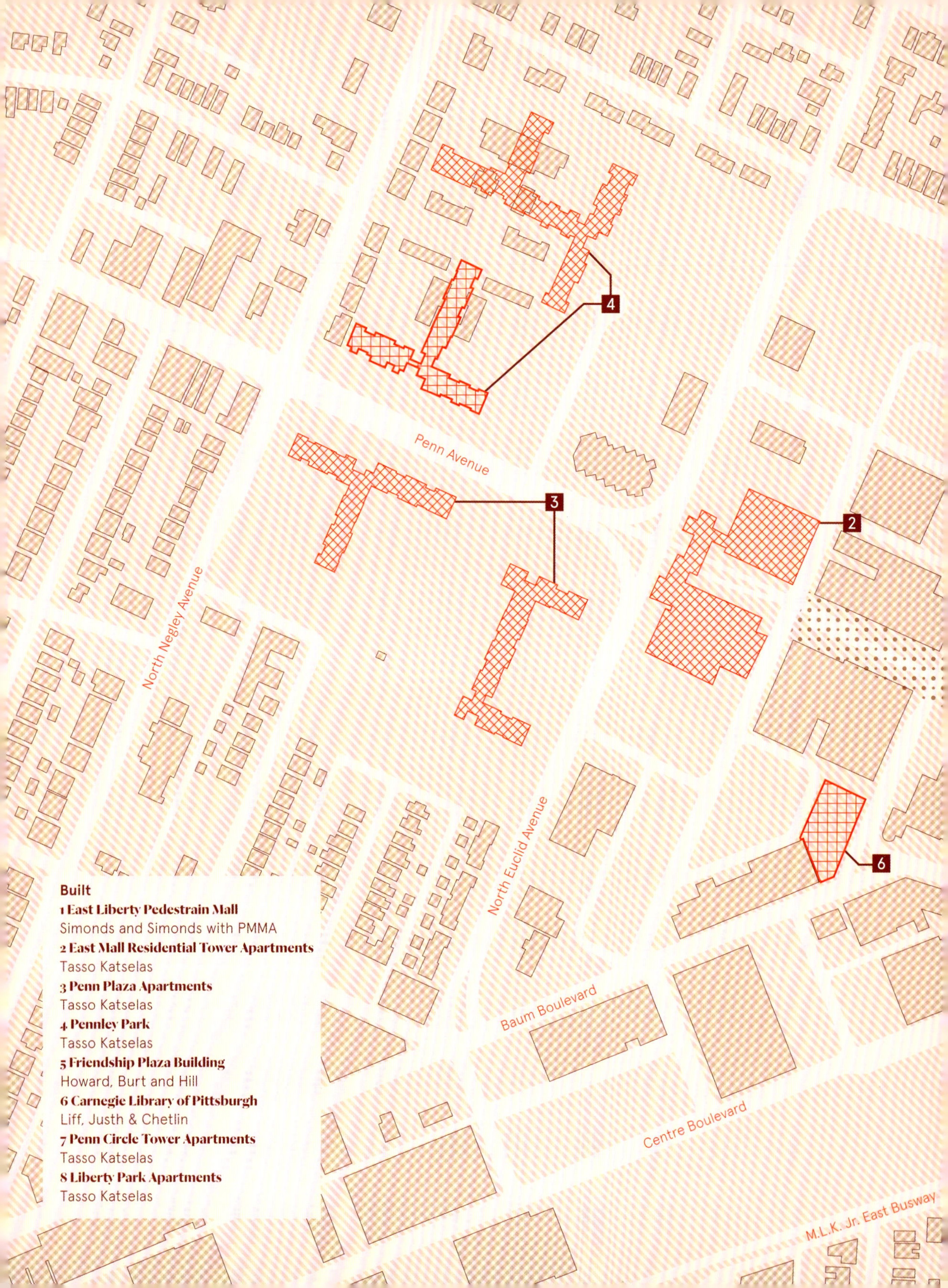
Penn Avenue
North Negley Avenue
North Euclid Avenue
Baum Boulevard
Centre Boulevard
M.L.K. Jr. East Busway
2
3
4
6
Built
1 East Liberty Pedestrain Mall
Simonds and Simonds with PMMA
2 East Mall Residential Tower Apartments
Tasso Katselas
3 Penn Plaza Apartments
Tasso Katselas
4 Pennley Park
Tasso Katselas
5 Friendship Plaza Building
Howard, Burt and Hill
6 Carnegie Library of Pittsburgh
Liff, Justh & Chetlin
7 Penn Circle Tower Apartments
Tasso Katselas
8 Liberty Park Apartments
Tasso Katselas

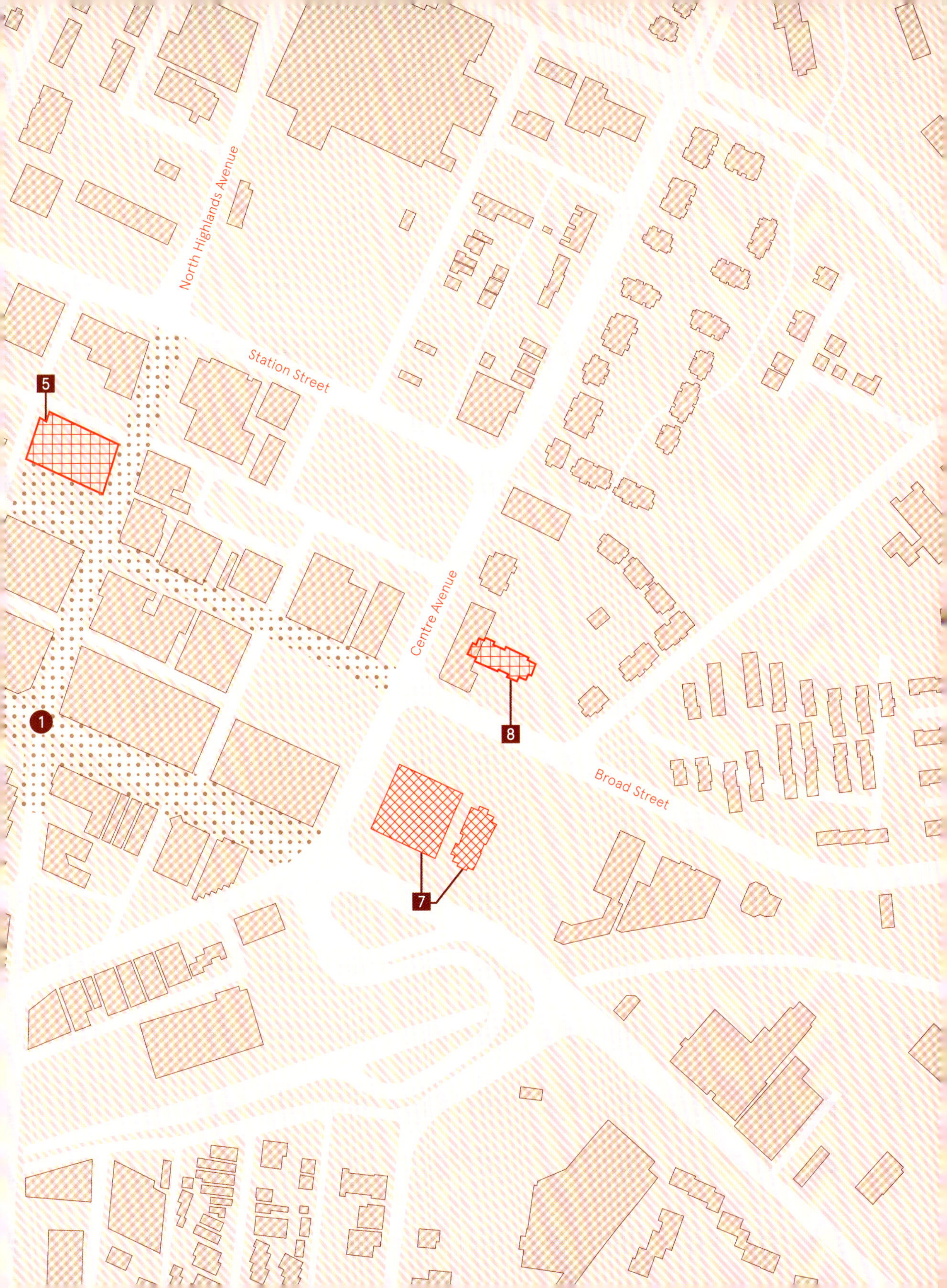
North Highlands Avenue
Station Street
Centre Avenue
Broad Street
5
1
8
7

EAST LIBERTY

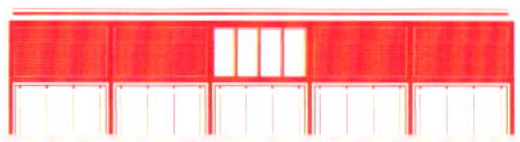

Carnegie Library of Pittsburgh – East Liberty

Liff, Justh & Chetlin, 1967

The East Liberty branch of the Carnegie Library of Pittsburgh stands near the heart of the community, across from the East Liberty Presbyterian Church. Originally designed by Liff, Justh and Chetlin, the library added a civic dimension to the neighborhood's ongoing revitalization. Constructed in the midst of a larger effort to build or renovate public libraries in the 1960s, the original design was emblematic of its time. The simple two-story building was composed of a thin concrete column structure with floor-to-ceiling glass along the street level, and brick panels infill above, with the exception of the central bay, which had four punched windows. The open floor plan was punctuated by a sculptural staircase that led to upper-level stacks and a reading room.

Forty years later, the building was updated and added to, in an effort to accommodate increased space needs, but also to indicate city attention to the area after decades of neglect. A 2010 redesign reflects EDGE studio's deconstructivist approach. A rainscreen facade of folded black zinc panels lines the exterior, defines points of entry, and revealed a large glazed ground-floor reading room and children's library. The library also provides a backdrop to Virgil Cantini's relocated 1969 sculptural fountain, *Joy of Life*, which was initially placed on the East Liberty Mall.

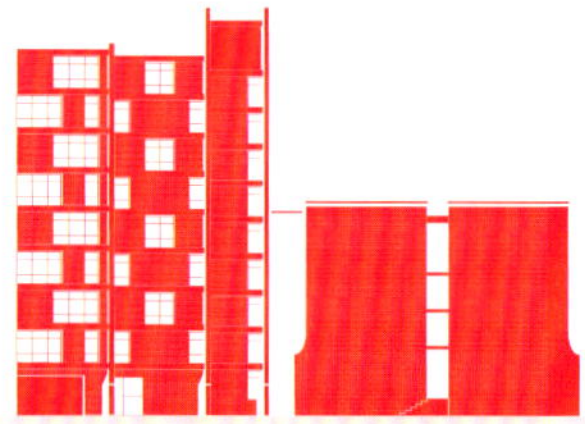

East Liberty Housing

Tasso Katselas, 1965, 1967, 1971

As part of the urban renewal plan for East Liberty, 1,800 new units of housing were constructed in the late 1960s and early 1970s. Designed by Tasso Katselas Architects, the mix of towers, mid-rise apartments, and townhouses changed the landscape of the neighborhood. As a result, the project inevitably came to symbolize all that was wrong with urban renewal, despite its best intentions and interesting use of basic materials in a low-budget endeavor.

The most notable element was the tower that straddled Pennsylvania Avenue, establishing a brick and concrete gateway to East Liberty, and allowing vehicles to pass underneath. This landmark was complemented by a series of low- and mid-rise apartment buildings, arranged in T-shaped plans that helped define the public spaces around them. The brick walls running perpendicular to the long facade of the building are load-bearing; protruding beyond the main elevation, they are expressed as fins that cast shadows along the length of the project. The facades are further enlivened by a playful placement of floor-to-ceiling windows. This playfulness is not arbitrary, but instead determined by the dimensions of the structural bay and its ability to accommodate one-, two-, and three-bedroom configurations.

Despite earning some early accolades from critics and new residents, the projects have been much reviled. In 2005, the towers were demolished, and several of the lower and mid-rise elements as well. Many of those remaining were given face-lifts beyond recognition. The owner recently asked tenants to vacate the premises, and it has since been completely demolished.

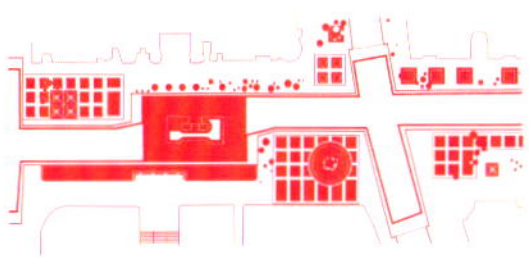

East Liberty Pedestrian Mall

Simonds and Simonds, 1969

The commercial core of East Liberty, the Pedestrian Mall was weakened and threadbare by 1960. Local merchants and other civic leaders asked the Urban Redevelopment Authority to help combat through-traffic congestion and a high rate of commercial vacancies. The URA's largest redevelopment project to date included the diversion of through traffic via an enormous loop around the commercial core; the creation of surface parking lots available for those intending to shop; and the transformation of business corridors into a system of interconnected pedestrian malls.

The Penn Avenue Mall, Highland Avenue Mall, and Broad Street Mall were designed by landscape architect Simonds and Simonds, with wayfinding and signage by Peter Muller-Munk. The malls occupied existing commercial streets that were redesigned for pedestrian use but permitted varying degrees of motorized traffic including buses, taxis, emergency vehicles, and some private vehicles. The new pedestrian environment included widened sidewalks and other pavings (including a giant EL logo), planters and plantings, benches and shelters, bollards and globe lighting, and a playground for children. Two focal points were *The Joy of Life*, a 1969 sculpture and fountain by artist Virgil Cantini; and Highland Square, a ½-acre landscaped public space with additional fountain.

Many of East Liberty's commercial buildings were preserved, unlike at other urban-renewal sites; but many were demolished as new buildings were built to fill vacant lots. But the pedestrian malls and new buildings failed to arrest the area's commercial decline, and the streets were gradually rebuilt and reopened to traffic. *The Joy of Life* was relocated to a nearby intersection, and part of Highland Square remains as a shadow of its former self.

Perspectives

Interviews

Interview with Robert Pease conducted in Pittsburgh on December 10, 2015, by Rami el Samahy with Matthew Newton and Shamus Fatzinger.

Robert Pease

Robert B. Pease was born in Nebraska in 1925. He served during World War II as an Air Force navigator before coming to Pittsburgh to study engineering at the Carnegie Institute of Technology (now Carnegie Mellon University). Upon graduating, he worked for the university, working with a group that focused on postwar development of the campus.

In 1953, he joined the Urban Redevelopment Authority of Pittsburgh (URA) and by 1958 became its Executive Director. During his tenure at the URA, Pease worked on more than forty projects in the city, including the neighborhoods of the Lower Hill and East Liberty. Pease subsequently became the Executive Director of the Allegheny Conference on Community Development (ACCD) in the late 1960s. Under his leadership, the organization secured grants for public schools and the expansion of the Pittsburgh International Airport.

After leaving the ACCD in 1991, Pease became the Senior Vice President of the National Development Corporation, a private real estate development and construction firm. He also served as a consultant for urban redevelopment projects around the world, including in Japan, India, Ireland, and the United Kingdom. He has won several awards for his work, including being named an Honorary Member by the American Society of Civic Engineers in 1994.

What were your impressions of Pittsburgh when you first arrived?

I came to Pittsburgh in August of 1946. Sometimes when I'd get up in the morning—I lived at the corner of Forbes and Morewood in a fraternity house—I couldn't see across the campus because of the smoke. My upper lip would be grey just from breathing Pittsburgh air. So Pittsburgh was a thriving city, industrially, but as a place to live, I didn't think much of it. I came from the Midwest with clean air and had no plans to stay in Pittsburgh. I thought I would leave because the city was a pretty lousy place then, smoky and dirty, and I thought, "Well, I'll get a job anywhere west of the Mississippi," but it never happened.

Of course the winter of '48 was the last smoky winter and the change was dramatic. I've often told people that was one of the reasons Pittsburgh began to have successes in terms of its rejuvenation; people had the feeling, "Well we got rid of the smoke, now let's do some more." At the same time, the flood-control dams were being built, which meant that the flood of '36 would never happen again, so that was another plus. In those days the mills and industries were going crazy, employment was strong, and it was a great city to be in economically.

So it was almost happenstance that you stayed here.

I worked at [Carnegie] Tech for four years after

I graduated. A fun job. I tell my kids and grand kids: Your life happens, you can't even try to make plans. Take advantage of the messiness.

What drew you to work at the URA?

An accident. I was working on the campus and Web Jones, who was the Dean in Engineering, called me to his office one day, and he said, "You know, there's a friend of mine who's head of the Redevelopment Authority in Pittsburgh, and he's looking for an engineer." So he called this fellow, Jack Robin, and said, "I'm talking to a man named Bob Pease. Here's his record -" and he had turned over the back of it and he said, "and he has a distinguished flying cross and five air medals..." He had read my war record, not my school grades! My grades were okay but not great.

I went downtown and I met with Jack. After fifteen minutes he offered me a job. The URA was just starting. Jack Robin was the first executive director, a man named Ted Hayes was the attorney, and I was the engineer. We were a staff of three, plus clerks. And it just gradually began to grow to what it is today.

Was there a sense early on that you were doing something unprecedented?

Personally, no. I didn't appreciate that. As I grew in the job and became head of the URA, I began to have an appreciation because I was able to travel with Mayor Lawrence to some different cities, and I realized we were becoming an example for other cities to follow. So I didn't have this personal feeling that I was doing these great things, but I felt that Pittsburgh was special and was becoming a good place to live in.

What are some of your proudest achievements at the URA?

I think one was to collect and manage a good staff. In terms of projects, the Lower Hill was underway when I got involved. Allegheny Center, East Liberty, the North Side, were other projects we started ourselves. The Allegheny Center was the best designed project we had done.

THE HILL

Was there support for the Lower Hill redevelopment initially, even from the Hill community?

There was really no opposition during the early public hearings. Now that may have been a sign of the times, because that was a 'You can't fight City Hall' period of life, but there was a general consensus that the Hill was in need of change.

There's one story I like to tell about a landlord who owned two buildings in the Hill District. He asked me if we would leave those two houses for him. So I went to look at them. There were two houses, with four families living there. Each family had three rooms: basement, first floor, second floor. There was no plumbing, just an outhouse. The only heating was through open grates. It was bitter, bitter cold the day I went up there. The air quality, the carbon monoxide levels, was just awful. The saving grace was that the walls were full of cracks, so they got some fresh air. There were a lot of buildings like that in the Hill District.
It always interests me that historians talk about this beautiful neighborhood that was torn down. If you walked through there in the summertime, you could smell the outhouses. I think it was a slum, by almost any definition.

[Urban critic and historian] Louis Mumford visited Pittsburgh, and I took him for a walk through the Lower Hill one hot summer afternoon. He told me that he would like to see old brick houses, to see what could be saved. At the end of the day, Mumford said, "You know, I really don't see any redeeming grace; I don't see anything that is worth saving." That's not published, but that's what he told me. And being in his company was kind of a thrill for me.

We were excited by the Pittsburgh Art Center development at the east end of the project. Gordon Bunshaft was the lead architect. There was a theater, underground parking, a sculpture garden and an art museum. Several foundations put almost $2,000,000 into the planning and guaranteed that the land would be bought for that purpose. In those days, you had to have the land guaranteed to be developed in order to have a project approved for federal funding.

Why was a project for a cultural acropolis on the Hill incapable of accepting and incorporating the culture that was already there, which included a phenomenal jazz scene?
It's a hard question and it deserves a hard answer—but I would surmise that racial segregation was an issue. The population to the east was pretty black and there was growing sensitivity or fright to that. People would gather from the Hill at the church up at the corner of Center and Bedford, and then march downtown to Mellon Square; and the head of Mellon Bank would call me and say, "We got all these blacks out here in the square, what should we do?" I said, "Nothing, just keep on doing your business." They meant no harm; they were just demonstrating and they were developing strength through the demonstrations. But that, I think, did a lot to cool off the desire to build this great art center in that area.

EAST LIBERTY

Was the process different in East Liberty? What lessons did you learn from the Hill experience?
East Liberty was so big—250 acres—and we were trying to do so much rehabilitating old structures, tearing down others and building new, it was almost too big to handle. In retrospect, it wasn't a great success. Yes, there was some new housing; yes, we shrank the commercial area, from three million square feet of commercial space to about a million-nine, and maybe sometimes inhumanely to some of the small businesses, which is a small regret. But I don't know what the answer might have been to save those either.

I think the concept was good; it tried to organize traffic, to divert the 80% of traffic that was through traffic, and in doing so create a viable pedestrian realm. But people complained about the traffic pattern. They didn't know how to get from Point A to Point B by going around the circle. The pedestrian malls seemed like a good idea at the time, but they didn't work because people didn't use them that much. In the end, we couldn't get the store owners to beautify their buildings or build back entrances [for access from the new parking lots]. It just didn't come off as well as we thought it might.

Three of the most frequent critiques leveled at the urban renewal era are the wholesale removal of existing fabric, the automobile-centric planning, and the lack of public participation; yet in East Liberty, the URA engaged in preservation, pedestrian-oriented open spaces, and a serious public engagement process. Is it true that there were 296 community meetings during the planning phase?
Something like that, yes.

And the project was initiated at the behest of the merchants?
The businesses, merchants, right.

And it was largely pedestrian. It didn't fit the villainous profile of urban renewal—there's preservation, there's public engagement, there's public realm—and yet it's seen as this—
—colossal failure, as some people say.

Would you agree that its failure was part of something larger, chiefly the suburbanization of America and the building of large malls outside of the city? Those who could were leaving the city in large numbers, choosing to live and shop elsewhere. It was a problem larger than city planning could solve.
I think that's exactly what happened. People wanted something new, they wanted either a new house or a new road or a new playground or a new school, and that was all available in the suburbs. It was also affordable; through FHA you could borrow money and buy a house. People moved to the suburbs for those things, but the lack of knowledge as to the implications of living there and working in the town, I don't think were foremost in anybody's thought. Now it's reversing but slowly.

East Liberty is now coming back because of the rise in commercial activity rather than people just saying 'I want to live in East Liberty.' Now there's a real reason to live in East Liberty, with what's happening economically. You have companies like Google coming there, stores and restaurants opening, lots of apartments occupied and more being built. Today, it has become a hot center and convenient to a lot of things. Though I don't know if anybody can take any credit for it, it just happens.

ALLEGHENY CENTER

How would you characterize the North Side planning process that led to Allegheny Center?

A study by the regional planning commission proposed a huge cut through Monument Hill to get the expressway north, which would've wrecked the neighborhood. We fought that and successfully stopped it. But out of that, Allegheny Center looked like an opportunity for development because of its location, its history, and because it was surrounded with the North Side Commons. The housing wasn't horrible but not good. The redevelopment was an opportunity to select a smaller area and try to build something that was really attractive.

1968 came along and there was a lot of racial tension. Following the assassination of Martin Luther King, a lot of social events occurred that made it difficult to finish the project. Gradually there were apartments added. It's a pretty good place to live, especially for those who work in the North Side, work in the hospital, or even Downtown. I still think the plans for that project were among the best the URA produced.

Both East Liberty and Allegheny Center were designed shortly after what Victor Gruen's projects in Kalamazoo and Fort Worth and followed his pedestrianization of commercial districts. For whatever reason, most of the pedestrian malls built in the sixties have been torn up; they just haven't succeeded in the United States.

I visited Kalamazoo, I visited Rotterdam. I was totally mesmerized with the thought of separating pedestrians from cars. When we designed East Liberty, we designed the ring road around it for circulation. We designed parking spaces where you could continue the left hand traffic pattern but still go left into the parking areas and park. And then you could walk on pedestrian ways to stores, both from the front and the back. We talked to the store owners about building new entrances on the back side for pedestrian access. They didn't do it. The commercial operators didn't have the money to successfully rehabilitate the store buildings. Later on, the city didn't put money into maintaining the pedestrian ways, and they were gradually opened up to taxis and buses and finally to cars.

ON CONTEMPORARIES

Could you speak about some of your contemporaries outside of Pittsburgh with whom you were in dialogue?

Ed Logue [Boston's Development Administrator] and I were very close, a similar history. He was a bombardier in World War II and I was a navigator. We both flew in B-24s and we used to compare our experiences. Charlie Farris ran the program in St. Louis, he had all kinds of problems. He had built a lot of new stuff; high rise, slab building apartments, highly touted at the beginning but later not touted at all except as a mistake. Lawrence Cox from Norfolk, Virginia had the first publicly financed renewal project in the country, which was a small housing project. I went to see that. The way they charted out the row houses was fascinating because they'd back a truck up to the front of the house, put blocks behind the wheels, put a cable around the house, and tighten a winch and just tear the house down in five minutes. It was wild. In San Francisco, the head of planning, Al Jacobs, came from Pittsburgh. San Francisco was more complicated, the mayor was more influential on the planning commission than Al thought it should be. He fought like mad against that triangular shaped [Transamerica] building, but it was built in spite of him.

For a while the Ford Foundation supported an organization of about twelve people who worked

Grandview Overlook, c. 1963.

in cities in regional ways. We used to meet a couple of times a year and just talk about issues. Just comparing notes. "Here's what we're doing, what are you doing?" and "What kind of problems are you having?"

There are some who argue that urban renewal was not the right thing to do. I don't know, I could make a case either way. Given the lack of building during World War II, the lack of maintaining what was built before the war, the recovery after the war was important and urban renewal was part of that excitement.

ON JANE JACOBS

Were you in Pittsburgh when Jane Jacobs came to town?

I was not. I read her book.

Did you read her book at the time?

Yeah, I was teaching at Pitt at the time and I wanted the students to read it as well. And she had a lot of good points, I disagreed with some of it but agreed with some of it. She had her viewpoint, which is legitimate. I don't think it was universally correct but that's okay. She had a good voice, she was bright and respected.

ON PITTSBURGH EXCEPTIONALISM

What distinguished Pittsburgh in that era from other cities?

Steel. We were producing for the war effort. 24 hours a day, 7 days a week, just going gangbusters. Fortunes were made. Pittsburgh became the arsenal of the world; well, that's an overstatement, but it was.

How would you say the dynamics of working here differed from Boston or St. Louis?

I think one of the keys here was that we had a mayor [David Lawrence] who was smart enough to know where politics belonged and where politics didn't belong. For example, all the time I was at the URA, he never once asked me to hire anybody. He kept that separate from his political life, and he recognized that was important. The other issue that I think was important was the complete devotion to the city by the business leadership. The Allegheny Conference is a good example where the executive committee was made up of chief executives of major corporations. Under their own rules they had to serve personally, they couldn't send any substitute to a meeting. You get those eighteen guys in a room and a decision is made, the decision sticks. Then the staff knew they had the backing of that kind of group. Whether it meant raising money, or policies or action, all that came together to make Pittsburgh a special city during that period.

Demolition of Carlton House, 1980.

Civic Arena under construction, n.d.

Jaye poses with the Lower Hill models, 1959.

It was an interesting time. I don't think it's a Camelot, but you could get dang close.

What is your favorite building from this era?
I always liked the Alcoa Building and I liked the U.S. Steel Building, that external structure was fantastic. I worked there for ten years, when Allegheny Conference was there; and it was a great place to be, a beautiful building, first-rate. I've always liked Gateway Center because of the open space; the open space is important, maybe more so than the buildings themselves. The buildings aren't great, but they were designed at a time when material was short.

Do you have any regrets?
Any regrets I have would not be about a huge project but about some little thing that we might have done better, usually with regard to the small businesses or relocation of some people. I don't have any huge regrets. Sometimes I wish things would've gone faster but they never did. Rebuilding an area is very difficult. It always takes more time than we think. The Gateway Center took over twenty years from beginning to end.

I think Pittsburgh has a lot to be proud of. I always thought Mellon Square was a great addition to downtown Pittsburgh. Living here is fairly easy compared to other cities. Commuting is not that difficult; you sometimes have traffic jams but it's not horrible. Mass transit is good, could be better, could be used more. I use it all the time since I've moved to Oakland. My car sits for days without being touched. It's a good system.

Any advice to those who are planning and designing today?
Just keep on keeping on, do your best and keep trying. Since I first got involved, the involvement of people has become much stronger than it used to be and that's for the better. In the beginning, it was, "Here's a plan and here's a hearing for city council and here's what we're going to do and it's all approved and let's start buying property." That's all been changed. Some folks say, "Well now it takes longer." Yes it does, but it's a better process. I sometimes think that the urban renewal process encouraged citizen involvement and changed a lot, including highway development. Maybe that's too simple a statement, but I think there's some truth to it.

One of the things we're struck by about this era is the willingness to think big, really big, for better and for worse. Afterward, the pendulum swung towards a timidity on the part of planners and designers and politicians because they didn't want to get their fingers burned again.
I think you're right. Citizen participation, particularly if they were against something, made it difficult for planners. I remember we had developed big plans for Oakland, because the schools and health centers were expanding. I remember a huge public meeting one night, and I was on the stage, and some guy way in the back of the room stood up and raised his hand. "I have a question: how can we stop this thing?" So I said, "You all get organized, all decide what you want and what you don't want, and let it be known to the public you'll stop this particular project." And they did.

In those days there was a federal regulation that if a university or hospital spent money to develop something, we would get credit for that money against a future project. So we saw this as a gold mine. In this case, I think we were greedy and we failed. But I'm not sorry we failed, it was a great experience.

In the fall of 2015, artist and photographer Shamus Fatzinger was driving through his neighborhood of Edgewood when he spotted a mountain of slide boxes out on the curb. Naturally, he pulled over to investigate. As he was rummaging through, a voice called down from the dark porch: "You want me to just tell you what's in there?"

The voice belonged to Robert Pease, director of the URA during most of Pittsburgh's Renaissance. Over 5,000 slides chronicle the life of the Pease family through more than six decades, celebrating their lives and their travels. Among these memories are traces of the city's evolution, as seen by someone intimately involved.

Allegheny Center, 1973.
Robert Pease in his office, 1980.
Hurricane Agnes, 1972.

Interview with Tasso Katselas conducted in Pittsburgh on April 10, 2016, by Rami el Samahy and Chris Grimley.

Tasso Katselas

Tasso Katselas was born in 1927 in the Pittsburgh area. After military service in World War II, he returned to Pittsburgh to study engineering and architecture at Carnegie Tech. Following apprenticeships at modernists Mitchell & Ritchey as well as Pittsburgh mainstays Ingham, Boyd & Pratt, he embarked on an extended tour of Europe. Returning to Pittsburgh, he taught architectural design while continuing his studies. He received a Master of Architecture degree in 1954 and established his own practice two years later. Perhaps the city's most prolific architect of the era, Katselas designed several of the region's best known projects, including the East Liberty Housing Project (1965–71), the St. Vincent Monastery at Latrobe (1967), the Community College of Allegheny County in Pittsburgh (1973), and later the Carnegie Science Center (1991), and the Greater Pittsburgh International Airport (1992). He also designed a number of buildings in Oakland, many projects for the Allegheny County government, and a scores of single-family homes across the Pittsburgh region. Katselas received numerous local and national accolades over the course of his long career.

You grew up in Pittsburgh? And then practiced here?

I ended up here by accident, even though I was born here. It's a long story, but I had met Frank Lloyd Wright and he offered me a job working for his office in San Francisco. At that time, I was teaching in Kansas City. When he made the offer, I packed everything up and drove to San Francisco. When I arrived there, the studio didn't know anything about a job. They called Wright and he said, "Well, oh yeah. He's from Pittsburgh. Let me talk to him." He told me, "I want you to go back to Pittsburgh." I said,"I want to be in San Francisco." He says, "Well, look. We're doing a chapel at Fallingwater for Mrs. Kaufmann." I said, "Mr. Wright. I spent all my money getting here." He assured me, "You're going to enjoy it. Go back and see Mr. Kaufmann and he'll know all about it." So I got my wife in the car and we headed back. On the way back, Mrs. Kaufmann died.

And so did the project.

What a "welcome home"...

At that time, driving across the country, you didn't have access to news. I got to Pittsburgh, called Mr. Kaufmann, and his secretary, thank God, said that Mrs. Kaufmann died. I called back, and of course, the deal was dead. So in a strange way, I ended up here. John [Knox] Shear was head of the Architecture Department at Carnegie Tech, and he took pity on my predicament, and gave me a job teaching students an introductory course in architecture. I got my Masters simultaneously while also working part-time. One of those projects was a student hangout called The Greeks—they were friends of mine. It was a sequential space of brick wall dividers, with a very soft undulating wall on one side, and a very abrupt wall that divided the eating area from the dining area. The students loved it and it got a lot of attention.

I wasn't a registered architect at the time. I used an engineer to stamp my drawings, but I did get attention for the project. On seeing it, another group asked me to look at doing an upscale restaurant. I was so egotistic I said, "I'll do it, but I want no interference." One of those dramatic statements that you really regret later. They said, "Are you full of shit? We can't trust you. We have budgets." I said, "Forget it. I'm leaving." I left and went to New York and got a job with Tishman. I told Tishman I needed two weeks to go to Maine to work on some cabins that a friend of mine had. His father was maître d' at the yacht club in New York and he had a wonderful place in Maine. While I'm in Maine, I get the telegram that says, "Okay. We agree to your conditions provided you meet this budget." I turned around and came back and did the restaurant, which was a big sensation.

This town was totally square. If I had just done papier-mâché, it would've been wonderful. As I look back on it, it was a nice space. It had a moving wall that opened up after the dining hours so that the cocktail lounge and the restaurant melded into one space. People would "ooh" and "aah" when the doors opened. Sliding doors were fantastic in 1953. While working there one day, two guys walked in and said, "Hey. Do you do apartment buildings?" I said, "Right on. Apartment buildings." They were the prime developers in Pittsburgh known for being the most difficult clients anyone could work for, and they had built these red brick things that you see. I said, "I'll do an apartment, but I don't do red brick things." They said, "No. We're looking to make a breakthrough." Well the result was 5100 5th Avenue. Again, I wasn't registered so I had to find someone to stamp the drawings. I said, "I'm not registered, but I'm willing to design." They said, "We'll get you an architect. Don't worry." Then they got me an engineer who just stamped everything I did.

Once that was done, I ended up doing four buildings for them, one after the other. By then it was 1956. Meantime, I got a call from a man saying that he was thinking of developing housing with a new program of the federal government, Section 8. He said he'd like to meet me and we ended up doing most of the East Liberty buildings, a couple of high-rises downtown, a whole town in Norfolk, Virginia, a town in New London, Connecticut, a couple of towns in Ohio—all under the Section 8 program. The one in Norfolk and the one in New London were competitions that we won.

There's an interesting story about that New London one. Doxiadis Associates entered it and we beat them because I knew just what to do. Years later, I was in Greece and Constantinos Doxiadis invited me up to his office. It's right in the center of town; you have to walk up this steep hill. He had me sitting in the waiting room although he told me what time to come. While I'm waiting, I started leafing through some leaflets on the table I opened up and there is my project in Norfolk listed as a Dioxiadis project! So I held onto it, walked in, we shook hands, he offered me something to drink and I said, "You've done unbelievable things." I said, "Magnificent, huge projects. Why are you claiming this one?" Well, he stumbled and fumbled. I said, "You know, you're a bit of an asshole. You want to take credit for everything. You didn't do this. I did this." Anyway, that's just an aside. It intrigued me.

You said you knew exactly what to do. What was that?

Well, I knew what people needed by talking to them. I spoke to people that were looking for housing, that were being displaced, and the result is we had to find economy. Which is not a bad word in architecture. It's probably a word that the poet can use, but not the businessman. That led me to seek the least amount of space to provide the maximum amount of housing. The program that is written for Section 8, I finally stretched it to its limit in the Allegheny East Commons housing. The only reason that happened is because the director of HUD at that time in Pittsburgh trusted me after he saw what we had done and signed off on everything. I mean, the spaces between the buildings are much smaller than HUD regulations.

Could you speak about the process of designing and building the East Liberty housing?
We built the first batch of housing for eight dollars a square foot. Then it went to ten. Then it went to twelve. Then went all the way to fifteen. It was getting tough. When it jumped to twenty, we knew that we were in trouble. Today, you couldn't do the buildings we did for a $150 a square foot. They were all exposed brick walls. Wall bearing buildings. Repetition of the highest element. Efficient economy. We did it with oversized bricks. We had to educate the brick union and we had to educate the brick layers. They said that there was no way the oversized brick would work and it was no faster than regular brick, so I said to them, "Look. We'll have a guy manufacture us some oversized bricks and we'll have your worst brick layer lay a section and you have your best bricklayer layout a section and we'll see what happens at the end." It was a huge difference. The oversized brick was 12 inches long (as opposed to the standard 7 and 5/8 inch). We signed the contract that night.

The next morning, the brick layer that used the oversized brick couldn't lift his arm because he had to reach out further. So we redesigned the 12-inch brick with a notch in it, so that the mason could reach the same amount and that is what made a lot of the low cost housing work.

The one they're going to tear down [Penn Plaza Apartments] is the classic. The historical architects are happy to see my buildings disappear because I do not belong to the American Institute of Architects, I do not belong to any professional societies. I don't belong to any country clubs. I don't belong to any churches. I don't belong to anything but this office. I am not surprised that they're not trying to protect that building, but they will be forced to protect Kentucky Avenue apartment building because it broke new ground.

You also did a considerable amount of work at St. Vincent University.
I got a call out of the blue saying that the Abbey of St. Vincent wanted to interview me for a job. "They're not going to hire a Greek atheist to do their monastery," I thought. "Once they ask me what my religion is, it would be all over."

I came home, I said to [my wife] Jane, "These guys are really peculiar up there. They don't want to know whether I believe in God or not, they want to know if I believe in architecture, and I think I convinced them that I do." They called me to—I love this—they called me to give a talk to "the community." I thought they meant the community of Latrobe, the officials. They wanted me to speak to the two-hundred hooded monks. When I walked into that room, I had to catch my breath. I was just in my thirties. After the presentation I was asked to wait in an adjoining room. I waited for an hour and a half and I thought well, I guess the jig is up. But the Abbot came back and said that I was chosen unanimously. I worked for St. Vincent for forty-four years.

Marty Griffin saw the work, came back and said to the county commissioners who were trying to do a new airport, "You should talk to this guy." I met the commissioners. In the meantime, Griffin hired me to remodel the existing airport. He said it would be a five-year remodeling. What I did lasted thirteen years with that extension for TWA. Well, TWA went bust. All I got out of it was a lifetime membership to TWA.

Was it a real shift in thinking from a monk's abbey to an international airport?
I did do a lot of research and the fact that I remodeled the existing airport was a big compensation: I got to meet all the characters. I realized the biggest mistake made in designing airports

St. Vincent Monastery
Latrobe, Pennsylvania

"Twentieth century monastic life is not a refuge from the mortal condition. It is bound up explicity with religious man and his inner community and implicity with secular man. Architecture must act as an effective background for this commitment."

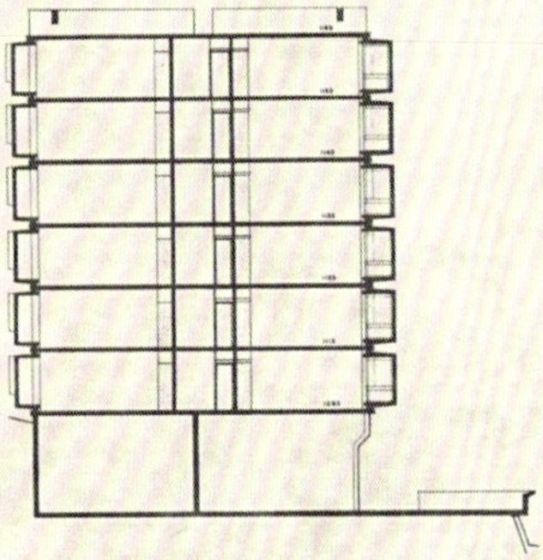

"The cell as the primary element offers a rich variety of personal space and light and time. A sequence that respects the individual but in turn manifests a relationship with the community as a whole through the common spaces; circulation spaces; in-between spaces; that link and bind each element. Each unit, each chapel, every terrace and garden and niche, build toward a unity of intention."

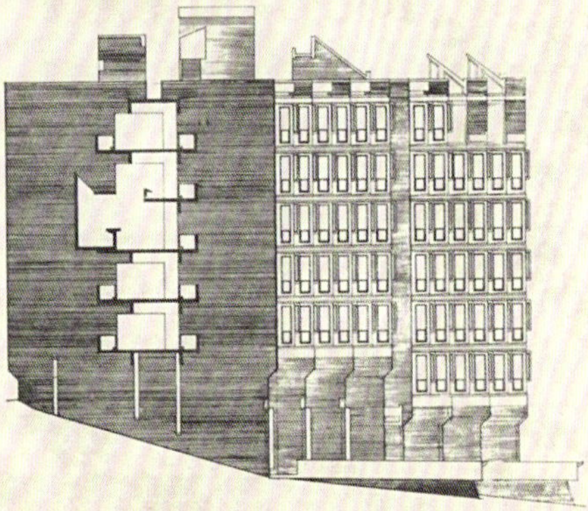

"This relationship was established through an almost tender exchange between client and architect until understanding became a growth out of a sense of monastic process. Final expression was generated as a reflection of this life—a life whose pulse is human, but whose impulse is devine."

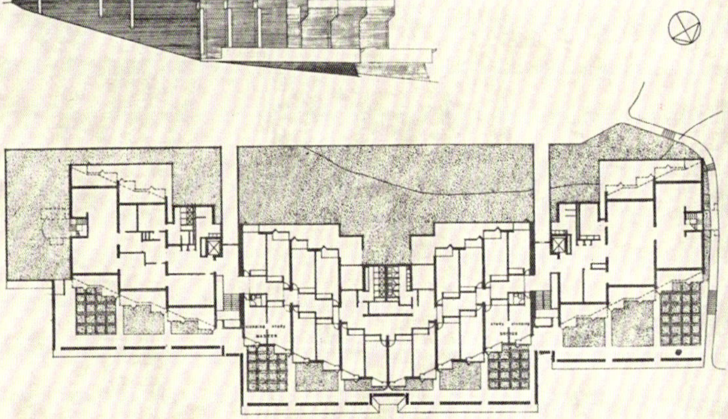

Drawings of St. Vincent Monastery, from self-published book, *Tasso Katselas Architect Planner,* 1969.

was in understanding where design begins. It begins when the guy makes his reservation at home, packs his bag, and gets in his car and heads for the airport. Then you start talking to the vendors: you talk to the guy that removed the refuse, the people that deliver the food. The airplane, that's all stock. It's all defined in a ledger. The FAA gives you that, but what about the human element? That isn't defined. That's the one I picked on, to make it user friendly. To make it such that when you arrived there would be no questions about where you go.

Everybody had been parking aircrafts wrong for years. I designed what's now called the Pittsburgh X, which all the airlines vetoed at first. Well, I fought like a tiger for that. I showed that not only would this be a more efficient way to park aircraft, it would also save fuel, which at that time was hugely expensive. It was the only thing airlines couldn't control.

Once it was finished, Norman Foster sent a team to visit us. They gathered enough information that they were able to duplicate our layout in Hong Kong to a tee. We won all kinds of awards and acclaim, but I never designed another airport.

I ended up doing a lot of housing for the elderly and nursing homes. I designed a nursing home for a group of doctors and it's one of my favorite buildings. It's in the middle of Oakland, it's now a dorm for the University of Pittsburgh. It's on Forbes where Simple Street bumps into it. It's a totally concrete building and it was revolutionary. The university has painted it and repainted it, but they can't destroy the integrity of it.

Could you describe what Pittsburgh was like when you were growing up and how it changed or how you saw it change once you started working in the city?
When I was a kid, one of my friends' fathers owned a restaurant at the Point. We could often not be able to see across the street. That's how bad the environment was. The biggest transformation is that the sun shines.

After the war you came back to Pittsburgh to study architecture at Carnegie Tech?
Yeah. While there I volunteered to work for Mitchell & Ritchey. I worked for free for them for two summers. They had me involved in the *Pittsburgh in Progress* exhibition where they made fantastic suggestions for the city. They made me tear out from the periodicals what was being published in different segments; apartments, hospitals, schools… Here I was, a freshman in college being exposed to everything that was being done in modern architecture, and getting fed in my brain the possibility that you can build these things instead of what I was watching being built.

Was it different from what you were learning at the time?
It was different because we were still square, not quite Beaux Arts, but just emerging. In my third year, John Knox Shear appeared from Princeton full of excitement then the whole category changed, and we changed with it. Mitchell and Ritchey were the guys that helped change things. As it changed, I thought I wanted to be part of this.

I've been told that I revolutionized stores and I think I revolutionized apartment buildings with what I did. At least I stretched the envelope so that other guys had the freedom to change and point to it. There are articles that I'm the godfather of Pittsburgh's modern architecture and I don't buy that. I think the seed was there and I think Mitchell and Ritchey planted it before me.

In the meantime, I was doing houses all the time. I did forty or fifty houses. When I got really busy, I still did a house a year. I wanted to deal with people. I wanted to know what a housewife did and what her problems were. It brings you down to earth.

It's interesting to note that one of the distinguishing characteristics of the postwar era is the relative youth of many of the architects. But even among those who were older, more established, there was room for innovation, experimentation. There were developers who were willing to give you that trust. There were city officials who were eager to project a new face of the city. This spirit is hard to find today.

If you're searching for a formula to get people to think creatively, I think you're going to have a hard job, because what's being produced now is minimum compliance architecture. It's cardboard stuff. That's ingrained and developers have taken over. As cheap as possible. Put some colorful panels up and that's it. They're tearing down one of the last pieces of solid apartment in the city (Penn Plaza apartments). Every apartment built in the last ten years in Pittsburgh is made out of wood, which is morally wrong. No matter what kind of wood you use, it's going to shrink. Drywall and wood. That's the formula, today.

Now, if I were to go public with what I'm saying, I would be attacked as sour grapes. Look, I'm almost 90 years old, I'm still working, we're busy, we still have fun, but I will admit that the developers are shying away from us because we demand something different and it costs a little bit more, but they don't see that the initial cost is really a preventive maintenance cost. How do you convince them of that? I was very good at it back then when I was young, I had the energy. I had the charisma. I could smile and talk them into anything.

I also think that the nature of development has changed. When you do a business plan as a developer you're looking at an eighteen- or thirty-six-month return on investment. You don't give a shit about the deferred maintenance cost or any of the issues that come later because they're not your problem.

And all this wood that we're seeing everywhere is being done in the name of sustainability, that this is all somehow more environmentally sound, this for me is the biggest offense; when the new construction is literally not built to last.

You know, I love this town. The bad, ugly, things that I thought were horrible are starting to look awful good to me, because they were built properly.

That's the sequence of events. Minimum compliance is the worst possible thing, and they even violate that! I guess if a big developer wants to build hundreds of apartments, we can have some leeway. But there's no such thing as leeway in human needs and human spirit.

What we're so intrigued by in this discussion, and in your writing, is a principled call for the need to elevate humanity, which flies in the face of the stereotypical caricature of modernism being all about the rigid form and it didn't take into account the human beings that were going to inhabit it.

Take Mies van der Rohe, Le Corbusier, even Wright… Mies believed in the ethic and moral principal of construction. If you didn't do it that way, then you don't build it, and he fought and twisted and turned and got his buildings built the way they should be built, and they're icons.

Corbu, you may not agree with him either, but if anybody ever fought for it, he did.

When I met Corbu, he took me to his office. At that time he was just beginning the Chandigarh commission, so it was a very exciting time in his office. He gave me to an elderly guy. This guy took me aside and he started showing me drawings and asks if I've seen any of his work? I said, "Yeah. I went to Savoye; it's a wreck." He says, "Oh there's a terrible story about Savoye. Mrs. Savoye was going to sue him and then the war came and then the whole thing dropped, and now they're talking about refurbishing it." He says, "That's not only it," he says, "The building in Marseilles that had full floor-to-ceiling glass, they had to put shutters…" and so on. So here I am, one of my gods is up there and this guy's maligning my god. I'm getting pissed off. Fortunately Corbu calls me over and showed me the preliminary drawings for Chandigarh. Amazing work. This was priceless stuff for a young kid.

St. Vincent Monastery, 1969.

St. Vincent Monastery, 1969.
Community College of Allegheny County, 1975.

Information Sciences Building, 1965.
Penn Plaza Apartments, 1965.

PENN PLAZA
APARTMENTS

Interview with Troy West conducted in Rhode Island on July 30, 2015, by Rami el Samahy and Chris Grimley.

Troy West

Troy West was born and raised in Pittsburgh. After graduating from Carnegie Tech he won the prestigious John Stewardson Memorial Fellowship in Architecture, traveled through Europe, and worked in Philadelphia with Louis Kahn and Oscar Stonorov. He returned to Pittsburgh in 1963, a tumultuous period in the city's evolution, and was soon drawn to the vibrancy and culture of the Hill District. His advocacy style of teaching and collaborative practice enterprises (under the names Architecture 2001 and Community Design Associates) presented a counter-narrative to the more top-down approaches that had developed the Point and the Golden Triangle. His architecture embraced the expressive ideologies and forms of modernism, which, when coupled with his unwavering belief in architecture as a social project, became powerful forces in their own right to elevate the voices of those not heard during the Renaissance.

You grew up in Pittsburgh.
Yes.

What are your memories about the way that Pittsburgh changed from your childhood to when you came back after your time in Philadelphia?
Well, growing up, they sometimes had to turn the streetlights on at 3 o'clock in the afternoon, the pollution was so bad. David Lawrence, the democratic mayor, and Richard Mellon said this has to stop. So there were people that just did it.

Architecturally, I didn't come of age until after I went to school. John Knox Shear was the Head at Carnegie Tech, and we had a field trip to Princeton—all of the faculty were from Princeton—and he knew everybody's name except mine. I was totally invisible. I got under the wing of one of the Korean war vets who introduced me to the work of Frank Lloyd Wright, and that was such a poison pill with these Princeton people—that I flunked, got a D-, the lowest in the class. Along the way I had some good teachers, and I won the John Stewardson Scholarship. The lead juror of the Stewardson was Oscar Stonorov. He built Carl Mackey Homes, the first public housing in Philadelphia in which the community was involved. I went to Philadelphia to pick up three checks, I think the whole thing was worth $1500, which ultimately kept me in Europe for almost a whole year. His secretary said 'Mr. Stonorov wants to meet you" So I go up to the office, and here is this guy, completely bald head, Russian accent, and he gave me introductions to everybody—Paolo Venini in Venice, people at Iittala in Finland, and then he said at the end "And when you're finished, you come work for me." I thought that was great.

In Philadelphia you also worked for Louis Kahn...
For two years at Kahn's I was fortunate to work on the Salk Institute. A great part of the two years I was there I was working on studies for the building. I worked a little bit on the Indian Management building, a tiny bit on Dacca. The office was on two floors, the Salk project was on the top floor, and that's where Lou's office was. The people working on Bryn Mawr, UVA, they hardly didn't see him, but upstairs we saw him all the time.

Our Way, axonometric sketch, Community Design Associates, 1971.

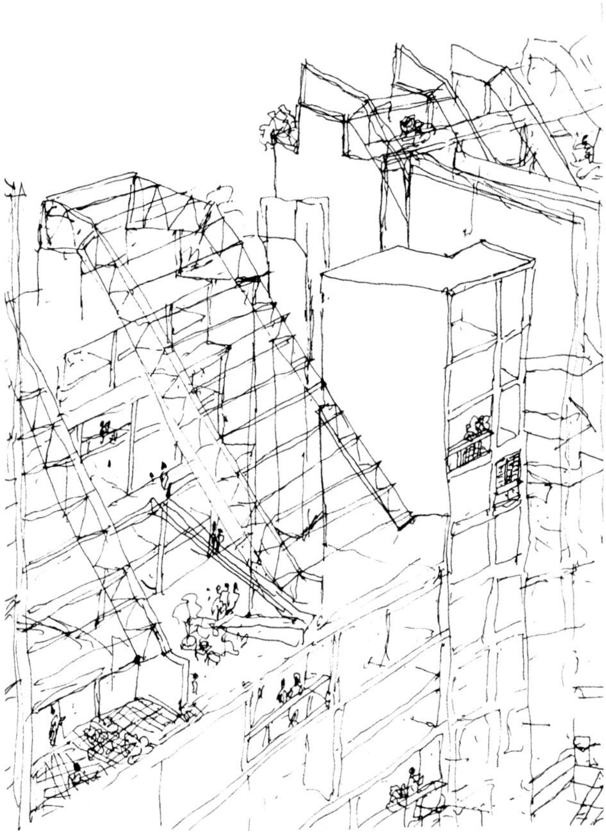

But I was working two dollars an hour, and I couldn't hardly live, I sold my wedding presents! But it was a good experience working there. Things went slow and he had to let the youngest people go, I tried to get another job in Philadelphia, but I couldn't, so I went back and went to see Tasso Katselas, worked for him for a couple years.

...and then you came back to Carnegie Tech under Schweikher?

There's that saying about when Brancusi had the chance to work for Rodin, an acorn can't grow under a big oak tree, and I think it was probably... I'd never taught before, but I thought I'd do it. I came at the same time as [artist and urbanist] David Lewis and [visiting UK urban designer] Peter Stead.

So by this time would you say that what now we call modernism is pretty much the agenda of what was being taught at Carnegie Tech at that time?

I think that under Paul Schweikher, it was definitely modernism. He would have faculty meetings every week, we'd have lunch together, we'd talk about everything. I said something about, "I know the painting and design department has an exhibition in the Fine Arts building, maybe the architecture department could have one." Schweikher was a larger-than-life figure. He would take an idea and say, "Why do you want to have it here, let's have it at the museum!" So we put a show called *Buildings by Pedagogs* at the Carnegie Museum. He was definitely favoring the younger faculty, because he had a lot of tenured people, but it was by and large all of the things in there were pretty modern.

What's fascinating to us about the projects that you were working on is that they were part of the time when real creativity came out of very small budgets. We don't see a whole lot of that anymore, especially with public housing, which now seems much more formulaic...

It's just awful. In the '60s, the best projects you could get were public housing. I was into public housing and low-income housing for sure, including the house that I built for myself, which cost $25,000! So Kahn was doing public housing, Stonorov, Norman Rice, every really good firm had public housing projects and they were great. I went out to Kahn's Mill Creek Housing a couple of times. I also worked on public housing for Stonorov, and I think his Schuylkill Falls project is maybe better than Mill Creek. He based it on what he did with Mackey Homes in the '30s—he really interviewed people.

So when you came back after that the city felt like a different place in terms of it's fabric?

No, the fabric was still intact. The only thing gone was the Lower Hill, and the Civic Arena was there. A friend got tickets for me and my buddy to go see the Rolling Stones at the Civic Arena. David Lewis was a big hockey fan, he had season tickets to see the hockey games, it was great. But then there are these ideologies, these are the people that will drive you crazy—the New Urbanists. They led the fight to stop the Civic Arena, but that's another story. I get these professional magazines, and there's one article about tearing down the Civic Arena, what are we going to do? Some housing? And guess what? There's this horrible building that the Penguins are building there— just a horrible piece of crap.

You were offering alternative proposals parallel to the more established efforts of the Renaissance, and very distinct from what is happening today, which is a neo-traditional response. I think this is part of what interests us in your work. It was modern, and unapologetically of the era.

When I came back from Philadelphia in 1963, I went to the Hill District. I'd take the 87 streetcar and ride up to the Hill District and go around sketching. I was just taken with all those narrow streets, and the place had so much energy. I made all of these drawing and paintings up there. And the first time I was up there sitting on the curb drawing, and it takes forever, some black guy comes up to me and he says, "we thought that you were from the CIA, but they wouldn't sit there that long!" I had a little bit of cache there, and I got introduced to and became friends with all of the local artists including the playwright August Wilson and painter Ewari Ed Ellis. They were a very interesting lot. So it was the place to be, the Hill District.

I got involved in trying to stop urban renewal. What they did in the Hill District was really horrible and opaque. But ironically, once we started Architecture 2001, there were some really good people at the Urban Redevelopment Authority who reached out and we were awarded the commission to build temporary relocation housing. It was a really enlightened program. They wanted to go into the Hill District and do some rehabilitation, but they didn't want to kick anybody out of their house, or have to leave their school or church. The first thing they wanted to do on vacant land was to build temporary relocation housing. People would be there for maybe six months, and then they'd bring another family in, when their place was finished. The first one we did at Bedford and Roberts and that was three units. The contractor was Jesus Inc.! I mean there were some real characters going around the Hill.

Our buildings were very modern, and were well received. We then did another four infill houses, and I'm not sure if it was on Summer or Arthur Street. Those were four units, and then we had the commission to do fourteen more units. We worked with the citizens up in the Upper Hill.

Then we got work through David Bond. He and I were classmates, and he arranged to have us do the Our Way project. So then we were working officially for the Urban Renewal Authority.

Community Map, Hill District, Community Design Associates (Troy West, Douglas Cooper; Delineators: Damion Austin, Chuck Culbertson, Jay Greenfield, Sharon Keeton, Joe Nagy, Robert Phipps, Emily Eckel, Sanders Woodall, Sir John Banks), 1971.

Construction meeting, Lower Hill, c. 1967.

Court of Ideas, c. 1967.

The first models and drawings of Our Way were as a paid study, and at that time Architecture 2001 was really rolling, the Court of Ideas was finished, we had a few projects, remodelings that we did. So we were holding on to the construction part and Ed Ellis, and organizers and all of these kids—Dickie Morten, a 17-year-old was in charge of trying to get things done. Finally, we met Chuckie Dial who had been in prison and knew how to build. Because in those days when you went to jail, you got some training.

At any rate, that was when we teamed up with [psychologist] Jay Greenfield and with [lawyer] Paul Titus, and his firm, Kaufmann and Harris. Paul took a big interest in what we were doing. We partnered up with Mellon Stewart Construction company to build the floors, pour the concrete, and implement the major mechanical systems. Our own construction company, Construction 2001, would do the infill.

The community was in part made up of 501c3 community board; Ruth Petrell who lived in the projects was head of it. It was a really heady time. Really exciting. It was getting published all over the place, including *L'Architecture d'Aujourd'hui*, who did an issue on American architecture in 1971. We were pretty well covered in that issue with Forbes Field, Our Way, and some others.

Everyone has talked about the Hill as this real cultural hotbed, past tense, and the jazz legends, everybody came through Pittsburgh.
Exactly...

And at the time the city is attempting to build a cultural acropolis there—with the Civic Arena and the Center for the Arts. These are two very different kinds of culture, it's almost as if the civic leaders felt that another definition of culture would be a detriment. Is that your sense of things at that time?
When I won the *Progressive Architecture* award for the Lower Hill Development for the Citizens Committee for District Renewal in 1966 I was working with the radicals, the organizers, and the militants. At the same time I was also working with Mrs. Frankie Pace, Mattie Addis, and Bob Lavelle, they were the establishment. So when they proposed to build the Symphony, it was adding insult to injury, because the URA had already constructed the Civic Arena, and nobody from the Hill liked what it stood for, and Skidmore, Owings & Merrill wanted to build the Center for the Arts on a big plinth, it was huge! So I came up with the idea of an alternative, and that's how we ended up building the housing.

I was always in two camps, even when we had Architecture 2001. In some ways I was an *enfant terrible*, but at the same time, I was working with these extraordinary people at the Urban Renewal Authority. Architecture 2001 was more than just an office, it was a bridge. Everybody came through, from Aldo van Eyck from Holland, to church groups, to the militants. We had many events in the Court of Ideas. The bridges we built there. There was one militant person, Topper Carew from Washington. He came in and he demanded that a collector of African art with an exhibit at the Carnegie Museum return the art to him! I was scared of him. He was also part of this an event we had called the Spring Thing, and we brought Bob Goodman and Hans Harns from MIT. We had a Christmas party, and we made a poster, it showed a little black kid and it said, "Is Santa Claus really white?" That was the poster. One of the construction crew, Dokes, dressed up as Santa, he was this big, black guy—I have a lot of pictures of that. We did a lot of different things. Art Blakey and Abbey Lincoln came... but then it very quickly it came apart.

Today the Court of Ideas is covered with the debris of nearby buildings. What's sad today is, even though that the Hill looks great, it's got tree-lined streets, single-family houses, it's a joy to walk all around the Hill, but the synergy, the whole thing that drew people there, it's not there!

When we look at your work, we don't see the indebtedness to Kahn, or to American modernism, but we do see van Eyck, the Dutch...

I met him, he came to the Court of Ideas.

So what was on the walls of the studio, what were you reading, what were you interested in, was your time in Europe influential in your own architectural language?

We were reading the *Autobiography of Malcolm X*, I don't know... I think whatever influences there were, they were subconscious.

They usually are.

The best ones are.

What's your favorite project from the time period, both your own and in general in Pittsburgh.

Our Way was my favorite, but it didn't get built. What was built? Some of the buildings by [Frederick] Scheibler, they were really good. And they were right close to Paul Titus's house, so I got to see them every day. In the Hill District, some of the things we tried to save, the Passavant Hospital was fabulous, the Irene Kaufmann settlement house was there, and we use to have our meetings there. That building was phenomenal. It had fireplaces, oak-panel meeting rooms, art, and the saddest thing was, they tore it down. Edgar Kaufmann jr. was interested in what we were doing, he came to the office a lot. He said, "Anything you guys can do?" and we made some sketches, but it was too late. That was just a gorgeous building. So you had all of the jazz clubs, you had the Halfway art gallery, our little operation, and you had all the poets, and you had the Irene Kaufmann Center.

Peter Berndtson [and Cornelia Brierly, both students of Frank Lloyd Wright] built a house practically on the Carnegie Campus. It was for Dr. Abraham Steinberg, and his art collection. I entered Associated Artists, it's the oldest artists' group in the U.S., and they would always have their annual exhibition at the Carnegie Museum. They would bring jurors like David Smith, and Clement Greenberg. The first year I won the best in the show, so Steinberg bought my sculpture, so it sits in his house. It's a beautiful little house. Behrensen built quite a few. I never met him, but I knew all about him. I went to see Frank Lloyd Wright and I got to meet with him, but I didn't get to meet with Peter!

And, of course, Schweikher was instrumental in getting Mies to do the building at Duquesne, and Schweikher did the Student Union. I won the sculpture prize at the Three Rivers Arts festival, it was purchased by DU, who put it in their student union, so that sculpture sits in a Paul Schweikher building!

The Schweikher Duquesne Union building was gorgeous. They gummed it a little bit. They do that. What they did to Tasso's airport was just terrible.

At a certain point you leave the Hill.

Yes. Not by choice.

You were advised?

No, I was fired. But Paul Titus and I were smart. When we incorporated Community Design Associates we paid into workman's comp. So I collected unemployment for a year. I'd stand in line, and I'd say, "I'm getting my scholarship," but we couldn't live on it so I had to do something.

At that point Architecture 2001 was kicked out by Ed Ellis as well, who had become really militant anti-white. We'd arranged to have a big conference, and Ed takes that moment to announce that, "Whitey's gotta leave the Hill." There was a meeting that they wanted to have, and Chuckie Dial said, "Don't go," and I said, "I think I have to." It was really tough because these were people who I thought were friends and they just proceeded to say, "You whiteys just gotta get the heck out of here." That's how we ended up out in Bloomfield. Ultimately we were invited back, and that's when we had the Pythian Temple, we had the whole space. We had the top floor where we did the map of the neighborhood. It was 40 by 24 feet, because that was the size of the room. Doug Cooper and I worked with the

Lower Hill Development for the Citizens Committee for District Renewal, model, Troy West, 1966.

Lower Hill infill housing, Troy West, 1967.

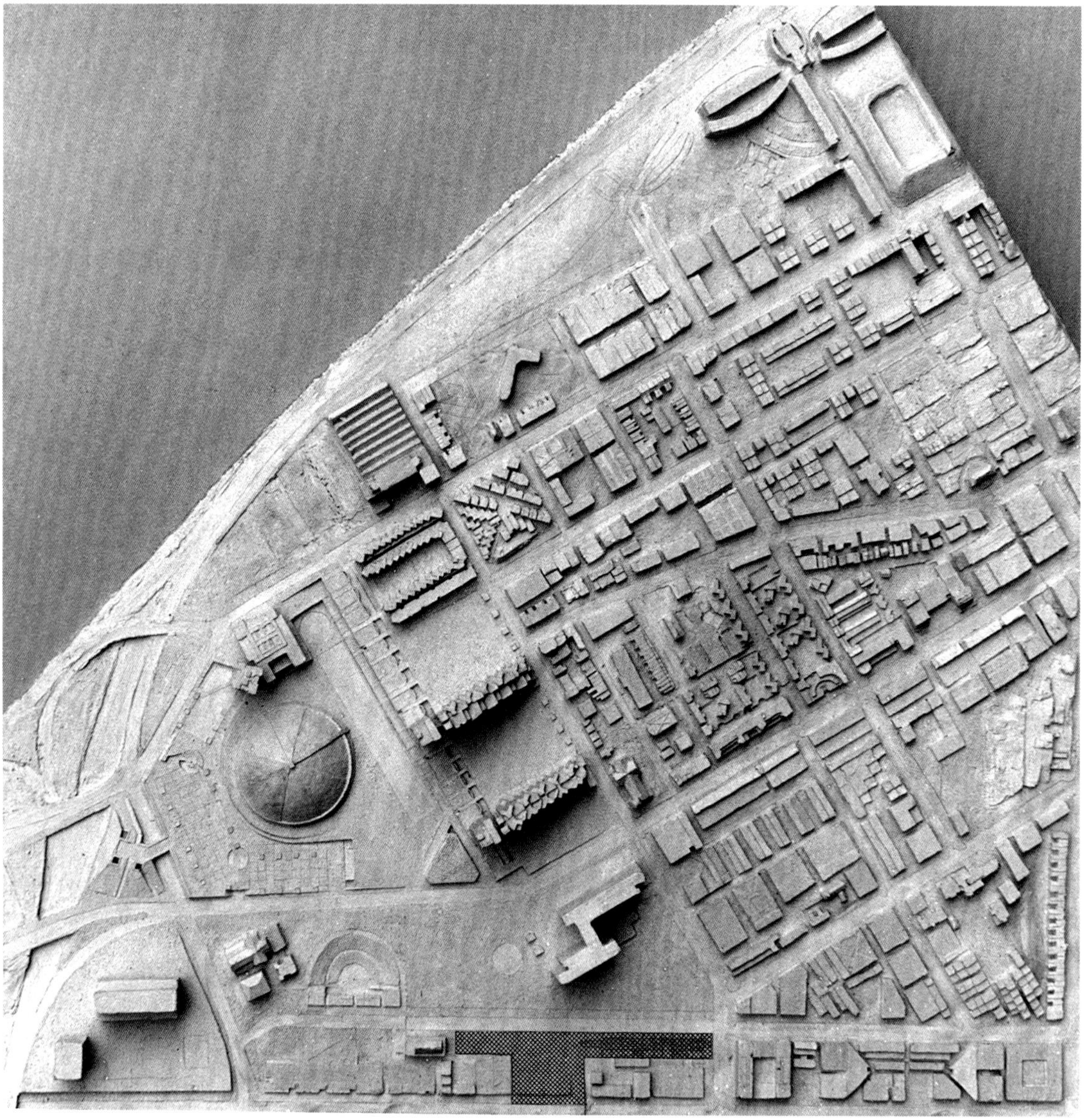

community to draw a map of the neighborhood from the point of view of the people living in it. It was a big hit with the community and started to get a lot of national attention. So that was very exciting.

Why did you leave Pittsburgh?

I knew that Harlyn Thompson had become Dean of this new school in Newark [NJIT]. When Thompson was leading North Dakota State University, I'd been invited to go to Fargo to give a talk. It was one of my best talks. At one point he said, "Maybe you'd like to come out here and work with the Indians or something," but then he left and became the dean of this new school. It was highly competitive. It was in the New York area and was the first new school of architecture on the East Coast in fifty years, so he became the dean. So I figure I'm going to go say hi to Harlyn, so I went to Newark and it looked kind of beat, but then he said something about starting the school. What he did was he picked all architects [for the faculty], but he picked one architect who had a minor in sociology, one in history, one in mechanical engineering, one in structural engineering, and he had one slot for advocacy. He said, "I could put you in that category." I went back to Pittsburgh and talked it over with my family, and said it will be alright, I'll have a job. We were in really bad financial shape. So I did it.

Perspectives

Salons

The HACLab salons were informal but informed discussions around a set of key topics, for the entertainment and education of invited participants and audience alike. All present were encouraged to participate.

IMAGINING THE RENAISSANCE

Thursday, February 18 2016

The organization of how we live, work, move and play is an essential component of successful urban design. Landscape and infrastructure were radically reconsidered during the post-war era. In what ways were cities including Pittsburgh reimagined? What drove these changes? What worked? What didn't?

PRESERVING MODERNISM

Thursday, March 10 2016

One consequence of modernism was a burgeoning preservationist movement, a largely grass-roots effort to halt the removal of traditional urban fabric as occurred in some areas of Pittsburgh. Today, these modernist projects were increasingly under threat of demolition, couched in efforts to "re-stitch" the city. Does this removal merely repeat the mistakes of modernism? What is worth saving? At what cost?

MAKING THE MODERN

Thursday, April 7 2016

It is important to understand not just the products created by modernism (books, buildings, and urban blocks) but also the processes and policies that brought about their creation. What lessons can Pittsburgh learn from their city's recent history? Can past experience be recalibrated to make the architecture and urbanism needed for tomorrow?

PROJECTING PITTSBURGH

Thursday, April 28 2016

Previously invited salon speakers were asked to return to help us review the exhibit and related events, and to assist in determining what, if anything, should be done next.

IMAGINING THE RENAISSANCE

Thursday, February 18 2016

LIZABETH COHEN
RAY GASTIL
KAI GUTSCHOW
SUSAN RADEMACHER
JOEL TARR

Ray Ryan This is the first of four salons held as part of what we are terming HACLab, our attempt to make exhibitions that are more flexible, interactive, and centered on Pittsburgh and related subjects. For the first of these HACLabs we decided to take on the important and thorny subject of modernism in Pittsburgh after World War II. We've asked OverUnder, architects and educators, to put together this exhibition and studio about Pittsburgh and the legacy of modernism here. These four salons will feature invited participants both from outside the city and from Pittsburgh itself, because it's important that the discussion include folks who know the history of the city intimately, but also people who can bring a bigger, broader perspective to the subject. This evening is the first of these discussions, so you are in a sense all part of this experiment.

Michael Kubo Because the purview of the exhibition attempts to relate the history of Pittsburgh to its present, I want to begin the discussion along similar lines, to start with a historical lens and then discuss the consequences of that history today. The exhibition and the discussion here tonight are about modernization and architectural modernism in Pittsburgh, understood as separate but related concepts, as part of a broader current of movement in major U.S. cities after World War II. Another way to describe this is that the exhibition deals with the history of what became known as the urban renewal era. For our panelists, I wonder whether we can begin by trying to pick at what this period meant more generally for architecture and urbanism, and to situate how urban renewal was conducted in Pittsburgh within this broader national story. What do we see as similar or different between the history of this era in Pittsburgh and what was happening elsewhere?

Lizabeth Cohen First let me say how delighted I am to be back here. I lived here from 1986 to 1992, and it has been interesting for me to go back and remind myself about postwar Pittsburgh because I have been investigating urban renewal nationally as well as specifically in New Haven, Boston, and New York City, most recently for a forthcoming book on urban renewal that is built around the career of Edward J. Logue.

I've been thinking about what is typical about Pittsburgh and what is distinctive about it. In a lot of ways, Pittsburgh's situation was very typical of U.S. industrial cities in 1945. All of these cities had been through a very rough time with the Great Depression and then World War II, which resulted in very little building. Here were all these GI's returning and there was a big housing crunch.

Many industrial northern cities had a boost with wartime production but it wasn't at all clear what would happen after that. The big pressure was suburbanization. The housing crunch that cities faced was essentially addressed through a federal policy that favored suburban development, creating mortgages through the Federal Housing Authority and Veteran's Association loans, rebuilding highways, and promoting decentralization and suburbanization. In this sense Pittsburgh was typical of what was happening in other cities.

Among the things that make Pittsburgh distinctive, I'll point to two to get us started. One is to look at many of the cities you could compare Pittsburgh to in this era—Detroit, Boston, New Haven, Cleveland. These cities were in trouble. They were worrying about losing residential population, particularly the middle class. Department stores were developing shopping centers in the suburbs and they were becoming the anchors for this exodus. But Pittsburgh had the added problem of being a region in crisis, even versus a city like Boston that faced many of the same urban problems as Pittsburgh, but which actually saw a lot of regional development, particularly around the opening of the Route 128 ring road and all the technology companies that began building out there. So while there was a fear that the city itself was going to lose its purpose, there was confidence that these industries were going to stay in the New England region. In Pittsburgh, however—where you could argue that the industrial base of the economy had already been in decline for much of the 20th century— there was tremendous concern that the region itself was in trouble.

The other thing that I think is distinctive is that the Renaissance in Pittsburgh gets started earlier than urban renewal in many other places. In 1943-44 the Allegheny Conference on Community Development is founded. In many cities, redevelopment didn't get started until the passing of the Housing Act of 1949 and the federal government's investment of resources into the project of revitalizing downtowns. Pittsburgh's renewal started earlier, and was in fact a collaboration between the city and its mayor, David Lawrence, and many of the major industrialists and businesspeople in the area, particularly Richard King Mellon and Edward Kaufmann. They become invested in promoting a strategy that they argue is very much driven by the private sector. In most of the country—and in fact I would argue in reality in Pittsburgh—government money was actually crucial to this whole project. For example, once the Housing Act passed, Pittsburgh did receive federal money; there was also a lot of state money and state legislation. Yet while the city was very much engaged, the story is in how these industrialists and the Allegheny Conference and the business elite became invested in promoting the narrative that this was primarily a private sector project.

So, even though there was a lot of government endorsement and investment, there was an outside influence of the private sector in the way things played out. We'll be talking about that, how very corporate the emphasis was in Pittsburgh, with less housing than in many other cities. Urban renewal wasn't talked

David L. Lawrence swinging baseball bat in dirt lot with chain link fence and children in background, circa 1956.

about as a public project the way it was, say, in New Haven or Boston, two cities I've looked at very closely. There was less room, I would argue, for citizens to actually have a say in the process, though that process of course does change over time. In many places in the 1950s, urban renewal was very top down. By the 1960s, there was a lot of pressure put by citizens' groups to open up the process, and the federal government requires much more citizen involvement. In Pittsburgh, though, there is a way in which citizens never quite achieve that kind of influence in the planning process.

Joel Tarr I'll point out a couple of things I think are relevant. First of all, Pittsburgh in 1950 had a population of 640,000 people. Today it has just about 340,000 people. In contrast to what Liz has said, I want to point out that Pittsburgh also had a very long tradition of public/private partnerships and that you can look at the Renaissance, as urban renewal was called her, within that tradition. In Albert Tannler's book, *Pittsburgh Architecture in the Twentieth Century*, he describes the Pittsburgh Renaissance as a reverse welfare state. I think there's some truth to that, but it's also true that you did have public involvement because of David Lawrence, the mayor during this period, as well as Democratic organizations in the city, which certainly made a difference in terms of how and where things were done.

Let's go back to the question of why urban renewal. There was a well known theory at the time that the way to bring the middle class back into the center of the city was by clearing the old housing and providing new housing, that the draw of the suburbs was basically the availability of new housing. What we needed to do was to get rid of the old structures—Pittsburgh had a very old housing stock—and replace them with new ones. Hence, urban renewal.

One of the things that's happened with urban renewal, as it is studied and talked about, is that it has become seen as a very negative thing, involving a lot of negative factors, primarily black removal in the Lower Hill, East Liberty, or on the North Side. But I think there's sometimes a failure to anticipate or to understand the extent to which some of the things that we've done have been in collaboration with certain leaders in those neighborhoods. Did they represent the population? Were they elected? No. They were elites in many cases. Were there black elites? The black newspaper, *The Pittsburgh Courier*, supported the Lower Hill renewal, for example. There were editorials.

When urban renewal started in East Liberty, the same thing happened. I have been fortunate enough to interview Robert Pease, the director of the Urban Redevelopment Authority at the time. He was in charge of both the Lower Hill and East Liberty renewal projects. As a classic example of urban renewal, Bob argued that conditions in the Hill were horrible, that the city was going to offer new public housing for the people that lived on the Hill, and that the quality of their lives would be improved tremendously through urban renewal processes. Of course, it also meant that these projects were scattered around. You have the destruction of neighborhoods and of the bonds that come from people living together. But I think that you cannot only look at urban renewal through the prism of being a negative experience. There were many associated expectations of hope that went into it. I think that was certainly true here in Pittsburgh. But there was also a refusal to acknowledge how people would be affected by the massive dislocations that occurred.

Ray Gastil One reason why this exhibition is so strong is that it takes you into the viewpoints of that era, where you can

Robert Moses and New Haven mayor Richard Lee, 1958.

see the critical eye, but also why Mayor Lawrence was on the cover of *Progressive Architecture*, in the same way that Richard Lee in New Haven or Ed Logue in Boston were heralded on magazine covers as the saviors of their cities.

I happened to be reading the 1959 progress report on urban renewal. What's interesting for the narrative of non-public investment that Lizabeth mentioned is that the report begins by claiming there has been about $197,500,000 of private investment and that the only place that they actually had much public investment was the Lower Hill. I realize this is a more complicated story, but it is also interesting that they say one percent of the city's buildable land has been part of this project.

I will mention something about the private side of the public-private partnerships that Lizabeth and Joel have mentioned, which in some cases had some remarkable public benefits. This goes to the fact that Pittsburgh's renewal was already underway before urban renewal legislation. I'll just mention smoke abatement, when we finally got the sky cleared. The smoke story is fascinating. As I understand it, the Equitable Assurance Society, which was the main investor for the construction of the Gateway Center, essentially told the city that if it didn't clean the air, there would be no investment.

JT Let's clarify how it was that Pittsburgh really cleaned its air. I'm not saying there wasn't a sincere effort or that the Allegheny Conference wasn't involved, but the key factor here, in fact, has to do with German submarines. From 1942 to 1944, the German submarine fleet was lurking off the Gulf coast and sinking oil tankers as fast as they could come from the ports. Those tankers were coming up to the industrial cities, and the federal government became increasingly concerned that we were going to be starved for oil. In response, Standard Oil built the two largest oil pipelines ever built, Big Inch and Little Inch. Those come to Pittsburgh in 1944 and oil once again flows into the industries here. At the end of the war, as companies began selling surplus property, Standard Oil sells these two big pipelines to private entrepreneurs who have investments in natural gas. Mr. Mellon had some too, and decided to convert the two pipelines from oil to natural gas. This means that at the time when the Allegheny Conference was beginning to enforce smoke control based upon the 1941 Smoke Control Act, cheap, clean natural gas was flowing into the city. Between 1945 and 1950, half the residences in the city changed from burning coal to natural gas. There was a transformation of the railroads also, from coal burning locomotives to diesel electric locomotives.

Laying the Big Inch and Little Inch pipelines, 1942.

The ones that got screwed the most in this transition were the working class. If you're middle class and you live in a house with a coal burning furnace, all you have to do when natural gas becomes available is to buy a convertor for $150 to change it to a gas unit. If you're a working-class person who heats their house by room stoves, kitchen burners, and things like that, you can't do that. The financial burden of smoke control really was harder on the workers than it was on the middle class. The air became cleaner, which is terrific of course, but the story is more complicated than traditional narratives will tell you.

LC Smoke abatement really goes to this desire to tease out the differences, or rather the specificity, of urban renewal history in Pittsburgh versus in other places. One of the extremely strong features that was totally distinct in Pittsburgh was the smoke abatement campaign and its history. It's a big part of the history of Mellon Square too, and the apocryphal story that when General Mellon came back to Pittsburgh in 1943 from his service, he and his wife stayed their first night at the William Penn Hotel, from which the Mellon Bank Building was just catty-corner across the block. It was daytime. As the story goes, they looked out the window and could not see the bank building. His wife is supposed to have said, "Honey, you've got to do something about this."

I think the stage was set in so many ways for the Renaissance well before World War II. There was this long history in public-private partnership of seeking excellence in design and planning. In the 1930s, the city's bond rating hit the lowest possible standard, which really alarmed people. In the early 1940s, both Alcoa and U.S. Steel announced plans to leave Pittsburgh for Manhattan. That was a very strong trigger, at least for Mellon Square, and I think also for the Gateway Center and the Point. These developments were about creating an environment that would entice corporate citizens to stay in Pittsburgh and also entice young executives to bring their families to Pittsburgh, to a place that was worth living in.

MK I want to cycle back to this question of public-private partnerships. We were struck not just by the role of private companies but specifically by the corporate character of these initiatives and, on an architectural level, of what these corporations produced. As with the history of smoke abatement and the sense of Pittsburgh as a dark, polluted city prior to those efforts, this specificity gave us a different way of seeing the buildings that were produced here, as opposed to Boston, New Haven, or other cities in which many of the emblematic buildings of the urban renewal era were designed and built in concrete. That was much less the case in Pittsburgh, where the character of these buildings was heavily marked by the corporations that commissioned them, particularly material producers like Alcoa and U.S. Steel or, somewhat later, Pittsburgh Plate Glass. These companies commissioned buildings that would express the materials they produced, and the results were dramatic architectures of glass and metal, from the gleaming aluminum of Alcoa to the rugged Cor-Ten of U.S. Steel.

Kai Gutschow I do think a figure like Mellon, and the legacy of his and several of the other families in town as titans of industry and heads of corporations, made Pittsburgh different from what we see in other cities in the U.S. But in other ways, they had given their art collections to the national government;

Gateway Center, one of the first built projects intended to reinvent the Point, on the cover of the Charette*, 1951.*

some had served as Secretary of the Treasury. They were more like government officials than many corporate heads were. I don't know if that led to the spirit of the Allegheny Conference as not just a greedy bunch of corporate capitalists, but as having a sense of public responsibility and ownership. Clearly they were trying to make a profit. Their buildings do have that sense of promoting the city's material industries, whether these were aluminum or the stainless steel of the Gateway Center. But if you look at the advertisements in contemporary journals, any one of these buildings housed many different companies, whether these were making wire or roofing materials or insulation. So I don't think it was about expressing only one company selling one material in each case. You see in some of the brochures the idea that a certain building will help revive the entire metalworking industry, from copper to aluminum, to stainless steel to other sorts of things, even though they were direct competitors and often had offices across from each other. I don't know if it's collusion or civic-mindedness; others would know more about how these companies were treating each other in this quest to build something that was corporate-led, perhaps more so than in other cities.

LC These corporate leaders were tastemakers, in terms of their personal investments and properties. They brought leading architects and landscape architecture firms here. I think that there was a competition for taste. I think that Kaufmann's legacy with the exhibits at his department store, his patronage and promotion of Frank Lloyd Wright to the public as well as for private commissions, had a big influence in opening up the sense of possibility, of thinking about what these new structures of the future might be. Then Kaufmann's sponsored the *Pittsburgh in Progress* exhibition and publication in 1947. His downtown department store was thronged with people. There were models of future Pittsburgh on display that had some horrifying suggestions, but there were also some wonderful ideas in it, and the authors of that document, Mitchell & Ritchey, went on to create a number of really signature works of architecture.

MK In the exhibition, we set out both *Pittsburgh in Progress* and another document from 1947, *Pittsburgh: Challenge and Response*, produced by the Allegheny Conference, as parallel launching points for what would come in terms of urban renewal proposals. Some of these came to fruition, others

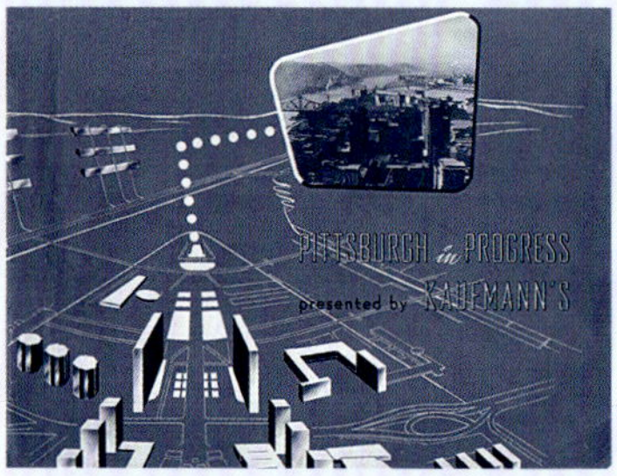

Cover of Pittsburgh in Progress presented by Kaufmann's.

did not. These documents also lay out the different public, private, and institutional actors that became key in that transformation. Beyond the Allegheny Conference there were other entities like the Oakland Corporation, a consortium of business elites that proposed to fill in all of Panther Hollow with a megastructure by Harrison & Abramovitz.

LC I want to speak to the distinctive way in which public-private partnerships worked out here and the impact it had on architecture. All urban redevelopment, as it was first called in 1949, depended on the public/private relationship. That was the whole concept, that the state would write down the cost of land and make it more attractive to private developers to develop land downtown. But in Pittsburgh—and this is what's interesting for us to think about—the private side led the pack in a way that was not the case in other cities. And you get the kind of architecture that reflects that. In Boston, by comparison, you had a very settled, long-standing Yankee Brahmin elite struggling against the politicians and their working-class Irish base. The Brahmin movers and shakers of Boston were very much locals, so in that sense they were no different from elite Pittsburghers. But they were not going to invest a penny in Boston.

What's interesting is that these are two very locally grounded elites, yet their influence plays out very differently. In the case of Boston, you couldn't get anyone to put up buildings. The city had to use federal money as leverage to ultimately change the rules of the game, to produce optimism and to change the real estate story so that the private sector would then invest. As a result you have public civic buildings, brutalist (or what you call Heroic) structures designed in cutting-edge architectural style. They're not corporate or glass and steel buildings. The architectural expression is different from Pittsburgh because the city took the urban renewal money and said, this is going to be our opening wedge. We'll use it to build a government center and then private interest will come around, and it did. The banks started building buildings downtown and eventually there was private investment.

The new Boston City Hall, designed by Kallman McKinnel & Knowles, as seen from the roof of 26 Court Street, the Annex of the old City Hall, c. 1968.

MK In Boston, the iconic urban renewal project that represented the era was Boston City Hall. Its construction was a major statement of civic investment in the city. By contrast, if we went around the room and asked what the iconic buildings of that era in Pittsburgh are, would people say Alcoa, or U.S Steel, or the Civic Arena?

Rami el Samahy Even before those, if you think about the important projects of the 1950s, there are two. There is the Gateway Center, which was as radical as the perceived smoke abatement. Where there had been a derelict railway terminal and an old expo building, a traditional fabric of warehouses, all of a sudden you have these shining new buildings that in fact didn't have an architect attached to them, but were essentially designed by an insurance company. These are gleaming towers in a park, in an equally new landscape adjacent to the Point. The other major project is Mellon Square and the buildings around it, which is the inverse of Gateway Center. It's a park surrounded by city street walls. If you put yourself back into the mindset of that era, you see these two projects that are fairly radical changes to downtown. We've been talking about the political elites and the businesspeople, but there were also users of the city who were powerfully affected by this new architecture, by this new landscape. All of a sudden there's modernity in the city in a real, palpable way.

LC In a way, the ensemble of Mellon Square, the Alcoa building, and the first U.S. Steel building was the first to be completed. 1955 was the opening of Mellon Square. Alcoa was 1953, because they started building it as soon as the design was announced. That was the first to be completed and available to experience. You've got these two lovely buildings, with really interesting detailing, and you have this never-before-seen creation of an urban plaza with integrated shops and parking below, sort of like Pittsburgh's version of Rockefeller Center, which was one of the things that had inspired Mellon to suggest this. In a way, this allowed people to experience modernism at a scale that they could understand, unlike Gateway Center, which was much bigger and more complex, not comprehensible at a glance or from th e everyday experience of going shopping or taking a lunch break from your office building.

KG In Pittsburgh, there is also the geographic sensibility of the Point and the lack at the time of any ability to see it or to find ways to weave through it. Once land was cleared in the Point, you couldn't help but notice radical changes, whether these were considered modernist or not. Change was in the air. For the average person driving through the city, one day there's a bridge across the tip of the Point, and the next day they move it. That's a profound change that affected everybody who was coming downtown. With the opening of the tunnels in the 1950s and 60s it accelerates much more, but for the common man, that might be how I would first notice these urban changes on a grand scale.

RG I think the Point was also the postcard of the city. That postcard advertised a powerful message about modernity and the new world; it offered a very different picture of a city, one that was accomplished not just through urban renewal but through the work that began with Frederick Law Olmsted Jr. saying, in 1910 or '11, that there needed to be a good park on the Point. It only took until 1972 for it to open. Whatever people perceived as right or wrong about that story, it's one that predated urban renewal. The Renaissance narrative in some ways returned The Point to a role in the city that it had held previously, but which had been forgotten.

JT The Allegheny Conference and the Renaissance had a relentless PR machine going all the time. They flooded the journals with pictures and articles about what was going on. I think this aspect of the story is very important, and it gets to the essence of what was happening.

MK Susan, you have made the comment that urban renewal isn't finished. What did you mean by that?

Susan Rademacher On my mind right now is what's happening in East Liberty, on the North Side around Allegheny Commons, and in the Lower Hill District. Those urban renewal projects, which changed the fabric and the organizational structure of those neighborhoods in a way that the downtown projects didn't, are still very much in contention and under developer pressure to bring them forward in a way that supports the community's goals for attracting residents and continuing to build the economy, meeting diversity goals, and balancing various economic interests in protecting the rights of people who are living there.

The platforms that did not exist in the 1940s and 50s for people of color and for people with low incomes to really be active participants in planning—that's changed. That's a huge change that began in the 1960s, and I think it's much more sophisticated today, to the point of creating its own kind of roadblocks. Pittsburgh is still, and probably always will be, undergoing a remaking and re-envisioning and trying to get ahead of its problems.

There's an issue right now with a little park in East Liberty that was created in the urban renewal age and which has come to have value. There's a need for new housing, so suddenly we have a combustion of issues around that, and a call for new involvement in design. On the North Side, we have a group of new developers, all around Allegheny Commons, the oldest park in the city, who are making some massive investments and are really interested in how the green space can relate to their investments in an integrated and balanced way. To me, it's just a continued unrolling of these same questions, with more tools at our disposal, and I think with more goals to balance.

RG That's in large part correct, but I do think the issues of diversity in this town are slightly different than in some of the other big cities in the U.S. If we have a problem it is in what we consider to be diverse, and whether people are as included as we think they are. I think we believe that we're asking for community input and getting it, but certainly there is a lot of complaining from different groups who feel they are not being represented and whose voices aren't being heard.

JT How many apartment units are being constructed in East Liberty and Highland Park and who's going to live in all these thousands of units? Do these one-room apartments and efficiencies that are being built anticipate where the new population around Google in East Liberty will go?

RG Let me answer this in a couple of ways. First, I do think we're going to see more young people staying in Pittsburgh, and more coming, who are attracted to the new jobs that we're creating right now. We are still barely moving the dial on population, but that's largely because we have an older population which is not replacing itself, so this new influx doesn't register in population terms. But it does register in terms of choices and where people want to live. People who watch the market as their job may have different opinions about whether the new apartments are going to be filled, but I'm pretty confident that there's a strong market.

On one level, this is a great thing. We have new industries, new jobs, high-paying jobs. I think Pittsburgh needs it. We cannot be an island of wealthy suburbs. This continues to be a challenge for us, despite the anecdotal impression of change. What we're trying to do is get it right and be a city, to have this kind of growth but remain unlike some other U.S. cities where other people are getting pushed out. We are not at that stage yet.

LC One of the things that Pittsburgh has going for it is that it makes your dreams possible. It has decent schools for the middle class, and I would hope that the investment continues because that was an issue that people took on in the urban renewal period and didn't get very far with. Many of the cities going through similar hopes of revitalization have come up against the fact that when people have school-age children, they move to the suburbs.

I want to pick up on the point about this being an interesting moment of polarization. On the one hand we have, as Susan said, much more expectation today on the part of citizens to be involved in the process. There are lots of community meetings, lots of demands that are made, so there is a lot of community mobilization. But I think that private development is calling the shots a lot more than it was in the past when you had a real public presence, with the federal government spending money. In a way, it really matters who's in the driver's seat in the public-private partnership, and I do think that private development is currently in the driver's seat in most cities in this country. You have this strange phenomenon of activism and the public being mobilized, but usually responding to proposals that come from private development. I'd be interested to hear how Pittsburgh fits into that.

RG Every single developer stood up and opposed our intro and planning overlay for the riverfront a week ago, so

I don't know what to say to that, but there is absolutely a high level of participation. Again, the first question is participation. Impact is the next level. It's uneven, but you can go through every type of demographic in the city and find a very active community group. We can argue about the impact but they do have a voice regarding development because it's built into our system. Now we are trying to develop a more formal way of recognizing these organizations in our planning, rather than doing this in an anecdotal way. That's something we're charged with trying to do with neighborhoods as we move forward, so that we can really begin to have an official shared vision.

SR I just want to add to this from the perspective of park development. The Parks Conservancy is working throughout many different neighborhoods in Pittsburgh. Typically we work where we're invited in by a community that has a clear voice and has developed some capacity to stick with it, and those relationships are fantastic. What I worry about are the pockets of Pittsburgh that don't have that yet. I'm wondering what can be done to help build that ability to care about common space. From the perspective of parks and development, we are really focused on trying to leverage the value of parks such that developers will make an investment in park improvements, not to serve themselves directly but to serve the goals and needs of the park to support the whole community.

[From the audience] One problem is that the apartment complexes that developers have put up along the rivers, standing opposite the suburbs, are ugly. The Alcoa building is gorgeous, and it's sad to watch the riverbank be populated with ugly buildings. It's like we lost our river. I've lived in this city for seventy-six years, and we first lost our rivers to industry for a long period of time. Now that we have it back, we're starting to lose some parts of it to a different kind of ugliness.

ReS I think "ugly" is a good word here, a useful word, because ugliness is often in the eye of the beholder. For many people, the buildings of this era—the architecture that we've been celebrating here—are ugly. You can like or dislike those buildings, but they were built with an intention and a care that is not as prevalent in architecture today. That has to do with economics. Personally, I think most of the new stuff is ugly, but more importantly, the construction methods are much different. They're more short-lived, and maybe that's a good thing.

The Tasso Katselas designed East Liberty Housing, built in 1971.

MK The Alcoa building and Mellon Square are essentially patronage projects. There is a great divide in architecture between the museums, university buildings, and other prestige projects that we all study in school and admire, which are paid for in a very particular way, and something like housing. The question is how to develop stronger models of contemporary housing that can push through those divides. Some of this is a matter of regulation, some a matter of design guidelines, but some of it comes down to the dollars and cents of contemporary construction.

ReS I'm not talking about the showcase buildings. I'm talking about the housing. I'm going to go out on a limb here, but I think that the East Liberty housing that Tasso Katselas designed, which many people hate, is better built than most of the stuff that is replacing it.

RG That building is a great

exception. It could survive another fifty to a hundred years. I'm interested in the fact that these questions come up over and over again. Are the lessons learned really learned? There was beautiful work done during the Renaissance, to the credit of the city and others, but it was also based on an attitude of having left the downtown alone for fifty years until you could scrape it clean and start again. I think we have to avoid certain lessons. If we don't, we will be left wondering about the problems that were repeated but that didn't have to be.

MK Among the comments that have been submitted by visitors to the exhibition, I want to read one:

> I lived in Ten Allegheny Center from 1976 to 1979—they were the happiest years of my life. I lived car free, as I do now, unmolested by vehicular traffic. I am now a preservationist for the East Allegheny community council. I lament two things: the destruction of Allegheny Square and the aluminum fins around the Church. I also lament the destruction of the original buildings demolished for Allegheny Center, of course. But there is nothing wrong with Allegheny Center in my opinion, its concept and execution. It contained all the necessary elements of a city.

RG Some of the most attractive aspects of Pittsburgh in terms of the critical mass of places that people want to be are based on the historical centers that have historic identity. What's exciting about some of the work of HACLab, and the studios related to it, is that it brings Allegheny Center back into the story as an interesting place to be. It's an amazing transition, to bring attention to the actual complexity and interest of specific places. Gateway Center at some point will be doing better even than it is today because people are going to begin recognizing its real strength. I think these are the kinds of things that form the way we see ourselves as a city, the way we tell our stories. Urban renewal was this historic, heroic, and scary story. As Susan said, the most important thing is that it's not actually done, and the way we finish it will either add to that critical mass of historic places or it won't.

[From the audience] The architecture of Allegheny Center doesn't always feel like it represents what we think is important now. There is lots of brick and not very many windows when I walk through it, and making things more visible seems to be prominent right now. In order to revitalize it, do we need to blow a hole through the middle of it so we can see the city through it? Do we need to take it out completely, or should we renew and reenvision and repurpose it?

ReS I love modern buildings but I don't consider myself a preservationist. I don't think buildings should be mothballed and live only as monuments to their own era. Building are living artifacts that should be reinterpreted by different generations for different purposes, by finding new uses, without necessarily tearing them down.

JT I have mixed emotions about what should be done with Allegheny Center, but just retaining the frame itself would be so striking. What are your feelings about demolishing it?

ReS It makes me crazy that this city has repeatedly removed layers of its history. Does Pittsburgh have any of its industrial relics left in the city? No. They're all gone. Compare that to how Bethlehem has turned their steel plant into a cultural destination. Here, the Civic Arena was this phenomenal emblem of the city's history, and now it's gone. I think the big question is, what do

we protect now? Many old buildings are regarded as ugly at some point in their life. The trick is to let them live long enough for people to like them again.
MK It's beyond liking or not liking, beyond taste.

LC Victorian stuff, for example, was hated in a certain era.

MK This is an argument that we started making in our *Heroic* project on Boston's concrete architecture. It has led us into the history of ugliness, and especially into accounting for the particular historical period that often becomes the danger zone for a building's survival, forty to sixty years after its construction. We refer to this window as the ugly valley. It happened for Victorian buildings just as it is happening now for buildings of the urban renewal era. We forget that by the time of its demolition, fifty years after it opened, Penn Station had been subjected to all sorts of terrible alterations. It was in awful shape and was seen by many people as obsolete, in disrepair and not worth saving, not as the iconic Penn Station whose loss we lament today.

We've tracked the language that was and continues to be used around many of the buildings from the urban renewal era, whether concrete buildings in Boston or steel buildings in Pittsburgh. Exactly the same terms, like monstrosity, were once applied to Victorian buildings, for example. In fact the preservation movement in the U.S. originated largely with a set of people that had the same generational relationship to Victorian buildings that we have today to the buildings of the urban renewal era.

KG The caution here is in using the aesthetic argument as the reason these things happen. I don't think the primary reason that the Civic Arena is no longer with us is because it was considered ugly. It's that it wasn't valued. It was pressured out by money and it didn't matter if people thought differently from what the financial industry values, or the way that real estate runs. It doesn't matter what a building costs or what its value is: if it needs to go, it will go. Only a few escape that pressure.

SR It's not only about ugliness. It's also a question of the social vantage. With the Civic Arena, we did a lot of playing with residents of all ages to find out what they considered beautiful. Children saw the arena as a thrilling shape to them. They did not have all of the negative associations with what that building symbolized, which the community could not or would not give up in their own relationship to the building in order to consider other options that had been suggested.

I want to mention that there's a significant and serious parallel here with modernist landscape architecture. There are a number of significant urban works across the country that are either imperiled or already destroyed. Mellon Square, before we undertook our planning study to see what we might do with it, was talked about in terms of removal to turn it into something that would meet other needs that may not exist downtown. Urban landscapes are constantly evolving and changing, even more so than buildings. There's the question of time that a designer has to anticipate. There are also new needs like accessibility or secure design. The approach of trying to understand and rehabilitate the original design intent, which is about experience, is to me the vein that we can try to mine to reinvigorate a place.

[From the audience] I think the lesson of the Civic Arena experience is that history is being constantly rewritten by the powerful. A lot of the people that were involved in the urban renewal era are still alive, and their stories keep coming back. I'm really concerned that we don't lose those stories. The fate of the Civic Arena turned into a political discussion about reconnecting a street grid, and the politicians got a hold of that. That was it. It was done. It had nothing to do with how the people in the Lower Hill felt.

JT There was nothing more stunning than sitting in the Civic Arena and seeing the view of downtown. It was just incredible.

Lizabeth Cohen is Howard Mumford Jones Professor of American Studies at Harvard University and the former Dean of the Radcliffe Institute for Advanced Study at Harvard. She is the author of numerous books including *A Consumer's Republic: The Politics of Mass Consumption in Postwar America* (2003), *Making a New Deal: Industrial Workers in Chicago, 1919 to 1939* (1990), and the forthcoming *Saving America's Cities: Ed Logue and the Struggle to Renew Urban America in the Suburban Age*.

Ray Gastil is Director of City Planning for the City of Pittsburgh, and teaches as Adjunct Professor in the Masters of Urban Design Program at the Carnegie Mellon University School of Architecture.

Kai Gutschow is Associate Professor at the Carnegie Mellon University School of Architecture, where he is Co-Director of the School's design-based graduate programs, founder and Track Chair for the M.Arch program, and a coordinator of the year-long B.Arch Thesis program.

Susan Rademacker is Parks Curator for the Pittsburgh Parks Conservancy, where she was project leader for the renovation of Mellon Square. She is the author of *Mellon Square: Discovering a Modernist Masterpiece* (2014).

Joel Tarr is Richard S. Caliguiri University Professor of History at Carnegie Mellon University, with joint appointments at the in the H. John Heinz III School of Public Policy and Management and the Department of Engineering and Public Policy. He is the editor of *Devastation and Renewal: An Environmental History of Pittsburgh and Its Region* (2003) and the author of numerous books including *The Search for the Ultimate Sink: Urban Pollution in Historical Perspective* (1996) and *Technology and the Rise of the Networked City in Europe and America* (1988).

PRESERVING MODERNISM

Thursday, March 10 2016

MARTIN AURAND
MATTHEW FALCONE
ROB PFAFFMAN
ALBERT TANNLER
GWENDOLYN WRIGHT

Michael Kubo Tonight's salon addresses the challenges of preserving modern architecture. One unintended consequence of modernism, particularly in Pittsburgh, was a burgeoning preservationist movement, a largely grassroots effort to halt destruction of the traditional urban fabric, as occurred in some Pittsburgh neighborhoods during the urban renewal era. Today modern architecture is increasingly under threat of demolition, often in an effort to restitch the city together. Does this removal merely repeat the mistakes of modernism? What is worth saving and at what cost?

Chris Grimley Gwendolyn, could you outline what you think preservation means to modernism and particularly to the work in Pittsburgh?

Gwendolyn Wright You captured it with the title of this exhibition—preservation is about imagining. It's about imagining what the past was and engaging what the modern is. There's always a conflict and an overlap.

The history of preservation began in the late eighteenth and early nineteenth centuries, which we consider to be, in almost every field, the beginning of a modern era of new sensibilities about how change happens, about conflicts within a society, about different ways of thinking about the commonalities and the differences between different groups. Part of what I find fascinating in this history is that preservation has always involved a set of experts who decide what the key categories are, what the shifts are, and how you identify things. It's always gone in terms of these waves: what are the high points and the low points of a particular aesthetic? While preservation at its best tries to engage a range of people about the cultures and places they live in, it has also been a way to pose these oppositions and often to insist that the people who live in a place don't know enough to understand what the issues are.

The reality is that preservation and modernism can coexist. In every instance of a debate, there have been exaggerated ways in which these two groups oppose each other. Preservationists hate modern buildings because they think they are responsible for tearing down older buildings, and modernists dislike preservationists because they seem sentimental. But in fact the two overlap. In looking at Pittsburgh you see that buildings, places, and historic sites had to be torn down to build postwar Pittsburgh. But that's constantly going on, and there is no perfect past. There is no tradition; even the words "tradition" and "traditionalism" suggest that there is something static, which isn't the case. Just as the terms "modern" and "modernism" presume that there is a set of improvements which we can hold on to. And we fall prey to that too easily. Perhaps in the U.S. even more than in other places, we fall prey to the notion that one can only be either a modernist or a preservationist. This or that. And just because you can't draw the line that nothing in the past or the present is absolute, it doesn't mean that there aren't values.

I gather that this exhibition is about opening up room to see how people act, how they think about changes to the city, and how Pittsburgh became a model for so many cities around the country. What I think is captured in the evidence that you have gathered is that we now see it wasn't all as clear as it seemed at the time. People tend to want to say, "Here's the real lesson; here's what's was really going on." But if you look back, it was always more complicated than that. What good historians learn is that when you form an opinion, you have to then say, "Okay, what's another way of looking at this? I could be wrong, or too narrow, or arbitrary; in fact I'm bound to be to some extent. So how can I try to find another path and explore a different way of doing things?" And you did that. It's so rare for exhibitions to go outside of making an argument.

MK Let's talk about the origins of preservation in Pittsburgh.

GW I want to interject a little conflict if I could. What are the commonalities and differences among those of you who practice preservation? What do you see as the scope for preservation versus that of modernism?

Martin Aurand At this point in my life, I don't really practice preservation in the real world, although I think arguably some of what an archivist does is preservation of a certain sort.

I was interested in your statement about the lack of a steady state, that our environments, and cities in particular, are always changing. To me that's the fascination, these layers. In trying to understand and unpack this era, I think we would miss a lot if any of those layers were missing. Some of these are academic; some involve a sort of preservation on the ground, and some are experiential, to do with how one experiences the city. To be able to perceive those layers and, for our purposes, to be able to experience the Renaissance era in Pittsburgh I think is vitally important.

GW Albert, what's your definition?

Albert Tannler One of the realizations I had in my research was that Pittsburgh was probably the ugliest city in the United States. For a good two hundred years it was horrible, mainly because of the pollution. And no one cared about those immigrant people who were making very little money while they made certain other people very, very rich. Let me just read a passage from that book very briefly:

> In 1900 British designer and architect Charles Ashbee visited Pittsburgh and was profoundly shaken by what he saw and experienced. He later wrote that Pittsburgh, one of the "greatest and wealthiest" cities in the United States, was "everything that a city should not be." He noted the natural beauty of the landscape and the impressive bridges but found: noble rivers... covered with a black slime, the scum of her works and factories.... All around was a chain of hills of such natural beauty that the lie of the land seemed to rival that of any city in the world. As little regard was paid to the trees as to the streams, the finest points of view were disfigured by advertisements and used as midden heaps. As the city burnt soft coal... the city was always covered with a dense pall of smoke and soot. I looked into the history of the... city and found her full of records

> of the heroism of past times, the early war of Independence and the struggle with France; one little landmark alone had been saved by some pious ladies from afar. I asked one of her leading citizens if nothing could be done to record or accentuate these things. "Nobody knew of them," he said, "and nobody cared."

Pollution was a serious, serious problem. Efforts were made before World War II to do something about it but the war intervened, so that plans that were put together in the 1920s and 30s didn't materialize until after 1945. If you go down to the Point today and you look along the Ohio River, you see the Block House and the Fort Pitt Museum, along with the extraordinary fountain that is there. We recognize that place today because of what has happened to it. When you look at the photographs that were taken in the 1930s and 40s, the conditions were unspeakable.

Automobiles in the smoke and smog of industrial Pittsburgh, circa 1940.

What I think makes this city special is the discovery of these extraordinary landscapes by a lot of men with money. To a large extent, they decided to put that money back into the community. The Heinz family for example, the Carnegies, or the Fricks. Then people were able to see these landscapes cleaned up, to look around and say, "This is an absolutely gorgeous place—this is amazing." And that led to the extraordinary architectural things that were built in these places, something that has continued up until the present.

I've been in Pittsburgh for twenty-five years. When I first came here, only crazy people would live downtown—nobody would consider it. You look around now and there are 20,000 people living downtown who weren't there before. The improvement in quality of life has had a great deal to do with cleaning the air and then building on that. The Point, which had been full of railroad yards, became a park. And it was because of the Democratic mayor, David Lawrence, and the Republican financier, Richard King Mellon.

MA Do you think the better quality of life in Pittsburgh now is because of modernism or despite modernism?

AT I think it's both. There's a real sense in which it attracted some of the best architects of their day. We have the largest house designed by Walter Gropius and Marcel Breuer in Pittsburgh. We have a whole community of wonderful buildings just outside of the city designed by two of Frank Lloyd Wright's most important assistants, Cornelia Brierly and her husband Peter, with Wright's help.

The Point with active railroad yards, circa 1915.

GW I think that we should try to open beyond suggesting that there's one form of modernism. We shouldn't define them according to which architect is passing along, what particular genetic code. Modernism and modernity has as much to do with the development of the department store as it does with the ways in which Kaufmann's department store has had influence through Kaufmann himself, or through the different architects he hired. One of the things that seems especially interesting

Kaufmann's Department Store as seen from the corner of Smithfield Street and Forbes Avenue, 1912.

about Pittsburgh as a place is that you had industry, you had commerce, you had social conflict in which there were efforts to try to keep the city innovative; you had recreation and you had efforts to try to engage and contain the natural environment which is an extraordinary benefit here. So there are many ways of thinking about what modernity and the modern world were and what should be preserved.

Again, it comes back to the question you've asked us: is this interrelation between preservation and modernism not just about one particular aesthetic but about various modern aesthetics? These have always been in conflict but inevitably overlap, build on, and challenge each other. And that's one of the things that has made this city so dramatic.

As an outsider, I want to pose a question to all of you, but perhaps to the two curators in particular. To what extent were different neighborhoods in Pittsburgh, and therefore different socioeconomic and different ethnic groups, involved in these debates about improvement and modernization? Modernization has always to do with the notion of improvement, but here it also has to do with these efforts, from early on, to ask, for example, how do we preserve aspects of the Hill? How can we think about different groups who have lived here?

Rob Pfaffmann I think I'm the only practitioner here who works on both modern buildings and preservation. In fact, most of my work is in preservation.

In the 1970s, right when we were shifting gears from late modernism to postmodernism in architecture, the preservation movement was growing and so were architecture schools. We were all in conflict between those things. I studied under Erik Stallman, a German modernist, but I had also grown up in a traditional New England town, and I saw the incredible destruction of urban renewal in Boston. And so I learned to navigate those poles and say, it's not either/or, it's both/and. Fast-forward to Pittsburgh and trying to understand the North Side along with the Market House, or the Lower Hill with the Civic Arena. When I had an opportunity to design the library on the Hill, I realized that there are the histories that aren't written in the traditional history books by those in power. You have to find out how people in the Hill really felt about urban renewal, to read the newspapers where you can see both sides of those issues. In the middle of that history is how economics affected whether these plans could be followed through or whether they led to other things, like displacement, which was not supposed to happen but did because the federal urban renewal program cut back on housing funds.

Exterior of North Side Market House, future site of Allegheny Center, 1936.

I'm frustrated that our preservation discourse has become all black and white—you've either got to put the original streets back or you have to save something exactly the way it was. It's not one or the other, it's both. That attitude has guided our work as architects and preservationists, not to be too pure about things. I think that people tend to back into their different corners and demand that if you don't do things exactly one way, then you're out.

CG At what point does getting backed into that corner trigger the need for action? I think we're skirting the issue about what gets torn down and what is preserved. In our work in Boston, for example, the architectural threat is predominately about civic structures, which are more likely to be demolished, whereas the Pittsburgh version is very much about private investment. How do we start to think about what buildings matter and, perhaps just as importantly, when buildings matter?

Matthew Falcone At Preservation Pittsburgh we don't take the first step toward preservation; it's usually a community group that comes to us that initiates things. The question is, how do we identify ourselves as Pittsburghers? I think part of the reason that modern buildings remain in danger here is that Pittsburghers don't see in them an architectural reflection of themselves, of their city. You have a later development like PPG Place that's a hit, that people see as wonderful because it incorporates and re-envisions elements that reflect traditional features of Victorian-era buildings.

It's interesting to look at the map of designated historic districts in Pittsburgh. For example, there are four

The Philip Johnson and John Burgee designed Pittsburgh Plate Glass Company Building, completed in 1984.

different residential districts that surround Allegheny Center. There are several landmarks in Allegheny Center thanks to the Pittsburgh History & Landmarks Foundation that are a reflection of what was seen as important to preserve when redevelopment was occurring during urban renewal. So, in essence, the residents around Allegheny Center decided that these sites were important to them as Pittsburghers, that they are important to their community. But they have not taken ownership of Allegheny Center itself, the Commons and the garden, as designated historic sites. There are planned alterations in the works and yet no community group has come forward to us saying, we want a voice in this process or we see these modern landscapes as part of our community.

GW Why do you think that is? Is it because of the process of how it was designed and used?

MF I think that's part of it.

GW Let's go back to your point about the process. The fact is, if ten years ago architects could have said, we don't care about modernist legacy—I'm just going to build my building—they can no longer do that. You can't simply say anymore that you don't care. It's the same thing with preservation, The histories of these sites is always there, though it maybe hidden, or it may be harder to find or to read. There are always multiple histories, not just one history that later gets fixed. That's the case with Allegheny Center, where what was there before it was built has become part of it, and of ways of thinking about that site.

RP It's really interesting to see how people respond. For example the residents of the high-rise towers in East Liberty, as Chris Ivey captures in his film *East of Liberty*. While we may look at them and say, those are ugly buildings, people began to adapt and they had very eloquent descriptions of why they liked living there. It was the beauty of the green landscape; they didn't want to lose that back to an urban street grid. And so they adapted to a different culture and really appreciated the tower in the park—it actually worked for them. So we have to be careful. I think this is the idea of the old fifty-year rule, that we have to get some distance, to wait for a new generation, It isn't the old generation that's making these judgments, it's the generation coming up that's looking at these places with fresh eyes.

MK Some of the audience members at the first salon who lived in places like Allegheny Center offered exactly this sort of nuanced commentary. They described on the one hand how exciting and modern these places

Still from the documentary East of Liberty: A Story of Good Intentions, *2006.*

once were, how valuable they were as improvements in their way of living, but at the same time they were clear about recognizing their problems, some of which extended from their partial realization or from a lack of maintenance. This points to Gwendolyn's comments about the fragmentary nature of these histories, where it becomes difficult to cleanly separate a before and an after. All of the material in the exhibition testifies to just how much what exists in the city today is the result of a series of residues or fragmentary traces of proposals that were partially built, modified, and so on. One of the questions that we want to pose here how one begins to make decisions in that kind of condition, where there is a fluid combination of things that have existed in different temporalities, often layered onto each other.

RP The different preservation organizations in Pittsburgh all got together a couple of months ago and met with the new planning director to talk about how to extend the preservation plan for the city. We asked, how it can become a living document, one that recognizes that the layers of what we value are constantly changing? How do you create a register of historic structures that includes the histories that aren't recognized in the modernist way of looking at history? In talking with people on the Hill, for example, you realize that all the sites that August Wilson inhabited or was involved with have importance to them, maybe not architecturally, but socially.

CG The more this conversation goes on, the more it may be complicated by the buildings that are not going to be taken down. No one is going to tear down U.S. Steel, or the Alcoa building.

MA Using the examples of Allegheny Center or the Civic Arena may be a bit of a mistake, because they live in isolation. The Civic Arena might have been more lovable if it had developed some context. I think to a large degree, we're very lucky here in terms of what remains. The Civic Arena, Three Rivers Stadium, the Old Airport, and Kane Hospital represent our four biggest civic investments, and they are all totally gone. What's left are the public spaces that were created by corporate business. We have Point State Park, we have the Gateway Center, we have Mellon Square and the buildings around it. And I have to think that those

Three Rivers Stadium, early home to the Pirates, Steelers, and short-lived Maulers, before its demolition in 2000.

spaces are better integrated into the city as a whole.

GW You also seem to be making a point that it's a question of spaces, not buildings. And it may be that those are easier for many different kinds of people to integrate into their lives.

MA But I'm also speaking to the buildings around these spaces. Many of the buildings we're talking about are not isolated and dull and off-putting by themselves. They're with other buildings or they're with complementary civic spaces. And so I think they can be evaluated in a different way, which might change the whole question of what you save from a list of buildings to something much bigger than that.

CG What about the Tasso Katselas buildings in East Liberty? Those are still an amazing testament to civic investment in social housing. Is that civic legacy something that should be reconsidered after the lessons of Civic Arena and its demolition? We have a plethora of civic buildings in concrete around the country that are coming down. What happens when these buildings disappear?

GW The space surrounding these buildings is where we can see and acknowledge change, to bring in more people to engage and take part in it. What's interesting to me in your example of public housing is that preservation has now become a major position, whereas in the past it was all about tearing down postwar housing and building cute little New Urbanist projects instead. But that model is now clearly seen as ethnologically and socially wrong, as taking away any sense of people having a connection to the places in which they live. Instead, there has been a major move to ask, "How can we make this housing work better?" Because it's not enough to leave it the way it is either. How can architects not just make these buildings function better or look more beautiful but add services, because we now know that housing is not just living units but also has to do with social services? Many projects are now moving in that direction, and that's clearly one of the things that has happened in Pittsburgh. There seems to be an understanding here of this complexity of different meanings and ongoing changes of action.

RP I think there's an underlying problem that we are repeating our history, something that was talked about at the last salon. You hear this a lot about the re-planning of the Lower Hill by the Bjarke Ingels Group. We see

A model of BIG's Lower Hill District Masterplan, a reimagining of the empty plots where the Civic Arena once stood, 2015.

that at Pennley Place, where there's not a transparent community engagement. I think the dangerous part right now is that we talk the talk but we don't always walk the walk. Things become more expedient, especially in the economics of the real estate development world. I think this is unique to the last five years in Pittsburgh—we didn't have to worry about those issues as much in the past. Whereas if you brought the Mayor through today and said, "If you didn't have to worry about the owner of Pennley Place, would you see any value in keeping the building and adapting it to new residential use with mixed income housing?" It would probably work really well. It's better built than the new stuff going up.

[From the audience] Why do some of these buildings no

longer function as they should have functioned? What are the reasons why that building might still have merit even if it isn't functioning well anymore?

GW Maybe we need to open this up a bit. Rather than saying something works or doesn't work in terms of use, maybe we should ask: for whom doesn't it work? It may function in ways that we may not be totally aware of. One of the greatest problems with post-World War II public housing in the U.S. was upkeep and maintenance. But it's still not worth tearing these buildings down, rather than finding ways to make them work better. That has been a real turn, to find ways of engaging the residents of these buildings and ways of putting in services. There's a wonderful housing project in Chicago, for instance, which ended up with a largely Chinese-American population. So there are a lot of pavilions for doing things like Tai Chi out in the garden, taking over the public spaces and corridors and making them into really beautiful, pleasant places to be. Public involvement is obviously easier said than done, but you've got to start there.

[From the audience] Why is it easier said than done? Is it harder to do than to knock a building down and start over?

GW It's easier said than done because there's a great desire among architects to just tear it down and start over, to decide they're going to come in and solve the problem.

RP I wouldn't blame the architects. I'd blame the leadership.

MA The politics of it.

[From the audience] I wanted to point out that low-income high-rises are frequently looked at as not working. They say that high-rises are not conducive to looking over Washington Plaza or the Gateway Towers, but it's not the buildings.

GW No, it's not.

CG It's never the buildings. There are numerous films and documentaries that have appeared recently that have dispelled the tired cliché of modern architecture, or modernism itself, as being the sole culprit for these things.

[From the audience] I would ask the question: Who is preservation or modernism for? Who is concerned about it and why? To give an example, what is now called SoHo in New York City was a neighborhood with at least a few vectors affecting its transformation. You had a preservation model because of the cast iron buildings, which were originally inhabited by small manufacturing. You had the vector of artists moving in and working there. We were there in 1968, when there was very little there but the buildings. But what it became between the preservation and modernizing efforts was then represented by commerce. And now it's essentially a very high-end mall.

At the last salon there was a gentleman who lives in one of the new parts of East Liberty. He was saying that he was glad that things were changing, but that he's also finding that there are places there where he can no longer afford to eat. What were the places that he could go to, and are they gone? Do they have to be preserved? Does there have to be an effort to preserve the local grocery store or the pizza place?

GW You're talking about something really important,

Building implosion during the demolition of the Pruitt-Igoe complex in St. Louis, Missouri, 1972.

which is economic preservation and making sure that there are all kinds of jobs, as well as social and cultural preservation. Those are crucial because all too often preservation in the U.S. is just about buildings. That's not preservation, telling people that they can keep the buildings, but without the neighborhoods. Not that they can ever stay the same—they can't—but there should be some effort. We've never had city governments really take on the challenge of giving people a say in what happens without totally deferring to them. I'm sure there are neighborhoods here in Pittsburgh where there needs to be engagement without deferring entirely.

RP We should make it a social discussion. Architecture is right in the middle of that discussion and how we use architecture is essential.

GW This is where I get angry with some of my preservationist colleagues who want everything to be about labels, about which particular style a building is in. It becomes really tedious.

MK Part of the pre-history of how SoHo came to be what it is now was the threat of demolition because of the planned Lower Manhattan Expressway that would have cut through the neighborhood. This was one of the last projects of the Robert Moses era, and there was a whole series of movements to protest the project in which many artists in New York City, like Donald Judd, were involved. This kind of story very quickly becomes enmeshed in a chain reaction of histories and counter-histories. For example, part of the reason why these buildings were available to these artists is that landlords stopped putting money into them once the Expressway was planned, and so they became cheap, inhabitable spaces that could be occupied. That occupation led in turn to the recuperation of the neighborhood, which then kicked off certain economic interests, and eventually the conversion to lofts and other forms of high-end development. Would we call that process preservation, and if so, what does the word preservation mean? Does this history count as preservation because in the end the bones of the buildings are the same as what was there before, or does it no longer count as preservation in any meaningful sense?

Perspective rendering of Paul Rudolph's plan for the Lower Manhattan Expressway, 1970.

RP In preservation, I think we have a challenge about how to communicate with the public and public officials about what's important. We need to achieve consensus and maybe architects should know how to have a strong say in that. Nevertheless, a public official has to look at the balance between the future residents of that neighborhood and the existing neighborhood.

Residents are often very vocal, but they may not be around in five or ten years. It's not about being paternalistic, but about but looking forward to the future to maintain flexibility. I think that's one reason why these loft buildings have done so well, because they're easily adaptable. That's a cue for us as architects, to make sure we design buildings that can be changed easily.

[From the audience] I often become an apologist when I'm faced with the question of preserving modernism and specifically postwar modernism because there's often this perception—sometimes not wrongly—that what we have are missteps, failed projects, ambitious and idealistic attempts that just didn't seem to work. A lot of the solutions that people present is about erasing that history, which frightens me. How do you make the argument for preserving those attempts in some sense because they are part of the history of neighborhoods and how they have developed?

GW It's interesting that beginning in the middle of the nineteenth century there were books on "modern" houses that showed what we would today call Victorian houses and see as traditional or old-fashioned stylistically, but which were seen as modern at the time. They were considered part of modernism in residential architecture in that they came out of all the industrial production that took off after the Civil War, which enabled cheap ornament, inside and outside, that would make your house look different from all the other houses on the block. That was part of what defined a modern house. In part, then, we need to be able to tell people that the definition of what is modern keeps changing. It's not only what people are criticizing now. There are certainly buildings of the postwar era or the Brutalist era of the 1970s that exemplify what modernity meant at the time. Not all of them should be kept but certainly not all of them should be torn down.

MF One of the most interesting things about preservation for me is that it has a generational component, where those that are raised in a certain era respond to certain architecture with which they grew up. We had a mass exodus in which a lot of people left Pittsburgh, so we have an older generation that's missing here, but which is very well represented in Boston, Philadelphia, or Washington, D.C. Some are coming back, but they weren't part of the history for thirty, forty, fifty years. It becomes interesting because there's a gap, where there are people who don't identify with that neighborhood or that building from the era. It doesn't really have any resonance with them; it wasn't the Pittsburgh that they remembered when they left.

[From the audience] This goes to the example of the main tower at East Liberty. I understand what has been said about not wanting to blindly tear it down. But at the same time how do you reinterpret it in a way that removes the stigma of alienation and isolation for many of the people who live in that neighborhood? How do you address it as racial segregation because that was part of the creation of Pittsburgh and particularly with the new climate we see?

RP In 2008 I went to the Docomomo conference in Rotterdam, titled "The Challenge of Change," which looked at urban renewal sites around the world. I was the one American there, and nobody had heard anything about the Pittsburgh story. It was exciting to be able to show Pittsburgh to people who had gone to study cities in former Eastern Bloc countries in Europe, and I was amazed by their ability to adapt some of the "ugly," communist-era concrete buildings in these cities into interesting places to live. There was very a different cultural attitude towards these buildings. Yes, these were also negative experiences in their history, but they claimed them back. It was a more mature approach.

MK There are positions that vary by place, or by constituency, on this question of what to do, if a certain history is seen as negative, with the buildings associated with that history. One attitude is that they should be removed as quickly as possible, so that we can try to go back to a state where we allow ourselves to believe that the history never happened. The counter-attitude is that whatever history has become a part of these physical spaces can and must be taken into the present, that it's a matter of working with them and accepting those histories as something that is always layered into the present, but which do not determine it in its entirety.

CG One subject we had hoped to frame in this conversation is the importance of archives and of historic resources for what we understand as preservation. We went very quickly to discussing the physical and political issues that endanger these sites. But I think we have to acknowledge that institutional histories and the histories of individual protagonists are just as critical to maintain. We're running out of time, both for the recording of these histories and for the projects that were produced. There are surviving architects, community activists, and others who have been integral to the making of Pittsburgh in particular. Historicizing these actors becomes crucial to what we mean by preservation.

RP I think what we have uniquely in Pittsburgh are some very human modernist buildings. If you look at the Alcoa building, there's an urbanism there that doesn't often exist in other towers. I think that may offer a cue as to how we communicate with those who haven't understood this yet, or to understand what works well about the U.S. Steel building as a social place. I would ask, how do you get this exhibition outside of the walls of the museum? The next time we have a preservation battle over a modernist building, how will we have prepared for that future dialog? I think these exhibits help us do that. And I think we have to find more ways to reach out to the communities about these issues.

[From the audience] I moved to Allegheny Center in 1976 when I was twenty-two. I moved there because I liked new buildings. I now own a house from 1873 and two other hundred-year-old buildings, but at the time all the old buildings that I had seen were falling down and turning ugly, and I hated them. Allegheny Center was new and clean, and it was a little pedestrian oasis. It was self-contained. It had four residential towers, a planetarium, shopping, retail and food, a radio station, my dentist, a library, a theater, and the old Post Office Museum was right next door.

Market Square prior to its renovation as a pedestrian plaza, 1996.

I think the whole idea of rethinking Allegheny Center that the exhibition poses is insulting because there is nothing wrong with Allegheny Center. I don't know why it needs to be altered. Since I've lived in Pittsburgh, Market Square has been "renovated," as a nice term for destroying the previous version and building a new one. It seems to me to be the war of the present city planners on the previous city planners, with whatever reasons they find for destroying the previous plan and coming up with a new one. And then the next generation develops yet another version.

CG I think you're absolutely right. Part of the experiment of HACLab has been to examine our constant need to reinterpret. Do we need to tear everything down in order to learn from our mistakes? If you like what happened in the past, do you simply replicate it, or just eradicate it if you don't? When does reexamining a particular place become a critical agent in understanding and perpetuating a particular moment in time? What we did with the students in reexamining Allegheny Center was in some ways meant to get someone like you to say that it's insulting and it's not what should be done. We need those voices in the room saying, "There's nothing wrong

with it, why mess with it."
GW There's the wonderful notion of John Dewey, the philosopher and educator, of the "constituted community." In his opinion, every profession and group that makes decisions should constantly push itself to expand beyond the people who come to their meetings, beyond the people who are officially part of that debate, because otherwise it gets too comfortable. He insisted that every group should be a little bit uncomfortable, and that you have to have people who raise opinions that you aren't comfortable with. I think that speaks to this edge between modernism and preservation, two words that none of us really like but which we are seeing in opposition, when they shouldn't be. They've always co-existed and we need to find ways of encouraging a whole range of people, starting with professionals but extending into many other groups, here and elsewhere, to be able to have a voice in saying what we hold onto in certain neighborhoods. Where are these different people and how can you bring them in? It's not all going to all in some easy way, but there need to be stakes that people can have, that will get them involved in that discussion.

Martin Aurand is Architecture Librarian at Carnegie Mellon University and Archivist of the Carnegie Mellon University Architecture Archives. He is the author of *The Spectator and the Topographical City* (2006), *The Progressive Architecture of Frederick G. Scheibler, Jr.* (1994), and *Pittsburgh Architecture: A Guide to Research* (1991). He was Curatorial Consultant for the Imagining the Modern exhibition.

Mathew Falcone is Associate Dean of Faculty at the Art Institute of Pittsburgh's Online Division and President of the Board of Preservation Pittsburgh.

Rob Pfaffman is principal of Pfaffman and Associates, an architecture and urban planning practice established in Pittsburgh in 1996. His firm's projects include the Oakland Civic Center Conservation Plan (2005) and the ongoing adaptive reuse of the Heinz History Center.

Albert Tannler is Historical Collections Director for the Pittsburgh History and Landmarks Foundation, where he oversees the James D. Van Trump Library and Frank B. Fairbanks Rail Transportation Archive. He is the author of numerous books including *H.H. Richardson's Allegheny County Courthouse & Jail Guidebook* (2016) and *Pittsburgh Architecture in the Twentieth Century: Notable Modern Buildings and Their Architects* (2013).

Gwendolyn Wright is Professor of Architecture at the Columbia University Graduate School of Architecture, Planning, and Preservation. She is the author of numerous books including *USA: Modern Architectures in History* (2008), *The Politics of Design in French Colonial Urbanism* (1991), and *Building the Dream: A Social History of Housing in America* (1981). Since 2003 Gwendolyn has also served as co-host of the PBS television series, *History Detectives*.

MAKING THE MODERN

Thursday, April 7 2016

CHRISTINE MONDOR
MARK FATLA
JUSTIN P. GREENAWALT
COREY ZENGEBOT

Rami el Samahy In our third salon we hope to go beyond the products of urban renewal—the drawings and the architecture of the buildings that are on display in this exhibition—to examine the procedures and processes, laws, regulations, and changes of attitude that were required to make urban renewal happen in Pittsburgh. There is often a caricature of urban renewal: that it didn't take the people into account; that it was a top-down process that ultimately failed because it failed to reach the people on the ground. Justin, if I'm not mistaken, you mentioned that the planning process for East Liberty in the 1960s included some 296 community meetings. How do you reconcile the caricature of urban renewal with that fact?

Justin Greenawalt One of the biggest things about East Liberty was how different it was from many of the other projects here in Pittsburgh in taking the community into consideration. Prior to East Liberty, you had a tabula rasa approach that prioritized wiping a site clean and building something new. East Liberty is one of the very few places where you'll find late nineteenth-century architecture at the core of an urban renewal project. It was a new way of doing things, and it relied on someone completely new at the helm: Al Jacobs, a young planner for the Pittsburgh Regional Planning Association who worked with Robert Pease on the project, was very community-oriented in discovering what people wanted. One of the most interesting things about Al Jacobs's process was his attitude toward saving structures. There was a whole row of houses on what is now West Sinclair. The Urban Redevelopment Authority (URA) was prepared to pick up these houses and move them. The fact that he talked to people and was willing to move their houses in order to realign the street was something I had never come across before.

An aerial view of East Liberty during the area's redevelopment, 1968.

Christine Mondor East Liberty had a much stronger sense of community to begin with. It was much more intact as a neighborhood, and more people lived there.

Corey Zehngebot It's interesting to hear this history. In Boston two of our earliest urban renewal plans are probably the ones that have come to represent its scope in the eyes of the public—Government Center and the infamous West End, which took a similar tabula rasa approach as some of the Pittsburgh plans. There was immediate blow-back in terms of how the Boston Redevelopment Authority (BRA) went about planning in the city at large. As a result the BRA was forced very early on to change their approach; they moved away from that sort of totalizing strategy to one that was much more strategic and nuanced, with less wholesale demolition, more engagement with the community, and the strategic building of schools, fire stations, police stations, and so on. But the reputation of urban renewal in Boston still dates back to that original approach, even fifty years later, and it has proven nearly impossible to overcome that to open up a dialogue.

ReS That's also the institutional legacy. We now have to be much more engaged with the community and much more economically and environmentally responsible, something that wasn't really in the language at the time. Yet there are these nuances.

If you trace the chronology in Pittsburgh, Point Park and Gateway Center were really the first large-scale planning efforts of the Renaissance, and they were considered huge successes. These projects signaled a new era. There was optimism, and perhaps with that optimism, some hubris. But then the planners moved up to the Lower Hill and really got it wrong, producing a backlash similar to the West End in Boston. East Liberty happened ten years after that and it was a much more community-engaged effort. But the tools that were enacted early on—eminent domain being one—and the creation of large government or quasi-governmental agencies to administer change at a large scale were things that didn't exist in the pre-Renaissance era and were very much a part of the time.

We still have those tools, but we don't use them in the same ways today. I wonder if any of you have thoughts on why that is.

CM *Pittsburgh Plans* has just completed our first ever comprehensive plan. Prior to that, if you look to the plans for the city by the Olmsted jr. in 1910, or the efforts of the 1960s, all of the changes were incremental. I'm not saying that they weren't big infrastructural changes, but they were building incrementally on things that already existed. Through some of these large moves, Pittsburgh saw a shift in the scale of administrative authority for making change in the community. I think today we're much more conscious of using that scale of administrative authority within the existing fabric. So even in areas where there are large blank slates, there's still a fairly incremental approach to how development is going to happen, and I think we're still wary of those big, one-time master plans that attempt to fix everything in one fell swoop. When you take away the opportunity for individuals to function, you remove the capacity of that community to exercise their own autonomy, and I think we're much more careful about that now.

Mark Fatla I'm not sure that that's accurate. The Mayor's four biggest priorities are all large-scale projects: Hazelwood Home on the riverfront, the Lower Hill, a section of the Strip, and an unspecified redo of Homewood. So I don't think this administration's shy at all about large-scale planning. When Thomas J. Murphy Jr. was elected as Mayor in 1994, he was also the "vision guy"—he was talking about large-scale projects for

Rafael Viñoly's David L. Lawrence Convention Center, completed in 1981.

the riverfront, the convention center, the stadiums, and so on. Not to say bad things came out of that, but I don't think that politicians here are shying away from those things. How do you think they get elected? Not by standing up in front of little projects or incremental improvements in neighborhoods and business districts, but by standing in front of big projects and hero deals.

CM I don't disagree. It's not to say that we don't deal with big pieces of property, but that we don't expect them to be done in a ten-year cycle.

CZ You don't necessarily expect to use the same tools either, and you don't fund them in the same way. To answer the question as to why we don't use those processes in the same way, I think there are two major reasons: politics and money. The politics of the 1960s was based on a population that believed in the public servant as an agent of good. I don't know if we, for better or worse, subscribe to that same philosophy. The current political reality does not make it such that people would ever go out and promote eminent domain, or the wholesale clearance of neighborhoods for large public projects. Those ideas would be totally unpalatable today.

The second reason is money. Urban renewal was basically a blank check from the federal government to do whatever you could in these cities, and that is just not happening anymore. Neither the federal government nor the state is paying for things, so it's really up to municipalities to be creative, and to leverage public investment for strategic private investment.

One outcome of urban renewal were the citizen advocacy groups that emerged directly as a consequence of these large-scale projects. People mobilized to stop what they saw as being bad for their neighborhood, and those vestiges remains in cities across the country. Redevelopment authorities had to become more responsive and transparent in how they do business and make decisions.

I think those are the reasons why we can't use the same processes today, even if legally we have the same tools; we have to be more careful about how we use them.

MF Politically, eminent domain is off the table, but I'm not sure that the process has become much more transparent with redevelopment authorities. Deals are still struck among big-money interests at tables that we're not at, and neighborhood activists often have to break down the door to sit at the table. Thankfully there are processes that give us entry—planning commissions, the zoning board—but the practical reality is that the process isn't more transparent. Maybe I'm old, or a cynic, but I think power and money will do what they want. They won't use eminent domain anymore, but there are other ways to assemble these big sites. We're seeing it right now with the four sites I mentioned, which are the priority for this administration.

ReS Do you see any difference between projects that are funded by governments, whether these are federal, state, or municipal, and projects that are funded by private individuals or corporations?

MF There may be more restrictions on the government money, but in terms of transparency, not a lot. It's money, and you have to be on guard because money's going to do what it has to do, whether it's governmental or private. And there aren't a whole lot of government projects anymore—fortunately. Pittsburgh's getting to the point where a lot more can happen without government money.

JG This brings up a very interesting point. Christine, I was curious to hear you say that Pittsburgh had engaged in a comprehensive master planning effort. This exhibition demonstrates that only a small number of distinct areas in the city benefited from the Renaissance. If you un-silo the city and start to look at it in a comprehensive way, is a governmental organization able to act as an agent for ground-up change in a way that private investment has never been able to do?

CM It's very interesting that you mentioned the term "ground-up" and government in the same sentence. Historically Pittsburgh hasn't had a particularly strong governmental ability to exercise large-scale control over our own environment; we haven't had a comprehensive plan. The state of Pennsylvania has recently required that every municipality produce a comprehensive plan. The plan doesn't design the municipality, but it helps the municipality prioritize how it might make decisions or design certain things moving forward. So it's not really a complete comprehensive plan, but is more fragmented, with specific focus categories. But in a city that's already complex and fragmented, doing a comprehensive plan in a complex and fragmented way is not helpful. It doesn't help us understand when affordable housing crises come up. We don't always have the data or the strategy to deal with fast changes throughout the system, and that's difficult. On the flip side, it is a very organic process and it allows us to have much more ground-up input.

I think that our biggest asset here in Pittsburgh is that we have incredibly robust non-governmental organizations and a community of Community Development Corporations and non-profits such as the Design Center, the Pittsburgh Community Reinvestment Group, and the North Side Leadership Conference, who have advocated for and carried these ideas forward. At some point this also breaks down, especially in relation to infrastructure. The only entities that can deal with infrastructure are governmental agencies, and we're seeing that with storm water. No amount of non-profits dealing with storm water or watersheds are going to solve a problem that is system-wide, and a governmental agency needs to set the table for that conversation. The conversation at that biggest scale is no longer about form but about resources, and that's different from what is on display here.

JG Public-private partnership gained traction as a concept among planners in the 1990s, but Pittsburgh pioneered public-private development in the 1950s, even in the 1940s. There was a very close alignment between the city and business leaders. But even during this era of cross-cooperation, there was no comprehensive plan for the city. At that time, comprehensive plans were everywhere—almost every city had some sort of large vision for the entire metropolitan region. Pittsburgh never did. It may speak to the way politics work in the greater Pittsburgh region, or it may be that it wasn't considered necessary.

MF It's totally new to me, by the way, that there is now a federal requirement to produce a comprehensive plan.

CZ The federal government said, we're going to stop giving you money unless you show evidence of comprehensive planning. Money is the great motivator, which is why Boston did one back in 1965.

MF Inertia aside, I think our geography also contributed to

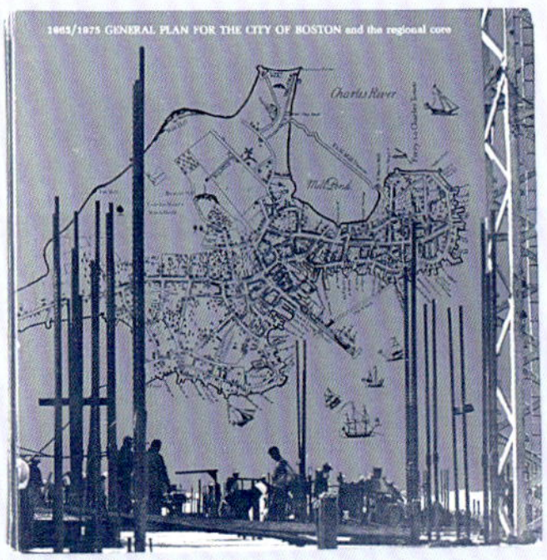

Cover of the General Plan for the City of Boston, *1964, the first comprehensive plan for the city.*

the lack of a comprehensive plan. Physical things divide us: ravines and rivers and hillsides and steep slopes make it difficult to plan this city, and this creates micro-markets where you can go four blocks over and the market for housing is dramatically different. It's damned tough to think about synthetic, comprehensive planning when geography creates these little micro-markets.

JG The underlying question is how to comprehensively rethink plans for urban areas when, for decades, urban areas were not the places that people wanted to be. Today there's a new influx which creates issues of housing, equity, equality, and access to living near the place where you work. There's an immense pressure on urban areas to adapt to what could be called a private paradigm of ownership. There is a strange friction between a city that was ignored for so long, that lost its tax base and the ability to upgrade its infrastructure, but where now everybody wants to come back, and the city isn't ready for it. How does an activist, a planner, or an urban historian respond to sudden, exponential growth?

CZ You've just described the impossible scenario that cities are currently encountering. It is impossible to do just-in-time planning with limited resources, and at the same time to try to think comprehensively while engaging different advocacy groups. You have to be a pathological optimist in the face of almost clear failure and impossibility, every day. You keep trying, because eventually you hope you are going to get something right.

ReS In some ways, Pittsburgh has an advantage over cities like Boston, New York City, or San Francisco in that there is still a lot of potential here. As much as things have improved in the last few years, there's still a lot to be done. But there are neighborhoods that are still affordable, where people can still move into the city. That's not the case in Boston or in San Francisco, where people are being priced out. That hasn't yet happened here, and it will probably be quite some time before that will happen here, because we have so much available housing stock.

MF We have to understand that you can't seal neighborhoods under glass like a snow globe. Markets are always changing, always growing. People say, "We're getting priced out of our neighborhoods!" Well, the flip side is that the people who owned for twenty or thirty years did very well—their family assets improved. So you have low-income families in places like the East End who are saying, "This is great! I can send my kid to college, or I'm going leave a legacy for the next generation because my asset value went up." So gentrification is not all bad, and it's not always preventable. Some people think that we have to freeze all our neighborhoods so that every place is the same, and has the same affordability. I think we have to protect people at all levels—don't get me wrong. But the market is going to change, and we're going to have to adapt as that changes.

CM It's hard to overstate what's happened in Pittsburgh. Affordable housing used to mean that you put people like me, who were young and just out of college, into neighborhoods where the average income was much lower than the measly architectural salary I was making. Now, in that same community, having affordable housing in the conversation means keeping people like me in that neighborhood, even at my current salary. This is a big flip from weak market to strong market. The issue is not to fear change but to prepare communities to understand it, and to give them the tools to deal with it. So if I come from a background where I understand how to do real estate deals, and I have some assets that I can use to make that deal, then the change that Mark is describing is awesome for me because I can go and reinvest with an understanding of the next market. But if I'm somebody who doesn't have assets, or has never been involved in that culture of real estate, and I don't understand the mechanisms by which I can capitalize on these changes, then it becomes a very threatening situation.

Chris Grimley To shift the conversation slightly, Rami and I had a remarkable interview with Tasso Katselas this morning. Tasso designed an extraordinary range of buildings in every kind of typology you can imagine. The thing that is repeated in conversations surrounding this era is this idea that architects didn't care about other people, that it was ultimately about their own ego, about coming in and exerting their influence. But there was this remarkable, heartfelt humanism when we talked with Tasso about his investment in challenging the norms of design to the point of failure, in testing new ways of making things to the point where they might not work. For example, he talked about working closely with the design of Section Eight housing to create better spaces for people to live.

ReS He talked about it down to the resizing of the brick, so that it would be economical to build these projects. The brick was a little bit larger than a typical brick, and they built a section of it to test because everyone said they couldn't do it. Since the bricks were bigger, the bricklayer's arm hurt a little bit more, so they designed each brick with a little hand-hold so that the bricklayer could grab it more easily. In fact the building was completed in one third of the time because the design used fewer bricks. There was a real consideration of the human, the human body, the inhabitants, the laborers, and the contract.

CG Ideas are meant to be pushed, and the way people live and how they occupy space are in constant evolution. Sometimes things don't work. This raises questions about the state of building practice in Pittsburgh today, and whether there has been an effort to introduce an idea of design excellence into the current conversation about gentrification, expansion, and rapid development, particularly given the number of units that are needed to house the city's population. With Tasso, there was a realization that the new development model in Pittsburgh—steel base, concrete deck, and wood above—is a recipe for disaster. So a broader question here is in how we refocus efforts on developing design excellence programs within cities that, by necessity, challenge the perceived norms of what development means.

ReS Alternately, how can we think about the processes and procedures that would make the built environment a little less awful than it is right now? Not much of what we're building is built to last. It's not because architects are lazy or bad. The situation that we find ourselves in—whether it's the economic environment, the regulatory environment, or maybe even the way we're educated—all of those things conspire to create a built environment that's far from ideal.

CZ I disagree. We've had this conversation many times, and I do think that a city like Boston has a particular agenda when it comes to architectural excellence. You're architects, as I am. A bit of background. The Boston Redevelopment Authority isn't just a redevelopment authority. Over time we've accrued additional functions, so we're also the planning department, and we do review for all development in the city. So in my job as an urban designer I work on planning initiatives, but I'm also there to do design review for all the development projects that are being processed. There is an aspiration to do good design, but it's different from what it was in the 1960s, when I do think that there was an aspiration for design quality, but it was somewhat misplaced. Not all architectural ideas were good ones. We can all look back and agree that the way those aspirations manifested themselves in the built environment has created what today we would call bad urbanism. Maybe some of their architectural qualities are notable and worth celebrating, but I'm not sure that the urban qualities that were created as an after-effect are desirable.

It was also all men, too, for the most part. You have to point this out.

JG In that respect there's a remarkable newspaper article in the documents room of the exhibition, titled "36 Men and a Model." If you haven't seen it, please go. The model is actually an architectural model—we'll leave it at that.

CZ There used to be an a priori understanding that if you were going to build something it had to have an aspiration to high design quality. Now the aspiration is to just get something built. If in the past you had a line item in the budget for design, now that gets moved to the process column. There is only a finite amount of resources that you can devote to a particular project, and it's hard to get projects approved. Nevertheless good projects do get built, and they're better urbanistically, but architecturally maybe they don't aspire to the same bombast as in the urban renewal era.

ReS That approach treats design as a soft cost. Design should be a hard cost.

CZ I totally agree.

MF Interestingly, I think CDCs, particularly in low-income neighborhoods, are driving the higher-quality work that gets done because we don't have to just hit the bottom line all day. We do as much as we can within the financial limits that we have—practical, basic economics. A brick, a two-by-four, or a sheet of drywall cost the same on the North Side as they do in Cranberry. But what you can build rents or sells for a lot more in Cranberry than it will on the North Side. CDCs are often the ones who drive the quality in a neighborhood, consciously so because we're trying to set a standard for everybody else to match. So when we do a historic storefront facade, the hope is that the person next door is sitting there thinking, "Oh man, now my building looks like hell—maybe I'll talk to these people about updating mine and doing the right thing."

JG It's a bootstrap approach.

CM Pittsburgh's an incredibly bootstrap place. I agree with you that design quality comes out of the CDCs, because they are about building common values in a community. When you look in the commercial markets, there's no similar conversation about what makes good design—it's really a bottom-line driven thing. We don't produce great corporate headquarters anymore either—we no longer have that budget. Some of Pittsburgh's greatest assets came from the largess of corporations in the urban renewal era. So now we're back to working incrementally. I think most places in the country are struggling to define what makes good design when we no longer have that scale of budget. CDCs end up being on the frontline of that, because you can't legislate it.

ReS What would you recommend?

CM I do think that there is a conversation happening right now with city agencies about what makes good design. We can go from knowing what good design is to talking about it and getting people out there. I think you're doing that with this kind of salon.

CZ There are two strategies for pursuing good design that government can help to facilitate. The first is to look at design guidelines at all scales. You can develop design guidelines that don't subscribe to a particular taste regime, but that make it clear what successful building is at a variety of scales. Ultimately my charge as a steward of the public realm is to ask what the components of a successful building are in terms of creating good urbanism. If you can get those things right, it frees you to think more creatively about the design solutions on a particular site.

The second strategy is to promote design excellence, as Chris alluded to, through building by public entities that sets the bar and leads by example. The public buildings that we're going to build will be exemplars of good design and that sends a message to the larger community.

ReS How do you get design excellence out of private development?

CM It's values-driven. The projects you mentioned have strong values behind them, where the community, the government, or an institution cares and wants to communicate those values. Commercial real estate doesn't have the same values, so decisions are made on a different basis.

CZ Having a Mayor that's willing to use the bully pulpit and say something about design would go a long way.

MF Isn't it not so much about values as it is about ego? When corporate headquarters were great designs, it's often because there was a corporate leader whose ego was bound up in that building.

ReS It's also a way of saying, "We're here for the long term." You don't have that today.

CG To Corey's point, I think conversations about design excellence have to shift away from what public institutions are doing and really force the hand of private development. That's part of our challenge in Boston. We are also seeing enlightened developers there who bring an ethos that is much more about investing in very specific neighborhoods within the city. The interesting thing about the developers that I'm thinking of is that there's no ego involved. Rather, there is an understanding that what they're doing has ramifications for the public, and therefore that they should invest in the public good.

CZ I just came from a national planning conference in Phoenix. I took a tour the last day, run by a city representative for an adaptive re-use program with a series of incentives to facilitate the refurbishment of existing buildings in a smart way. The city basically gives developers credits that cover all their permitting fees. It struck me that we don't have a program like that in Boston because people are already very sensitive to the historic fabric and more naturally want to preserve the buildings. At this juncture in Pittsburgh's development trajectory over the next ten years, programs like that may be well-suited to this city.

JG Pittsburgh desperately needs an incentive for reusing historic structures. Right now we have a historic preservation ordinance. You can nominate any building for historic status as long as it's not a religious building, in which case you have to have the consent of the owner. But there's no incentive for it. We've seen out-of-town developers come in and use historic preservation credits, but developers who are based here in Pittsburgh have no idea that they can do such things. There needs to be a conversation with developers about the tools that they have and about how to develop tools to better facilitate the adaptive reuse of historic buildings.

MF Designing buildings is one thing. It's an important

issue, and there are lots of talented architects who can do that. But there's a need at the level of systems design as well. You have to design the system-level interactions so that they work. Incentives are a great idea for that. There can be alternative building codes based on community usage, or aesthetics, or a percentage devoted to artwork. Designing that system is as important as designing the buildings. You don't want every little group to be able to veto something that's good for the larger community, but you don't want to roll over them either.

CZ Architecture often becomes the punching bag for systemic change that is already happening. The architecture in East Liberty, for example, has become a punching bag for huge demographic and economic shifts that were happening anyways.

We don't let people have big ideas, and big ideas happen when you think at the system level. This is going to sound like I am not a community person—and I am very strongly a community person—but I worry, with the incrementalism that comes from always listening to a community, that sometimes the big idea comes not from looking at what you have in front of you, but from understanding these bigger systemic changes and then using that collective intelligence to come up with the big idea. In the 1960s, planners told the people that they didn't have a collective intelligence. The message was, we're not figuring this out together—we, the planners, are figuring it out for you. I think that's a big difference. If we can deal with communities and indigenous knowledge on a systems level, then maybe we can produce big ideas.

I think the pendulum has swung to where now we are completely tied up in community processes. We used to be in a think-and-do tank, and now we're think tanks that would like to do a bit more. It's frustrating because there are people who have great ideas, but they're stymied every step of the way. We need to recalibrate and find that balance between efficiency and oversight, and not feel like we're just going in the name of expediency or efficiency without the proper oversight mechanisms. These are design problems. How do we create the proper mechanisms to ensure that we don't raze an entire neighborhood again, but that big ideas can still flourish and actually do something?

MF I worry that you think things have changed. I'm at the other end of this. I think that planning is still a top-down approach. Neighborhoods still have to fight to have a voice at the table. Most community engagement processes are complete and utter bullshit. It is a checkbox.

CZ I can point to many big ideas that have taken hold and been transformational. The High Line in New York City is an example; Atlanta's Belt Line, San Antonio's reimagining of the Riverwalk, the 606 initiative in Chicago, or the Big Dig and the Rose Kennedy Greenway in Boston. I can also point to many examples where that has not been true. Those have been ground up, advocacy-led ordinances.

The BeltLine *stretches over 20 miles on reclaimed rail tracks to wrap Atlanta, Georgia's core.*

Chicago's 606, *a linear park, is one of the longest converted elevated railways in the world.*

MF I didn't say they don't exist.

CZ You implied that they are bullshit.

MF I said that in this town most community engagement processes around development are bullshit. It checks off the boxes to have the community meetings, to prove there was a community engagement process. But it's not real, and any consultant who tells you they can do it faster or easier is selling you a contract.

I would also suggest that this city's reclamation is not based on any of those big projects and big ideas, but that ordinary people, who have sweated and built and saved their neighborhoods, created the overall base for all of these other things to now flourish. We are benefiting today from a growing city and improved markets not from anything any politician or big corporation has done, not from any stadium or convention center. We are benefiting from the fact that for the last thirty or forty years, ordinary people were preserving historic districts, sweating over places like Bloomfield, building back little business districts one small building at a time.

CG Our strategy with these salons has been to avoid viewing this history with rose-colored glasses, just as you are right now. The goal is not to have an either/or conversation, but to be able to look at other issues, like the smoke abatement campaign and the scrubbing of the city's pollution. It had to come from high authority that the city could no longer tolerate not being able to see the sun at 12:00 in the afternoon—no neighborhood was going to be able to do that.

MF I agree.

CG So it can't always be a dichotomy. There's a nuance to the both/and argument that can get lost in the good-guy/bad-guy dichotomy.

CM It's a question of identity. If you only think of identity as being my house, my block, or my neighborhood, then you lack the capacity to stand up when the big capitalist comes in and says, "I want to develop all this space in your neighborhood." That's the friction that we feel right now. We've been bootstrapping for so long, and now there are forces that are affecting our communities at a scale that we haven't seen before, and we're trying to figure out what the mechanisms are to support that conversation. Pittsburgh has a lot to learn from other cities, because our governmental agencies aren't necessarily set up to be the protectors of that conversation, because they haven't had to. We've just been making it happen one building at a time.

MF Let me just say that I don't mean to imply that it's an either/or. The point is that everyone always gives credit to the big-money projects, and nobody ever really talks about the grassroots, Main Street, historic district, or neighborhood side of things. That tends to get lost and doesn't get its due credit as a process.

[From the audience] I wonder if you could comment on what's happening in the Lower Hill, where Bjarke Ingels Group was given an extraordinary opportunity—one that doesn't exist everywhere—to think through twenty-eight acres of nothing. How does that design fit in with the conversations that we're having here? It's extraordinary what they accomplished. Was the community 100% engaged? Not at all. Is it a gift to the city if we can figure out how to manage the cost and bring that incredible environmental quality to the site? It could certainly be construed that way. What does the black community in the Hill think about it? At some of the meetings where the design was presented, there were reactions from "Do I deserve this?" to "I hate this," to "I don't know if I like this or not." There were side conversations about whether it was good design, but also people asking, "What is this? Is this good? I don't even know what I'm looking at." It's an extraordinary opportunity that happened in a big way in a project that's contentious and fraught with incredible agreements made between the community, the stadium authority, and the Penguins. Can you provide some context on what's happening there?

CM I think you just provided all the context.

ReS You've done a wonderful job of summarizing all the complexities of the project.

[From the audience] People don't know what good design is. I think the difference between our time and the 1950s and 60s is that we are more open to ideas, that we have the capacity now. There are enough enlightened individuals in any room now. Even the average suburban family is more enlightened than when I was growing up. So we're at an incredible inflection point where I think it's possible to have these conversations, and I think we're all figuring out how to do that together.

CG You're saying something that I think we should take to heart as designers. The populace is ready and willing to absorb ideas, but they don't know what design is. It's up to us as a profession to give people agency through design literacy and how that manifests itself in the city.

CZ I applaud the curators and the Carnegie Museum for taking on such a challenging subject, and for this idea of bringing the community into the museum, which I think is already a space where you let your guard down a little bit. You don't come into the museum with the charged emotional state that you might if you were going to a community meeting, ready to be angry. There are already codified behaviors that you agree to respect, there's a social code. Just being here, I'm very heartened that folks will come and have this conversation in a museum space around these very difficult issues. I think that is really fabulous.

Mark Fatla is Executive Director of the Northside Leadership Conference, the non-profit community development corporation serving Pittsburgh's Northside. He has more than thirty years of experience in community development and has been a Northside resident since 1984.

Justin Greenawalt is President of the East Liberty Valley Historical Society and a member of the Board of Directors of Preservation Pittsburgh.

Christine Mondor is Principal at EvolveEA, a Pittsburgh-based multidisciplinary design practice. She serves as Chair of the Pittsburgh Planning Commission and teaches architecture and landscape architecture at Carnegie Mellon University and Chapman College.

Corey Zehngebot is a Senior Urban Designer and Architect for the Boston Planning and Development Agency (formerly the Boston Redevelopment Authority), where she is responsible for leading, managing, and participating in the formulation of urban design guidelines and planning initiatives.

PROJECTING PITTSBURGH

Thursday, April 28 2016

MARTIN AURAND
RAY GASTIL
CHARLES ROSENBLUM
MIMI ZEIGER

Chris Grimley I want to begin with a prompt that comes from Martin Aurand, one of our panelists tonight. Martin offered the idea that through the discussions we've had so far about spaces of living, working, playing, and preservation, among other topics, we have yet to focus on the actual buildings and landscapes from Pittsburgh's modernist era. Tonight we would like to discuss what these sites are today, how we move forward with them, how we think of them in the future, and what they mean to us.

I'd like to start by asking Mimi for her take on it as an outsider, as someone who is new to the Pittsburgh context over the last 36 hours. Mimi, you recently wrote an article titled "In Defense of Difficult Landscapes," about the Long Beach Civic Center and the contested history of this Brutalist, if not to say Heroic, complex of buildings. That complex has suffered a fate similar to what we've seen with certain sites in Pittsburgh, particularly the Civic Arena site, which was loathed by some and loved by others, and has ultimately been subject to the same issues of demolition and possible renovation. Can we invoke your notion of the "difficult landscape" as a way to situate the different sites in Pittsburgh that we've looked at over the course of the exhibition, and what it means to think about those today?

The original Long Beach Civic Center, design headed by Gibbs & Gibbs, Architects, 1977.

Mimi Zeiger Long Beach is a suburb or port of Los Angeles, as well as a city in its own right. The Long Beach Civic Center is a city hall, library, and civic center that takes up an enormous multi-block site—Allegheny Center is very similar. At one time there was some retail around it, embedded in it. There was a library that's still there, but soon the whole site will be demolished. It has a Peter Walker landscape that covers the entire top of the library, which was meant to be an outdoor space for the city. So this difficult landscape was initially a utopian environment of the type that we saw in the 1960s and 70s and have seen again more recently, as with the High Line and attempts to recreate that model in other cities.

As the roof of the library in Long Beach started to leak, the landscape died off, and the city ended up taking out the whole carpet of green and concretizing it, then painting it with a white surface. They put up fences so you could no longer go up onto it. This is a democratic space of the first order, yet it failed, for many of the reasons that I think a lot of these projects fail. The buildings themselves are subject to failure. The whole neighborhood started to go into decline and with that, people lost interest. It became populated by skateboarders and homeless people and became the back end of the city, rather than this expression of civic space.

At the time I was writing in defense of the complex, there had been not only a resurgence of interest in Heroic buildings, including an interest in preservation around the time that Prentice Hospital in Chicago was under threat, but also small tactical urban garden projects that were starting to find their way into this landscape. There were still people who loved it and were trying to make something happen. The question of the article was, how do you let a landscape reactivate on its own terms? That is something that I was arguing for.

Prentice Women's Hospital during its demolition, 2014.

CG It seems like part of the argument in that piece, and in other recent work of yours, has to do with the difficult idea that despite their failures, people love some of these places. We've heard very strong statements about Allegheny Center through multiple presentations here, both from members of the audience and from panelists, that despite all of the claims about its problems, many people recall the area fondly, and that there should be an intent to mediate the negative perception about it.

Martin, what did you mean in your prompt about thinking about the actual buildings and landscapes of modern Pittsburgh, and how do you see that as being different from the discussions we've already had through these salons?

Martin Aurand There are clearly very many elements and aspects to this period and the exhibition does a tremendous job of trying to lay out those different points of view. The last four salons have covered many parts of that terrain in many different ways. It seemed to me the one that has received the least attention is architecture, if not the buildings themselves. That's the chord that I wanted to touch. There are a couple of different ways to do that, at least from where I sit.

One is that we've had a number of people comment on the amazingly unique and interesting buildings we have in Pittsburgh. We have the Alcoa building that's wrapped in aluminum and the U.S Steel Building that's wrapped in steel, and we have a wonderful way of putting our industries and their corporate presence up on the skyline. At the same time we've heard comments that put down the idea of corporate architecture because it was a top-down affair and should be looked at that way.

Yet it's clear that the corporate presence is one of the things that most distinguishes postwar Pittsburgh architecture and urbanism. We are talking in many cases about industry buying into the architecture of this particular period. So I think this is at the heart of where are we going. We should explore this history of corporate development and architecture in Pittsburgh in depth in ways that I don't think have happened yet. This has to do with corporate headquarters downtown, and with the materials that appear in these buildings, many of them produced by industries that were getting into building materials during the postwar period in ways they hadn't before. These industries had geared up during World War II, they had excess capacity, they looked around, the building industry was taking off, they tried to find niches for their products, and they tried to show them off in their own buildings. There's an awful lot of work that still needs to be done to understand all of this, including the suburban research centers that all of these industries built around Pittsburgh in the same period, often using important architects. Each one of these office buildings downtown radiates out to a research center or two out in the surrounding county. So there's a whole history and understanding of the corporate presence in Pittsburgh that I don't think we have a particularly good grip on right now.

The other thing that interests me is more experiential, and that is the ways in which we continue to experience postwar Pittsburgh. There are certainly some difficult landscapes, to use Mimi's term, but there are also some places that are not so difficult. For example, two experiential sequences I'll just throw out very quickly. One of them is infrastructural. In 1952 Pittsburgh built a new airport. Since then the city has swapped out its architecture but the infrastructure is essentially in the same place, with some of the same runways. From the airport, you come into the city along the Parkway West that was built during this time; you go through the tunnel that was built during this time; you cross a bridge that was built during this time. The iconic sequence we all talk about entering into Pittsburgh is totally a postwar thing. It dumps you onto the edge of Point State Park and the Gateway Center. All of this was new construction and new space, in a way that was never there before; we still experience it, and we still love it.

Aerial view of the original Pittsburgh airport, designed by Joseph Hoover and Simonds and Simonds, 1968.

The other sequence begins from the fountain at the Point, going up through Point State Park, underneath the bridge, through the two parts of Gateway Center, jumping to Mellon Square and the old U.S. Steel building, and jumping again to the later U.S. Steel tower. This is a backbone that comes all the way up through the Golden Triangle, one that speaks entirely to postwar Pittsburgh, that we could visualize and understand and celebrate in ways that we don't.

CG There is an almost scenographic sequence that stitches these sites together.

MA You could say that. These are important to me partly as somewhat designed sequences, but mostly because these are something that we can still experience.

CG In the case of the Golden Triangle, this seems interesting given the claim that these sites are specifically stitched together by a sequence of private, corporate entities.

MA And public spaces too...

CG ...and also by agencies like the Urban Redevelopment Authority. Many of the documents and artefacts that we have throughout this exhibition were selected to reflect what we think of as a very conspicuous conjunction of private and public entities in Pittsburgh. I wonder if you would argue that the character of this delicate tethering of corporate spaces through a particular kind of civic sequence provides a physical manifestation of this unique condition.

MA Yes. Its text reads "Renaissance."

CG What is called the Renaissance in Pittsburgh is more generically referred to as the urban renewal era in other places. Charles, I wonder if you could address this question of reassessing the urban renewal era. You brought it up in a couple of pieces you wrote about the exhibition, and it seemed you felt in those pieces that one should take a harder line on the urban renewal era.

Charles Rosenblum At the immediate level I agree with the things that Martin said about these vignettes that are under-examined and that reflect a great amount of Pittsburgh's urban identity and the culture of this era. Moreover, I appreciate the elucidation of these areas that have yet to be further explored with substance. So if I want to be contrarian, I have this non-disagreement with Martin's point of view that I have to foil.

To offer another perspective, I might quote from *Ghostbusters*, when Bill Murray's character says "I'm confused about this whole good/bad thing." We operate under the presumption that the two are very easily distinguished from each other and in fact the premise of the show, in a very artful and shrewdly conceived way, is that we aren't going to say, "Oh, Brutalist architecture is just dreadful and I hate it." Those different sensibilities that exist simultaneously, sometimes in different constituencies and sometimes in the very same ones, are very frequently unresolved for precisely the reasons which Martin has articulated with great clarity.

We don't like that these projects are top-down. We have difficulty with the astringent nature of modernism, yet some people love it very much. There are very difficult issues of social and economic justice and inclusion that accompany these issues of urban renewal. Pittsburgh calls this period a Renaissance, and other cities frequently don't. I delight in the complexity that engages these issues in a multivalent way and tries to see them in the conflicting presence of those things that we admire, that we think of as achievements, and simultaneously those that we think of as abhorrent, lasting errors. The question then becomes, how do we make progress? How do we learn from mistakes? How do we sift out the accomplishments from the terrible errors?

I think at a micro-level it's possible to pick some of these things out, and I think that a process like the one in *Imagining the Modern* that engages archival material in depth and that recovers people who are important voices at the time—someone like Troy West, who is substantial and involved and yet not easily characterizable—lends nuance to the reanimation of these arguments. That doesn't mean that these arguments are resolved; perhaps they never will be. There is simultaneously a critique that I engage in affirmatively, though I wonder if we are still suffering from "architect-itis," the idea that if something is wrong here, the solution is clearly a building.

Obviously I'm being reductive and am poking fun in a circumstance where your engagement is enormously thoughtful, both as a serious way of thinking multivalently and as a genuine process of engagement with communities of different kinds. But it does come back to the issue of what's good, what's not so good, and how we perpetuate a process by which those assessments are made substantially and some of the evaluations continue forward in a way that reflects good conclusions.

Michael Kubo One interesting aspect here is that unlike Boston, where many of the iconic structures of the urban renewal era were civic and cultural, Pittsburgh presents this specific confluence of public-private partnerships that sought to remake whole areas of the city. Unlike civic monuments here and in other cities, many of the corporate projects are not necessarily in danger of going away. You can put "UPMC" on the U.S. Steel tower, but no one's proposing to tear it down. It's generally public and/or cultural projects that have

Harrison, Abramovitz & Abbe's U.S. Steel Tower, completed in 1971, now home to the University of Pittsburgh Medical Center.

been demolished, the Civic Arena being the most prominent example.

Our research for this exhibition has been interesting as an unraveling of how a city in the urban renewal era reinvented itself through a very specific framework of civic and corporate partnerships to change the trajectory of its development. At this hinge moment in Pittsburgh's history, we might ask questions about how to realign these private, public, and institutional interests and make all of these desires coherent and commensurable with what different communities want.

Ray Gastil When David Lewis [a founder of the community-based city planning firm Urban Design Associates] describes coming to Pittsburgh in the 1960s, he says that he sat down with all of the people who were involved with planning the Point, and they told him, the vision here is that there will be the downtown, and then outside of downtown there would be corporate "islands of excellence." This is a foundational story about Lewis's relationship to Pittsburgh and the recognition that he needed to find something else, not only to address the needs of low-income neighborhoods and mill towns outside of this purview, but also to fight against this idea that there was nothing else about the city that was of interest, when the vision was to go from downtown right out to these beautiful corporate pastoral office parks. When you talk about the social problem, this is the simple version. If you think of the world as islands of excellence and then everything else, this everything else is completely devalued. This is something that we struggle with, but it's not how the city sees itself today. Today, like in many other cities, the result has been little business districts located along where the streetcars went, which is how people see their city, and what they value in that story. And it's a story that some people in this room have helped tell.

That said, I agree with Martin. We have a remarkable set of buildings. They don't make 'em like they used to, in the sense that only a very unusual corporation today would actually spend money on projects like these. This doesn't mean that they're all perfect buildings, it just means that they were conceived through design and a detailed conscience about their relationship to the city. These are very conscious and deliberate sequences and as such are rare in the hard world we live in. For better or worse, corporations, especially publicly held corporations, have no interest in developing projects like these anymore. So I think we need to look at the built heritage of this era and value it for its claim on the ground as well as in its built form. I recognize the value of this heritage despite recognizing the issues of social history that we have to face, not just because of urban renewal, but because of all the other things that are involved in that story. I truly think we have to value it and keep valuing it, though I'm not quite ready for all of it to be landmarked. Not right away.

For example, one of the reasons you can run this interesting studio on redesigning the Allegheny Center is that for the most part—and this is a generalization that will be challenged by many of the people here—unlike many of your students, the builders of Pittsburgh in this era resisted the megastructure. The reason Allegheny Center actually works is in part, that you can play with it and imagine a future for it; that for the most part it resists the urge to

Students present their work to critics as part of the HACLab studio.

become a megastructure, to become overwhelmed by that kind of scale. I'm not in love with megastructures, but you can't reuse a city or rethink the city if you had too many of them, so to speak.

CG One of the megastructures that was resisted quite explicitly in Pittsburgh was the Frank Lloyd Wright project for the Point.

MZ Maybe I can ask some questions of the locals, or put some things out there. From what I'm hearing, in these public-private relationships, certain corporate towers or apartment buildings have become iconic in our experience of the city. In fact yesterday I did the same Golden Triangle walk that Martin described, though not from the Point but from Allegheny Center, over the Warhol Bridge and then up Sixth and through Mellon Square.

Coming from outside, I can see the kinds of projects that people might want to put in to start to knit these things together. A Bloomberg-ian green street, for example, with bike lanes that start to cut through a pocket park here and there. I speak to those because as something like the Alcoa tower becomes a residential building, it changes the relationship of the corporate building to the plaza or to the downtown as its use changes. As adaptive reuse happens to more of these buildings— as the tech hub incubator or the festival marketplace begins to happen—how do we change our relationships to what has been seen as a pervasive corporate landscape? And how does that change our interest in preservation or not?

RG I don't know that it is overwhelmingly a corporate landscape. I think that the skyline certainly is in terms of what dominated it, but the experience of downtown also involves a lot of civic buildings from an earlier era. They're very present, as well as a lot of warehouse-era buildings. I also think that some of the corporate building identity of Pittsburgh disappeared as the corporations left. And so they became symbolic, in the way that everyone calls these buildings by their names from four owners back.

It's actually been hard to have any urban narrative in this situation. What I often think our downtown has lacked in narrative is in many ways rediscovered because of the bridges, the experience of crossing the bridges and the movements that happen, the back-and-forth to and from downtown. But a lot of it beyond the skyline is a story that hasn't been very clear because the corporate presence is largely gone.

MK I think this discussion of programs as they change over time is at the heart of the story here. This is at the core of what happened to Allegheny Center, and of what might happen with the downtown. What's especially meaningful here is the question of the relationships between program and form.

MZ If you talk to someone at the Getty Research Center or the conservation institute there, they'll tell you that one of the biggest problems with buildings of this era is that they are usually designed for a single function. They were built primarily for one corporation or one civic institution to do a very particular set of things and so it is very difficult to apply an adaptive reuse approach to them.

Ann Lui I want to ask a question about programming and whether megastructures or other scales of intervention are the answer. When we were working on the exhibition, something really struck me about Troy West. While his buildings were really interesting, in fact a lot of his work was in organizing, in collaborations, in getting people together. He would probably disagree with me, but I think that part of his work is in many ways more influential than his built work. You'll notice for example that when you look at other architectural photographs in the exhibition, there are rarely people in them, maybe a scale figure or two. When you get to Troy's photos, they're bursting with people and with color. Maybe this relates to the example Mimi gave of the Long Beach Civic Center where there was guerrilla farming happening, as an attempt to bring that space back to life.

Lately I've been thinking about how we talk about public space, and how we use the term "public," in the sense of state-owned or state-run. But in cases like the Black Lives Matter protests or the Umbrella Revolution, public space is made by people activating space. It doesn't matter if they're in the city square. You can be a Hong Kong citizen with an umbrella in the street or in a mall, and you make public space wherever you go. Maybe this is a caution about redefining the architect's role, and the need to get out of the mid-century trope that architects respond to problems with buildings, but instead to say that architects can be guerrilla farmers or activists or community organizers, invested in a whole other range of functions. What's next might be to try to reprogram these spaces through this kind of choreography of activity, rather than proposing new structures.

[From the Audience] Mimi, you mentioned the idea of difficult landscapes, but nobody here has discussed landscape architecture. I hear a lot about built structures. But I don't hear too much about the logic and dynamics of the landscape, of street patterns, of infrastructure and so on. And it seems to me that these are very, very critical shaping elements.

MZ I hear what you're saying. For me, walking the Golden Triangle was similar to what Martin was suggesting about knitting together certain kinds of landscapes. You come onto this incredible modernist landscape when you hit Mellon Square and it refocuses you and the space, like Union Square in San Francisco. You've removed yourself from the city, you've become part of a stage. The broader movements within landscape urbanism and also strategies like placemaking today are much more about using street-level landscapes. I am a fan and have written quite a bit about these things. But I also take caution about abandoning the architectural gesture within these strategies, because once you do, you lose the architectural agency of form.

Martin, in a way, isn't the moment of creating Point State Park the beginning of the resetting of this relationship to the larger landscape? It's a very architectural gesture.

Union Square, a 2.6 acre park in San Francisco, provides an escape from the city while being surrounded by skyscrapers.

MA There are other strips and streams too. The first bits of Riverfront Park, Three Rivers Stadium, or the strip of overlooks along Mt. Washington are all from this era. There are all sorts of elements of the city that speak to landscape that are from this era.

CG I also want to invoke the highways again, the notion of this roadscape that is also a landscape, as in the work of Kevin Lynch. In Pittsburgh's case I mean less *The Image of the City* and more the Lynch of *The View from the Road*, which is precisely about the notion of a certain scenography of infrastructure.

MA It's hard to love the infrastructure for the infrastructure or to love the parkways for the parkways, but they certainly did have that effect.

Still from Kevin Lynch's View from the Road, *a short film documenting car travel in Boston, 1965.*

Rami el Samahy Among the interesting things about this exhibition is that, while we concentrate on the city of Pittsburgh, the other half in the background is the planning framework of this era, which is all about suburbia and the highway system.

MA These were linked to the corporate campuses that were to attract many to live in the suburbs, where they would be comfortable in the white middle-class environment.

[From the Audience] Those are the reasons why East Liberty was redeveloped into a pedestrian mall, or why Allegheny Center became a mall. These were answers to suburbia.

[From the Audience] In terms of the rationale behind the original Renaissance, the corporate influence by the 1980s had collapsed completely. So you were left with all these buildings that were built for one group of people. How does that play into all this discussion? When I was a kid growing up here, every year the Fortune 500 list came out, and it was a real source of pride that Pittsburgh had the third most corporate headquarters after New York City and Chicago. That notion would be laughable today. The whole world that the Renaissance was built for disappeared, and we were left with the structures, but the economic rationale behind it vanished for the most part.

MA It sometimes feels like cows grazing in the ruins of the Roman Forum. The head-scratching mystery is what to do with this legacy. But I think there is an advantage in the persistence of architecture as something that is conceived and constructed at a premium and with a vision that is, in a sense, about idealism—even if it's a very capitalistic brand of idealism. We have this paradox now that we're experiencing some welcome economic prosperity, but the culture of good, artistic, thoughtful construction is just not where it was previously, and a lot of that is financial.

So I think, as the cows are grazing, that we can look around and ask: do we want to go back to the old days? We don't. But what are the ways in which a sense of architecture as an artistic premium, not simply a commodity but an intrinsic ingredient in our urban lives and identities, can be part of our lives in the current moment and not just in the past.

MK These are very interesting comments that raise questions about the scope of what we were looking at in the exhibition, and about possible expansions to ask what happened in the era immediately after the Renaissance. In revisiting urban renewal we dealt with what we felt were very natural historical cutoff points—the beginning of the oil crisis in 1973, or the U.S. Bicentennial in 1976, for example. Perhaps we've been remiss in not engaging more with the 1980s, a difficult period for most U.S. cities?

[From the Audience] Pittsburgh had a difficult 1970s too. We had a complete rejection of the Renaissance and the corporate elite. [Richard] Caliguiri was elected mayor and his focus was on the neighborhoods, not on the downtown. The U.S. Steel

Building, which opened in 1973, is the last of that period, and then Pittsburgh goes through a rejection of the public-private partnership model until Murphy becomes mayor.

MK I wonder whether this cycle of the public-private partnership and its rejection happened earlier in Pittsburgh than in other cities. I'm thinking of Los Angeles as a place where the city's modernist heritage is now talked about in similar terms, as largely a legacy of corporate building or private houses, much of which was built from the 1960s through the 1980s, rather than in the '40s or '50s. In that sense, it may be possible to argue that the corporate heyday of Pittsburgh, as with New York City or Chicago, took place somewhat in advance of that. Does this mean that Pittsburgh is also confronting certain current problems in advance of questions that are going to come up in other cities?

MA To add on to that, is there anything in the way that the city is handling what's happening today that is advanced compared to what other cities are thinking about? In other words, could we say Pittsburgh is now at the forefront of something, or is it catching up with others?
MZ I think there is a parallel between Los Angeles and Pittsburgh, which seems like a strange thing to say. In the later part of the twentieth century, downtown L.A. saw the impact of suburbanization and the fleeing of the civic core. Old theaters became swap meets, office buildings were filled with sewing shops. By the 80s and 90s artists and designers started to move into lofts, a few galleries opened, but it wasn't until the last ten years that developers have started to reinvest and restore the area.

MK The fact that L.A. has a downtown is probably news to a lot of people.

MZ Yes—brand-new news. My point is to look to L.A. as a caution. Downtown L.A. is rapidly gentrifying, SROs are turning into hotels, and new development displaces not only artists, but the first wave of businesses that ventured to the neighborhood— there's an Ace Hotel and an Acme shop. The idea that tech firms are becoming established here in Pittsburgh, or that streetcar suburbs are developing as places for the hipsters who work in those buildings—this all happened in L.A. a little bit ago. And then people started to see downtown L.A. and thought, "yeah, I don't need my car." So the idea that downtown Pittsburgh is being viewed in similar terms while L.A. doesn't have enough housing now, doesn't have enough green space—these are things that still exist in Pittsburgh that maybe we need to preserve precisely to ward off some of the difficulties that are occurring in other cities.

[From the Audience] Pittsburgh was built on streetcars and the railroads. The railroads are all still there and the streetcars are just as important as they were. I don't think Allegheny Center would be having problems today if the streetcars still went there. There are so many areas that are really interesting, and that were designed when it was easy to just take the streetcar everywhere, and now even though there's a line that goes near Allegheny Center, you can't really get out there without having to walk into the middle of nowhere, under a big highway and up a hill until you finally get there.

Trolley Cars gather on Fifth Avenue in Oakland with the Mellon Institute in the background, 1939.

ReS I think there were two things that made the

Renaissance possible. One was federal funding; the other was corporate investment. We don't have either of those today. What we do have is real estate development. How do you harness that energy in ways that make a lasting city and an interesting environment to work in? Do you fight development to prevent it from happening? Or do you try to jujitsu it so it actually does happen in ways that are meaningful? I would argue for the latter.

CG There's a turn of phrase that came up in our previous work on Boston's urban renewal era that I think is relevant to the opportunity we've been given here. During a conversation about our Heroic project, Christopher Lydon said that architecture isn't frozen music, as the cliché goes—*architecture is frozen politics*. I think if we start to look at cities, and particularly Pittsburgh, through the approach that we've tried to develop in this exhibition, frozen politics is really an apt metaphor for how the city was made. By thawing or at least revisiting some of these frozen politics, maybe we can give some agency to people in the room to take this project forward and work through the hard problems and issues that Pittsburgh faces as it moves forward in the next ten to twenty years.

AL One of the hopes that we had for this exhibition is that it would serve as a kind of infrastructure, an appeal to go forward and think about these issues and work on them, with the further hope that maybe one percent of those ideas would be radical speculations. For example, Rami was saying that we need to channel real estate development, but the SEC has just approved equity crowd funding, so instead of more patronage projects, could people in Pittsburgh pursue equity fund projects from the ground up? Some of these may be pipe dreams, but I hope that some of the take-away from this exhibition is that people can go forth and do things that are not driven by developers, that might serve as the basis for a salon in this space fifty years from now, as the beginning of a whole series of future conversations.

CG We might end this discussion by recalling the title of the exhibition, *Imagining the Modern*. Perhaps this is the moment, at the end of the last salon, for us to come clean about the double temporality of the title. It was meant to evoke all of the ambitions that you see throughout the rooms of the exhibition, to point to the breadth of imagination, beyond good and evil, across the spectrum of possible Pittsburghs that were produced in that era. But it is equally a call to designers, and to the power of tools like architecture and landscape, to think about the same questions in the present. So *Imagining the Modern* was meant to encourage everyone to be emboldened by all of the things that appear in the exhibition, to think what it would be not just to imagine the modern of that time, but also to imagine the modern of this time, as well as the modern to come.

Martin Aurand is Architecture Librarian at Carnegie Mellon University and Archivist of the Carnegie Mellon University Architecture Archives. He is the author of *The Spectator and the Topographical City* (2006), *The Progressive Architecture of Frederick G. Scheibler, Jr.* (1994), and *Pittsburgh Architecture: A Guide to Research* (1991). He was Curatorial Consultant for the Imagining the Modern exhibition.

Ray Gastil is Director of City Planning for the City of Pittsburgh, and teaches as Adjunct Professor in the Masters of Urban Design Program at the Carnegie Mellon University School of Architecture.

Charles Rosenblum is a journalist, critic, and scholar who writes about architecture, art, and other facets of visual culture. He taught at the Carnegie Mellon University School of Architecture for nineteen years and writes regularly for the *Pittsburgh City Paper* and *Pittsburgh Quarterly*.

Mimi Zeiger is a Los Angeles-based critic, editor, and curator situated at the intersection of architecture and media cultures. She teaches in the Media Design Practices MFA program at Art Center College of Design and was co-curator of the US Pavilion for the 2018 International Architecture Biennale in Venice. She is co-editor of *Made Up: Design's Fictions* (2017) and the author of numerous books including *Tiny Houses in the City* (2016), *Micro Green: Tiny Houses in Nature* (2011), *Tiny Houses* (2009), and *New Museums: Contemporary Museum Architecture Around the World* (2005).

ONE WAY

ONE WAY
WYLIE AV
CRAWFORD

Chatham Center

UPMC
STOP

UPMC

Acknowledgments

This book has relied on the input, guidance, feedback and support of many over the years who gave their time during the creation of the exhibition, who attended our student reviews as studio critics, or who participated in the salon series—both invited guests and audience members alike. We are also appreciative of the scholars who framed the introductory section of the book. We are especially grateful to Tasso Katselas, Robert Pease, and Troy West, who generously gave us hours of their time, and in doing so, helped us gain first-person insight into this remarkable era of Pittsburgh's development. In the lead-up to the exhibition, Ann Lui was our key researcher and associate curator. A special note of thanks is also due to Martin Aurand, who as curatorial consultant, writer, researcher, and fact checker provided a plethora of information, images and advice, without which this project could not have been. We are also deeply in debt to the remarkable Raymund Ryan, curator of the Heinz Architectural Center at the Carnegie Museum of Art, who selected this project as the inaugural HAC Lab, and provided us with the opportunity to dive into this rich and complex subject with the care it deserved.

Publication of this book would not have been possible without the Graham Foundation for Advanced Studies in the Fine Arts, Bill and Janet Hunt, Furthermore: a program of the J. M. Kaplan Fund , Preservation Pittsburgh, the Carnegie Mellon University Berkman Faculty Development Fund and the Carnegie Mellon University Architecture Archives.

This book has been produced with the invaluable assistance of:

OverUnder
Claire He, Makena Janssen, Shannon McLean, Win Overholser IV

Additional research and writing of project texts
Adam Himes, Phillip Denny, Martin Aurand, and Kelly Hutzell

Carnegie Mellon University School of Architecture
Stephen Lee, Kai Gutschow, Mary-Lou Arscot, Jonathan Kline, our students over the years 2005–2015

Preservation Pittsburgh
Melissa McSwigan, Brittany Reilly, Justin Greenawalt, Matthew Falcone, James Mohn, and Brian Bevan

City of Pittsburgh
Ray Gastil, Andrew Dash, Pat Hassett

Pennsylvania Department of Transit
Dan Cessna, Cheryl Moon-Sirianni

Buhl Foundation
Frederick Theiman, Diana Bucco, Linda Weaver

Children's Museum
Jane Warner, Chris Seifert

Other
Shamus Fatzinger, Artist
Nicholas Ross, HDR
Andrew Wickesberg, ACCO

Archives
Allegheny Conference on Community Development Philip Cynar
Avery Library Janet Parks, Shelley Hayreh, Margaret Smithglass, Pamela Casey, Katerine Prater
Bjarke Ingels Group Jesslyn Guntur
Brady Stewart Studio Brady Stewart III
Carnegie Library Gil Pietrzak
Carnegie Museum of Art Laurel Mitchell
Center for Creative Photography at the University of Arizona Leigh Grissom, Shandi Wagner
DRS Architects S. Philip Hundley
East Liberty Development, Inc. Elizabeth Sensky
Esto Erica Stoller, Caroline L. Hirsch
Frank Lloyd Wright Foundation Margo Stipe
Pittsburgh History & Landmarks Foundation Frank Stroker
New York Public Library Thomas Lisanti
Heinz History Center Matthew Strauss
Pittsburgh Post-Gazette Linda Parker
Skidmore, Owings & Merrill Karen Widi
University of Florida Smathers Libraries John Nemmers
University of Pittsburgh Laura Brooks

Imagining the Modern was exhibited at The Heinz Architectural Center, Carnegie Museum of Art from September 12, 2015 to May 2, 2016.

Carnegie Museum of Art
Catherine Evans, Tom Fisher, Sarah Minnaert, Matthew Newton, Katie Reilly, Marylin Russell, Raymund Ryan, Hannah Silbert, Alyssum Skjeie, Lynn Zelevansky

Curators Chris Grimley, Michael Kubo, Rami el Samahy
Associate Curator Ann Lui
Curatorial Consultant Martin Aurand, Carnegie Mellon University
Design Chris Grimley
Production Andrew Potter, Brett Pierson, Cameron Longyear, Claire He, Panharith Ean, Kelly Hutzell, Mark Pasnik

Special thanks from the exhibition
Katherine Abramovitz; Dee Briggs, Dee Briggs Studio; Phil Cynar, Allegheny Conference on Community Development; Thor Erickson, Design Center; Philip Hundley and Kathryn Jolley, DRS; Gabriel Kozlowski; Steve Lee, Mary-Lou Arscott, Kai Gutschow, Charles Rosenblum, Spike Wolff, School of Architecture, Carnegie Mellon University; Miriam Meislik and David Grinnell, Archives Service Center, University of Pittsburgh; Gil Pietrzak and Marilyn Holt, Carnegie Library of Pittsburgh; John Roman Nemmers, University of Florida; Eugene M. Sawa, University Library System, Microforms, Government Documents & Maps, University of Pittsburgh; Erica Stoller and Christine Cordazzo, Esto; Mike Stewart and Brady Stewart III, Brady Stewart Studio; Margo Stipe, Frank Lloyd Wright Foundation, Matthew Strauss and Sierra Green, Heinz History Center; Frank Stroker and Albert Tannler, Pittsburgh History and Landmarks Foundation; Janet Parks and Nicole Richard, Avery Library, Columbia University; Troy West, Troy West Architecture

^ **Wylie Avenue at Crawford Street intersection looking toward downtown, with Civic Arena construction in background, Lower Hill District,** Charles "Teenie" Harris, 1959.

^^ **Civic Arena from Wylie Avenue, 9.27.2011, from the series Last Light,** Ed Massery

^^^ **Civic Arena Yields to the Pittsburgh Skyline, 3.6.2012, from the series Last Light,** Ed Massery

Contributors

Martin Aurand is Architecture Librarian at Carnegie Mellon University and Archivist of the Carnegie Mellon University Architecture Archives. He is the author of *The Spectator and the Topographical City* (2006), *The Progressive Architecture of Frederick G. Scheibler, Jr.* (1994), and *Pittsburgh Architecture: A Guide to Research* (1991). He was Curatorial Consultant for the *Imagining the Modern* exhibition.

Caroline Constant is Professor of Architecture Emerita at the University of Michigan and visiting scholar at the Graduate School of Design, Harvard University. She is author of *The Modern Architectural Landscape* (2012), *Eileen Gray* (2000), *The Woodland Cemetery: Toward a Spiritual Landscape* (1994), and *The Palladio Guide* (1985). Works in progress include *Cambridge Modern Architecture and Landscape Architecture, 1930-1970*, probing the disciplinary contributions of educators and professionals associated with Harvard, MIT, and the Cambridge School of Architecture and Landscape Architecture for Women.

Kelly Hutzell is an Associate Professor and Director of the Graduate Programs in the Architecture Department at the Wentworth Institute of Technology in Boston. She previously taught at Carnegie Mellon University, where she and her students conducted studies on the urban renewal era, the results of which comprised some of the initial research for the *Imagining the Modern* exhibition. Her work has been published in *Architectural Design* (AD), *ArchitectureBoston*, UCL's *Urban Pamphleteer*, and *Volume*.

Chris Grimley is an architect and designer at OverUnder, an architecture and design firm in Boston, Massachusetts. He has taught at the University of British Columbia, Rhode Island School of Design, Northeastern University, and Wentworth Institute of Technology. He is coauthor of *Heroic: Concrete Architecture and the New Boston* (2015), and the deisgner and editor of *Henry N. Cobb: Words and Works 1948–2018* (2018).

Michael Kubo is Assistant Professor in the History and Theory of Architecture at the Gerald D. Hines College of Architecture and Design, University of Houston. He was previously the Wyeth Fellow at the Center For Advanced Study in the Visual Arts, National Gallery of Art and Associate Curator for the US Pavilion at the 2014 International Architecture Biennale in Venice. He is coauthor of numerous books on twentieth-century architecture and urbanism including *Heroic: Concrete Architecture and the New Boston* (2015) and *OfficeUS Atlas* (2015), and is currently preparing a book on The Architects Collaborative and the authorship of the architectural corporation after 1945.

Rami el Samahy is a founding principal at OverUnder, an architecture and design firm. Currently a Visiting Professor at MIT, he has taught at Carnegie Mellon University, Boston University, the Boston Architectural College and Wentworth Institute of Technology. His research has focussed on a wide variety of urban issues including the contemporary Arab city, the logics of main street retail, and the legacy of urban renewal.

Credits

4–5 © Brady Stewart Studio; 6–7 William V. Winans Jr. Photograph Collection, Detre Library & Archives, Sen. John Heinz History Center; 8–9 Paul Slantis; 16 Clyde Hare; 19 Detre Library & Archives, Sen. John Heinz History Center; 21 Newman-Schmidt Studios; 24 Courtesy of Troy West; 358–359 © Carnegie Museum of Art, Charles "Teenie" Harris Archive; 360–361 © Ed Massery; 366–369.

Positions

31 Otto Krebs, Library of Congress; 35 Reprinted from Robert Moses, *Arterial Plan for Pittsburgh*; 38 Kaufmann's Department Store Photographs, Detre Library & Archives, Sen. John Heinz History Center; 41 Reprinted from *Fortune*; 45, 52, 63, 66, 70 Allegheny Conference on Community Development, Detre Library & Archives, Sen. John Heinz History Center; 51 Reprinted from Mitchell & Ritchey, *Pittsburgh in Progress presented by Kaufmann's*; 54 Joseph W. Molitor architectural photographs,1935–1985, Avery Architectural & Fine Arts Library, Columbia University; 56 Reprinted from Ben Rosen Associates, *Equitable Builds a Gateway*; 64 Westinghouse Electric Corporation Photographs, Detre Library & Archives, Sen. John Heinz History Center; 67 Carnegie Mellon University Architecture Archives; 69 Reprinted from *The Steel Triangle in the Golden Triangle*, Carnegie Mellon University Architecture Archives.

Media

84, 86, 89, 90 Reprinted from Mitchell & Ritchey, *Pittsburgh in Progress presented by Kaufmann's*; 85, 92–97 Reprinted from Allegheny Conference on Community Development, *Pittsburgh: Challenge and Response*; 100 Reprinted from Robert Moses, *Arterial Plan for Pittsburgh*; 101 Reprinted from Patrick Horsbrugh, *Pittsburgh Perceived*; 102, 105 (top), 112–113, 139, 202 Carnegie Mellon University Architecture Archives; 104–105 (bottom) Reprinted from *The Auditorium: From Blueprint to Reality*; 106–107 Reprinted from Deeter Ritchey Sippel, *Allegheny Center*; 108–109 Reprinted from Oakland Corporation, *This is an Urban Area: Panther Hollow Project Plans*; 114–115 Reprinted from Tasso Katselas, *Tasso Katselas Architect Planner*; 116–117 Reprinted from Paul Schweikher, *Buildings by Pedagogs*; 118, 120, 127, 140–141 Courtesy of Troy West; 119 Reprinted from John O. Simonds, *Landscape Architecture: A Manual of Site Planning and Design*; 124, 136–137 Harrison & Abramovitz; 125, 130, 132, 135 Mitchell & Ritchey / Deeter Ritchey Sippel; 126 Copyright © 2019 Frank Lloyd Wright Foundation, Scottsdale. All rights reserved. The Frank Lloyd Wright Foundation Archives (The Museum of Modern Art | Avery Architectural & Fine Arts Library, Columbia University); 128, 133, 134 (top), 204 (top) Avery Architectural & Fine Arts Library, Columbia University; 131 (top), 205–209 © Ezra Stoller/Esto; 131 (bottom) SOM Archives; 133, 134 (bottom) Helmut Jacoby; 138 University of Florida; 144, 146, 148, 152, 156 Reprinted from the *Pittsburgh Courier*; 145, 154, 162–163 Reprinted from the *Pittsburgh Press*; 149, 150, 153, 157–159 Reprinted from the *Pittsburgh Post-Gazette*; 164, 165, 167, 168 Reprinted from *Architectural Record*; 166 Reprinted from *Architectural Forum*; 169 Reprinted from *Industrial Design*; 171 Reprinted from *Holiday*; 175–177 © Carnegie Museum of Art, Charles "Teenie" Harris Archive; 178–179, 194–201 Allegheny Conference on Community Development, Detre Library & Archives, Sen. John Heinz History Center; 180–183 W. Eugene Smith; 184–187 Clyde Hare; 188–191 © Brady Stewart Studio; 192 Aerial Photographs; 193 Charles R. Martin; 204 (bottom) Harold Corsini; 210–213 Joseph W. Molitor architectural photographs,1935–1985, Avery Architectural & Fine Arts Library, Columbia University.

Perspectives

272–283 Courtesy of Robert Pease; 284 Rami el Samahy; 288, 292 (top) Reprinted from Tasso Katselas, *Tasso Katselas Architect Planner*; 292 (bottom), 293 (top) Adam Hines; 293 (bottom) Martin Aurand; 294–303 Courtesy of Troy West.

Salons

308 © Carnegie Museum of Art, Charles "Teenie" Harris Archive; 310 (top) Associated Press, photo by John Rooney; 310 (bottom) Farm Security Administration - Office of War Information photograph collection, Library of Congress, photo by John Vachon; 311 Carnegie Mellon University Architecture Archives; 312 Reprinted from Mitchell & Ritchey, *Pittsburgh in Progress presented by Kaufmann's*; 313 Boston Redevelopment Authority photographs © City of Boston; 316 Martin Aurand; 323 (top) Detroit Publishing Company photograph collection, Library of Congress; 323 (bottom) University of Pittsburgh; 324 Pittsburgh City Photographer Collection; 325 Derek Jensen; 326 (left) Chris Ivey; 326 (bottom) Allegheny Conference on Community Development, Detre Library & Archives, Sen. John Heinz History Center; 327 Bjarke Ingels Group; 328 U.S. Department of Housing and Urban Development; 329 The Paul Rudolph Archive, Library of Congress; 331 Susie Post for the *Pittsburgh Press*; 335 *Pittsburgh Post-Gazette*; 336 TheZachMorrisExperience, licensed under CC-BY-SA 3.0; 338 Reprinted from Boston Redevelopment Authority, *General Plan for the City of Boston*; 343 (left) Stacy Funderburke; 343 (right) Colin Hinkle, courtesy of The Trust for Public Land; 347 Wayne Thom; 346 David Schalliol; 349, 355 *Pittsburgh Press*; 351 Jorge Castro, licensed under CC BY-NC-SA 2.0; 352 Tom Fisher; 353 Benson Kua, licensed under CC BY-SA 2.0; 354 Kevin Lynch.

Editors Chris Grimley, Michael Kubo, and Rami el Samahy

Library of Congress Control Number: 2018967823

ISBN 978-1-58093-523-4

10 9 8 7 6 5 4 3 2 1

Printed in China

Design by OverUnder Chris Grimley and Shannon McLean, with Claire He, Win Overholser IV, and Makena Janssen.

The Monacelli Press
6 West 18th Street
New York, New York 10011

monacellipress.com